BALDWIN
OF THE Times

BALDWIN

OF THE Times

Hanson W. Baldwin,
A Military Journalist's Life, 1903–1991

ROBERT B. DAVIES

Naval Institute Press
Annapolis, Maryland

Naval Institute Press
291 Wood Road
Annapolis, MD 21402

Library of Congress Cataloging-in-Publication Data
Davies, Robert B.
  Baldwin of The times : Hanson W. Baldwin, a military journalist's life, 1903-1991 / Robert B. Davies.
    p. cm.
  Includes bibliographical references and index.
  ISBN 978-1-61251-048-4 (hard cover : alk. paper) 1. Baldwin, Hanson Weightman, 1903-1991.
2. Journalists—United States—Biography. 3. War correspondents—United States—Biography. 4.
Foreign correspondents—United States—Biography. I. Title.
  PN4874.B26D38 2011
  070.92—dc23
  [B]

                                                                                    2011023455

♾ This paper meets the requirements of ANSI/NISO z39.48-1992 (Permanence of Paper).
Printed in the United States of America.

19 18 17 16 15 14 13 12 11   9 8 7 6 5 4 3 2 1
First printing

To the next generation:

Audrey, Gavin, and Flynn—may they never know war.

Contents

Acknowledgments

Historians frequently work alone, but we are helped in many ways by the kindnesses of librarians, archivists, colleagues, former students and spouses. Over the years of research, many people have helped me in ways both large and small.

This biography could never have been written had it not been for the willingness of the Baldwin family to be interviewed. Hanson Baldwin was a private man whose profession required that he comment publicly, and almost daily, on the passing parade of current events. But he never wrote about himself. My taped interviews with him at his home in Roxbury, Connecticut, reflect his views on many subjects, including his own personal biases. His wife, Helen, joined us on one occasion, and their daughters, Elizabeth and Barbara, in separate interviews, were willing to share many anecdotes about their father. In 1975 Dr. John T. Mason, the director of the United States Naval Institute's oral history program, interviewed Baldwin on eight separate occasions. The Institute's 790-page transcript covered Baldwin's entire life and career.

Before listing those persons whose help I want to acknowledge, I would like to single out Dr. Roland Dille, the president emeritus of Minnesota State University, Moorhead. During the 1980s, when I was doing my initial research, he had the foresight to fund several of the summer travel grant requests that enabled me to use the resources of five libraries and archives in three eastern states and in the District of Columbia.

Others who helped in many ways are: William Beecher, William Colby, Vincent Demma, Gail Hanlon, Greg Harness, John B. Oakes, Thomas Paterson, John Rothman, Charles St. Vil, Abigail Tom, and the Joseph Muse Worthington family.

Other institutions that were helpful were: the Boys' Latin School of Maryland, Baltimore; the Clark County Historical Society, Springfield, Ohio; Columbia University Oral History Research Office, Butler Library, New York; The Library of Congress, Manuscripts Division, Washington,

D.C.; George C. Marshall Foundation and Library, Lexington, Virginia; *New York Times* Archives, New York; Enoch Pratt Free Public Library, Maryland Department, Baltimore; Franklin Delano Roosevelt Library, Hyde Park, New York; Hollins College Alumnae Affairs Office, Roanoke, Virginia; Hood College Library, Frederick, Maryland; the State Historical Society of Wisconsin, Madison; United States Air Force Historical Research Center, Reference Division, Maxwell Air Force Base, Alabama; University of Virginia, Alderman Library, Manuscripts Department, Charlottesville; Yale University Library, Archives and Manuscripts Division, New Haven, Connecticut; and Wittenberg University Library, Springfield, Ohio.

My wife, Mary, initially took no interest in this project, correctly assuming that it was my hobby. In time, however, she began providing invaluable editorial comments for which I will always be grateful and I am indebted for her assistance. I also wish to thank my children, Peter and Rachel, for their continuous love and support.

I am solely responsible for the book's content and willingly accept all criticism of errors of omission and commission.

BALDWIN
OF THE Times

Introduction

The eighty-four-year-old grandfather moved slowly and hesitantly toward a wingback chair next to the fireplace, over which hung two objects: a Steuben eagle given to him on the occasion of his retirement by his employer, and an oil portrait of his beloved wife, Helen, painted by his son-in-law. The old man sat down abruptly, positioning himself so that his right ear faced his guest, having been deaf in his left ear since a stroke in 1978. He replied to questions about his long career in a soft voice, carefully weighing each word, as if he wished to make sure that their meaning would not be misunderstood. He listened to each question attentively, followed by a pause, and then his reply would well up, increasing in volume as one topic after another brought forth events, issues, and personalities of our nation's military and political past. It seemed to me as if his memory was organized in a web wherein every event and every person of the past was related in some way.

In his day, Hanson Weightman Baldwin (1903–91) was America's best-known military writer and analyst, whose principal forum for thirty-nine years was the *New York Times.* He was the consummate journalist whose knowledge of military affairs was admired in his lifetime. His tall and lean presence, and his no-nonsense demeanor, made him a formidable professional. His writing style was fact driven, impersonal, and clear headed. "Realistic" was a word often used to characterize his writings, which conveyed to his readers the seriousness of contemporary military and political situations. His reputation was based upon his ability to make independent judgments. His sources were the best, those who made national military policy in the Pentagon, a number of whom, in time, became his personal friends.

His writings frequently went beyond a narrow military focus to include political and economic and social factors that Baldwin considered necessary to a fuller understanding of news development. His tendency to editorialize in his writings often provoked reproving memos from the *Times* publisher, who took sharp exception to Baldwin's broader view of military issues. In reply, Baldwin would simply restate his strong views about the unity of political and military factors. In 1960, a Harvard professor referred to him as the "dean of American military writers," an approbation that pleased him to the end of his life.[1]

While the public man was often blunt and forceful in his writings, the private man was a Maryland-bred gentleman of the old school: soft spoken, courteous, civil, and well mannered at all times. He assumed that a person's character was more important than his rank in uniform or the title of his political appointment.

He had no illusions about the permanence of his extensive writings, once commenting that there was nothing quite as evanescent as a journalist's writings. In retirement, Baldwin dismissed the suggestion by the archivist of the *Times* that he write his memoirs, saying, "A newspaperman's memoirs are . . . a dime a dozen; and I don't think that I have enough material to warrant publication in any event."[2]

He was the first American newspaperman to be given the sole assignment as the military writer and analyst for a major newspaper, and this was in 1937. For this assignment, he was indebted to the new publisher, Arthur Hays Sulzberger, who foresaw the possibility of another war in Europe and wanted his staff to be prepared. Baldwin's writings, taken as a whole, serve as a public diary that followed the changing public perception of the role of the American military in our national life during World War II, the Cold War, the Korean War, and the Vietnam War. In the 1930s, the American public ignored the military; in the 1940s and 1950s, they admired it; and during the late 1960s and early 1970s, they often despised it.

He was a prolific writer, a Pulitzer Prize winner, and the sole author of eighteen books and numerous articles in national magazines. For the *Times*, his primary forum, he wrote literally thousands of articles that appeared in the daily and in the Sunday magazine, as well as hundreds of book reviews.[3]

Given the limitations of daily journalism, often writing in a hurry to meet a deadline, Baldwin did not see the world through a porthole, nor did he adopt the "drums and trumpets" school of military writing that focused on heroic action. Rather, he always felt that human beings were the heart and soul of any battle, more important than any machine. In this he was a humanist. He was not a war lover. He accepted the balance of power among nations as the tried and true method for keeping the peace. The world was a nasty and brutish place where a nation's survival depended as much on luck as it did on power politics backed by military force. Neither was he a historian, though, over time, he observed the passing parade of people and events on which he commented. He was a cold warrior, who lived in a post–World War II world divided into two competing political systems, Communism and democracy. He never doubted which system would prevail in the end, though he did not live to see the collapse of the Soviet Union. He jealously guarded his independence from influence by his sources, lest he be dismissed as an apologist for the military establishment. His words were the basis for his reputation for balance, fairness, and integrity. Above all, he knew that without that independence he was just another scribbler whose words in a daily newspaper would be thrown out with the fish in the garbage.

CHAPTER 1

A Baltimore Youth, 1903–20

anson Weightman Baldwin was born on March 22, 1903, in Baltimore, a middle child, the only son of his father's second marriage. His older sister, Frances Elizabeth Baldwin, was his senior by four years, and Dorothy Sheffey Baldwin was his junior by three years. His parents were Caroline Frances Sutton Baldwin, who was fifteen years younger than her husband, Oliver Perry Baldwin Jr. He was fifty-three when his son was born.

Caroline Baldwin was related to the Sheffey and Hanson families of Frederick, Maryland. Her son's middle name, Weightman, was a family name, as well. Her husband's relations were originally from Connecticut; some of them had moved south during the antebellum decades. There was a naval tradition of sorts in the Baldwin family. Hanson's great-grandfather had either admired Commodore Oliver Hazard Perry, the hero of the 1813 Battle of Lake Erie, or had actually served under him. Hanson's grandfather, Oliver Perry Baldwin Sr. (1813–78), had served as a midshipman for a few months on the Navy sloop USS *Falmouth* during the 1830s.

On leaving the Navy, he sought a life of adventure that almost killed him. He was a rafter on the Mississippi River for a time, contracted yellow fever, and sought recuperation in the Shenandoah Valley of Virginia. There he became a country newspaper editor in Staunton and in Lexington. It was there that he met and later married Eliza Lee Sheffey, whose father was a prominent local judge. The couple moved to Richmond, where he became the editor of the *Richmond Dispatch*, a paper with a large circulation that was outranked only by the New Orleans dailies.[1] The father of nine children, Oliver Sr.'s only surviving son, Oliver Perry Baldwin Jr., was born on September 2, 1850, in Richmond.[2]

The senior Baldwin became a well-known public speaker whose topics varied from dedicating a local cemetery to eulogizing the death of former president Zachary Taylor.[3] Though he was a Whig, the party that favored government aid to businesses, railroads, and telegraph companies, Baldwin was a Southern nationalist first and foremost. The election of Abraham Lincoln in November 1860 was viewed by the South as a definite threat to slavery, a system that had been repeatedly castigated by the fiery abolitionist talk in the North during the previous decade. On July 20, 1861, the Congress of the Confederate States of America met in Richmond, Virginia, the capitol of the new nation.

Oliver Baldwin Sr. felt that Richmond might not be a safe haven for his large family. He sent them westward to his wife's home in Staunton, Virginia, with the belief that they would be out of harm's way in the mountains. He was mistaken. The area soon became a battlefield. In May 1862, General "Stonewall" Jackson's six thousand troops passed through Staunton en route to McDowell, a small village twenty-five miles west of Staunton. On May 8, 1862, he successfully headed off the Union forces under General John C. Fremont who were marching eastward.[4] Fearing that his family would be caught in the cross fire of the opposing armies, Oliver Sr. quickly resettled his family in 1862 in Ashland, a small railroad town sixteen miles north of Richmond that seemed to have no military value to either side, and it was closer to Oliver Baldwin's work in Richmond.[5]

Two years later, on May 4, 1864, General Ulysses S. Grant ordered his entire 12,000-man cavalry, led by Major General Philip H. Sheridan, to move south from the Rapidan River to Richmond. Two days later, the war arrived at quiet Ashland. On Wednesday, May 11, a brigade of Union cavalry entered the town, drove off the small defending force, and proceeded to cut the Fredericksburg railroad by burning a locomotive and a train of cars. Later, Confederate cavalry moved through Ashland pursued by Sheridan's troopers en route to Mechanicsville.[6]

Viewing all this military action, fourteen-year-old Oliver Baldwin Jr. never forgot what he saw that day. The sights, the sounds, the thundering hoofs of the cavalry, the rattle of their sabers, the firing of their carbines, the shouts of the troopers, and all that dust swirling behind the passing cavalry was heady stuff. Almost a year later, on Sunday, April 2, 1865, General Robert E. Lee's army evacuated Richmond for Appomattox Court House and his surrender took place a week later.

Oliver and a friend found a railroad handcar in the bushes, put it onto the tracks, and rode south far enough to see the glow of the burning city of Richmond. That view remained in his memory for the rest of his life. It is not surprising that he became an unreconstructed rebel after 1865 when the "Lost Cause" became a nostalgic rationalization for the South's defeat.[7]

With the Confederacy defeated, the presence of Union soldiers in Richmond, and the Southern economy in shambles, Oliver Sr. moved his large family back to Staunton, Virginia, in 1866. Oliver Jr., then fifteen, remained with relatives in Ashland and later moved to Baltimore, one of the Southern cities that had not been physically damaged by the war. In May 1867, Oliver Baldwin Sr.'s application to fill a vacancy in its editorial department was accepted by *The Baltimore Sun*. That newspaper would serve as the link between three generations of Baldwin men, Oliver Sr., Oliver Jr., and Hanson.[8]

Hanson Baldwin's father, Oliver Jr., received his Bachelor of Law degree in July 1873 from the University of Virginia at the age of twenty-three.[9] Two months later, he received his license to practice law in Baltimore County, Maryland. His was not a lucrative practice, though he stayed with it for the next nine years. To supplement his income, he ran for public office and was elected in 1875 to Maryland's House of Delegates. His interest in national politics was evident in 1876, a presidential year, when he spoke in favor of the candidacy of New York governor Samuel J. Tilden, a reform-minded Democrat who had gained notoriety by attacking the corrupt Boss Tweed ring in New York City.

In January 1882 Oliver Jr. joined the staff of the *Sun*. One of his early acquaintances at the paper was a twenty-two-year-old night telegraph editor who joined the staff in 1886, stayed for two years, then moved on to New York City and great fame. Carr Van Anda became the managing editor of the *New York Times* in 1904, a post he kept for twenty-one years. The paths of these two men would not cross again for forty years when Baldwin wrote a letter of recommendation to Van Anda about his son, Hanson, who was looking for a newspaper position in October 1929.

As the years passed, Oliver Baldwin rose in the *Sun* organization. He became its managing editor between 1906 and 1912 and he remained at the *Sun* for fifty years. His last assignment was as the editor of the editorial page from 1921 until almost the day he died in June 1932, aged eighty-two.[10] He wrote many of the editorials and feature articles over the years and is best remembered for strong personal partisan journalism that was popular early in his career. One of his former colleagues once remarked to Hanson, "Your old dad was right—tell the truth and shame the devil."[11]

While he was tolerant of the opinions of others, he made no compromises with his own strongly held convictions. He opposed prohibition and women's suffrage, was convinced that "ladies" would never wish to vote, and those who were not ladies ought not to be allowed to. He championed individual liberties and world leadership by Christian men. As a Southerner with a long memory, he disliked all Yankees and was always surprised when he met one who was both civilized and pleasant.[12]

Hanson's formative years were spent in a loving, stable family. The family lived at 147 West Lanvale Street in Baltimore. The house was a typical three-story row house that was connected by a common roof with all the other houses on the block. A thick wall was all that separated the houses from each other, and the marble steps in front of each house were a distinctive Baltimore feature.[13] The first-floor rooms were a front parlor, a dining room, and a kitchen in the rear. The second-floor family room faced Lanvale Street, and the only bathroom was on that floor. The back room was his mother's bedroom. The third floor contained bedrooms for the other family members.

The tone of the family was set by his father, whose love of Shakespeare made him a self-appointed theater critic who would castigate, often in print, the abilities, or lack thereof, of actors attempting to perform the Bard of Avon's plays. On Sunday afternoons, Oliver would read Shakespeare and the Greek classics to his family. He liked to recite poems of a heroic tone, then popular, in the "I am the Master of my Fate" genre.

Oliver was trained in the classics (as well as the law) at the University of Virginia and had developed a long friendship with the famous classics professor Basil Linneau Gildersleeve (1831–1924) of Johns Hopkins University. Their mutual admiration of ancient Greek culture led them to exchange birthday cards written in ancient Greek, as well as books with inscriptions in that language. Hanson absorbed literate, humanist values from his father and an intellectual interest in putting ideas to work. From his father he learned the value of a broad humanist education. Later in life, he also came to appreciate the value of self-discipline.

One of Oliver Baldwin's legacies was his emotional tie to the "Lost Cause." He would often tell to his son stories of his youthful experiences in and impressions of the Civil War, or, as he referred to it, the War Between the States. He would also include stories of the hardships the Baldwin family had endured during the harsh Reconstruction years. He once took his son to visit the widow of a Confederate general, George W. Hall (1832–67), whose home in Richmond was a private museum of the Confederacy. Before they left the widow's parlor, Hanson recalled, she "took me by the shoulder and said, 'Son [pointing to the stars and bars flag in her parlor], if that flag is ever raised again, follow it!'"

That sense of Southernness surrounded Hanson as he grew up. The South, he later recalled, was almost a separate country that believed its culture was different and superior to the North. He commented that anyone born around 1900 north of the Mason-Dixon Line would not be able to understand the deep feelings of brotherhood and of ties to a Lost Cause. He claimed that it was not simply a question of racial discrimination or a question of slavery, it was part of the mind of the South. Since young Hanson was surrounded by such views, it was not surprising that the heroes of his youth were Robert E. Lee, Stonewall Jackson, and J. E. B. Stuart, rather than U. S. Grant, Philip Sheridan, or Winfield Scott Hancock. Such heroes reflected more of Oliver's views than Hanson's mature assessment later.

He was secure in his home life and in his neighborhood. Baltimore, at the beginning of the twentieth century, was a sleepy Southern city whose streets were, for the most part, covered with cobblestones. The streetlights were fueled by gas, not by electricity, and public transport was the electric trolley car.

Religion played an important part in the Baldwin home. Regular attendance at an Episcopal Church was expected. The church calendar was followed, especially at Lent, Easter, and Christmas. In one church pageant Hanson played an angel whose part, which he found thrilling, was to look down upon "a beautiful blond with beautiful blue eyes."

Hanson also remembered how in 1912, as managing editor of the *Sun*, his father used the paper's influence as a progressive democratic newspaper to persuade the city leaders to invite the Democrats to hold their national convention in Baltimore's 5th regiment armory. During the convention, the paper's editorials favored Woodrow Wilson over Champ Clark of Arkansas. After forty-six ballots, New Jersey governor Thomas Woodrow Wilson, a Virginian, was nominated. Hanson remembered the excitement of that occasion when his father returned home with the news. Occasionally, he was allowed to stay up past his bedtime to hear that day's convention report.

In 1912, at the age of nine, Hanson was enrolled in the Boys' Latin School of Baltimore, founded in 1844 by a professor of classics at Princeton University.[14] The school was close enough to his home on Lanvale Street that he could walk the few blocks. For most of his eight years there, the headmaster was the beloved James Annesley Dunham, a Canadian who was once described as "a manly man . . . who knew everything that was to be known about a boy's psychology."[15] So great was his influence at the school during his twenty-three-year tenure that the BLS was popularly called "Dunham's."[16]

James Dunham may have been the American equivalent of "Mr. Chips," but his curriculum was standard for preparatory school, including Latin, French, and German; English literature; mathematics; and physical education. Art and music were not taught. Memorization was the preferred teaching method. Hanson took many years of Latin but "learned very little of it," except for a few Latin poems and phrases. Scholarship, while stressed, was secondary to the development of a well-rounded student during his impressionable adolescent years. "Sound mind and sound body" was the school's motto.

Two teachers who left a lasting impression upon Hanson's youthful memory were Edward Lucas White and Christian Beuerlein. In class, "Whiskers" White, who taught Latin, was noted for classroom pranks on his students. He told all sorts of funny stories in class, which demonstrated his other talent for writing. The author of eight books of poetry, fantasy stories, and short stories books he was, as Hanson recalled years later, "a professor you could never forget."[17]

Physical training was also held in high esteem at BLS, as it imparted the positive mental and physical attributes of manhood. The head of the physical education department was Christian C. Beuerlein, a Swiss tumbler, gymnast, and fencer, a small, bald, mustachioed man with a German accent. He was trained in the European *turnverein* method, in which the boys' muscle sizes were carefully noted and built up with special strengthening exercises. It was a system that was used at the U.S. Naval Academy, at whose gymnastic exercises Beuerlein often served as a judge. The boys used the horizontal and parallel bars and other equipment.[18] He always insisted that a boy complete whatever it was he had started. Hanson recalled how he once tried to jump through the bars, caught his toe on a bar, and fell, but Beuerlein caught him in the nick of time. Scared, Hanson was told to do it again immediately, but this time to do it correctly.[19]

Hanson's innate shyness during his Latin School years was exacerbated by his sudden growth to six feet two inches at the age of sixteen. Tall and gangly, he tried all the sports at school but excelled in none, except track, where his new height enabled him to win one match in the high jump and one in running.[20]

Although he had two sisters, he was uncertain about how to behave around girls. One girl who attracted Hanson's attention for a time would look up to the second floor of the Latin School as she passed by daily on her way to the neighboring Bryn Mawr School, which his older sister Frances attended. To alert him to the girl's presence, his classmates would shout his moniker, "Hans, Hans, there she goes!" much to his embarrassment. Because of his height the girls loved to tease him by calling him "Handsome" Baldwin, but he was very insecure. When he asked his father about human reproduction he was sent to a well-known surgeon who was not much help, and once on a date with a neighborhood girl they went to a play where a stage prop was a nude statue, and the sight embarrassed him.[21]

As graduation from school approached in 1920, his parents began to ask about his future plans. Why did Hanson turn his thoughts to a Navy career? He had long been aware of the Baldwin family's naval tradition, which his father had broken by becoming a lawyer and later a journalist. Oliver Baldwin did not express a preference about his son's vocation, other than recommending that he avoid being a newspaper reporter. Aware that many of his classmates and friends were thinking about attending The Johns Hopkins University in Baltimore, Hanson may have thought that if he lived at home he could save on room and board expenses. But the tuition costs would have been a financial burden on his father. Hanson most likely recalled family discussions about money and did not want to impose an additional burden on his father.

America's entry into World War I in April 1917 sharply narrowed Hanson's future plans. President Wilson's challenging declaration that America's task was to make the world safe for democracy generated extreme patriotism. The anti-German sentiment over the sinking of the liner *Lusitania* in 1915, the 1917 revelation in the Zimmermann telegram that Germany planned to bring Mexico into the war against the United States, and the German announcement that it would renew unrestricted submarine warfare convinced President Wilson that the United States could no longer remain neutral during World War I. Caroline Baldwin demonstrated her patriotism by buying Liberty bonds through the *Sun* offices. A year later, in 1918, Hanson thought of running away to join the U.S. Marines. His father put a quick stop to that idea.[22]

It was in that climate of awakened wartime patriotism that Hanson began to read a series of boys' adventure stories that were very popular and widely read by adolescents of that era. Those quickly written, low-priced, and mass-distributed stories with dramatic confrontations with evil forces enabled the pure hero of the story to act swiftly and decisively in defense of the nation's interests and those of the heroine. Their attractiveness appealed to the desire of youth for action and adventure. Life, as portrayed by those authors, involved fair play by honest and sober heroes who were called upon to demonstrate their physical fitness in the process.[23] Those books reinforced Hanson's perception of how the world ought to behave, where everyone played by the rules.

The Dave Darrin series most impressed Hanson Baldwin. Written by the prolific Harri Irving Hancock (1868–1922), who produced at least ten series of boys' adventure stories between 1910 and 1919, the Dave Darrin series told of the hero's adventures at the Naval Academy and on active duty in the Navy in the Caribbean, the Mediterranean, and in European waters during The Great War. In *Dave Darrin on the Asiatic Station* (1919), the hero was in China defending missionaries against Chinese bandits aided by a slippery and completely untrustworthy local governor. In the racist language of the period, he faced a threatening "mass of yellow fiends, crowding, yelling and shouting," whom he repulsed by emptying his service automatic into the "mass of yellow humanity" at the foot of the wall. Later, he was forced to turn the machine gun on the hostile mob with the remark "you've got to do it."The racial stereotypes were clearly drawn.The Chinese were sullen, their streets were foul smelling and their houses mean looking. The inevitable victory of our hero was owing to "the superior athletic physique of the Anglo-Saxon [that] bore up before the rushes of the Chinamen with seeming tireless energy."[24]

Another book described Darrin's fourth year at the Naval Academy, where the hero accepted the discipline of the naval service with the remark that it will be "part of the whole professional life ahead of me."[25] As June Week approached, Darrin doubted if he could command a rowboat. But on graduation day he accepted his ensign's commission, as an officer and a gentleman, signed by the president "as a sacred trust given by the nation."[26] In 1924 Hanson Baldwin may have been thinking those same thoughts.

While Dave Darrin was a fictional hero, his vigorous defense of America's right to defend its interests around the world was generally accepted by many Americans at the time. A serious-minded adolescent Baldwin sought a guide to behavior and those Darrin stories may have shaped his idealistic perception of what a Navy career was all about.

That innocence was challenged in the autumn of 1919 when he attended a post-season football game between the midshipmen and the Great Lakes Naval Training Station on Farragut Field at Annapolis. The midshipmen were leading 6 to 0. A fumble at the Great Lakes' goal line was picked up by a Great Lakes player who ran, unopposed, down the field toward the Annapolis goal line.The Navy coach sent in a substitute player to tackle the opposing player before he had crossed the goal line, and the tackle caused a fumble at the Annapolis goal line.This unsportsmanlike behavior resulted in a near riot by the spectators, which the referees defused by conceding the goal to the Great Lakes team. They kicked the goal and won the game by one point. That was not the way the boys at BLS had been taught to play, but winning was not everything at BLS; instead, the way the boys played the game was considered all-important. Baldwin never forgot that incident.[27]

In 1920, at the age of seventeen, Baldwin was a serious-minded, patriotic youth who had set his mind on a career in the U.S. Navy. While many other American adolescents enjoyed the hedonistic pleasures of American society in the Jazz Age, Baldwin chose the difficult career path of discipline, duty (a word that he had heard often from his mother), and national service. Buoyed by America's successful role in the Great War, Baldwin looked forward with eagerness to his chosen career.

CHAPTER 2

The Annapolis Years, 1920–24

In the spring of 1920 Baldwin attended, for about six weeks, the Severn School, which was designed to coach students for the Naval Academy entrance examination. The Latin School had prepared him well. The results of his entrance examination, in six subjects, including algebra and arithmetic, ranged from 3.0 to 3.5, with the exception of geometry, where his grade was 2.9. The Academy rejected candidates with a grade of less than 2.5 in any subject. He also passed the physical examination, although there was a momentary setback when the examining doctor found a heart murmur but thought it not serious enough to reject him on medical grounds.[1]

Since all appointments to the two military service academies required nomination by a U.S. senator, Oliver Baldwin had written to Maryland's U.S. senator Joseph I. France, urging him to nominate Hanson. He was nominated as the second alternate to the primary candidate and, as it turned out, one candidate failed the entrance examination and the other failed to appear for his physical examination. On such a chance occurrence, a career was launched.[2]

On Friday, June 18, 1920, seventeen-year-old Baldwin entered the U.S. Naval Academy as a fourth-year classman. Filled with fictional expectations about travel and adventure, he quickly learned that his plebe year would be very stressful. One writer has referred to Annapolis as "a place of obligation," in which plebes (fourth classmen) agreed to perform duties and conform to obligations of the institution.[3] For example, the eighty-five-page book of regulations was comprehensive, specific, and detailed. All aspects of behavior, dress, and conduct were spelled out. There were 165 offenses listed, each with the number of demerits assigned. The maximum number of demerits was forty for an unauthorized absence from class, exercises, chapel attendance, or "shirking" at drill. The most heinous offense (fifty demerits) was the unauthorized use of tobacco. There was another list of offenses that included "moral turpitude," a "hardened disrespect for authority," or an "incorrigible" lack of energy.[4]

Of the 875 men who entered Annapolis with Baldwin in June 1920, 50 left before the end of the first week. He was not a quitter but one of his fears was that he would flunk out, or "bilge," in the slang of midshipmen. There was much to learn about the many traditions of the Navy. The curriculum was designed to teach officer-trainees how to navigate a ship and how to shoot. While engineering and related technical subjects were taught in the classroom, there were other opportunities to learn by practical applications. There were no elective subjects. The only exception was the choice to study either French or German. Baldwin recalled that over one hundred pages of assigned reading from the textbooks had to be partially memorized every day to be recited in class if one was called upon, which was frequently the case. All learning was by rote. Instructors were "referees" between the student and the textbook.[5]

One exception to the uninspired teachers was Charles Alphonse Smith, the chairman of the English department. He arrived at the Academy in 1917 after a long college teaching career, most recently at the University of Virginia. Baldwin remembered him as an "inspirational" teacher who stood out in sharp contrast to the others and was beloved by the midshipmen. He died just after Baldwin's class of 1924 graduated and his last words were reported to be, "I greet the unknown with a cheer."[6] Baldwin always remembered him with fondness.

The class of 1924 was notable for being the first class in which the plebes were physically segregated following reports of a hazing incident during Baldwin's first months there. Hazing had been a traditional yearlong initiation rite at the Academy for all plebes, the rationale behind it being that before someone could command others, he had to learn to be commanded by upperclassmen. Thus, plebes had to be constantly reminded of their inferior rank.

Hazing events in the autumn of 1920 caused the superintendent, Rear Admiral Archibald H. Scales, to order an investigation. Since the first classmen could not assure Admiral Scales that hazing would cease altogether, he ordered the immediate segregation of all plebes on two floors of Bancroft Hall and in the dining areas.[7] In a letter to his father, written in November 1920, Baldwin wrote, "A great change has come at the Naval Academy. Three or four yellow plebes complained, in other words, 'squealed' and said that they had been 'hazed.'" Superintendent Scales acted "promptly and stuck the accused upperclassmen in the brig and, in addition, he segregated us in Bancroft Hall," at the time, the world's largest dormitory.

The forced segregation also took away two of the four days of liberty each month given to all plebes, and their days of liberty were not the same days permitted for upperclassmen. Baldwin was concerned that this segregation would "practically ruin our Navy careers," because the Navy would "look down upon us as the class that couldn't stand the guff and we are somewhat despised." He asked his father, as a well-respected editorial and feature writer at the *Sun,* to use "a little pull and write to one of your friends in Washington to ask them to investigate this and have it [segregation] repealed."[8]

The segregation order was rescinded on Monday, November 22, 1920. Five boards of inquiry met with the fourth classmen to determine the degree and extent of the hazing; the boards found no cases of "brutal" hazing and concluded that the hazing incidents were few in number.[9] However, three upperclassmen were dismissed from the Academy and nine others were confined to the station ship *Reina Mercedes* that served as a dormitory for staff employees, as well as a prison for midshipmen.[10]

Baldwin was called before one of the boards and told to report whether or not he had been hazed and, if so, to name the upperclassman who did it.[11] Years later, he recalled how terrified he was to face that board of senior naval officers. The questions became more and more difficult; "finally, faced with some lying or, perhaps, wrecking the career of some upper classmen I admired, I stood mute, sweating and scared to death. The Captain ordered me to answer, and when I said nothing, [he] thundered: 'You are exactly the type of young man not wanted as an officer in the United States Navy. I shall recommend you to the Superintendent for the highest punishment he can give.'"[12]

Later, at a noon formation of the entire regiment of midshipmen in front of Bancroft Hall, the demerit list was read out loud: "Baldwin, H. W., 4th class,

4th Battalion, Deliberate disobedience of orders—100 demerits." When his demerits were announced, one of the first classmen whispered "good show," or words to that effect. Baldwin did extra duty during his plebe year by walking back and forth, in dreary repentance, in front of Bancroft Hall with a rifle on his shoulder, but since he had expected to be kicked out, his "heart leaped with joy" when he received only demerits and not a dismissal.[13]

Aside from the hazing drama, plebes were also made aware of their low rank by other means less violent. Baldwin recalled standing on his head in a running shower, being forced to sing "Anchors Aweigh." He was tone deaf and the racket he made brought great amusement to the first classmen observing his humiliation.[14] Other forms of harassment included the old practices of "cuckoo" and "asymptotes." The first had the plebe under a table saying "cuckoo," and then poking his head out and saying "cuckoo," while an upperclassman standing on the table would hit the plebe with a broom or other hard object. The latter practice required a plebe to put his nose on a downward curved chalk line on a wall and then try to erase the line with his nose. This meant doing deep knee bends.[15]

In July 1921 Scales was relieved by Rear Admiral Henry Braid Wilson, the former commander of the U.S. Naval Forces in France during the Great War. As superintendent he faced the effects of the Washington Naval Arms Conference, which reduced the need for new ensigns in a smaller navy. Congressional parsimony during the 1920s forced budget cuts for all the armed forces. It was an era of naval stagnation and no capital ships were built for a decade.

Admiral Wilson defined the Academy's mission as indoctrinating educated gentlemen who had a loyalty to the nation with practical rather than academic minds.[16] Since he sought to develop character, he introduced a new course in leadership. He believed that the best motivation for proper behavior was not fear of disciplinary action, but the expectation of a reward for efficient behavior.[17]

Baldwin recalled Admiral Wilson looking like a sea-faring admiral, with his cap at a jaunty angle and an air of "consummate dignity."[18] A model for many midshipmen, they nicknamed him "Uncle Henry." His reforms were designed, in his words, to make the Academy "more human, more livable."[19] Some of his reforms were cosmetic: granting Christmas and Easter leaves and changing the choke-collar service coat to the double-breasted officer's style coat.[20] Other reforms were more substantial and long lasting, such as the rule that no midshipman would ever question the honesty of another midshipman: "There is no place in the Navy for anyone who is untruthful." Another rule stated that the tone of voice used by seniors toward lower classmen should not be loud or overbearing: "A forceful command is not a tyrannical one."

The hazing incident of 1920 was dealt with directly. Specifically prohibited was the practice of laying hands on plebes in a brutal fashion.[21] Seniors could no longer expect personal service from juniors. But to preserve the habit of obedience that hazing encouraged, Wilson included many traditional practices into the Academy's regulations, such as the requirement that plebes report to all formations "on the double" to indoctrinate the value of promptness.[22]

Public relations, which did not exist in the Navy before 1921, were important to Admiral Wilson. The imposing walls that surrounded the Academy were designed to keep the public out as well as to keep the midshipmen in. The annual report of the superintendent became an illustrated booklet that was sent to the parents of midshipmen and to other interested parties. He encouraged parental support of their sons in the Academy during the years when Baldwin was a midshipman. Oliver P. Baldwin wrote favorable articles about the Academy in the *Sun*. The superintendent was fully aware of these articles, but is not known whether Midshipman Baldwin received any favorable attention because of his father's writings.[23] Wilson's attempt to reduce the isolation of the Academy from the outside world was not lost on Baldwin, who would in later years use his writings to stress the importance of the Navy to the nation and the role of the Naval Academy to train future officers.

During Baldwin's first year, plebes were permitted off campus on only two occasions. Church parties permitted them to leave the grounds on Sunday mornings, and since he had been raised as an Episcopalian, Baldwin attended St. Anne's Church in Annapolis. There he met Joseph Muse Worthington, a fellow plebe, and his two sisters. He and Worthington made an official request to be roommates, but it was turned down because Academy rules forbad any change of roommates during the school year. When Hanson told his father about the matter, he, in turn, contacted Maryland governor Albert Ritchie, who called Superintendent Wilson. Within a week Baldwin and Joe Worthington were roommates. It was the beginning of a beautiful friendship that forged a bond between the men, and later their families, that lasted for more than five decades.[24]

The Army-Navy football game was the only occasion on which the entire regiment left the Academy. They marched to the Baltimore and Ohio railroad station at Annapolis, en route to New York City. Bets were made with Army cadets. If Navy won the game, the top prize was a West Point bathrobe. Baldwin never won one but his Latin School classmate, Cadet Randall Sollenberg, gave him a West Point dress hat with plume, which Baldwin kept as a trophy. During the years 1920–24, Navy won twice, tied once, and lost once to Army.[25]

An important part of every midshipman's education was the two three-month summer cruises. The first cruise was after the plebe year and the second one was after the third year. On the day after the graduation of the first class, the remaining three classes were assigned to one of three older battleships: the *Michigan* (BB 27), the *Delaware* (BB 28), or the *Florida* (BB 30), all of which had been commissioned between 1909 and 1911. The purpose of the cruises was to give the midshipmen a variety of practical lessons and experiences on board a capital ship. Some of the ships' regular crew and officers were on board to instruct and to guide the midshipmen in all aspects of running a ship.

All the crew shared crowded quarters and all slept in hammocks, there being no space for bunks. Freshwater was in short supply; there was limited personal bathing and uniforms had to be washed in a bucket. All on board had to keep the decks clean and the brass work polished. Every morning, with trousers rolled up and in bare feet, they would holystone the deck with a saltwater hose and then squeegee it.[26] The deck gang would alternate midshipmen between the turret division on the casement guns, or in the fire control division. Everyone spent time belowdecks in the fire room shoveling coal as experienced sailors instructed midshipmen on the need to maintain the water pressure in the boilers at all times, a very important responsibility.

There were many challenges to living in close quarters on board these old battleships but none quite as onerous as "coaling." It was an "all day, all hands" operation that was dirty and tedious. To offload coal from the colliers alongside the ship onto the deck, the crew used wheelbarrows and shovels to push the coal down into the scuttles and chutes to the coalbunkers below deck. Only the ship's band members were excused from this duty. The band perched on top of the aft turret, playing popular tunes to urge everyone else to greater effort.[27]

Baldwin recalled that as a coal passer he had to work in airless bunkers filled with coal dust. The one positive lesson of fire-room duty was to finally see at close hand how Babcock and Wilcox boilers, which midshipmen had for years been required to diagram in their steam engineering course, actually worked. They also learned the proper use of the ash-ejector system, which removed the coal ashes by water pressure. It was a tricky process that if done improperly would result in ashes being blown in a person's face.[28] Years later Baldwin wrote about that system that contributed to the sinking of a passenger ship.

One of the pleasant benefits of the cruises was to visit the many ports of call in Europe, where midshipmen had an opportunity to see the sights.[29] In retrospect, Baldwin felt that the learning by doing was a good teaching technique, though without modern navigation equipment those old battleships were "navigated by guess and by God, and by sun and star signs."[30]

His plebe year behind him, Baldwin devoted many of his recreation hours to athletics, especially water polo, where he made the team in his final two years at the Academy. He was also on the crew squad and played some football on his class team. Although his profession would be journalism, Hanson never wrote for *The Lucky Bag*, the class annual, or *The Log*, a weekly student publication.

In 1923, during his junior year, two dramatic events stood out. Every year, at the traditional "baptism of the class rings" at the beginning of June Week, second classmen would jump or be thrown off the sea wall at Dewey Basin, an inlet of the Severn River. Amid all the horseplay when everyone jumped into the water on top of each other, one midshipman, Leicester R. Smith, drowned.[31] The following year, the Ring Dance replaced the traditional going-over-the-wall high jinks.[32]

The other event (which could have ended Baldwin's career) occurred while a group of midshipmen were practicing at the rifle range. A Marine corporal was instructing the group on how to disable a .30 caliber machine gun, with the partially disassembled gun on a wooden table with steel leg supports. The corporal was using a live cartridge to press on the springs to take the gun apart. One of the midshipmen inserted a cartridge into the breech when the bolt was removed, and it went off. The bullet first hit the buttocks of the Marine who was sitting on the table, then went through the table and down a steel leg and entered Baldwin's Achilles tendon. Both men were taken to the Naval Academy hospital. The attending doctor split Hanson's tendon to remove the bullet fragments, but infection soon set in. Against Baldwin's instructions, Joe Worthington told his parents about the accident. Oliver Baldwin then hired a Johns Hopkins specialist and together the doctors drained the wound and stopped the infection.

Oliver Baldwin was devastated by the accident. He wrote to his son that the bullet that had hit his heel "hit me in the middle of the heart," adding, "I pray [to] God this will be the last time you get hurt in peace or war."[33] This unusual outpouring of parental concern illustrated the close bond between them. Hanson remained in the hospital for about a month, recovering slowly. The first class cruise had already left by the time he was released from the hospital and had taken his final examinations, but he joined the fleet in July on board the recently commissioned scout cruiser, the USS *Richmond* (CL 9), on its shake-down cruise. Having no specific duties on board, he stood watch as the junior officer of the deck tried to use the sextant to determine the ship's location, and visited the chart room.[34] He joined the first class cruise in Lisbon, Portugal, and recalled that port being "the dirtiest, filthiest place on earth . . . full of prostitutes." Many Americans found the easy access to alcohol a new and exhilarating experience that they were not prepared to handle responsibly. Accustomed to prohibition in the United States, many midshipmen found alcohol enticing and became drunk in public. Baldwin was not one of them.[35]

As his graduation day neared, Baldwin shared some doubts about his future naval career with his father. The Department of the Navy had offered to all midshipmen the option of resigning from the Navy immediately following their graduation, the direct result of the Washington Naval Arms Limitation Conference (1921–22), at which the United States had agreed to scrap thirty of its capital war ships by 1924. As a result, the Navy had no need for all of the newly commissioned ensigns. He told his father that he wanted to take a sabbatical resignation to attend the University of Virginia for a year, to "take any courses I like, mostly in literature." He then wanted to travel "for six or seven years" in the Orient and "end my days in peace undisturbed by the cares of the world in the gentle climate of the South

Pacific."[36] Whatever his father's response, and it was probably a negative one given his father's devotion to duty, Hanson let those vague thoughts lie dormant for the next three years.

June Week comprised five days of athletic events, dances (called hops in 1924), a dress parade, and the presentation of athletic awards. On Sunday, June 2, at the baccalaureate service in the chapel, the chaplain's sermon had political overtones. He criticized the "flabby patriotism" of those who "under the security of our flag, by their blind and senseless mouthing of peace, peace, when there is no peace, would force us into a policy of lamb-like defensiveness." He charged the graduates that in its national self-defense, the Army and the Navy must be "sufficiently" strong to guarantee America's ability for "full leadership abroad," which did not mean aggression or a desire for world conquest, as the pacifists claimed. Americans instead are, he concluded, "eager Samaritans."[37]

Midshipman Baldwin,
USNA class of 1924
*Courtesy of the Nimitz Library,
Special Collections Division*

On the night before graduation, the class of 1925 hosted the Farewell Dance for the class of 1924 in the cavernous Dahlgren Hall, decorated with blue and gold streamers and lights. The midshipmen were dressed in their high-collared summer white uniforms, and their dates wore pastel dresses. More than two thousand spectators watched from the balconies as the couples danced the night away, a colorful and romantic scene that Hollywood would re-create later in films with Ruby Keeler and Dick Powell.

On Wednesday, June 4, 1924, 515 members of the class of 1924 graduated and received their ensign's commission as officers and gentlemen, signed by the president of the United States. Baldwin remembered very little about the graduation ceremony, other than his mother and one of his sisters pinning his ensign bars on his uniform.[38] He graduated in the middle of his class, 228th out of 522. Of that number, 7 did not graduate because of incomplete grades, and 58 chose the Navy Department's offer and resigned immediately from the service. All of Baldwin's grades for his spring term were 3.0 or better, with the exception of navigation (2.93) and electrical engineering and physics (2.96). Perhaps more indicative of his future in the Navy was his mark in "Aptitude for the Service," 3.70.[39]

Oliver Baldwin's long editorial, "June Week at the Naval Academy," in the *Sun* praised Superintendent Wilson for instilling the principles of "honor, uprightness and truth that would insure that the American flag, the American name, will never be sullied by our Navy" so long as those principles were observed. He contrasted the "simple, direct character" of the Academy graduates and their "courage, manhood, honor and duty" with "the scholastic subtleties and the foolish disputations of the so-called highbrows." Hanson was less interested in his father's literary prose than in getting on with his chosen career, in which he looked forward to joining the Asiatic Fleet on the Yangtze River in the future, a hope that was never to be realized.[40]

In later years, Hanson reflected that although the Naval Academy tended to offer only a narrow range of courses, "it did shape character, it did teach concentration and self-control and above all it inculcated tradition, spirit, morale [and] patriotism." The phrase that he used later to describe his life-long bond with his classmates was "the band of brothers," a phrase from Shakespeare's *Henry V* that he most likely had heard his father proclaim, as he tended to: "For he today that shed his blood with me shall be my brother, we few, we happy few, we band of brothers."[41]

The graduation speaker was Curtis D. Wilbur, the recently appointed secretary of the Navy, who urged the newly commissioned ensigns to rule over enlisted men with firmness and courtesy, and warned them to avoid sarcasm and always to put themselves in the other man's position. He also cautioned the newly commissioned ensigns to keep intellectually active, warning them against becoming "the shirker, the slacker, and side-stepper,"[42] but most likely Hanson's attention was elsewhere during the address. He had invited three Baltimore girlfriends to join him for June Week activities, but at separate times. To his chagrin, they had compared notes and discovered his scheme.

Former president Woodrow Wilson had died in February 1924 and the Republicans had nominated Massachusetts governor Calvin Coolidge. On Broadway, two romantic operettas, *The Student Prince* and *Rose Marie*, enjoyed long runs, and George Gershwin's *Rhapsody in Blue* was first performed with the Paul Whiteman Orchestra and the composer at the keyboard. Leopold and Loeb were sentenced to life imprisonment for the murder of Bobby Franks in Chicago, and the Republican principals in the Teapot Dome oil scandal were indicted. There were more than two million radios in American homes,[43] but Ensign Baldwin paid scant attention to such larger events as he began to devote all his energies to his first duty station.

CHAPTER 3

Showing the Flag, 1924-27

While awaiting the arrival of their ships, Baldwin and other ensigns were assigned temporarily to the Washington-Dahlgren-Indian Head stations where the Washington Navy Yard gun factory personnel showed the ensigns how guns were made. The optical shop taught them how to use range finders, stadimeters (to measure the distance to the target), and other optical equipment. At Indian Head, Maryland, they were shown the various forms of gunpowder that were stored in glass jars. Baldwin recalled the instructor taking a jar of fulminate of mercury and commenting on how delicate that powder was. The instructor handed the jar to the same classmate who had put a live round in the machine gun that had gone off and hit Baldwin in May 1923. This time, the classmate pretended to drop the jar, but caught it before it hit the floor. This joke did not endear him to the other ensigns.[1]

During that ordnance summer, Hanson lived at home and commuted to Washington. To escape the heat and humidity of the capital city, he used the eighteen-feet-deep ship-model basin at the Navy Yard as a swimming pool after hours.

Dahlgren, Virginia, on the Potomac River, was where the naval guns were tested. Another attraction there was Letty Shield, who was a sister-in-law of one of the officers at the station. To Hanson she was a "lovely and delightful girl" and they shared a love of swimming. The friendship blossomed and he was enamored of her for several years, the first, but not the last, of his romantic interludes while in the Navy.[2]

On Thursday, August 29, 1924, Baldwin and three other ensigns reported to the battleship USS *Texas* at Hampton Roads, Virginia. That ship, commissioned in 1914, had been detached from the U.S. fleet with three other American battleships in November 1917 to form the 6th Battle Squadron of the British Grand Fleet in World War I.

There are two versions of the day Baldwin reported to the *Texas*. To his mother he wrote that the officers, including the captain and the executive officer, "seem a fine bunch and they have all treated us wonderfully."[3] But years later he recalled how he and three other ensigns, following protocol, put on their dress whites, their swords, and white gloves. So accoutered, they reported to the executive officer, who shouted, "What in the goddamn hell have you got all that silly stuff on for? Take it off and get over the side into the coal barges and help coal the ship."[4]

The ship's captain was Ivan C. Wettengel, a "Prussian type, very dour-looking and tough." He was not at all the benign fatherly figure Baldwin tried to portray to his mother. The closest he came to revealing anything to her was a comment that an officer's life on board ship is "different from [that of] a midshipman's."[5] Instead, he told her quite a bit about the ample food on board, including steaks, potatoes, ice cream, and cake.

He thought himself very fortunate to have been assigned to the F Division (gunfire control) on the ship. As an ensign, Baldwin was under the more senior officer Lieutenant (jg, or junior grade) Theodore R. Wirth, who, in the position "of becoming a god or devil, . . . became a god." (Meaning he had the power to make life difficult or easy for Baldwin.) They became lifelong friends and later Baldwin would turn to "Turk" for advice about his naval career.[6] Another officer in that division was Bill Sebald, class of 1922, who later became the naval attaché in the American embassy in Tokyo.[7]

Baldwin served on the *Texas* for sixteen months, and much of that time was spent on routine port calls along the East Coast of the United States and, during the winter months, at Guantánamo, Cuba. In late November 1924, the USS *Texas*, together with other ships, participated in secret tests against the partially completed *Maryland*-class battleship USS *Washington* (BB 47). It was one of the U.S. Navy's ships to be scrapped under the terms of the 1922 Washington Naval Arms Limitations conference. In 1924, a rusting hulk with no turret guns and no steam power, it was towed to a point sixty miles off of Cape Henry, just inside the 100-fathom curve.

Captain Wettengel issued a written notice to all hands that the tests were "strictly confidential," and all officers and men on board were warned not to tell anyone by "word of mouth or letter" about what they might see.[8] Simulated torpedo and mine explosions were detonated underwater close to the *Washington*'s hull. Ensign Baldwin was in the fire-control division below deck. The *Texas* fired shells at different ranges, but the ship did not sink. On November 23 two planes from Hampton Roads dropped practice bombs onto the deck of the *Washington*. Gale-force winds from the northeast suspended further tests. Anchored, waves broke over the *Washington* and she began to settle down by the bow. The following morning she was still afloat. The *Texas*, at a range of seven thousand yards, fired its 14-inch guns. Baldwin was again below deck watching the dial on the Ford range finder when the order "Cease firing" was given. He went topside to see the USS *Washington* sink as the *Texas* moved closer to inspect the shell damage. As Baldwin later wrote, "On the *Texas*, a bugle blew and we above the decks stood at attention. Her stern lifted, her bow sank. . . . She began her last plunge." The bugler blew "Taps" and "we saluted."[9]

The first death in the class of 1924 was that of Henry Clay Drexler, whom Baldwin knew. During gunnery drills on the recently commissioned light cruiser USS *Trenton* (CL 11), a powder bag for a 6-inch gun exploded in the forward turret. Five were killed and seven were injured. Apparently, Drexler had tried to dump the powder bag into an immersion tank inside the turret, but not soon enough.[10] It had taken Drexler six years to get through the Academy, and he was killed just ten days after reporting for duty. In a letter to his mother, Baldwin commented on Drexler's death as a model for other naval officers: "If every officer could die as heroic a death as this," he wrote, " . . . our Navy need have nothing to fear." At the age of twenty-two, Baldwin thought losing his life for a cause larger than himself would be a worthy sacrifice. He then added a fatalistic comment about how "some must die that others may live," assuming that the Navy would learn important lessons from Drexler's death and be better for it.[11]

The next port of call for the *Texas* was New York City, where it would participate in Navy Day activities on October 27, the birthday of former president Theodore Roosevelt, the father of the modern American Navy. Baldwin always enjoyed the city and its many diversions. Usually on such visits he would stay with his uncle, the Reverend Joseph Wilson Sutton, his mother's brother, who was the vicar at Trinity Chapel on West 25th Street. Occasionally he would invite a few of his fellow officers to stay there, as well.

On that occasion, he took the opportunity to see various Broadway shows, including *What Price Glory* with Brian Donlevy, William Boyd (who would become television's Hopalong Cassidy), and Louis Wolheim. Of that grim play about the Great War, Baldwin wrote his mother: "[It] held my interest more than any play I've ever seen and I should like to see it again."[12]

Following his brief stay in New York, Baldwin was sent to the Ford Range-Keeping School in Long Island City, New York, together with Ensign Bill Sebald, for a two-week training period. The Ford Instrument Company built the Navy's mechanical analog computer, which in the 1920s provided a partially mechanized fire-control system to aim its main battery of guns and to set the fuse times on the 14-inch shells. It was a complicated instrument not easily mastered, at least in Baldwin's experience.[13]

After a five-day Christmas leave spent at home, Baldwin joined the fleet in the new year, 1925, as it headed south to Guantánamo Bay, Cuba, for its usual winter exercises in gunnery and maneuvers. Gitmo was hot, the base primitive, and there was little for naval ensigns to do. They shaved their heads to minimize the heat. As their hair grew back, the fuzz became a sort of a badge of honor to show others that they had been there.[14] Because of the heat, sleeping belowdecks was impossible, so they took their mattresses on deck at night. They also swam at every opportunity when they were not at the rifle range.

Another diversion was to visit the little town of Caimanera, the closest village to the base. It was off limits to all naval personnel except officers, who needed their captain's permission to enter the town, ferried by motorboat with a junior officer in charge. On one occasion, when Baldwin was the boat officer, he passed the time by reading Plutarch's *Lives*. After a few hours of waiting, he was alerted that a senior officer of the *Texas* was returning to the boat. Baldwin stepped onto the dock with one foot, the other on the motorboat. Once the officer was on board Baldwin told the coxswain to shove off, but he still had his finger marking his place in the book and his foot on the dock. Into the water he fell to the great amusement of all.[15] The fact that he was reading literature to pass the time indicated that he wanted to broaden his horizons from the narrowness of the naval officer's world.

This awareness that there may be more to life than this routine became more pronounced in the months ahead.

One of the most unpleasant duties was to attend the summary courts martial that were heard before three officers. On one occasion, Baldwin learned how to temper discipline with justice. The chief water tender in the fire room had smashed the water gauge glass while on a drunken rampage, but the court found him not guilty. As Commander Milo P. Refo, the gunnery officer on the *Texas*, explained to Baldwin, the sailor had a good service record that counted in his favor, but that kind of decision ran against Baldwin's Academy training, which had taught midshipmen to stick to the book and follow regulations.[16]

A junior officer of the deck was expected to make a ship's inspection, while in port, at least once or twice during a four-hour watch, and Baldwin took his duties seriously, following rules to the letter. On one occasion Baldwin was down in the bag alleys, the longitudinal compartments on both sides of the *Texas*, where the men stowed their hammocks and sea bags. Without meaning to, he overheard a sailor asking who was the OOD. A second one replied, "That son of a bitch, Baldwin. Get your hair cut."[17] He was amused by this outburst.

In the 1920s, the average American knew, or cared, so little about the armed services that a naval officer's uniform was often mistaken for that of "a railroad gateman, a bus conductor, or a messenger boy."[18] The public's opinion of the Navy had reached such a low point during the Jazz Age that one naval officer recalled his fellow officers being considered to be "one cut below the bootlegger who was providing the neighborhood with liquor."[19]

The *Texas* entered Portsmouth (New Hampshire) Navy Yard in late 1925 for a long-planned modernization that included converting coal-fired boilers to oil burners, replacing the two cage masts with a single tripod foremast, and increasing the armor on the decks. During these renovations, many officers were transferred to other ships. Soon, Baldwin found himself the sole officer in F Division. To while away the time he played on the ship's football team, and when his new orders arrived he left the *Texas* on a fifteen-day leave beginning on December 23, 1925, and reported to a destroyer, his first choice for sea duty, the USS *Breck* (DD 283), on January 6, 1926. It was to be his home for the next twenty months. In his fitness report for the final three months of 1925 on the *Texas*, Commander C. A. Blakely noted that

Ensign Baldwin was "very capable" and "gives promise of becoming a lead-ing figure among those of his profession."[20]

The USS *Breck* was one of 273 flush deck destroyers hurriedly completed by eleven civilian shipyards in 1918 and 1919. The crew called this ship the "USS Break," because of the numerous breakdowns in its engineering plant. These destroyers were long (314 feet), narrow (31 feet), and fast (over 31 knots), and they rolled easily, even in the wake of a passing motor boat.[21]

The authorized complement for the *Breck* was 9 officers and 144 men, but when Baldwin served on board there were only 6 officers and 125 men. On a small ship, junior officers had to learn many duties because, as Baldwin recalled, "nobody knew much more about some of these things than you did."[22]

On Thursday, June 17, 1926, the USS *Breck*, together with five other destroyers of Division 25, Squadron 9 of the Scouting Fleet, left Newport, Rhode Island, for twelve months of cruising in European waters and in the Mediterranean. They visited thirty-two ports in their mission to "show the flag" and to establish "amicable" and friendly relations with other peoples.[23]

On his maiden voyage across the Atlantic en route to the Azores, heavy weather hit. "As I write," he said in a letter to his mother, "the ship rises and falls and rolls and sways . . . and the spray and spume and spindrift would fly about the bridge and rattle against the glass window like hail."[24] Later he wrote, "We are the only five ships on a limitless ocean. . . . You feel small when you realize that there may not be other ships within a couple of hun-dred miles."[25]

On their safe arrival at Ponta del Gada, San Miguel Island, the Azores, the young ensign went ashore to see the sights, assuring his mother that he did not participate in the drinking or roulette gambling that flourished in the local clubs. His long letters home described a plan he and his sister Dorothy had to write a travel book using Baldwin's letters as the basis. As he had thought just before his graduation, Baldwin was still uncertain about whether or not to remain in the Navy or become a professional writer, but he did not have to make a career decision just yet.

At Gibraltar, which the *Breck* used for docking and machinery repair, it was apparent that Britain's Royal Navy was the dominant naval force in the Mediterranean. The U.S. Navy's role was to show the American flag in foreign ports. The *Breck* steamed independently of other ships, spending lots of time ashore to make the American presence visible to the local people.[26]

At Haifa (now part of Israel) Baldwin was the only officer on board when a strong easterly wind threatened to push the *Breck* onto the rocky shore, there being no docking facilities there. Sensing a real problem developing, he found a gunner's mate and a "fine old chief petty officer" and sent them down to the engine room to alert the fireman on duty to get up steam and, using a procedure called "veer the chain," let out the anchor chain while dropping the other anchor to turn the ship's stern into the wind. Baldwin proudly noted that the captain, once on board "gave me a pat on the back for doing the right thing. I felt very good about it."[27]

The *Breck*, like other destroyers of that class, was known as a "wet ship." In rough seas it rolled a great deal, and it was "unpleasant" to be on deck in a seaway because footing was difficult. To go from the bow to the stern a sailor had to go onto the open main deck and hang on to the lifelines. The ship also had portholes close to the waterline and they would leak if not secured. In the wardroom, tablecloths were kept wet to provide friction so that the dishes would not slide on the table. Unfortunately the chairs were not bolted to the floor; instead they were secured to the table by a rope line.[28]

It was not part of the showing the flag policy, but because Baldwin had become blinded by love, he foolishly agreed to take the pet dog of his latest girlfriend, a Gibraltar resident, Constance Wolfe, on board the *Breck* that was scheduled to leave Gibraltar for England. Since the quarantine laws in Britain were uncompromising, she may have hoped to evade them by shipping her dog home on a U.S. naval ship. The dog never got its sea legs and was off balance frequently, becoming seasick on the captain's bunk. On arrival at Portsmouth, the dog was taken off the ship and placed in a six-month mandatory quarantine, so perhaps the young ensign learned a lesson about doing a favor for a pretty face in a foreign port.[29]

The USS *Breck* also spent a considerable time at Marseilles, France. It moored at the foot of the Rue de Canabiere, which the crew called "Rue de Can of Beer," in the Vieux Port, a favorite among sailors on liberty leave. The *Breck* and its sister ship, the *Toucey* (DD 282), visited Marseilles in July and in December 1926. The American consul arranged for them to visit the exclusive tennis club and the local fencing club (Salle d'Armes), where Baldwin enjoyed conversations with a French artillery officer, the consul from Siam, and other members of the foreign community.[30]

In Marseilles, showing the flag was a duty that required that the officers and men of the *Breck* demonstrate simply and directly American generosity to those less fortunate. The "Christmas Ship," a tradition in the U.S. Navy, began in 1915 so that ships' crews could entertain local children in foreign ports. On Christmas Eve, the crews of the *Breck* and the *Toucey* entertained fifty boys and girls from a local Catholic orphanage. The ships were decorated with signal flags, branches of fir trees were lashed to the masts, and all the ships' lights were turned on, including the search lights. Santa Claus (Père Noël) made an appearance to hand out gifts to the children: pocketknives for the boys and dolls and handkerchiefs for the girls. Carols were sung and all the children had an enjoyable time. The nun, who accompanied them, thanked the crews in French. Though most of the ships' company did not understand her words, the expression on her face and the obvious sincerity in her voice overcame the language barrier.[31]

The British and the American colonies in Marseilles also entertained Ensign Baldwin and other officers on several occasions. At one dinner party at a French home, the host brought out a special cake called "Le Roi et La Reine." Hidden inside the cake were little figures of a king and queen, together with a few small spoons, symbols of future wealth. Whoever found a king, as Baldwin did, was invited to choose his queen by kissing one of the women at the table. "Shy and bashful by nature, and totally and entirely unfitted for what happened," forced to respond to the encouragement from the family—"*Choisez la reine!*"—he went over to the host's wife and kissed her on both cheeks, to the approval of all. "She pretended to be embarrassed," he recalled.[32] Such simple acts of friendship and good fellowship probably did more to overcome perceived differences between France and the United States than any number of elaborate diplomatic receptions and treaties.

In January 1927 the *Sun* ran a brief announcement that Ensign Hanson W. Baldwin was engaged to Miss Constance Wolfe (the owner of the previously mentioned pet dog), a resident of Gibraltar whose father was the officer in charge of the Royal Dock Yards there. Her parents lived on Hayling Island, adjacent to the harbor at Portsmouth, England. A June wedding was to be held in England. Baldwin requested a two-month leave, to begin on or about May 20, 1927, with travel time to return to the United States. The Bureau of Navigation granted his leave request. In 1975, he commented tersely that the engagement was broken off.[33] Years later, he admitted that he had been "violently smitten" with her at the time, and in 1987 he admitted that Constance's mother had not encouraged her daughter to continue the engagement.[34]

The *Breck* was docked in Plymouth, England, on Saturday, May 21, 1927, when Charles A. Lindbergh and the *Spirit of St. Louis* flew high overhead en route to Paris. Although Baldwin saw the plane, he did not know of its importance until later.[35] On June 3, the *Breck* was at Cherbourg, France, where the by-then internationally famous pilot boarded the USS *Memphis* (CL 13) for a safer trip across the Atlantic. As that ship passed close by the *Breck*, the ship's company cheered him. Lindbergh was overheard to remark, "I wish I were going back with you. I like a small boat."[36]

In Baldwin's day, promotion in rank was not automatic. Ensigns were required to serve in grade for three years, with an additional four years as lieutenant (jg). Before promotion, a candidate had to take daylong written examinations that thoroughly tested all the subjects a naval officer was expected to know. Baldwin took his examinations in Villefranche, France, on engineering, electricity, seamanship, ordnance and gunnery, practical and theoretical navigation and plotting, international and military law, communications, and aviation.[37] He passed and was promoted to lieutenant (jg) on June 5, 1927. The results were impressive: the lowest grade was a 3.26 in steam engineering, and the highest, a 4.0, was in international law.[38]

His officer fitness reports were also excellent. The captain of the *Breck*, Lieutenant Commander John H. Magruder Jr., noted repeatedly in his quarterly reports how Baldwin was energetic, industrious, reliable, and devoted to duty. In one report, the captain noted that Baldwin was "above average for his grade—a thorough gentleman—loyal, courteous and enthusiastic, abstemious" in his habits, and in fine "physical trim."[39]

Based on his professional performance, Baldwin could possibly have risen to flag rank during World War II, when promotions were more rapid than during the 1920s. But he decided to resign his commission and leave the U.S. Navy in 1927. From his letters home, it appears that he was interested in becoming a travel writer and was experiencing growing restlessness about his often repetitive and boring naval duties. At the age of twenty-four, he wanted more out of life than just waiting for some international incident to summon him to action. He vented his concerns to Ted Wirth, a fellow officer, who urged Baldwin to remain in the Navy, reminding him, "We're always tied down by something—family or business on the outside—duty on the inside. We take it or get out," but he added that if Baldwin was determined to leave the Navy, he should "get out while [he was] young and free." He also added a final observation: "You're one of very few men I know . . . who is just what your mother thinks you are. To me it is remarkable,"[40] alluding to the fact that Baldwin accepted without question the rigid straightforward values of his upbringing, such as not drinking any alcohol.

Another of Baldwin's correspondents was Lieutenant (jg) Frank O'Beirne, who was stationed at the Fleet Air Base, San Diego. He praised Hanson for having the courage to "get out and make your way in civilian life. You can do it. Competition is keener than most of us in the service realize—or perhaps we do, which keeps us in! I'm holding out for $10,000 a year so I guess I'll be in for some time."[41]

Baldwin applied to be with the Asiatic Fleet, the famed Yangtze Patrol, because he wanted adventure and the challenge of doing something different, rather than repeating earlier experiences. It was where his former roommate Joe Worthington was stationed. Baldwin's interest may have been spurred on by a letter from another classmate, Stephen Bedford, who had described, in dramatic fashion, the civil war in China and the Navy's role in trying to protect American businessmen and missionaries.[42] An alternative assignment requested by Baldwin was with the Judge Advocate General's office in Washington, D.C., but neither request was granted. He was to continue his assigned routine duty along the Atlantic coast, with winters in Guantánamo Bay.

Soon, however, a door of opportunity opened to him when three of his travel narratives about visits to the Azores, Gibraltar, and Spain were printed in the *Sun* in the spring of 1927, providing a glimmer of hope that perhaps he might become a successful commercial writer.[43]

The *Breck* returned stateside in June 1927, after a yearlong cruise in Europe and the Mediterranean. On September 2, all the destroyers in the Scouting Fleet proceeded as a group to Charleston, South Carolina. There, Baldwin left his ship for the last time, having previously submitted his resignation on August 31 while at sea, with a requested resignation date of September 30, 1927.

In his last letter to his mother while in the Navy, Hanson assured her that he had no reason to change his decision: "I am confident in my ability to take care of myself," he wrote, and to remain "master of my fate and captain of my soul. . . . I believe I am doing the right thing. No one can do more than follow his beliefs, no matter where they may lead."[44]

When the Navy's Bureau of Navigation, which dealt with all officer personnel matters, wanted to know why he was resigning, his answer was "limited opportunities, incompatible work, and personal reasons."[45] On November 5, 1927, Baldwin was one of 318 ensigns to resign from the Navy in 1927. Records show that during the late 1920s a number of junior officers left the service. There was little to hold them. Promotions were slow, pay was low, and congressional parsimony stopped any new destroyers, on which new ensigns had their initial sea duty, from being built. When he resigned, there were 5,422 line officers and 82,500 enlisted ranks in the Navy, a sharp drop from the 1918 Navy's personnel level of 448,600.[46]

However, not wishing to sever all ties with the naval service, Baldwin then applied to the Volunteer Naval Reserve, where he was commissioned as a lieutenant (jg) on November 29, 1927, for deck and engineering duties for general service. In 1930 he took one two-week summer cruise along the New England coast on the USS *Childs* (DD 241), but it was not a pleasant experience. The serving officers, who all shared a low opinion of reserve naval officers in general, did not welcome him. He quickly learned that he was now an outsider and there was no turning back. He had made his decision to leave the U.S. Navy, and it was up to him to take charge of his fate and future as a civilian.

CHAPTER 4

In Search of a Vocation, 1927-29

anson Baldwin was on his own for the first time in his life. At the age of twenty-four, he had traveled widely but was not satisfied with the idea that the Navy was to be a lifetime career. The structured life he had lived for seven years was over, at least for the next few years. He decided to live at home with his parents, with whom he got along well. They were very happy to have him around after so many months away. His vocational goal was simple: to travel, to write interesting accounts of the people and places he saw and visited, and to sell his travel articles to magazines and newspapers. He hoped that getting some name recognition would help him to further his writing career. To pass the time, he clipped quotations made by well-known and successful motivational and self-help authors from magazines and newspapers and pasted the clippings into several scrapbooks. All stressed the merits of sticking to one's goals, which would bring ultimate personal success.[1]

While waiting for success to materialize, Baldwin wrote about what he knew best, the U.S. Navy. On December 17, 1927, the Navy's submarine, S-4, was rammed by a U.S. Coast Guard cutter off Provincetown, Massachusetts, and all hands were lost. Bad weather delayed a prompt recovery, but later, divers heard a coded message from six of the remaining crew that said, "Please hurry." The *Sun* ran an editorial, "This Christmas Tragedy," that was critical of the Navy's slow rescue attempts and questioned whether naval authorities had developed the proper equipment for such emergencies.[2] The editorial provoked Baldwin to write a letter of indignation to the paper: "The Navy has never been slow in coming to the aid of their comrades," he wrote, chastising the editorialist for his "ignorant" criticism. He listed the many difficulties of submarine rescue. While this verbal invective initially satisfied him, he then remarked, "The wind was taken out of my journalistic sails when my father, chuckling with mirth, confessed that he had written the offending editorial and that he had put my letter in the paper." Baldwin vowed never to write another letter to any editor, though he admitted that some of his own future writings had given others "cause to do so."[3]

Wishing to travel again, Baldwin applied to be a member of Admiral Richard E. Byrd's 1928 Antarctic expedition. While he was waiting to hear about his application, Oliver Baldwin's health declined and the 78-year-old newspaperman required an operation and so, Hanson withdrew his application.

Beginning in January 1928, Baldwin began an eleven-month internship as a cub reporter at the *Sun*. In his *Reminiscences*, he recalled that he was uncertain as to his vocation and was just "looking for something to do and so [I] decided to try to get a job" at the *Sun*.[4] He had never been a reporter, nor had he previously shown an interest in being a newspaperman, an occupation that his father had advised against. In Baldwin's favor were the few travel articles written while in the Navy that showed some narrative skills, but most likely it was the good word from Oliver Baldwin to the managing editor that was sufficient to hire Hanson. At the *Sun*, Baldwin's mentor was Mark Watson, the Sunday editor, a longtime friend and colleague of Oliver. Despite his lack of reporting skills, Baldwin threw himself, with great energy, into his new assignment. Paid $18 a week, he often worked twelve hours a day, six days a week.[5] He had not planned for a newspaper career at that time, but perhaps not wishing to disappoint his father's faith in him, he took all reporting assignments that came his way. He compiled two scrapbooks that contained his *Sun* pieces, none was dated and most of them had no byline. A list of a few headlines will give the reader the variety of the news stories he covered.

"Assert Bride Placed Poison in his Coffee"

"Youth, 18, Dies After Bout with Brother"

"Woman Kills Herself in Her Sister's Home"

"Youth, 19, Wounded by Policeman Dies"[6]

Two pieces, written in 1928, for which Baldwin received bylines, were on the arrival of the *Graf Zeppelin* in New Jersey and on the sinking of the

SS *Vestris* off the Virginia coast. The German zeppelin, on its maiden voyage from Germany to Lakehurst, New Jersey, was delayed for two days around Bermuda before docking in New Jersey. Baldwin described its arrival with florid phrases, such as the "mistress of the skies" and "latest aerial conqueror of the Atlantic." U.S. Navy personnel, who had waited for seventy-two hours for its arrival, were upset that the ship did not make radio contact to note its position while en route to its docking site. A naval official in Washington was critical of the time and money the Navy spent just waiting for its arrival. Baldwin noted other carping comments made by American officials about the German officers and crew that replaced the initial popular interest in the airship's flight with "a degree of unpopularity."[7]

On November 12 the SS *Vestris*, a cargo-passenger liner en route from New York to Bermuda, sank in a storm two hundred miles off Hampton Roads, Virginia. Of the 325 passengers and crew on board, 112 were lost. Many reporters interviewed the survivors about their experiences, but Baldwin wanted to find the probable cause. The initial report of the sinking was that shifting cargo had made the ship unstable and that listing caused it to take on water.[8] Baldwin interviewed the three surviving fire-room stokers who told him about a cracked sea valve in the fire room's ash ejector. Baldwin's naval experience taught him that all coal-burning ships had ash ejectors. On the *Vestris*, the ash ejectors were clogged and water came into the fire room through the ejectors. As the ship listed farther, the coaling door on the side of the ship had burst open because of outside water pressure, thus increasing the list.[9]

One of Baldwin's early assignments as a cub reporter was to cover the Northwest Police Station in Baltimore. Baltimore was then a racially segregated Southern city. Since none of his classmates at the Latin School, or later at the Naval Academy, was African American, he had no understanding or racial sensitivity of their community. He wrote that the Northwest was not a neighborhood that most white Baltimoreans ever visited, nor would they want to. The docket of the local police station was filled with reports of assaults, shootings, and knifings on almost a daily basis, as well as reports for drunkenness and disorderly conduct. Baldwin ended his superficial report by observing that the Negro "with his racial pride . . . lives a complete life of his own, untroubled save by the laws of this white man's civilization."[10] This racial insensitivity reflected his Southern white middle-class values and biases.

At the end of 1928, after almost a year with the *Sun*, Baldwin wanted to travel once more, since his father's health had improved after an operation. He asked two editors on the paper for a general recommendation. Both had been impressed with his ability to handle both news and features. The city editor reflected upon Baldwin's ability "to sense news background beyond the boundaries of his routine and his natural turn for writing [that] soon took him to other fields. He became one of the best men of the special assignment staff."[11] The managing editor praised the clarity of his writing and his reliability.[12] Both editors wished that Baldwin would return to the *Sun*, but he never did.

In 1929 Baldwin made two voyages of discovery, one to South America and the other to Labrador. He signed on as a quartermaster on the Munson liner *The American Legion* for a voyage to Rio de Janeiro, Brazil, and to other ports of call in South America. His real purpose was to sell his experiences later in a series of travel articles to magazines and newspapers.[13]

The American Legion left New York harbor on Saturday, December 29, 1928, for a thirteen-day voyage to Rio. Baldwin's duties on board were to stand watch on the bridge behind the ship's compass twice every twenty-four hours, but his aim was to observe the officers and crew for his future articles: The master-at-arms was "fat and lazy" and wore "hideously loud pajamas." The boatswain's mate had a "close acquaintance with all the swear words in two tongues." Hanson couldn't wait to tell his mother the stories he had heard and to "start writing about these things."[14] He found the ship's crew to be filled with "queer characters and others [who had] odd eccentricities."[15] Baldwin observed that the Merchant Marine service had lax discipline, filthy crew quarters, widespread drunkenness (even on duty), and a crew who had no pride in the ship, which was why so many seamen jumped ship whenever they felt like it.[16]

At Rio de Janeiro, he observed from a distance at dockside women of the demimonde; at dusk, "drunken sailors staggered by, tightly clutching the arms of their ladies of the evening."[17] But he didn't seem to have engaged in any of these behaviors himself.

Baldwin's second voyage during the summer of 1929 was to Labrador. He signed on for fifteen weeks to work at one of the building sites operated by Dr. Wilfred Grenfell, a medical missionary. Baldwin was hired to supervise nine summer volunteers, all of them college students, to prepare a site for a new hospital at Cartwright. One of the stipulations he made to the Grenfell Association, before accepting this position, was that he be permitted to write later of his summer activities, and they had no objection.

Baldwin met Dr. Grenfell for the first time at a Sunday church service. The good doctor sincerely believed that he was doing God's work, but Baldwin wrote to his mother that Grenfell was "a man with thoughts dashing hither and thither."[18] He felt that the operations at Cartwright, Labrador, needed better organization with definite lines of authority established to push the summer projects to completion. He was proud that his volunteer group of nine had built a wharf, a storehouse, and a coal shack ready for use during the following summer. The hospital project was postponed until the following year.

During that summer, Dr. Grenfell and his wife lived on board the small steam yacht *Strathcona*. In late August, a few weeks before Baldwin planned to return to Baltimore, Dr. Grenfell was looking for someone to take the ship to St. Anthony, Newfoundland, where it would spend the winter in dry dock. When he learned that Baldwin was a former naval officer, he appointed him the captain of the *Strathcona*: "You are her absolute commander. . . . [Y]our being a naval officer you will use [your] authority rightly."[19] Baldwin expressed his doubts about steaming along an unknown coastline, but Dr. Grenfell dismissed those concerns, saying that there was a man on board the *Strathcona* who knew the coastline very well. The only problem was that he was blind. However, if Hanson described the features of each headland, then "he'd tell you which way to steer."[20] At night, while at anchor, Baldwin and Grenfell had many long conversations about "life and death and all the eternal verities."[21] So warned, the voyage reached its destination without incident.

Shortly before he returned home he wrote an enthusiastic letter to his mother expressing how "all pepped up" he was, and how he was "ready to write the Great American Novel and scoop all the papers from New York to Frisco."[22] With his travels over in September 1929, it was time, he later wrote, to be serious about "making a living."[23] His two years of searching for a vocation had ended. Like his father, he had decided be a journalist and would remain one for the next thirty-nine years, writing in a hurry to meet countless deadlines. His immediate problem was to open that door of opportunity again.

CHAPTER **5**

On General Assignment, 1929-36

To find that open door of opportunity, Hanson Baldwin traveled to New York City in September 1929 to find a position with the *New York Herald-Tribune*, then the "Mecca" of the newspaper crowd, but the managing editor turned him down quickly.[1]

Sensing his son's disappointment and aware of the obstacles of his being hired with little newspaper experience, Oliver Baldwin decided to try a back channel to the *New York Times* by writing a letter of introduction for his son to Carr Van Anda, the great and legendary managing editor of the *Times*, then in semi-retirement. Van Anda had been a night telegraph editor on the *Baltimore Sun* almost forty years earlier. In reply, Van Anda graciously commented that "any son of yours is entitled to anything he wants, as indeed is anybody with the training and experience you tell me he has . . . I shall be happy . . . to recommend that a place be found for him."[2] He suggested that Hanson "communicate with me," as he visited the *Times* about once a week.

On the strength of Oliver Baldwin's letter, the young Baldwin received a call to come to New York to meet with Frederick T. Birchall, the acting managing editor of the *Times*. His gruff manner made the interview a rather frightening experience. During that interview, Van Anda entered Birchall's office, who said, "I think this young man will make out all right," a view with which Van Anda agreed. Birchall had been Van Anda's principal assistant before the latter's retirement in 1926.[3]

At the age of twenty-six, Baldwin was hired on as a general assignment reporter on Sunday, October 27, 1929, two days before the New York Stock Market crashed—not an auspicious time to begin a career. His salary was $75 a week.[4] Had Oliver Baldwin not written to his former colleague, Baldwin would not have been hired. Though retired, Van Anda's peerless reputation and influence on the paper was still a force to be reckoned with.[5]

In hindsight, had Baldwin been hired by the *New York Herald-Tribune*, he would probably have been laid off as so many of the new hires were during the economic depression of the 1930s. Those who remained had their salaries cut by 10 percent on three separate occasions. By contrast, the *Times* staff had only one 10 percent salary cut, and no one was fired, or incidentally, was hired.[6]

Working for the *Times* during the early 1930s was not all prestige and Pulitzer Prizes. As a newly hired reporter with unproven skills, talents, and abilities, Baldwin eagerly accepted all assignments from the city editor, most of which dealt with the human flotsam and jetsam of New York City life. His pieces also appeared in the paper without a byline, a common practice at the time.[7]

One of his early assignments was to cover an incident in which a cat had become caught in the spire of St. Patrick's Cathedral on Fifth Avenue. A fireman later rescued it. The city editor, David H. Joseph, was not pleased with Baldwin's reportorial treatment of this incident, which he felt needed a sense of humor and a light touch. As a result of his momentary displeasure, Baldwin did not get good assignments for a while.[8]

Those early months on the *Times* were not particularly happy ones for Baldwin. Shortly after being hired his salary was reduced by 10 percent to $67.50 a week, and he had no choice other than to endure the deprivation. At no time did he even consider resignation, given the bleak employment picture in the newspaper business. Returning to active naval service was not an option, so he simply worked harder.

After two months at the *Times*, he poured out his discouragement to a longtime friend, a geologist working in South Africa. He said that his boss did not appreciate his reporting efforts and that the salary cut was a blow to his self-esteem. His friend advised him to be patient and not to see the salary reduction as a reflection upon his abilities. Things would improve, he wrote.[9] A murder in Times Square, a short distance from the Times Building, provided an unexpected opportunity for Baldwin. With the encouragement of Walter Fenton, the assistant city editor, Baldwin arrived before the police detectives and was initially thought to be one of them, so he used the opportunity to his advantage. On learning that he was a reporter, the police expelled him promptly from the scene. The happy result was that his front-page story pleased Joseph, who subsequently gave him better assignments.[10]

Another opportunity to prove his worth came in May 1930 when U.S. Navy ships paid a visit to New York City for a week. Having requested the assignment, Baldwin took full advantage of the situation to board many of the ships, to renew old friendships with his Annapolis classmates, and to make valuable contacts for future stories. And he enjoyed himself. "This has been a mad, glad, glorious week," he wrote to his mother, "the fleet, the fleet, and the fleet from early morn until far into the night."[11]

For the first time, he was writing about a subject he knew and enjoyed, and it was reflected in his work. He used descriptive nautical words that were not normal reportage for the *Times*. For example, his first story began, "Out of the mists of early morning, twenty-four units of the Navy's destroyer fleet came into port yesterday." "They entered port as destroyer sailors like to do, without frills and furbelows of the 'pig-iron babies,' as the 'dungaree navy' calls the battleships."[12]

On the following day, thirty-seven ships of the combined Battle and Scouting Fleets steamed into New York harbor to anchor in the Hudson River. Baldwin described their arrival with vivid detail: "A low-lying sea haze hung over Ambrose Channel yesterday when the fleet steamed in from the south. The bow wave, curling away from the prow of the USS *California* [BB 44], leading the parade, was tinged red by the mist-filtered rays of an early sun."[13] As the battleships, cruisers, destroyers, and other ships passed by, they were described as "ships with clipper bows and huge stacks, ships with rakish masts and fast lines, ships small and large." The seven battleships whose "screws thrashing the water under the great power of her electric-driven turbines," the cruisers with "their knife-like bows cutting the water. Their light hulls seemed to restrain their powerful engines with difficulty, as if the ships were conscious of their recently achieved importance in things naval." The visit gave civilians the opportunity to board a few ships for guided tours, while the crews eagerly awaited shore leave: "sailors with broad grins on their faces and money in their pockets."[14]

Later that week he met with Birchall, the managing editor, who praised his articles on the visit and informed him that he had restored his pay to what it had been in the previous October, $75 a week. Annoyed, he wrote to his mother: "I think I am worth considerably more—but shall have to prove it to them gradually. I suppose my self confidence and egotism are colossal—n'est pas?" The comment reflected his realization that the previous months of doubt and uncertainty about his new career were now behind him, especially since Joseph, the city editor, had told Baldwin that the fleet stories and his coverage of the event were "a good job," and even the copyreaders had praised Baldwin.[15]

Two weeks later, Baldwin was sent down to Lakehurst, New Jersey, with three other reporters to cover the arrival of the *Graf Zeppelin*, a German rigid airship that was en route to its home base in Friedrichshafen after a 13,400-mile trip to South America. When it arrived at 7:25 a.m. on Saturday, May 31, 1930, Baldwin, in a letter to his mother, described the docking as follows: "Her name in letters of crimson on her side, the dirigible descended easily and gracefully almost into the arms of 250 marines and some 50 navy [personnel] who 'walked' her to the mooring mast, whence she was wheeled by an intricate system of cables, pulleys and landing engines into her berth in the huge hangar." Though he wrote the main story of the event, no byline was given other than "a staff correspondent."[16]

Baldwin could look back on the month of May 1930 with satisfaction. Confidently, he wrote to his mother that, "I am now pretty well established on the Times—but I wonder if it means much. I have eternal discontent." He never forgot the ephemeral nature of newspaper work, which only drove him to try harder in his reporting assignments. To build upon the good reception his Navy articles had received, Baldwin covered the three-day joint Army and Navy maneuvers in June around the eastern approaches to Long Island Sound.

Fortunately for Baldwin, this opportunity to cover military and naval events came because few editors or reporters had any interest in military matters. Certainly the mood of Americans in 1930 was focused upon finding jobs, given the high rate of unemployment and the sense of national hopelessness and despair. Even President Hoover had little interest in the military. With millions unemployed, and jobless men selling apples on the streets of New York, national defense was not a political priority on anyone's agenda in 1930.

An early example of Baldwin criticizing the U.S. Navy for its lack of public relations efforts appeared in the December 1930 issue of the U.S. Naval

Institute's *Proceedings.* The problem, as Baldwin saw it, was that the American public was uninformed about the value of the U.S. Navy to the country's well being.[17] Many newspapers were anti-Navy. Naval officers looked down upon reporters as being "sloppy, half-drunk" lowlifes, whose aim was to get people in trouble, including officers who were misquoted by reporters, thus harming their already slim chances for promotion. Also, the Navy did not help reporters to get their facts straight. Even Baldwin, a Naval Reserve officer, was met on occasion "with a brusqueness and a condescension" by naval officers and with "positive discourtesy" and words "so insulting as to leave a hostile impression."[18]

The solution, he felt, was for the Navy Department to appoint public relations officers in each of the thirteen naval districts in the continental United States. They would provide human interest stories to local newspapers about those in the service, as well as general news about the Navy of interest to the public. Where appropriate, port calls by naval ships should be well advertised in advance of their arrival, along with the number of ships, the purpose of their visit, and the schedule of events to occur during their stay in port.[19] He noted that the U.S. Army already had public relations officers on each post to feed stories about the Army to the local press. This long article not only told the Navy what was needed to correct its abysmal public relations, it served to highlight the real problems that the author personally experienced while trying to get news of the Navy into print.

The article provoked an official response from the Navy Department's Office of Naval Intelligence in Washington, D.C. A Navy captain informed Baldwin that his criticism of publicity had already been dealt with in March 1930, and he included methods of contact with the press and recommendations for improvement. The captain denied that there was "any friction" with reporters, and his counterpart in the Army, who also read this article, agreed that there was no problem with the working press. Baldwin was invited then to drop by the Navy Department should he visit the nation's capital.[20] Obviously, no change by the Navy would be forthcoming, but his article demonstrated his early proclivity to stir things up with his words when necessary. One of the functions of the press is to be provocative, and young Baldwin was simply carrying on the tradition his father had been following for many years on the *Sun.*

Baldwin's first coverage of the U.S. Navy's annual fleet exercises was in February 1931 off Panama. Eager to get the assignment, he told Fenton, the assistant city editor, of his desire to cover naval assignments. New York cabled Richard V. Oulahan, the Washington bureau chief for the *Times*, to intercede with the Navy Department so that Baldwin could accompany the ships.[21] Baldwin left Guantánamo Bay, Cuba, on board the USS *Arkansas* (BB 33), the oldest battleship in the Navy that was to be the flagship for the Scouting Fleet in the maneuvers. The war games were to test whether the Panama Canal Zone could be defended by carrier-based planes and by fast cruisers (the Blue Fleet) against a simulated attack by battleships from the Navy's Pacific battle force (the Black Fleet).

Baldwin's dispatches about the exercise did not mention the many problems he had in filing his cables. As he had noted earlier, the Navy had little experience with public relations and did not understand the role of the press. Years later, Baldwin recalled that the Navy had this "old absolutist idea that everything had to be done under their thumb," and that naval officers were "really incredibly obtuse."[22] As the Navy was not equipped to send long press messages, which could take twelve to twenty-four hours to tap out to send to a shore station for re-transmission to New York, he found it easier and quicker to file his dispatches from a commercial cable station in Balboa, the Canal Zone. On one occasion, when a naval officer who came into the cable office attempted to alter Baldwin's copy, Baldwin sharply reminded the officer that international communications were private.[23]

A Navy patrol plane, on a regular scouting flight, spotted the two groups of the Black Fleet. It alerted the two carriers, the *Saratoga* (CV3) and the *Lexington* (CV2), the new, fast, 10,000-ton "treaty" cruisers, and their destroyer screen in the Blue Fleet, which was defending the Canal Zone. Later, the umpires of the Black Fleet ruled that the aerial "bombing" from the carriers did not seriously damage the battleships. Baldwin did not question the preferred Navy view that battleships had staying power in battle, while aircraft carriers became "extremely vulnerable" if their flight decks were damaged. He pointed out with assurance that the postwar modernization on battleships, including increased gun elevation, the addition of external blisters to withstand torpedoes or bomb explosions on ships' sides, and the rapid-fire 5-inch antiaircraft guns, made it possible for battleships to withstand air attacks.[24]

In his final briefing, Admiral William V. Pratt, the chief of naval operations, praised the 10,000-ton "treaty" cruisers, three of which took part in the fleet exercise. In response to a question from Baldwin about the future of the battleship versus the aircraft carrier, Admiral Pratt, "one of the country's foremost naval authorities," Baldwin dryly commented, became indignant, pounded the table with his fist, and dismissed as "piffle" the idea that the airplane would ever replace the battleship. The admiral did concede, however, that airplanes were "an important corollary" to the battleship.[25]

One unintended benefit for Baldwin in covering this fleet problem was the opportunity to talk at length with David S. Ingalls, the assistant secretary of the Navy for aeronautics, who was an observer during the exercise. He congratulated the young reporter for his article in *Proceedings* about the Navy and its poor press relations, suggesting that Baldwin return to active duty in the Navy Department as its director of naval publicity. The offer was refused on the spot. Baldwin would have had to take a salary cut as a lieutenant (jg), there was no organization in the Navy to help him, and most important, he would have to abandon any "possible future with the *Times* just when things [were] looking brightest," he wrote to his mother.[26] While in Panama, Baldwin bought two linen suits, two Panama hats, and a linen bathrobe in anticipation for his forthcoming marriage to Helen Bruce in June.[27]

On the lighter side, Baldwin described for his readers the Navy at work and at play. The former was "the carnival of cleaning," done every Friday as the crew scrubbed, cleaned, and polished their ship in preparation for the skipper's Saturday-morning inspection of the ship and crew. Decks were sanded down, "flushed with salt water, and dried and bleached white by the sunlight."[28] On shore leave, sailors in Balboa filled every café, "gulping great glasses of cold beer," while some of the officers played baseball in a pickup game.[29]

Baldwin's twenty-one dispatches on the fleet exercise were more reportorial than analytical. They were informative and filled with a considerable amount of detail sufficient for the *Times* readers to have a good idea of the purpose of the naval exercise and its results. The routine of Navy life was also described. He reflected the views of serving officers, two of whom were his former classmates and who would later be in his wedding party. His reports were limited in scope because he was staying on the flagship of the Blue Force, and he was not able to transfer to one the cruisers or aircraft carriers that participated in the naval exercise. But all things considered, it was a hopeful beginning for his future coverage of military and naval maneuvers. The *Times* editors wanted to improve the coverage in all fields and Baldwin was the only staff reporter with the training, the background, and the Navy contacts, all of which enhanced his value to the paper.

Baldwin enjoyed living the life of a bachelor in Manhattan. He shared an apartment with another *Times* man in Chelsea on Twenty-Sixth Street and he thrived on the irregular hours—very busy when writing to meet a deadline and idle at other times, as he sat at his third-floor desk in the *Times* newsroom waiting for something to happen—and he had no fear of walking home in the early morning hours from the Times Building on West Forty-Third Street.[30]

His letters home also showed a great interest in the welfare of his younger sister (by three years) Dorothy, whom he called Dots. A 1928 graduate of Hollins College in Roanoke, Virginia, she was writing book reviews, articles, and poems for the *Sun* and occasionally visited her brother in New York. She later became a psychiatric social worker with the American Red Cross.

To his mother, Hanson often expressed his admiration for Dots; "she's a swell kid and I hope she'll always love me," he wrote. He enjoyed her company and shared her dreams. "I am so glad," he commented to his mother, that her "happiness is all that is worthwhile in life."[31]

His older sister Frances (by four years) was also living in New York in 1930, following a yearlong research trip to England, where she had had a travel fellowship to study sixteenth-century English sumptuary law. A graduate of Goucher College, in Baltimore, she had received her Ph.D. in history from The Johns Hopkins University in 1923, the only woman so honored that year.[32]

Because he was busy, Baldwin had little time to meet new friends, other than his *Times* colleagues, and aside from occasional visits with his two sisters, he mentioned only Letta Shields, whom he dated occasionally in the summer of 1924. He confessed to his mother, "I like her a lot and we can, I think, have a good time together and that in New York for me is rare enough." On a date (perhaps the only one), they saw the play *The Last Mile,* a prison mutiny drama starring a thirty-year-old Spencer Tracy.[33]

He may have dated a few other women as well, but on Monday, June 8, 1931, Hanson Baldwin married Helen Finette Bruce, whom he had met a few years before at Hollins College when he was visiting his sister Dorothy.

In his recollection he had "demanded" that Dots introduce him to "the prettiest girls" at the college. On a little bridge over a stream that ran through the campus, Baldwin met a group of coeds, including Helen, and his naval ensign's uniform "made a sensation" with them. Nothing came of this initial encounter with Helen until five years later, when, after their graduation in 1928, both Helen and Dorothy came to New York City to find work. Helen worked as a secretary at both *McCall's* and *Scribner's* magazines, "in a very boring job in which [she] was not at all equipped," by her own admission. As an English major with no practical skills, she had to teach herself how to type on the job.[34]

Baldwin and Helen met again, by chance, when he brought another friend of Dorothy's to a place where she often changed for an evening at the theater. While his date was changing, Helen appeared and they chatted. A short time later he invited her to see a naval ship then moored at the Brooklyn Navy Yard. "And that is how it began," she later revealed. Baldwin's version of this story was that he met Helen at the office of John R. Chamberlain, the assistant editor of the *New York Times Book Review*. Looking for something to do after her secretarial work at the magazines, she would ask Chamberlain for a book to review for the *Times*. On one occasion, she had left her glasses in Chamberlain's office, which she retrieved the following day. Soon, she began to appear regularly at Chamberlain's office and Baldwin just happened to be waiting there for her.[35]

Baldwin's uncle, Reverend Sutton, the vicar at Trinity Episcopal Church chapel, married them on June 8, 1931. Helen's sister Elizabeth was her maid of honor, and her only attendant. Her uncle, Wilbur Love "Bud" Cummings, gave her away since her father, William Mansfield Bruce Jr., a well-respected engineer and inventor of electrical telegraph systems, had passed away.[36]

According to the *Times*, Helen wore an ensemble of slate blue crepe de chine with a Watteau hat of the same shade and a shoulder corsage of Talisman roses. Baldwin's best man was Lieutenant John Brewer Brown, his Naval Academy classmate. Three other serving naval officers, all his former classmates, were the ushers, as was Bosley Crowther, whose desk adjoined Baldwin's in the third-floor *Times* newsroom.[37] In addition, there were twelve other guests, most of whom were family members. Their honeymoon cruise was to Bermuda on the Holland-America ship *Veendam*.[38]

Bud Cummings hosted the couple's wedding reception at his Greenwich Village apartment. A "gentle, kind man" who had financially helped Helen's mother, a widow, since 1929, he invited Baldwin to dinner after their engagement had been announced to determine if he was a suitable beau and later reportedly informed Helen's mother, "Well, he [Baldwin] is better than the last one." As a senior partner in the famous law firm Sullivan and Cromwell, along with Allen W. Dulles (later the first head of the Central Intelligence Agency) and his older brother, John Foster Dulles (later to be President Eisenhower's secretary of state), Cummings helped Baldwin in more ways than just smoothing his way into the family.

Through Cummings, Baldwin was able to make many other useful contacts, including Eustace Seligman, a retired senior partner at Sullivan and Cromwell, and a longtime member of the Council on Foreign Relations. Seligman was a gregarious man whose home in the West Village was frequently the scene of informal gatherings that included people who were prominent in business and in public affairs. After dinner, Seligman would often pose a current political or social problem and require that each guest propose a solution. Such was Baldwin's introduction to an elite, intelligent, and well-connected people, some of whom proved helpful to him in later years.[39]

As heady and potentially useful as these prominent social and business persons may have been, Hanson and Helen had to return to their own small apartment in Greenwich Village at 189 West Tenth Street. Among their early guests was Walter Fenton (and his wife) who, as the assistant city editor, had been so helpful during Baldwin's shaky early months at the paper. On one occasion, when the Fentons had been invited to dinner, Baldwin and Helen took a walk, misjudged the time, and on their return found the Fentons sitting outside on a pile of firewood that had been delivered in their absence. The incident later became "a standard joke" in the Baldwin household. After their first child, Barbara, was born in 1932, they moved to a larger apartment, since the "only way to get sun and air was to go to the roof" of the Tenth Street apartment building.[40]

Another couple whose company the Baldwins enjoyed was Bruce Rae and his wife, Ishbel Ross. Rae was one of the *Times'* great reporters. He covered the sensational Hall-Mills murder case in 1926, as well as many other stories. In 1930 he became the night city editor and he put fear into the hearts of cub reporters with his caustic wit and sharp tongue, challenging them to write better. He would tell them how long a story should be and where cuts and additions should be made. Even though they were friends, Baldwin was not immune from the same treatment. In time, he learned how to argue with Rae, but he also learned from him how to report more fully than he had been doing. Eventually he saw Rae's warmer side and came to appreciate the sense of humor that was hidden beneath his gruff exterior. Ishbel Ross, *The New York Herald-Tribune*'s star reporter for fifteen years, also covered the Hall-Mills case and the Lindbergh kidnapping case. She retired from reporting in 1932 to raise her daughter and to write novels, and she and Helen got along "famously."[41]

In the early 1930s, just as Baldwin's career at the *Times* had begun to show promise, tragedy and loss came to him. On July 4, 1931, less than a month after his marriage, his older sister, Elizabeth, died of pneumonia after a brief illness in New York. She was only thirty-two. Dorothy wrote to her brother a few months later, "I am naturally introspective and morbid, and Elizabeth's death has made me more so."[42] All in the close-knit Baldwin family were saddened by her early death. One obituary referred to her as being "cut off" while on "the road to a more enduring fame."[43]

One of Baldwin's early successful assignments was his coverage of the national rifle matches beginning in late August 1931 at Camp Perry, Ohio, near Port Clinton. The *Times* managing editor, F. T. Birchall, made it clear to the sports desk that Baldwin's dispatches were to be treated as general news and not as a sporting event. The telegraph desk was told not to cut Baldwin's pieces "to ribbons" if they were good, and to give him a byline that was contrary then to normal practice. He told Baldwin that he was less interested in the rifle scores than in "picturesque dispatches" about the personalities and the scene at Camp Perry.[44] During the two weeks of this rifle match, about six thousand persons, including participants, their families, and spectators, lived in a "canvas city," ate their meals cafeteria style, and watched "the world's largest shooting meet" along two miles of the shoreline of Lake Erie. The participants were a mixture of U.S. military personnel, both officers and enlisted men, as well as policemen, cowboys, miners, men in chaps and sombreros, "in dirty overalls and padded shooting jackets, politicians, lawyers, journalists, state, county and municipal officials, men of nearly all the professions and occupations."[45]

At night, this crowd of shooters dressed in "riding costumes, beach pajamas, and polo suits" made Camp Perry resemble "a Hollywood movie lot
during rehearsal time."[46] During the day, the shooters sent "bullets shrilling
out over the waters of Lake Erie . . . from the muzzles of nearly every modern type of firearm." In trying to explain why this event attracted so many,
Baldwin observed, "Perhaps it is the thrill of a slow trigger squeeze or the
feel of a rifle butt" but certainly it is that "wherever guns are fired and targets
are pulled, many soldiers of fortune and world wanderers will be found."
He added, "By day they fire, by night they read or write, and occasionally
they yarn of the far places and strange sights they have seen."[47] Birchall was
very pleased with the quality of the eleven stories filed by Baldwin. "Your
dispatches have been excellent," he cabled. "Congratulations and thanks. You
never disappoint me."[48]

Given the positive encouragement by the *Times* editors on his 1931
fleet exercise coverage and his reporting on the Camp Perry rifle matches,
Helen later recalled Hanson remarking one evening, while writing at home,
"I think I'm going to concentrate on the military." She thought his comment was made in late 1931 or in 1932. She knew how excited he became
when covering military and naval stories or other national defense issues.
Unfortunately, those were the issues that were not uppermost in the public's
mind in 1932. Baldwin would have to bide his time.[49]

Less than a year after Elizabeth's death, Hanson's father died on June 21,
1932, at age eighty-two. Oliver had been in fragile health for over a year
preceding his death but still insisted on going to his office at the *Sun,* even
if only for a few hours in the morning. Although he told an associate that it
was his hope that Death would find him at "his worn desk, pencil in hand,
and his eyes on his task," he died at home.[50] The belief that both Oliver and
Hanson shared was that character determined a man's worth, not his rank
or title. Another shared belief was the idea that a journalist needed to keep
his independence, for without it his words carried no significance and his
carefully built reputation for balanced analysis would be lost, never to be
regained. Another trait Hanson learned from his father was that one should
defend his position in his writings and avoid compromising his position.
Like his father, Hanson believed the purpose of a journalist was to be fearless
but not reckless, balanced but not irresponsible. All judgments must be made
"without fear or favor," as it said on the *Times* masthead statement adopted

by Adolph Ochs in 1896. Years later, Baldwin admitted having a "very strong dislike for being forced to do things . . . [because force is] completely contrary to the concept of individualism" any newspaper writer embraces.[51]

In 1933, he tried to test the waters to see if any other newspaper needed a military and naval writer. He wrote letters of inquiry to the editors of *The New York Herald-Tribune* and to the Scripps-Howard newspapers, all in vain. The editor of the *Baltimore Sunday Sun,* Mark Skinner Watson, an old family friend who had first encouraged him to "take up the typewriter" a few years earlier, advised him to stay with the *Times.*[52]

With his marketability limited and his desire to increase his income intense, especially after the birth of their first child in July 1932, he hired a literary agent, Willis Kingsley Wing. His hope was that magazines would prove to be a profitable outlet for his writings, especially since he still wished to pursue semi-fiction. Wing's previous experience had been as an editor at Doubleday and on *The New Yorker* staff, and their letter of agreement was limited to fictional or other writings for a general audience. "I have no stories ready now," he wrote to Wing in December 1932, "but I am not lazy, just busy." At the time, in addition to writing for the *Times,* Baldwin occasionally wrote for the *Sun* and the U.S. Naval Institute's *Proceedings.*[53]

While Baldwin's reporting was praised by the *Times* management, the Office of Naval Intelligence (ONI) believed his articles on newly commissioned warships revealed too much "confidential information." For example, he had revealed that the new heavy cruisers of the *Astoria* class, the "treaty" cruisers, had thin armor on the decks and sides, excessive vibration from the struts bearing the propeller shafts, and a "tendency to roll heavily." Captain Hayne Ellis of the ONI demanded to know Baldwin's sources, but he refused to reveal them.[54]

Later, when he wrote an article for the *Sunday Sun* on the new *Farragut* class of eight destroyers commissioned in 1934 and 1935, Captain Ellis cited the article as "proof" that Baldwin had given too much information, beyond the ship's tonnage, class, and length, as permitted by the 1930 London Naval Treaty. This was true.[55]

Such a detailed description of the new class of destroyers would not have been possible if he had not had access to at least some of the blueprints, possibly at the Brooklyn Navy Yard, where two of the destroyers were then under construction. But Baldwin denied that he had leaked confidential information that could be "construed" as being of "aid and comfort to any potential enemy."[56] Much of the information about the new destroyers had been previously released by the Navy Department, while other information he said he had estimated from available statistics. He asserted that while his article went into some detail about the new ships, "it was harmless detail."[57]

When Admiral W. W. Phelps, the commandant of the Third Naval District (New York), ordered Baldwin to reveal his sources, he refused, citing an "unwritten law" in the profession of journalism that unnamed sources were "never revealed," and that it would be "a tacit breach of faith" to reveal his sources. Admiral Phelps rejected this line of defense and recommended to the Bureau of Navigation in Washington that Baldwin be given "disciplinary action," but Baldwin denied that the admiral had jurisdiction over him or the right to give him orders.

The Navy rejected Baldwin's appeal. He was reminded that the U.S. Navy was charged with the nation's defense and that it alone had the exclusive right to withhold information from the public that it deemed to be confidential, saying that disclosure in the press "cannot be justified on any such theory as that of the freedom of the press or that the public has a right to know."[58]

The matter became very serious when Rear Admiral F. B. Upham, the chief of the Bureau of Navigation, demanded that if Baldwin continued to refuse to accept the "ethics of the Navy," including an obligation of loyalty to the "interest and protection" of the nation, his resignation was the only option open to him.[59] As weeks became months in that futile letter-writing campaign, neither Baldwin nor the Navy altered their well-stated positions. Though the Navy did admit that Baldwin's "pen" was "capable of rendering excellent service," he was allowed to do so only on the Navy's terms, and their terms were that Baldwin resign his commission, which he refused to do in 1933.[60]

Baldwin felt it was a basic right of the American press and of the American people to express "the free and unabridged statement of fact and expression of opinion," that it should not be denied to him because of his Reserve commission, nor should it be "an instrument of suppression in time of peace," nor would he agree that the Navy Department had a right "to dictate what I shall—or shall not, write." He reminded the Navy that since 1930 not one of his writings had been "harmful to the best interest of the country or of the Navy."[61]

After months of trying to solve this battle with the Navy all by himself, and without success, he turned to Edwin L. James, the recently appointed managing editor of the *Times*. In a long memorandum, he summarized his own position and that of the Navy. James kicked the matter upstairs, as it were, to Arthur Hays Sulzberger, the son-in-law of Adolph Ochs, *Times* publisher and owner. Sulzberger appreciated Baldwin's dilemma, saying, "It is very difficult for a man to serve two masters," and recommended that he resign his naval officer's commission so that he would feel "freer" in his future writings for the *Times*.[62]

Ten months later, in March 1934, Baldwin received a letter from the Bureau of Navigation that stated that he was eligible for promotion to the rank of lieutenant if he made a formal application. This he did, citing his reporting for the *Times* on naval matters. He said he made it his business to increase his knowledge of not only the American Navy but of the navies of foreign powers as well. To this end he had renewed his study of the German language at the Berlitz School in New York City. His writings had appeared in various forums. He also referred to his 1930 article in the U.S. Naval Institute's *Proceedings*, which pointed out the weaknesses of the Navy's publicity policy. Forgotten for the moment was the controversy of the previous months over what the Navy thought was suitable Navy news.

In May 1934 Baldwin was promoted to lieutenant in the United States Naval Reserve. Perhaps the admirals realized that Baldwin was their best advocate for the naval service, an advocate who would not be censored by anyone. He was assigned to the "Intelligence Division for Special Services." His assignment, it was noted, was to be continued in excess of the quota of the office of the chief of naval operations, but, upon later reflection, he decided that resignation was the best option, and it was accepted effective September 21, 1934.[63] In his letter of resignation to Secretary of the Navy Claude Swanson, Baldwin admitted that being in the Naval Reserve could be considered by some as being "too close" a connection with the Navy, that it could be seen to jeopardize his fair and accurate reporting and analysis of naval news. He felt that if he had "bowed" to the Navy's wishes, it would have acted as a "handicap" to his work that was, in the words on the *Times* masthead statement, "the accurate and impartial reporting of the news without fear or favor." In addition, having been in the intelligence section of the

Naval Reserve could "prove embarrassing" should he report from foreign countries on their military and naval news in the future.[64]

After fourteen years of active and Reserve status, Hanson Baldwin severed his official connection with the U.S. Navy. It was time for him to move on to other matters, but the episode demonstrated how persistent he was when he considered an issue important. Oliver Baldwin would have applauded his son's sticking to the principle of the independence of the press and the right to print the truth as he saw it.

One of the events that shaped Baldwin's later views on labor unions was the 1934 attempt of the new American Newspaper Guild to organize the *Times* employees. The widespread layoffs of reporters in the industry had created a good deal of anxiety. Baldwin had joined the union in the hope of creating some job security for himself, but he became increasingly upset by the talk of union leaders about a national class-consciousness. He found himself a lone voice at union meetings in protesting the drift of the union leadership to include all workers in the newspaper industry. To his thinking, that development would sacrifice the objectivity of news reporting, making it pro-labor. It would also challenge the right of the freedom of the press in America. That brief union experience was to sour him on the idea for years to come.[65]

Through the efforts of Wing, his literary agent, Baldwin's articles for a general reading public appeared in such diverse forums as the prestigious *North American Review* and *Esquire* magazine. Not only were such mass media outlets useful in expanding his readership, they also enabled him to escape the tendency of other *Times* staffers to confine him to military topics.

An early example of the type of article that he wanted to write appeared in the March 1934 issue of the *North American Review*. In "Japan and the Future," Baldwin sought to evaluate the political implications of Japan's 1932 expansion into Manchuria and its economic and commercial inroads throughout Asia. Major obstacles to Japanese expansion were the United States' "possession" of the Philippines, backing by China, and the Open Door Policy. Baldwin suggested that, in light of Japan's recent moves, the United States ought to make a "complete withdrawal" from the western Pacific.[66]

This early attempt to write about international political events and their naval consequences was the sort of article that Baldwin came to write with frequency in the immediate years ahead as the European and Asian political and military fascist states threatened the democracies.

In another magazine article, Baldwin showed his irritation with Washington's naval policy since the early 1920s. Politicians spoke of naval parity with Great Britain but refused to authorize new ship construction to maintain the fleet up to treaty parity levels. The Navy Department had failed to educate the American public as to the value of a fleet and its mission to protect American interests around the world. The Navy League and its advocates urged the creation of a "navy bigger than the biggest," while pacifists and idealists rejected such goals as militaristic—a word that resonated with the American public's hostility to anything military at the time.

The larger problem was the isolationist foreign policies of the 1920s that gave the impression that the Navy played no role in U.S. foreign policy. This lack of understanding could be placed at the feet of both the press, which ignored the importance of naval affairs, and the Navy itself, which had "done everything it could to keep" the press ignorant of the importance of the Navy to defend the nation's interests.[67] Baldwin praised both President Franklin Roosevelt and Congress for the passage of the 1934 Vinson-Trammell Act, which authorized ship construction so as to achieve naval parity with Britain. Baldwin also praised Admiral William H. Standley, the chief of naval operations, for initiating a program for the annual replacement of obsolete and over-aged ships. In reply, the admiral called Baldwin's article "accurate" in its efforts to get the Navy built up to treaty levels and to maintain them by a program of ship replacement. He encouraged Baldwin to continue to write on public issues, saying, "More power to your good writing arm."[68]

To supplement his income from the *Times*, as well as to try his hand at writing sea stories, Baldwin wrote five articles for *Esquire* magazine in 1935 and 1936. They all dealt with stories of men against the sea, in which decisions, often made under duress, determined a man's fate. Only one of the articles was semi-autobiographical, "Navy Blue and Gold," which was about the life of a midshipman at Annapolis. Sailors, Baldwin observed, may look like the boy next door, but "the Navy is a world to itself, and yet it is a part— though a distinctive part—of American life."[69] He described the training and the traditions of the sea taught and experienced at the Naval Academy. He ended this yarn of sea incidents by reflecting that "because the business of the Navy is such a deadly serious one . . . and because Navy men feel so deeply about the service" they learn to accept all aspects of it, good and bad, and cherish the comic situations the years produce.[70] Waxing sentimental, he concluded that "the life of the fleet goes on from age to age in its laughter, in the tragedies, and in the great body of its brave traditions."[71] Keep in mind that he was writing for an audience who had little knowledge of the Navy and who cared little for those who went down to the sea in ships. His purpose was to inform and, if possible, educate the public that the United States had a Navy of which it should be proud and that it was important to the nation, despite arguments to the contrary. Those *Esquire* articles humanized sailors and their world.

These new writing opportunities in 1935 helped Hanson Baldwin's career. Through the contacts made by his literary agent, he was able to branch out from the confines of being a general assignment reporter at the *Times* to find a wider audience in new forums, and to write on a range of political and military topics. This trend in his career would continue for many years to come.

To make himself knowledgeable about the U.S. Army, about which he knew little, as well as to increase his usefulness to the *Times*, Hanson Baldwin sought out Army tutors on Governor's Island, the headquarters of the U.S. First Army. Two colonels, Joe Dalton and Stanley Grogan, gave him a number of books and some of the Army staff college publications, which provided some basic information about the Army, its organization, and tactics. Richard Ernest Dupuy, who, in 1935, was a major in the Army's field artillery, was also very helpful. Later, as a colonel, Dupuy wrote many books on the Army and on military history, as did his son, Trevor.[72]

Baldwin's first coverage of large-scale Army maneuvers was in August 1935 at Pine Camp (now Fort Drum), in upstate New York, near Watertown. There, 36,000 Army Regulars of the U.S. First Army and the National Guard from twelve eastern states engaged in mock battles for two weeks. The regular Army were full-time soldiers under federal control, while the National Guard were part-time soldiers under their individual state's control. It was the largest peacetime maneuvers since the end of World War I. The exercises tested the mobility of troops on trucks, the use of radio communications, and the value of airplanes as support for ground units.

Baldwin's reportage of the maneuvers had a flamboyant character to it. Machine guns shot "500 death pellets per minute," while in the skies above the troops "helmeted and goggled pilots [flew planes] with . . . roaring motors [that were] spitting birds of hell" over the battlefields. On the ground, soldiers played their war games "with blank cartridges popping and umpires flags waving."[73]

In hindsight, there was an innocent quality in 1935 about his reporting of what must have been very serious war games at that time. The *Times* gave a good deal of space to those games, as if trying to inform the public that military preparedness was important news, even in the midst of the Great Depression. The tone of Baldwin's reporting conveyed a seriousness of purpose, as if he were covering real battles as a war correspondent writing from the front lines for his hometown newspaper.

Such dime-novel characterizations did not hide the fact the National Guard's equipment was antiquated, its field training limited, and its officers and non-commissioned officers poor leaders. While some infantry units were "sped across" the country roads in trucks and in armored cars much quicker than in a forced march, as Baldwin dryly noted, "unfortunately the motorized First Division was coping with an imaginary enemy which was almost as modernly equipped as it was."[74]

The field maneuvers highlighted many deficiencies. To make up for the lack of trucks, the Army had to hire "hundreds" of taxis to quickly move troops about during the exercises. Station wagons were used as scouting vehicles. Those make-do steps could not cover the fact that the Regulars and the National Guard units were not ready for actual combat. In fact, there was only enough blank ammunition budgeted for these games to give each soldier three bullets.[75]

The Regular Army had its deficiencies, too. It had only five serviceable tanks, all of which were obsolescent World War I models. In full view of a number of foreign military observers, one tank "straddled a high stump and was 'bellied'—its treads moving aimlessly, like the feet of a turtle lifted in mid-air." The other tank, in that particular exercise, broke down behind "enemy" lines. This incident was not an impressive display of the U.S. Army's tank corps.[76]

At the critique following the maneuvers, the Army stressed its need for modern tanks, more motorized units, and more reliable communications equipment. In a telling observation, Baldwin noted that many National Guard and Regular Army units came to realize "how little they really knew of 'war' in the field," deficiencies observed by many of the 139 press reporters, radio broadcasters, and photographers.[77] The *Times'* extensive coverage made those war games public knowledge and contributed to the public's awareness that an increasingly violent world required that America's armed forces be updated with modern equipment for its future defense needs.[78]

An event in 1935 that directly affected Baldwin's career at the *Times* was the death of *Times* publisher Adolph Simon Ochs on April 8. He had bought the bankrupt paper in 1896 and turned it into the nation's leading newspaper of record. There were two contenders for the post of publisher, General Julius Ochs Adler and Arthur Hays Sulzberger. Adler was member of the Ochs family trust and a cousin of Adolph Ochs. He was the general manager of the New York Times Company. A decorated combat veteran of World War I, who had fought with New York's 77th Regiment, Adler remained very interested in the Army and was a brigadier general in the Army Reserves in the late 1930s. Adler's large office, on the east end of the fourteenth floor of the Times Building, was decorated with many military relics. He hired only ex-military men to be on this staff and, on occasion, he would inspect the uniforms of the *Times* guards at the first floor entrance for their proper neatness.[79]

Arthur Hays Sulzberger was the husband of Adolph Ochs' only child, Iphigene. During the many months of his father-in-law's declining health, Sulzberger had been the de facto publisher. In the weeks following Adolph Ochs' death it was not immediately clear who would become the publisher, Adler or Sulzberger. A month later, at a meeting of the family trust, Iphigene Ochs Sulzberger voted for her husband Arthur to be the next publisher, a post that he held for the next twenty-six years. He was in many ways Baldwin's mentor on the paper, as well as his sharpest critic.

Hanson Baldwin's rapid rise at the *Times* was based partially on the trends of European political events from 1936 onward, and from the decisions of both Arthur Sulzberger and General Julius Adler, who saw the need for a military specialist on the staff to prepare the American public for the possibility of war in the future, which could involve the United States.[80]

The year 1936 was crowded with potentially dangerous trends to world peace. In January, the second London Naval Conference ended in failure to stop a new naval arms race. Japan demanded parity in capital ships, and when the United States and Great Britain refused, it left the conference now free to abandon the previous 35,000-ton limit for battleships. Japan proceeded to lay the keels for the two gigantic *Yamato*-class battleships, which displaced almost 70,000 tons with their 18.1-inch main battery.[81] In March 1936 Hitler reoccupied the Rhineland, which had been designated a demilitarized zone under the Versailles Treaty of 1919, and in May Italy annexed Ethiopia. In July the Spanish Civil War began, which would last until 1939 and brought Italy and Germany closer together. In November Japan and Germany signed the Anti-Comintern Pact, which was aimed more against the Soviet Union than against the international organization of the Soviet Union's Communist Party. In January 1937 Adolf Hitler formally withdrew Germany from the war guilt clause of the Versailles treaty and from those clauses that he claimed denied Germany its equal rights with other nations.[82]

Against the distant thunder of these ominous trends, the *Times* management, in the autumn of 1936, began to discuss the possibility of sending Baldwin to Europe to investigate and to report on the military preparations among the major powers. His seven years as a general assignment reporter would soon be over and his new role as the paper's first military analyst was about to begin. It would last for the next thirty-one years, until his retirement.

CHAPTER 6

A New Assignment, 1937

anson Baldwin's big break came in the early spring of 1937 when he was sent by the *Times* for a three-month assignment in Europe to survey the scale of military rearmament of the major powers. The suggestion for this trip came from others, notably Frederick Birchall, the *Times'* chief European correspondent, who had hired an untried Baldwin in 1929 when Birchall was the paper's acting managing editor.[1]

The current managing editor, Edwin L. James, raised the issue with Sulzberger, who "was more than enthusiastic" about such a trip. To avoid problems in "some of these dictator-ruled countries," Baldwin suggested that the military and naval attachés in Washington, D.C., be contacted first, in order to "let the boys back home" know about his trip and its purpose. Sulzberger suggested that Russia and Czechoslovakia be added to his itinerary, as he considered those countries "a danger point in Hitler's plans."[2]

In order to give Baldwin some standing with his European contacts, he was appointed as the *Times* naval and military correspondent, a first for the paper, but a title familiar to the European press. Prior to Baldwin's departure in February 1937, Sulzberger told him, "You've learned a lot about the Army and Air Force, you ought to take a good look at the armies, navies and air forces of all the principal powers in Europe. War is certainly going to come over there sooner or later, and you'd better get informed about that. Then I think, when you come back, from then on you'd better specialize and do only military affairs."[3] Both James and Sulzberger thought it was a marvelous suggestion, as did Baldwin when the new assignment was proposed to him in December 1936. Realizing that his knowledge of Europe's armed forces was limited, Baldwin quickly filled this void by calling upon other *Times* staff, notably Arthur Krock, the Washington bureau chief, to get letters of introduction for him from the European embassies as well as from the U.S. War and Navy departments.[4]

Secretary of War Harry Woodring told Arthur Krock, after Baldwin's visit, that the *Times* was "rendering a splendid service to international accord [by] giving the public a more comprehensive knowledge of the armies and navies of the world." He hoped that Baldwin's reports would inform "Americans of the problems of Europe's national defense" and thus serve to lessen nationalistic fears and promote international peace. In short, to know the other country's fears would be a path to international understanding. Woodring agreed to inform U.S. military attachés in Europe to help Baldwin, assistance he later found to be invaluable.[5] James also informed the *Times* bureaus in London, Berlin, Paris, and Rome of Baldwin's trip, its purpose, and suggested that they offer him their assistance, if called upon.[6]

On Wednesday, February 3, 1937, Baldwin sailed on the SS *President Harding* for Southampton, England, with his wife Helen. He carried an $800 advance from the paper to cover his anticipated expenses. (Helen remained in London for a time, and later returned to New York.)[7] His trip came at an opportune time. Against the backdrop of German rearmament, Italy's successful conquest of Ethiopia, the beginning of the Spanish Civil War, recent French and British rearmament programs, and the collapse of the naval limitation treaties, the military was again poised to be "the [maker] of history."[8] Baldwin's assignment was to report objectively, factually, technically, and comprehensively on Europe's rearmament programs. In so doing he was quietly alerting Americans to the fact that Fortress America's neutrality might not be sufficient in another war.

In London he met many persons in the military and in the press who were willing to offer him some factual information and lots of opinions. After his arrival, Baldwin asked whom he should contact while in England and was told, "Oh, don't bother with Churchill, he's just a nut," advice he followed much to his later regret.[9] He met Captain Taprell Dorling, the naval correspondent for the *Observer*, who invited him to the Army and Navy Club where promptly at noon both enjoyed a whisky and soda, and then continued on to the posh Dorchester Hotel for smoked salmon, an omelet, a steak, and lager with another military attaché.[10]

He also found congenial British colleagues in the Fleet Street Press Gang, a group of naval correspondents in London that included Hector C. Bywater, the well-known naval writer whose 1925 book, *The Great Pacific War*, accurately outlined future U.S-Japanese naval battles. Previously, Bywater had covered the 1921–22 Washington Naval Disarmament Conference for the *Baltimore Sun*. When Baldwin met him in 1937 he was the naval correspondent for the *Daily Telegraph*. Also at this club was Francis L. McMurtrie, the editor of *Jane's Fighting Ships*, an indispensable annual reference book of the world's navies. These and other military specialists provided many details on Britain's military preparedness.[11]

Baldwin's first single-authored book, *The Caissons Roll: A Military Survey of Europe* (1938), was a compilation of his *Times* articles written during and after his three-month European assignment. The statistics that he cited on the armed forces of the various countries he visited are no longer of interest, nor were they always accurate at the time owing to government reluctance and military secrecy (as he later admitted).[12] Rather, it was his impressions of the mood of Europe that are of historical interest now. The reader should keep in mind that the *Times* wanted to inform the American public of the facts of European rearmament in order to counter the strong and popular isolationist thinking that led many citizens to feel that America should remain unaffected by Europe's mad rush to rearm.

Baldwin attributed the driving force behind Britain's and France's rearmament to be Germany and Italy: "There is evidence nearly everywhere," he wrote, "of a fear psychosis or of national inferiority complexes—the haste to arm, the blustering speeches, the braggart or defiant talk." For modern Europe is a "veritable Tower of Babel, with each man's hand raised against his neighbor."[13] The "have not" nations of Germany and Italy had demanded power, land, resources, and empire.[14] The Rome-Berlin Axis had become "more and more pronounced" as economic ties and shared political concepts between the two nations gave "an aura" of a reasonable and happy alliance.[15] Germany, Baldwin observed, was the stronger power, and Hitler was "a wily leader" whose policies of *"Drang nach Osten"* focused upon a push eastward through Poland and Czechoslovakia to Russia—"the Red Menace" of the German mind.[16] "It would not be astonishing," he observed, "if the next German move were in the south, probably Africa—merely as a prelude to bigger things to come."[17]

He dismissed any likelihood of an Anglo-German alliance. The "bogy" of Europe was the "specter of a Russo-German alliance." Economically, it would be "logical," but politically and psychologically such an alliance lay in the "kingdom of fantasy," Baldwin mistakenly thought. Two years later that fantasy became reality with the signing of the Nazi-Soviet Pact on August 23, 1939. The next war would come in the 1940s, not in 1939, as some had predicted.[18]

Baldwin also overestimated the abilities of France, Poland, Belgium, and Holland to delay any German invasion of their countries. As for France, he wrote assuredly that there were nine possible "paths of conquest" for Germany to take into France, three of which were through Switzerland. Five paths involved Belgium and Holland. The one path that he did not mention, but that Field Marshal von Rundstedt's Army Group A used successfully in May 1940, was through the Ardennes Forest in Belgium.[19]

Possible German invasion routes into Russia would have to overcome the anticipated stiff Polish and Czech resistance. The Annapolis graduate could not possibly have foreseen that in March 1938, Austria would be peaceably annexed by Germany and that western Czechoslovakia (Sudetenland) would be annexed in October 1938 with the acquiescence of Britain and France at the Munich conference that previous September.

Since he was writing in the spring of 1937, when there were only rumors of war, Baldwin's lack of foresight ought not to be censored. In hindsight, some of his assumptions were rather ill founded. For example, he assured his readers that England held "the master key to Europe" by being "the most powerful European nation." Financially, it was the strongest power, and its 1936–37 rearmament program would bolster its diplomacy.[20] Without England's participation "there can be no major war in Europe," Baldwin pontificated.[21]

However, to his credit, he noted some problems. The Royal Navy had not recovered psychologically from the indecisive result of the Battle of Jutland in May 1916, which had destroyed "the myth of British invincibility at sea."[22] In 1922 its naval supremacy was successfully challenged by the United States at the Washington Naval Arms Limitation Conference, and in 1935 Britain abandoned Malta, its principal naval base in the Mediterranean, because of Italian naval threats.[23]

As for the British army, it was limited by "the Kipling tradition." The days of empire building were over, but it "doesn't know it." The British soldier seemed, to Baldwin, "better suited to defense than to offense." Their officers were of two types: the officer who was both brilliant and ambitious, and the "Colonel Blimp" officer, reactionary and opposed to change, who was "glad to retire as a lieutenant colonel and to live the life of a country squire."[24] Unfortunately, he noted, the former were in the minority and did not make British army policy. With those drawbacks, the British army, Baldwin observed, was not prepared for a major war.[25] He also noted that British air power was increasing in the numbers of planes produced, but he made only a passing reference to the Hurricanes and Spitfires that were to play a major role, three years later, in the Battle of Britain.

Based upon the recent examples of war in Spain and in Ethiopia, Baldwin thought tanks would be best used as mechanized cavalry to operate on the enemy's flanks and in the rear of retreating forces once the enemy's breakthrough had occurred.[26] He did not foresee the massive tank-versus-tank battles that occurred a few years later. He assumed that Germany was planning for a war of quick decision, "a war to be won . . . within the space of a few weeks or months," by using its ground and air forces. Two years later, Germany's "blitzkrieg" campaign of 1939 and 1940 resulted in Poland falling in four weeks, France in six weeks, and Holland, Norway, and Denmark in less time than that. France, he noted, felt "secure" behind its Maginot Line of fortresses and assumed that the next war would end in a stalemate like World War I.[27]

Predicting the nature of a future war was always chancy. In general terms, there would be the bombing of cities and the use of propaganda to break the civilian population's will to resist. He saw military tactics as being in a state of flux. The current question was "mass versus mobility, the war of maneuver versus the war of position," for which he saw no clear answers in 1937. Should there be another war, which he thought was a real possibility, many civilians would be killed. He predicted that the next war would end "as wars always have ended and always must as a war of man against man," by which he meant that man's determination to fight would be decisive. Military tactics were then in a "state of flux," noted Baldwin, and the current question was whether air power should be used in the tactical support of ground forces, as a "weapon of terror" against civilians, or whether the selective bombing of purely military targets should be used?[28]

At sea, battleships were "still the strength of the fleet" and would "probably prove decisive." They were not. Submarines had proven their effectiveness in the previous war and would be used again in individual torpedo attacks or in groups against a common target. Indeed, the wolf pack tactic later became an all-too-common attack by U-boats.[29]

In summary, Hanson Baldwin drew a number of observations on the "awful" nature of the next European war. He felt that ground troops should seize and hold land targets and that while supporting tanks and airplanes would be useful, neither could gain "a permanent decision" on the battlefield. Bombing cities or military targets was "not likely to win wars . . . [because] wars cannot be won in the air." And finally, he ventured that propaganda broadcasts by radio, newspapers, and motion pictures would be "a major instrument of the future totalitarian war."[30]

His book was the first of its kind to make an informed survey of the level of military preparation in Europe. The secrecy that surrounded each government's military organization and war plans definitely hindered the accuracy of Baldwin's reports. He was aware of this limitation, yet, also in hindsight, his observations on the amount of mineral resources needed for war by each country and the public's attitude toward defense had value.

In France, Baldwin met with General Maurice Gamelin, the inspector general of the French army. In response to the question, "Are you satisfied with the French preparations for war?" the general replied, "My soul is at peace."[31] Other sources with whom he spoke also expressed confidence that the French army and nation were safe behind their Maginot Line. Baldwin was not so sure. He found an absence of a coordinated national strategy between those who believed that the next war would be won in the air and those who believed that a ground war would be decisive, or, as he put it, the "mechanized thinkers" and the "bayonet-stickers."

Reflecting upon his sources, Baldwin asserted that the French army was "perhaps the best army in the world." Its weakness was the "inferiority complex" of the French army in the face of the increasing German military might. Historically, France's defense was based upon alliances with other countries, with the result that France was committed to strategic defense, a war of position that would "degenerate into the horrible trench stalemate" of the last war.[32] The penetration of the Maginot Line in 1940 would be a disaster for France that required a quick shift of static defensive positions.

Baldwin observed French army maneuvers in the Champagne area on the site of the 1915 World War I battlefield. He noted that the soldiers' baggy uniforms, their reluctance to salute officers, and their general sloppy appearance made the typical French soldier appear to be a "veritable military novitiate" when compared with the German troops. He hoped that, when motivated, for example by a German invasion, the French poilu could be "whipped to prodigies of valor by proper leadership."[33]

French tank tactics were, as in other nations, in a "state of turmoil,"[34] with their principle role being to accompany the infantry. Likewise, its air force was to cooperate with the army as a weapon of defense and to attack the enemy's industrial centers.[35] French airplane designers were obsessed with a single plane design, a weakness that was the result of the Blum government's nationalization of airplane factories, which had resulted in a low rate of production.[36]

The French navy was "humiliated" by the inferior ratios established at the naval conferences during the interwar years. The new battleship, *Dunkerque*, would be the first of six battleships, all of which were then under construction. Baldwin was critical of the labor strikes, the compulsory short work week, and the influence of Communist ideas among the shipyard workers that only delayed new ship construction.[37] The greatest French naval weakness was its need to keep its fleet both in the Atlantic and in the Mediterranean: "But on the sea, as on land, it is always necessary to remember that France is counting upon the aid of England" he said, which it did three years later.[38]

Germany was well on its way to becoming "the greatest military power on the continent, if not the world,"[39] and he observed ominously, it may write "tortured chapters in the history of tomorrow." In Berlin, Baldwin was surprised to see so many uniforms on the street. Germany was "a nation in uniform," which, to his thinking, represented not only national honor and glory but prestige and strength. Its rearmament was under way with thoroughness and for "perpetuity."[40] Germany would not be ready for a war until untrained men were "fitted as human cogs into the military machine." While on the surface the appearance of so motivated and dedicated a society led by Chancellor Adolf Hitler seemed frightening, Baldwin reassured his American readers that what the dictatorship gained in unity, it lost in flexibility.[41] Germans could not comprehend other peoples' motives, which gave them an inferiority complex, and which made them "ranting, boastful, and loud." He also noted that Germany was not an economically self-sufficient nation, which led it to make barter agreements with Central Europe to gain access to those needed raw materials.

Baldwin's requests to inspect German military installations were always refused. The highest-ranking officer in the War Ministry with whom he spoke was Major General Wilhelm Keitel. It was a "futile interview," Baldwin later recalled.[42] His impression was that Keitel was more of a political officer than a combat officer. His slavish devotion to Adolf Hitler led to his rapid promotion to chief of the general staff in 1940.

Unable to learn for himself any of the details of Germany's military organization and war preparations, Baldwin had to rely upon the military attaché in the American embassy in Berlin, Major Truman Smith, U.S. Army.[43] He and his aide, Percy Black, and later Alan Vanaman, had no opportunity to learn of the progress of German airplane factories, airplane engines, or to inspect the new planes before 1936.

Major Smith had become well known for his arranging for and accompanying Charles A. Lindbergh's five visits to Germany between 1936 and 1939. The German Air Ministry was eager to accommodate this famous American guest's requests for tours of factories, airfields, and to meet with its personnel. Lindbergh's expertise about planes enabled Smith to send detailed reports back to Washington on Germany's growing air force.[44] During those visits the Luftwaffe leaders, including Reich Marshal Herman Goering, permitted Lindbergh to inspect not only the latest airplanes, but on one occasion permitted him to take a forty-minute flight in the ME 109, Germany's latest and best fighter plane.[45] Baldwin was given no such preferred treatment in 1937, which is why he relied upon Smith's information.

The growing size of the German army, Baldwin noted, was to become a "machine of men, whose marching tread again shakes the fundaments of Europe."[46] This generation of conscripts would not be fully trained until 1939. Tanks would be used in large numbers, while its anti-tank guns were of excellent quality. As for gas experiments, "no one [knew]" for sure if such were under way. So often Baldwin had to hedge on his descriptions about the German military, "for nothing is surprising in the Pandora's Box that is the *Drittes Reich*," but he noted that the great strength of the army was the willingness of the conscript to be "a trained cog in a machine of men."[47]

The German air force was in the development stage with new planes, including the Junkers 88, the Heinkel 111, and the Messerschmitt 109, which were "attracting attention," but Baldwin never saw those planes on his visit. He characterized Goering, the Luftwaffe's leader, as having a "queer, dogmatic, egotistic, artistic personality," but he did not attempt to describe his role in the Nazi hierarchy other than to mention that the Luftwaffe was growing in size.[48]

In 1937 the German navy was no match for that of any other European power, and it was the least important of its armed forces. The construction of the three so-called pocket battleships (*Deutschland, Admiral Graf Spee,* and *Admiral Scheer*) had started the naval arms race in Europe.[49] Submarines were a potentially serious threat, given how successfully they had been used in World War I. The German navy was being built for its potential use, not only in the Baltic Sea, but for service on the seven seas. Since capital ships took time to build, Baldwin assumed that it would be a long time for Germany's "voice upon the water [to be] as strong" as its voice on land and in the air.[50]

On the home front, German civilians had been assigned wartime tasks should a war commence. The propaganda network operated at "top speed," with the press, movies, theater, and radio all being "attuned to the Fuehrer's will."[51] Given Germany's careful military preparations for a future war, it was not surprising that Baldwin felt in 1937 that Germany could be a real threat to the peace of Europe.

Baldwin described Poland as having a "medieval atmosphere." Its farmers, though free, lived like serfs. The country was industrially weak with few raw materials needed for an arms industry.[52] He witnessed Polish cavalry maneuvers, including Marshal Pilsudski's, the dictator of Poland from 1926 until his death in 1935, own regiment. Horse-mounted cavalry demonstrated their prowess with the saber and the lance, as well as with troikas, those three-horse drawn carriages with machine guns mounted on them, capable of firing at the gallop.[53] Though archaic militarily, Baldwin could not help but comment favorably on the cavalry: "steel helmeted, spurred, and armed with sabers flailing or lances leveled, [with the] men shouting at full charge [it] was a terrifying sight."[54] However, forty regiments of horse cavalry were no match against the tanks and the mechanized infantry that were the new weapons of the twentieth century. Baldwin noted that the Polish officer corps "thinks too much in terms of the loosely knit, personal warfare of Poland's yesterdays."[55] He dismissed Poland's small air force and its navy as existing for reasons of national prestige rather than being of practical military value.

Politically, Poland relied upon alliances with other countries, rather than trying to develop its own industry and a transportation network. Geographically, its terrain was "too dangerous for any degree of military comfort," Baldwin commented.[56] Eighteen months later, it took Germany only four weeks to conquer the country. As predicted by Baldwin, sabers and lances and human valor were useless relics of a bygone era when faced with German tanks and planes.

In Italy, Baldwin found a "looser" Mussolini dictatorship, where the population had neither the national discipline nor the military ability of Germany.[57] The country imported 86 percent of its needed raw materials, especially oil. Despite the facade of a dictatorship, he saw Italian individualism as being a "doubtful factor" in the Italian military, a quality that would lead to self-expression, not regimentation. The Ethiopian victory, Italian road construction along the Libyan seacoast, and the Italian air bases at Benghazi and at Tobruk were sources of national pride in Mare Nostrum, an Italian empire in the Mediterranean.[58]

The Italian army assumed it would have a quick victory; if possible, by using air and ground mechanized forces, since Italy was vulnerable to a sea blockade. One weakness of the army command, as revealed in the Ethiopian campaign, was the number of generals who were important politically but had few military skills. Baldwin doubted whether the air force command and the general staff organization were as thoroughly trained as in England or in Germany. Baldwin's interview with General Giuseppe Valle, the under-secretary for air, told Baldwin that "wars could not be won by aviation alone, but the planes . . . were secondary to ground and sea forces."[59]

In 1937 the Italian naval policy was to build ships for "blue water" operations on the high seas, rather than those limited to the Mediterranean alone. The two 35,000-ton battleships, *Littorio* and *Vittoria Veneto* with their nine 15-inch guns, then under construction, would be commissioned in August 1940, whereas Baldwin thought that they would be commissioned in late 1939.[60] The new ship construction, when completed, would challenge Britain's domination of the Gulf of Aden, the Red Sea, the Persian Gulf, and the Indian Ocean.

A small but important part of Italy's navy was its torpedo boats. At the port of La Spezia, taken for a spin around the bay in one, Baldwin recalled the experience of "the fine sparkle of salt spray on the foredeck [and] the bitter blowing fingers of the sea wind in the hair." Such boats could be a potential threat to Britain's sea communication in the narrow "bottle-neck" between Cape Bon, Tunisia, and Sicily.[61]

In spite of the Italian trait of "individualism," Baldwin concluded that the Italian navy was well equipped and well trained, with both its officers and men exhibiting a "fine spirit."[62] His primary sources in Italy were the *Times* correspondent in Rome and the American military attachés, including Captain Thomas D. White, then the assistant military attaché for air in Rome, who retired in 1961 as chief of staff of the U.S. Air Force.

Finally, Baldwin's long-awaited Soviet visa was issued in Warsaw, so Baldwin returned to Poland from Italy. Meeting him at the Moscow train station was Harold Denny, the resident *Times* correspondent since 1934, very nervous and worried. He immediately told his visitor, "For God's sake, keep your mouth shut. They know you were in the Navy, and a naval reserve officer. My secretary's disappeared and my driver's disappeared and I don't know what will happen next." Denny's fear was justified.[63]

The latest victim of Stalin's purges was General Mikhail Tukhachevsky, who, with seven other generals, had been arrested recently by the NKVD, the secret state police. He had tried to create an army led by professional soldiers, rather than by political commissars; because Stalin feared such independence, his fate was sealed.[64]

The execution of Tukhachevsky in June 1937 demonstrated to Baldwin that the "political commissar system undermined the basic military principle of command and may well interfere with Russian tactics."[65] Baldwin recalled sitting in Denny's sparsely furnished Moscow apartment one evening with his wife (the niece of the U.S. ambassador William C. Bullitt)[66] and another American, talking in whispers lest their conversation be overheard and reported. The other American, a cousin of Denny's wife, was fascinated with Russian small arms and spoke openly, although Denny tried to silence him for fear that such talk could bring an arrest by the NKVD.

In Russia, another useful source for Baldwin was Lieutenant Colonel Philip R. Faymonville, the American military attaché at the embassy. Since Baldwin's applications to interview Soviet military personnel had all been denied, Faymonville agreed to host a bachelor cocktail party for a few Soviet military officers, none of whom were high ranking but were willing to be sociable, except about military and defense subjects, where they were closed-mouthed. Baldwin came to value the U.S. military and naval attachés as a group, not only as valuable sources of information, but mainly for the "atmosphere," as he phrased it, which they lent to the country where they had been posted. He could ask them questions that the Washington-based bureaucrats could not answer. As he later noted, "I found this was really valuable later on. It served as a great backlog for the future."[67]

He quickly realized that any notes he took on his visits to Germany and to Russia would be confiscated, especially as any information about a country's military program was secret and could bring the charge that Baldwin was a spy. "I made it a habit," he recalled, "when I was talking to somebody, to memorize the salient facts . . . and then, when I got a moment to myself back at the hotel or elsewhere, I would write them down to keep them in my memory." Where possible, he would type very brief notes and send them back to the United States in a diplomatic pouch or have the military attachés in Berlin and in Moscow forward the notes in care of his *Times* office in New York.[68]

In the Soviet Union in 1937, Baldwin observed Communism firsthand and saw a scared and frightened people. His previously latent anti-Communist views had their maturation during that week's visit. Communism, he wrote, was probably "the only political philosophy, except Nazism, which openly and actively, as well as secretly and insidiously, works for the overthrow of any and all potential enemies in time of peace as in time of war."[69] He added that the rulers of Russia worshiped "a mummy in a Red Square mausoleum" and prepared the country for a "war of ideologies with the crushing of Communism the Holy Grail of a new [anti-Soviet] crusade."[70] He felt that the official Soviet policy of secrecy only veiled its weaknesses and its suspicions of other nations. He reported on Stalin's attempts to transform Russia into an industrialized nation. The country's strength lay in its vastness, its self-sufficiency in important raw materials, and its diverse population "glued together by the amalgam of propaganda." Its weakness was the lack of a network of roads and railroads.

The size of the Red Army, including reservists, Baldwin put at 20 million, with perhaps only 1 million of these troops well trained. The chief asset of the Russian soldier was his "peasant hardihood, strength, and dogged courage,"[71] assets that were to be severely tested after June 22, 1941.

Soviet airplanes were copies of foreign models built in Russia under license. A medium bomber, the S.V., was powered by two American Wright Cyclone engines. The Soviet's best fighter, the I-16, was powered by either the Wright engines or by the French-built Gnome-Rhone engines.[72] Baldwin felt that Russian parachutists were "more spectacular than useful."[73] In short, the Soviet Union was preparing for war with weapons copied from other nations, but it was "one of the great unknown" military powers of Europe.[74]

Baldwin was eager to leave what he called that "black night" of the Soviet Union. His baggage was thoroughly searched by Soviet officials at the Polish frontier with "a fine tooth comb."[75] Fortunately for him, they found nothing incriminating in his baggage. While he was en route to New York City, on board the Cunard liner *Aquitania* (which left Southampton on May 26), Fred Birchall, the *Times* bureau chief in London, sent a cable to Edwin James, the managing editor, praising Baldwin's hard work and his ability to see "everybody worth seeing who could be seen." His ability to gather materials would be the basis for his future articles in the *Times*. Since Baldwin, Birchall observed, did not talk about himself, "it seems worthwhile to write this to you [James]."[76]

Baldwin brought back a number of maps acquired during his three-month trip that became very valuable and useful after September 1939. On his return, he spoke with military and naval intelligence personnel in Washington, though he could tell them little that had not already been printed in the *Times*.[77] As a rule, he never went on special missions for the military intelligence people because, to his thinking, newspaper work and intelligence work did not mix. The latter needed specific technical information about weapons, their ballistic characteristics, and their effectiveness on the battlefield that would be of no interest to the general newspaper reader. It is understandable that national security services would consider journalists useful as informal spies, since they were reputed to have access to all kinds of information, some of which could be useful to the military. No doubt some journalists fell into that trap, but always Baldwin resisted, as it blurred the separation between newspaper reporting and espionage.

The *Times* senior management was very pleased with his European articles. A week after his return, the publisher, Arthur Hays Sulzberger, invited

Baldwin to lunch in his private dining room on the fourteenth floor of the Times Building. That lunch, on Monday June 7, 1937, established his course with the paper for the next thirty-one years.[78]

Though Baldwin could not recall, decades later, what had specifically transpired at that lunch, there is, fortunately, in the *Times* archives a memorandum of understanding written by Baldwin two days later, in which "the mechanics of the new work" was outlined. Sulzberger asked Baldwin to devote all of his time to military affairs, the first such assignment for the paper. In response, Baldwin requested elastic working hours, day and night, for a five-day week. He would also continue to write for Lester Markel's *Times Sunday Magazine*, and do an occasional editorial for Dr. John Huston Finley, the editorial page editor. Baldwin wanted "a free hand" with which to select military topics, and the freedom to "dig up stories that are not routine." He wanted the city desk to understand that he was "not to be held responsible" for all routine assignments on military affairs. He would, however, keep Joseph, the city editor, informed of the military topic that caught his interest, hopefully with his concurrence. The arrangement made Baldwin almost independent and self-employed by the *Times*. He would, of course, be held answerable to Sulzberger, or, as he phrased it in his memorandum, "As you suggested, I shall . . . keep my eyes open . . . for all such assignments that might be profitably covered and shall pass along the suggestions to you—for the time being—and to whomever you may direct later."[79]

Sulzberger passed this memorandum on to James, the managing editor, for his comments. He suggested that Baldwin be attached to one department yet be free to work for the editorial and the Sunday departments, not wanting Baldwin to regard himself as independent of the news department, and this was agreed to.[80] Later that autumn, the publisher raised Baldwin's salary from $100 per week to $125 per week, to be charged to the news department's payroll. The pay raise was greatly appreciated, since Baldwin and Helen's second daughter, Elizabeth Decker, had been born a week earlier.[81]

In early 1938 Baldwin's first book, *The Caissons Roll*, mentioned earlier, appeared to generally favorable reviews. The *Times* reviewer called the work "timely" and noted that, after 1940, the major powers would be ready for war.[82] An academic reviewer noted that the figures cited in the book were incomplete, in that no one knew for sure how much money was being spent to rearm Europe. He noted that while the next war would begin quickly, with "machine against machine," the war would become a "stalemate of trench warfare." He thought the book contained little hope for the "future of mankind."[83] The reviewer expressed a widely held view that the next war would be static like the first Great War. *The New Republic* magazine thought that Baldwin's picture of European rearmament was "at times terrifying" and a grim reminder of "just how mad the world has gone."[84] Major Dupuy, U.S. Army, and Baldwin's aforementioned mentor on army subjects, criticized other newspapermen in general for their "crass ignorance of war and things military," while praising Baldwin for his military knowledge and accurate reporting.[85]

The generally positive book reviews did not necessarily result in good sales. Sensing the author's disappointment over the poor sales figures (they averaged about one sale per day), Alfred A. Knopf, his book publisher, consoled Baldwin by saying that booksellers took "little interest in works of this kind." America's reading public in 1938 did not want to buy any books that predicted a new European war within the next four years; at that moment, the nation felt reassured that the three Neutrality Acts passed by Congress after 1935 would keep the United States out of the next war.[86]

Baldwin took his new assignment as the *Times'* military and naval correspondent very seriously. He actively cultivated Army, Navy, and Air Force serving officers as potential news sources, fully aware that, in general, professional military personnel held a low opinion of all print journalists. As Major Dupuy noted in his review of Baldwin's book, too many journalists were out of their depth when dealing with the military. They had no understanding of why men would give the best years of their lives in the service of a country that did not appreciate their service, and allow themselves to be paid so poorly for that service.

As the only full-time military and naval correspondent on any American newspaper in 1937, Baldwin was the right man in the right job because he had the necessary background to succeed in his new role. The encouragement of the two senior *Times* executives, Sulzberger and Adler, would have meant nothing had not Baldwin already proven his ability and value to the paper. His previous eight years as an often anonymous general assignment reporter were now behind him. In those few years before the invasion of Poland, Baldwin felt that a military analyst had to be "a whole lot of things to all people."[87]

The *Times* recognized his talents and his increasing value to the paper by giving him several writing venues: both straight reportorial pieces and book reviews. His longer articles for the *Times Sunday Magazine* permitted him to elaborate upon his short pieces for the daily paper. He also wrote an occasional editorial on military issues in the news. What most upset Sulzberger were Baldwin's analytical pieces, in which he combined the reporting of facts with his own interpretation of those facts. The publisher believed that the editorial page was the only proper venue in which to express an opinion in a newspaper. The compromise was the Q-head, a signed article that represented Baldwin's views just short of an editorial. A larger headline font set it apart from the other articles on the page.

The main question was, "What are the limits of military analysis?" Increasingly, Baldwin came to see that narrow military topics often involved larger political, economic, and social issues that had to be cited to help his readers to better understand a topic. Sulzberger, whose censorious memoranda over the years expressed his concerns, did not appreciate that view, but the issue was never fully settled.[88]

Being an Annapolis graduate helped Baldwin with his Navy classmates, but not with the Army or Air Force where he was not well known. In an attempt to get Army officers to talk with him, Baldwin assured them that he would never violate their confidence. To a junior Army officer at Fort Leavenworth, Kansas, Baldwin wrote, "be assured that anything you may tell me remains safe with me, that your letters are and will be safe, and that wild horses couldn't drag any secrets from me."[89]

He was as good as his word. Decades later, when asked to name some of his sources, he refused, saying that either he had forgotten their names, or that, if they were still alive, he would need their permission. Baldwin was not a kiss-and-tell journalist. He was not an apologist or a sounding board for the military, though to some readers his articles may have seemed to be special pleading, and he was alert to that criticism. He valued his independence and sought to avoid having the appearance of being a military apologist, for without that independence his usefulness to the *Times* and to his reading public would end. In 1938 he put his views this way: "My motives in writing anything are not to please anybody or anything, or any institution, I am interested in . . . presenting the truth—and although that is always the most difficult of all things to do—I try to call 'em as I see 'em and let the chips fall where they may."[90] That view summarized his outlook and his approach to his work and did not change for the remainder of his long career.

However, from readers' letters, he learned that what he thought was a balanced piece of writing others often saw as a biased one. National defense was not a neutral subject, even during the 1930s. The never-again school was convinced that America should never have entered World War I. In the popular slogan of the day, "in war some get rich and others get shot." In its passage of the Neutrality Acts, after 1935, Congress reflected a popular sentiment that America should stay out of another European war. College students' hostility to anything military was well known. In that atmosphere, the retired U.S. Marine Corps general Smedley Darlington Butler's 1935 book, *War Is a Racket*, found a receptive audience.

As the decade of the 1930s neared its end and European events took on an ominous tone, Baldwin traveled more often than he had in the past to Washington, D.C. During his short visits he was ever conscious of invading the turf of the *Times* Washington bureau and its chief, Arthur Krock. Fortunately for Baldwin there was no one at the bureau whose full-time assignment was the military, and few journalists in Washington had bothered to develop any contacts in the War and Navy departments. He found that tact and deferring to those who covered Capital Hill went a long way toward minimizing any professional jealousy or friction.

Baldwin had to create this new specialty all by himself. His sources included serving officers in the War and Navy departments in Washington, D.C., as well as in military intelligence, whose offices were across the street from the old State-War-Navy Building. He made it his business to make personal contacts with the Navy chiefs and their assistants, one of whom was Admiral William H. Standley, the chief of naval operations from 1933–37, whom Baldwin later recalled having known "very well when he was the CNO."[91]

Baldwin also cultivated the civilian secretaries of war and navy and their assistants. He had grown up with a number of junior officers who "came up to high rank" in later years, and over time he developed a wide range of knowledgeable sources in the military services, many of whom became his personal friends and whom he could and did call for specific information.[92] One difficulty of his work, which he frequently encountered, was the mindset of the military. In an unpublished memoir, written in 1937, he observed, "it is a curious thing, despite the hardy positive virtues inculcated by the profession of arms, it breeds a single-mindedness which too often becomes a narrow-mindedness, a conservatism which becomes reactionary, a patriotism which tends toward chauvinism, a loyalty which may become blind and harmful."[93] He deplored the pettiness of the military in those prewar years, where limited budgets and public indifference bred jealousies, interservice rivalries, and the rejection of all constructive criticism. He recognized that the military profession bred loyalty, comradeship, physical courage—all "the vigorous positive virtues, but . . . also [begat] from generation unto generation the defects inherent in its limitations."[94]

He also observed that the Army was closer to the American people than the Navy, since Army camps in the United States permitted social interaction between soldiers and civilians who lived nearby, whereas the Navy's duty was to show the flag in distant ports far from the United States. In 1937 the Navy's public relations policy was too often "motivated by a bull-headed stupidity, a complete lack of understanding of public reaction. It has failed to make itself truly a part of the people as the Army has, and although it is the more glamorous . . . it is the less democratic one."[95] Particularly aggravating to Baldwin, who covered some fleet exercises, was the degree of Navy censorship that he considered to be both unreasonable and unreasoned. For example, in 1934, during the fleet athletic championships in Panama, a staff officer refused to give Baldwin the golf team's scores because they "might be confidential"[96]

In the late 1930s, when spy scares were in the news, very few naval officers were willing to talk to the press. The decision by President Roosevelt to build the U.S. Navy up to treaty limits also increased the official secrecy level and official suspicion, which even included the First Lady, Eleanor Roosevelt, and others being listed by the Office of Naval Intelligence as "dangerous Reds,"[97] and all cameras on board ships being locked away. Although Baldwin thought that dealing with the Navy was difficult in the 1930s, he had yet to encounter Admiral Ernest J. King, later the chief of naval operations, whose contribution to public relations during the war was limited to a terse statement—"we won"—at the war's end.

In the late 1930s Baldwin frequently relied upon his Naval Academy classmates, still on active duty, for information about the engineering and construction problems with new ships. For example, one technical issue on which Baldwin wrote attracted the attention of President Franklin D.

Roosevelt. It was the use of high-temperature, high-pressure steam being installed on the new *Mahan* class of destroyers. Problems quickly arose with the welding of the joints on steam lines. Baldwin was alerted to this problem by Lieutenant Stephen R. Bedford, one of his classmates at the Academy who was the engineer officer on the USS *Cushing* (DD 376), one of the new *Mahan*-class destroyers. Lieutenant Bedford was sharply critical of using steam pressure that was too dangerous. "Having seen a few blasts of live steam now and then," he favored the diesel-electric power plants on those thin-skinned destroyers.[98]

Baldwin wrote on this technical and complex issue that involved the conflicting personalities of the principals, including the personal bias of Secretary of the Navy Charles Edison, who sided with those admirals who favored the high-pressure steam system, the cumbersome Navy bureaucratic organization, and the big three shipbuilding companies. There were also other technical problems on the new cruisers and the construction delays on four of the new battleships. Baldwin attributed the construction problems to the inexperience at the shipbuilding yards because necessary skills had lapsed when capital ships were discontinued after 1922.[99]

On the day that his article appeared in the *Times*, President Roosevelt held a news conference, at which he cited Baldwin's article and commented that he found it "interesting . . . and very well written because it is a highly technical subject." The president proceeded to elaborate upon Baldwin's comment on the lack of shipbuilding experience over the past fifteen years and was critical of the delay between the congressional appropriation of funds and the commissioning of new ships as "altogether too long."[100]

A few days later, the *Times* editorial favored the use of high-pressure, high-temperature steam. "The Navy will have to make up its mind," the editorial concluded, "whether it wants to carry guns and armor or water and fuel."[101] Though unsigned, only Baldwin had the knowledge to write such an editorial. The high-pressure, high-temperature steam controversy faded after a year as better welds of the pipe joints were introduced that permitted higher temperatures and pressures than before.[102]

One of the more interesting foreign military attachés whom Baldwin cultivated was Lieutenant General Friedrich von Boetticher, the German military attaché in Washington. He first met him in 1935 at the Pine Camp, New York, Army maneuvers. As Hitler's expansion plans in Europe became obvious, Baldwin found him to be a valuable background source of the fundamentals and basics of the German army's organization, tactics, and ideas. He was alert to the fact that any information that von Boetticher gave him had to be checked carefully against other sources, lest Baldwin be considered a mouthpiece of Goebbels' propaganda ministry. From the general's point of view, talking with Baldwin could be worthwhile because he might learn something about America's military establishment. In 1938, von Boetticher returned from a long leave in Germany, during which time he had the opportunity to sit next to Adolf Hitler at a dinner. He had become another victim of Hitler's fatal charisma, "almost ecstatic about Hitler's charm and brilliance and knowledge."[103]

After the German victory in Poland in 1939, Baldwin asked the general for details about that four-week campaign. Eventually, he was given a German propaganda film on the Polish campaign and a booklet entitled "The Campaign of the Eighteen Days." Von Boetticher returned to Germany in early June 1941. In retrospect, Baldwin felt him to have been a decent, apolitical officer whose devotion to duty and love of Germany "tore him apart" as Hitler's war policies brought only death, misery, and destruction to so many in Europe.[104]

Serving officers in the naval establishment in Washington were good sources of information, especially Lieutenant Bernard L. ("Count") Austin, the Navy's press relations officer from 1937–40. Count Austin, whose moniker dated from his midshipman years at the Academy, was in the same class of 1924 with Baldwin and became his lifelong friend, probably supplying Baldwin with technical information on new ships and other factual details on the Navy.

Austin once recalled how being a public relations officer was a broadening experience after his earlier exposure to the press and radio. He commented that a military officer's training encouraged quick decision-making and quick responses. The drawback was that this "full speed ahead" attitude often led to an intolerance of other arguments and encouraged a simplistic and dogmatic behavior.[105] Baldwin was very familiar with the type.

Another valuable source was Commander Louis E. Denfeld, then an aide to Admiral William D. Leahy, the chief of naval operations (1933–39). In December 1938, Denfeld praised Baldwin's recent series of editorials in the *Times*, especially those on the Navy as being, in his opinion, "in complete agreement with our ideas on the subject and I believe the ideas of the President."[106]

An important Army source for Baldwin was Lieutenant Colonel Stanley J. Grogan, the chief of the press branch, Bureau of Public Relations, in the War Department in Washington, D.C., as well as the War Department's Military Intelligence Division, G2, of the General Staff. It is reasonable to assume that those military and naval contacts were the only sources then available in the late 1930s for technical data on ships and military equipment.[107]

Prior to the German invasion of Russia on June 22, 1941, Grogan sent a four-page mimeographed bulletin to nine journalists that gave data on the German army, together with a bibliography of books recommended by the German General Staff in December 1940 to its officers for their professional reading. Baldwin was on that short list, together with Walter Lippmann (*New York Herald-Tribune*), Mark S. Watson (*Baltimore Sun*), Walter Trohan (*Chicago Tribune*), and Drew Pearson, a freelance commentator.

The sinking of the American gunboat USS *Panay* (PR 5) on December 12, 1937, on the Yangtze River by Japanese planes alerted Baldwin to how little he knew about Japanese affairs. He began a correspondence with an Academy graduate, William Joseph Sebald (class of 1922), who had been posted to Japan in 1925 to study the language while attached to the American Embassy in Tokyo. When Baldwin began to make contact with him in early 1938, Sebald was no longer in the Navy and was practicing law in Kobe, Japan, where his reputation was based upon his four books on Japanese law.

As an American resident in Japan, his letters to Baldwin dealt more with perceptions than with specific political and economic issues, though those issues were touched upon. The Sino-Japanese War, begun in 1937, was "dragging out" much longer than the Japanese had expected. Despite the unfavorable balance of trade, Japan was in fair shape, he wrote, due in part to restrictions on the domestic consumption of raw materials and the restrictions on foreign currency exchange rates.[108]

A friend of Sebald, who had recently returned from Shanghai, China, told him of the public behavior of American naval officers who "get drunk and make fools of themselves in the lobbies of hotels." Sebald commented to Baldwin, "this sort of thing goes on right up through the ranks," the effect being that the Japanese officers looked down upon U.S. [naval officers] as a bunch of carousers "who cannot behave themselves, and who must therefore lack the first essentials of good officers."[109]

Politically, Americans considered Japan's leaders to be "demagogues" who exploited their people for "personal gain," a view Sebald rejected. The truth, as he saw it, was that Japan's political leaders acted only for the "welfare of Japan, the Emperor, and the Japanese people," not for personal gain. When a leader made a mistake, he would step aside for his successor. In some very serious cases he would even show his responsibility by committing hara-kiri, an acknowledgment that "a mistake can be vindicated and responsibility taken, only by death."[110]

Closer to Baldwin's interest, Sebald observed that Japan's military leaders believed that, for the glory of Japan, they "can do everything . . . much better and much more expeditiously than the [Japanese] civilian." The government bureaucracy had resisted this view that prevented the army from putting its ideas into practice. This tension would explain, he thought, why Foreign Minister Hirota Koki was a retired general and the prime minister, Prince Konoye Fuminaro, was "a compromise man who plays with both sides and keeps peace in the family."[111] Baldwin welcomed such perceptive comments on Japan by one who lived there and knew the language, and he used such letters as a background for future articles without giving attribution to protect Sebald.[112]

Hanson Baldwin's ever widening circle of news sources, from Annapolis classmates to bureaucrats in the War and Navy departments, kept him well informed about current military issues in those years before the hounds of war were let loose in September 1939. Being the first full-time military correspondent for an American daily newspaper gave him an initial advantage over other journalists in the field of military reporting, a field that would become very crowded during World War II.

To increase his public recognition, Baldwin began to make occasional radio broadcasts over the Columbia Broadcasting radio network beginning in February 1938. The *Times* management did not encourage such radio outlets, lest a reporter reveal new information that had not first been printed in the paper. Baldwin was made aware of this concern and was careful to paraphrase only previously published articles, but the issue would be revisited many times in future years.[113]

Upon his return from his European trip in May 1937, Baldwin was convinced that a general European war was "inevitable," but not before 1942 when Hitler's rearmament programs would be completed. Baldwin was not certain that the United States would be involved initially, but he agreed with President Roosevelt that America should prepare for possible entry into that war by rearming immediately. He hoped that Hitler and Stalin—"the two greatest tyrannies"—would "knock each other off."[114]

During the late 1930s, Baldwin developed relationships with the Washington political bureaucracy that he felt to be as important as any spot news that might come from those contacts. One source was Louis A. Johnson, the assistant secretary of war (1937–40), a politically ambitious man who had admired a number of Baldwin's *Times* pieces and welcomed his visits to Washington.[115] Those Washington contacts provided the necessary background, which Baldwin was to cultivate for profit, especially after the United States entered World War II in December 1941. "It was invaluable to have known them and then to be able to keep up the contacts," he later recalled.[116]

Baldwin met with President Roosevelt once or twice, in those prewar years, as a member of a small group of reporters interested in specific topics. On one of those occasions, he recalled "sitting in the chair beside him" in the Oval Office while the president commented upon the needs of the Navy. Roosevelt was charming, but said "nothing outstanding" that he could recall.[117]

Baldwin could not escape the demands of daily journalism that required that he write quickly to meet a deadline. His analytical pieces took time to write and still had to be timely to be considered newsworthy. He did not hesitate to print a correction to any of his pieces in a later edition of the *Times*. He took his work seriously, but not himself. It was his fate to live during the most momentous events of the twentieth century, and it was his duty, as he saw it, to report on and to explain those events, to try to reveal their significance. He was no militarist, but he did understand the relationship of military power to America's foreign policy. To his thinking, a nation disarmed was a nation vulnerable to hostile foreign forces, as America learned during the 1930s.

His style of writing was informative and instructive. He avoided moralizing or conjecture on decisions made by military leaders in war. But he always believed that men, not machines, were the heart of war. Unlike Ernie

Pyle, who wrote so movingly about the effects of combat on individual soldiers, or Bill Mauldin, whose cartoon figures of Willie and Joe so well summarized the war from the GI's point of view, Baldwin's writings dealt more
with military hardware, defense issues, strategic problems and people collectively, than with individual personalities. He worked very hard to develop
Army and Navy sources whose level of expertise on specific topics served
him well in the tumultuous years ahead. His reputation grew from reporting accurately on fleet exercises and Army maneuvers, to seeing the larger
political and strategic picture that his readers came to respect and to admire.

CHAPTER

Distant Thunder, 1938–39

Many of Hanson Baldwin's writings in the late 1930s continued to be limited to narrowly focused American military topics. Gradually, in 1938, his *Times* pieces began to include political issues, domestic and foreign, that bore upon national defense. His magazine articles tried to analyze the meaning of events, for which he later became well respected and widely read.

Baldwin entered what he called the "mental gyrations and verbal circumlocutions" of the congressional debate with an article that raised the key question, "What ought to be the size of an 'adequate' Navy for America?" He began with the statement that our foreign policy must determine our naval policy. If that policy was to meet all enemy fleets in their home waters, the United States would need to double the number of battleships being built or being planned. Since that was not the case, he concluded that the present construction program was "adequate" for a "simultaneous attack" on both American coasts. The U.S. fleet was "sufficient," he wrote, to protect the Panama Canal, Hawaii, and Alaska. But the Navy was "nowhere near adequate" to protect U.S. commerce and U.S. citizens everywhere, in addition to protecting the Philippines and Guam, and to support the Open Door Policy in China.

He praised Congressman Carl Vinson's call for a naval policy and for the proposed naval building program, which would "register [U.S.] determination" to have a "strong" foreign policy, and his article was praised by Walter Lippmann, the well-respected columnist then on the staff of the *New York Herald-Tribune*.[1]

In the prestigious *Foreign Affairs* magazine, Baldwin wrote of how over-extended the Army and Navy both were, especially if they were expected to defend our Pacific island possessions and to keep the Open Door in China, while protecting American citizens and our commercial interests every-where.[2] He was aware of the isolationists' "great strength," which reflected many Americans' determination "to keep peace at almost any price."

Baldwin noted two current trends in public policy, one pacifist, as represented by the isolationists, the other militarist, as reflected in the policy maxim of former president Theodore Roosevelt: "speak softly and carry a big stick." The time had come, Baldwin observed, for "a really big stick to come again."[3] He reviewed with satisfaction FDR's increased budgets for the Navy, "our first line of defense," that called for new ship construction up to the limits established by the London Naval Treaty of 1930, to expire in December 1936.

On December 12, 1937, Japanese planes sank the American river gunboat the USS *Panay* (PR 5) on the Yangtze River. This attack spurred President Roosevelt to call for a 20 percent increase in ship tonnage (or sixty-nine new ships). Baldwin praised this decision because more ships would require more sailors to serve on them. Enlisted personnel shortages in the Navy were a continuing problem during fleet exercises.

The U.S. Army was, in Baldwin's analysis, in a "complete state of flux."[4] Some of its equipment was modern but it had too little equipment to be effective. For example, the new Garand rifle (later to be called the M-1) was a superior rifle, but only seventy-seven were manufactured each week at a cost of $88 per rifle.[5] The new 105-mm Howitzer showed great promise, but only seven existed. While newer light and medium tanks were on order, few had been delivered. More importantly, there was no agreement as to which tank tactics the Army should adapt.[6] War Department plans called for mechanizing only those units needed to move their artillery, field kitchens, and other equipment, but not to use tanks as an independent fighting unit.

As then organized, the U.S. Army's infantry divisions of 28,000 men depended too much on animal transport, which made it a "ponderous" unit to move. During the Texas maneuvers in 1937, a small motorized infantry division of 13,512 men was used with success.

Unfortunately, there were too many "Colonel Blimps" in the Army who resisted change, and Baldwin eagerly awaited an influx of "keener"

American officers. Regrettably, they were few in number and the Army's promotion system, based on seniority, resulted in there being much "deadwood" among the officer corps. As evidence of this "dry rot," Baldwin publicized an article in *The Infantry Journal* authored by "Colonel X." The anonymous author contended that many Army officers who worked for the Civilian Conservation Corps had to be relieved of their duties because of incompetence. He remarked that the blame for this situation lay in the years of focus upon "spit and polish" routine, rather than on encouraging initiative and responsibility. The new challenge for the Army was to build an officer corps that would be judged by results and not by a "timorous conformity" to military routine. General George C. Marshall was fully aware of this condition, and when he became the Army's chief of staff on September 1, 1939, he dismissed officers who were not up to the job.[7]

As for U.S. bases overseas, Baldwin, to his later dismay, pronounced Pearl Harbor "probably impregnable to a foreseeable attack."[8] In the Philippines, he thought the fortress at Corregidor might "hold out a year or more" against a Japanese attack, and that fortress fell in one month's time in 1942.[9]

Aside from those optimistic speculations, the tone of Baldwin's report was cautious. He did not want to alarm the American public about the inadequacies of U.S. armed forces, yet he did support President Roosevelt's rearmament policies and the money voted by Congress to implement them, even though much of the funding went to the Navy. He was concerned that the Army and Navy were not prepared to defend U.S. insular possessions in the Pacific or American commerce and citizens overseas. He rhetorically asked, "Could we defend our interests in the Far East as well as in South America?" If so, "Would we need allies to defend those interests?" If there were no allies, "Would the Roosevelt administration favor enlarging the size of the Army and the Navy to a point where we could go it alone without allies to defend the American Empire?"[10]

In Europe, the importance of the Munich Conference in September 1938 was not lost on Baldwin. That conference resulted in western Czechoslovakia being ceded to Germany with the concurrence of Great Britain and France. Ironically, the agreement opened for Germany "a gateway to the East and an avenue to world power."[11] Strategically, the "bloodless conquest" of old Bohemia reminded Baldwin of a phrase attributed to Otto von Bismarck, Germany's famous chancellor of the last century, "whoever is master of

Bohemia is master of Europe," as it was rich in raw materials and industries, he observed.[12]

Politically, the Munich agreement demonstrated the fear of the Western democracies of another European war, as revealed in their negotiations with Germany. Baldwin saw three possible developments: an Anglo-German rapprochement, in which England would not oppose Germany's moves into eastern Europe; second, Germany and Russia would "[stand] face to face"; and last, the smaller European countries "defer[ing]" to Germany, since Britain and France could no longer be relied upon.

Whatever the outcome, in 1938, he foresaw a tripartite pact between Germany, Italy, and Japan. Such a pact was signed in September 1940. He also predicted that Hitler would seek "new worlds to conquer" in South America and elsewhere, correctly comparing the Munich agreement to a pool of international politics into which stones would "spread world-wide ripples for years to come."

While European events, both political and military, held real threats to peace, Baldwin was also concerned with the weakness of the U.S. military. Years of congressional neglect, the public's disinterest in military matters, and the Great Depression that focused many citizens' attention on finding work were the important domestic factors that affected the military establishment.

In the months immediately following the Munich Conference, events moved swiftly. Germany continued to partition Czechoslovakia and Japan announced its Greater East Asia Co-Prosperity Sphere, by virtue of which it would be the dominant economic and political power in the Far East. On the evening of November 9–10, 1938, Nazi party members attacked Jewish homes and businesses—an event known as Kristallnacht—to avenge the murder of a German diplomat in Paris by a young Jew. Despite universal criticism of this event, Germany continued to expand its dominion.

It was against this backdrop that Baldwin wrote a series of seven editorials for the *Times* in December 1938 entitled "A National Defense Program." "We are living in a new age of imperialism," he wrote, in which America must conserve its interests in a "disordered world." Those interests included South America and the defense of the Monroe Doctrine. In defense, America was "already armed," but his question was, "Should we increase the extensive armament we now possess?"

Playing the role of devil's advocate, Baldwin questioned why it was necessary "to invest in instruments of death" when the money could be used "more profitably" for slum clearance, new public housing, new roads and bridges, flood control, the reforestation of bare hills, and the building of schools, hospitals, and parks.[13] Baldwin's answer was that there was a great need to protect North and South America by having a better-balanced and modern machinery of self-defense. He called for a new rearmament program to be "intelligently conceived and specifically planned for our current needs." He warned against the dangers of "hysteria" that could be "swept along on a high tide of oratory" toward unreasonable objectives. Second, he noted that there was a dangerous tendency to oversimplify defense problems, such as the crash plan to build more airplanes while ignoring the need for a balanced Air Force. And last, he warned against a defense program that was motivated by job creation schemes and that favored certain types of armament over others.[14] Subsequent editorials in the series focused upon the specific military services and their organization of supply.

He dismissed as "fantastic" a situation in which an "alliance of hostile nations" would strip its own coasts of self-defense and sail across two oceans to attack the United States. The United States did not need, he wrote, a new Atlantic fleet, but rather a better-balanced and well-rounded single U.S. fleet. For example, America did not need additional battleships beyond those newly authorized, but it did need more destroyers and submarines to replace the aging types of ships then in the fleet. It needed more aircraft carriers, as well as an increased capacity in its shipbuilding industry. His sharpest criticism focused upon the well-entrenched and powerful Navy bureaus, whose red tape often impeded new ship construction.[15]

With the benefit of hindsight, it is clear that Baldwin's bold and ill-considered statement, "We do not need a large standing Army. Nor do we need conscription,"[16] did not stand up to subsequent events. He favored a modest increase of the size of the Regular Army from the existing 65,000 men to 185,000 to accommodate the growth of the Army Air Corps, and he was critical of the continuing existence of small Army garrisons at home and overseas that survived only as "relics of the past." In the United States, he said, too many "political Army posts" existed "primarily" for the "prestige" of local congressmen and should be closed. Baldwin favored the concentration of small Army units into large ones that would function as a modern Army. He favored longer training for the Reserve Army officers, to be increased to two weeks of active duty every two years.

The American public had the "partially mistaken" belief that air power was the dominant weapon of the day. Baldwin discounted the inflated number of German fighter planes, but urged that more government funds be spent for research and development of liquid-cooled engines, as well as long-range aircraft and helicopters, once called the "autogyro."

Baldwin believed that the Atlantic and Pacific oceans were "effective barriers" to any enemy air attack on the continental United States, but that obsolescent planes should be replaced. The Army and Navy air forces should be increased by three thousand planes for each service. America's manufacturing capacity should be increased. More ground personnel were needed, as well as more airfields from Alaska to Puerto Rico.[17]

While more equipment and personnel were needed in all the armed services, Baldwin felt that the U.S. national defense program was basically an industrial problem, not a military one.[18] He favored American rearmament but felt that the United States should not follow the example of those other nations that were willing to sacrifice their political freedoms as the price of their rearmament. Baldwin urged a gradual approach that would survey the capacity of American industry to manufacture war goods, and then encourage certain industries to experiment with highly specialized equipment needed by both the Army and the Navy, and to begin to stockpile essential raw materials that the United States did not produce. He urged that Congress continue to fund "educational orders" to certain industries for a few special items, so that in the event of a national emergency the personnel at those factories would be already trained to produce those difficult-to-make war items.

In this series of seven editorials, Baldwin emphasized the need for both industrial and political planning of America's defense program, and a smooth-running military organization to coordinate the needs of both the War and Navy departments. He suggested the promotion of "relatively young and vigorous" officers to key positions in administration who had proven themselves to be adept in planning and procurement. He favored the abolition of politics from officer promotions and the need to cut red tape in the service bureaucracies.

In short, Baldwin called for a planned defense program that would result in more ships—especially aircraft carriers, cruisers, destroyers, and submarines—but not more battleships beyond those already approved. He contended that the Regular Army and the National Guard ought to be increased in size, while existing Army units needed to be concentrated. The Army Air Corps needed a "gradual" expansion to the three thousand planes already authorized. The interservice and the intraservice rivalries were an "expensive luxury" that should be reined in. The goals of national defense, as outlined by Baldwin, were achievable, he thought, if Congress and the American public would support them.[19]

This editorial series not only helped to insure Baldwin's niche as the *Times* military correspondent, it gave voice to Sulzberger's belief that the world was rapidly becoming a dangerous place in which the United States must look to its own defenses. The conservative tone of Baldwin's editorials was not intended to raise an alarm about an immediate threat to the United States' national existence, but as a quiet and prudent argument to better assess its future role in an unstable world. He urged continued preparedness and the modernization of America's military defenses to better meet the challenges of that fateful year, 1939.

During the spring and early summer of 1939, there were many dangerous threats to world peace from Germany and Japan. In Europe, Germany completed its domination of Czechoslovakia, signed the "Pact of Steel" with Mussolini's Italy, completed barter agreements for Rumanian oil, and continued its pressure on Poland for territorial concessions. Japan continued to implement its Greater East Asia Co-Prosperity Sphere by occupying eastern China and Hainan Island, which threatened British communication between its crown colony of Hong Kong and its naval base at Singapore.

As mentioned earlier, it was through radio, a new and popular mass medium in the 1930s, that Baldwin found he could reach a very wide audience. In one 1939 radio script entitled, "Should America Re-arm?" he denied that he represented either a "Big-Navy" school, or isolationism. In his words, he was "a conservative believer in national defense" who favored the pending Vinson Naval Construction Bill then before Congress, as it "helps to maintain our relative naval strength and is therefore a definite aid to our international safety." He opposed the construction of any new Pacific island bases, as they would "tend to embroil us in any war in the Far East where, in my opinion, the United States has no vital interests . . . worth the red hell of war."[20]

National defense, a popular term in the late 1930s, was the theme of numerous writers. Baldwin's 1939 articles were informative and cautiously critical of U.S. national defense policies favored by senior military and naval officers. Writing in *Foreign Affairs*, the quarterly journal of the Council on Foreign Relations, Baldwin opposed the recommendations of the Hepburn Board, acting with a congressional mandate, that $65 million be spent to develop new airplane bases at Guam, Wake, Midway, Johnson, and Palmyra islands, as well as at Pearl Harbor and at other sites in Alaska and in the Caribbean.

Baldwin dismissed the board's argument that a Guam base would "assure the impregnability of the island" and insure "practical immunity" of the Philippines against hostile attack. Guam was over five thousand miles from any American supply base, was vulnerable to a Japanese air attack, and was geographically surrounded by Japanese-held islands. To develop Guam, Baldwin argued, would be to compete with Japan for dominance in the western Pacific and would commit America to meddling in "the problems of the Orient."[21]

However, he argued, to develop Caribbean bases would not carry any such "grandiose implications," since the Caribbean was already an "American lake."[22] Baldwin felt confident that taking steps to enlarge the Army and the Navy would make any invasion of the continental United States, even by a combination of powers, "virtually impossible in the foreseeable future."[23]

Oswald Garrison Villard, another writer concerned with America's defenses, a well-known champion of social issues, and a pacifist, deplored waste, incompetence, and confusion due in part to the absence of an established defense policy by the Roosevelt administration in a *Harper's* magazine article entitled, "Wanted: A Sane Defense Policy."[24] Citing various writers, including Baldwin (who agreed that U.S. armed forces could successfully defend U.S. coasts), Villard asked, "Why are we then told that 'we are in danger?'"[25]

Villard called for a committee on national defense outside of Congress and the military to study these important defense issues. He deplored the rearming of America, which would, he felt, subordinate the country's social and industrial life to the preparations for war, which he feared would result in the United States losing "its democratic soul."[26]

Baldwin praised the article, in particular for its call for a national commission that would plan for a "sane" national defense policy. Baldwin suggested that its members not be politicians or military officers, a point with which Villard agreed. Lest Baldwin think for a moment that his pacifist correspondent was seeing the light about the need for a rearmed America, Villard stated that he favored "the Gandhi position of disarming promptly for the great safety of the Republic."[27]

When Villard's article appeared in April 1939, Hitler had cancelled both the 1935 Anglo-German Naval Agreement and the 1934 nonaggression pact with Poland. He had also demanded territorial concessions from Poland, to include the return of the Polish port of Danzig to Germany and Poland giving Germany enough land to create a road linking the city of Danzig with the German province of East Prussia.

Always seeking new forums, as well as new sources of income, Baldwin was pleased by an offer to publish an article in *The American Mercury* magazine.[28] Baldwin's July 1939 article, "Impregnable America," stated authoritatively that the continental United States was "well-nigh impregnable,"[29] rejecting the popular view that a "military tidal wave could prevail against U.S. Continental and Hemispheric impregnability."[30] He advised against frittering away our "great strength" by trying to defend Pacific Ocean outposts, especially Guam and Wake Islands, the "way-stations of history." The Philippines could be made impregnable, but only if the United States was willing to pay a very high price. Hawaii was "impregnable" with the existing levels of Army and Navy personnel and equipment stationed on the islands, and the garrison there could hold out for months against any Japanese invasion.[31] He warned that the Panama Canal Zone's defenses needed modernization to include new airfields and a third lock system that would be able to accommodate the new and larger warships and merchant ships of the future.

In his view, if the United States went on the offensive "into distant seas, [it would] face an end in treasure, human life and national destiny."[32] Such foreign ventures, he thought, would destroy American continental and hemispheric security for the "American castle,"[33] a fleeting figure of speech that was soon discarded after the autumn of 1939.[34] Interestingly, the *Mercury* editor initially wanted Major R. Ernest Dupuy, U.S. Army, to write the article, but he had begged off and recommended Baldwin as a "capable writer [who] has a naval and military background and a very sane outlook."[35]

Villard read Baldwin's article "with great interest and satisfaction," and mentioned also that he would quote from it in his forthcoming book. The Baldwin-Villard correspondence illustrates how Baldwin's reputation for balanced reporting of military and national defense issues had become increasingly admired and respected by an ever-widening readership.

It was against this backdrop of gathering war clouds in Europe that Baldwin, on July 1, 1939, suggested to Lester Markel, the Sunday editor of the *Times Magazine,* that he travel to Europe to reprise his tour of 1937. "I think nothing can replace reliable source-information," he wrote. "Periodic trips of this nature seem to me to be an essential part of this job, and I think, absolutely necessary to supplement the data collected second-hand from military magazines."[36]

To bolster his chances of approval for the trip he cited his competition from other military writers, specifically Major George Fielding Eliot, the author of the recent book *The Ramparts We Watch,* who was going over to Europe in July for several newspapers. Baldwin suggested that his trip could coincide with "the scheduled big maneuvers in August and in September." Little did Baldwin realize that those maneuvers would be the real thing, the beginning of World War II in Europe.[37] Needless to say, the trip was never taken. In hindsight, it was naive for Baldwin to have assumed that he could visit the same countries as he had two years earlier, when the increased secrecy about their war plans and their weapons would have made the trip a futile exercise.

Instead, he had to content himself with reporting on Army maneuvers closer to home. In mid-August 1939, 52,000 Regular Army and National Guard units began two weeks of war games near Plattsburg, New York. As he had done in 1935 at Pine Camp, New York, Baldwin embedded himself with the units and filed long daily reports. The headline of Baldwin's final dispatch, "Maneuvers End With Troops Mired," had an unintended double meaning. While the heavy rains had dampened the troops' spirits, Baldwin quoted an unnamed officer as saying "nothing was well done" in the previous two weeks. Some Regular Army officers were "round pegs in square holes" who were not "fitted for their jobs, [while] some in the Guard probably never will be." There was too much caution shown by officers, as a group, who feared losing a battle more than trying to win one. He saw the need for air cover to aid the infantry. This limited use of airplanes gave "an unusual artificiality" to the scene as troops marched casually along roads or rode in speeding trucks into battles by daylight. Two "autogyros" (helicopters) were used as artillery observation posts, but Baldwin felt them to be vulnerable from ground fire that would limit their use over the front lines. Baldwin concluded, as he had in the past, that while new military technology was certainly useful, "the man on foot" was essential to win battles, using a phrase that he would use for years to come with variations.[38]

In a *Times* editorial, "'Soul of the Army,'" the writer, most likely Baldwin, sharply criticized the U.S. First Army for not being a trained army: "Most of its units were badly led, staff work was incompetent, orders were garbled or delayed, and units lost contact with supporting units and with the 'enemy.'"[39] There was no time to develop that "soul of an Army," that tradition of personal leadership so essential to success in battle. The editorial reiterated one of Baldwin's ideas that the U.S. Army, in general, must be a well-trained, small field army, with complete staffs and proper organization, whose training must be "continuous and uninterrupted," and that the National Guard, if it was to play any future role in the country's defense, should have frequent field exercises.[40]

Four days later, on Friday, September 1, Germany invaded Poland with massive military forces that quickly overwhelmed the Polish forces. In less than four weeks Warsaw fell. The contrast between the successful German blitzkrieg and the amateurish behavior of many American troops in the just-completed Plattsburg war games was an alarm signal for America to wake up to the new harsh realities of another European war.

On Sunday, September 3, both Britain and France declared war on Germany and, coincidentally, the British passenger liner SS *Athenia* was torpedoed and sunk off the northwest coast of Ireland by *U-30*. Thirty Americans lost their lives. The ripples of the 1939 German invasion were felt elsewhere, as other nations made preparations for possible entry into another European war. Passenger liners cancelled sailings to Europe, border crossings with Germany were closed, and many American tourists were stranded, unable to book immediate passage back to the United States.[41] Suddenly, the distant thunder of the previous years had become loud.

The beginning of another European war after twenty years was to change Baldwin's focus from one of general concern about America's rearmament program to a sense of urgency that the nation had better be prepared. As the country's only full-time newspaper analyst on military and naval affairs, he saw clearly his responsibility, which was to comment upon fast-moving events in an intelligent and informed manner.

The rapidity of the German advances surprised and challenged Baldwin's ability to comment on the fast-changing developments on the Polish plains. Initially he thought that Polish forces would hold out for at least six weeks, and that the French Army would seize the Saar region of Germany. He was wrong on both assumptions. He was impressed with the speed of the *Panzerdivisionen* that "roared along the ground" behind the wide use of German air power,[42] and that within nine days of the "Second World War," as he called it, Germany had given a "practical field demonstration of "Blitzkrieg.""[43] Their ability to disrupt Polish communications, to outflank Polish defenders, and to prevent the full mobilization of its forces enabled Germany's mechanized and motorized units to overwhelm Poland's "plodding foot soldiers" and its horsed cavalry "who still use[d] sabers and lances and still employ[ed] some of the tactics of Balaclava."[44]

Three days later, Soviet troops also invaded Poland, which prompted the *Times* to editorially comment, "Hitlerism is brown communism, Stalinism is red fascism. The world will now understand that the only real 'ideological' issue is the one between democracy, liberty and peace on one hand and despotism, terror and war on the other."[45]

In trying to sort out the meaning of these events, Baldwin thought that the encirclement tactics Germany used in Poland would bog down if it attempted to go into the Netherlands, Belgium, or Luxemburg. France's Maginot Line would deter German forces from making a land offensive in the West, as would the "difficult terrain" in the Ardennes forests. Though wrong in his predictions about the war's progress, Baldwin did correctly observe on September 10 that the "war promises to be long; Germany has won her first victory; she will probably win many more; but she will probably lose the war."[46] He based this observation on its lack of a manpower reserve and the industrial resources needed to win a "war of endurance," though Germany would protract the final outcome.[47] Looking to the future, he said "it is becoming apparent that the history of both the dim and distant tomorrows will be shaped by forces not yet clearly perceived."[48] Little could he envision in 1939 how widespread World War II would become, and the development of new weapons of mass destruction, including long-range rockets and the atomic bomb.

After the surrender of Poland, and Germany's apparent reluctance to invade western Europe for the time being, Baldwin used the lull in the war to toot his own horn with Sulzberger, the publisher of the *Times*. Baldwin had received offers to make radio broadcasts, personal appearances, and to edit a magazine, all of which would pay more than his current *Times* salary of $125 per week, a figure that had remained unchanged since 1937. Baldwin had increasing family responsibilities; in addition to their two daughters, his mother, Caroline, now lived with his family. He couched his request in terms of his increasing value to the *Times* and the increasing workload necessitated by his duties; they were more time consuming than those of a general assignment reporter, and he had also had to forgo the writing of sea stories and outside magazine articles that paid rather well.

He expressed gratitude to Sulzberger for the opportunity to specialize in military subjects, to write editorials and articles in the *Times Sunday Magazine*, as well as to review books at "little cost to the paper." As a result, he said, "my stories have helped to give the paper authenticity and distinction in a special field since so many of my articles have been widely quoted and reprinted in both the military and lay press in this country and abroad."[49] Baldwin said that a radio broadcasting company paid $200 to $250 a week for a broadcaster and the Houghton-Mifflin Company had offered him a $1,000 advance on a book, which he had to refuse given "the pressure of my work here."[50]

He argued that radio talks would give him a forum for an impartial and a "calm level-headed" presentation of the war news. Anticipating an objection from Sulzberger, who disliked staff controversy, he remarked that "war is, of course, a controversial subject, but so is fishing, and so are music and sports and international politics."[51] It was later agreed that in future appearances on radio programs, book tours, and public lectures, Baldwin would not take a position but give a "realistic, objective, analytic approach" to military events, which Sulzberger felt was of "vital importance" in the news columns of the paper.[52]

After a face-to-face meeting with the publisher on these matters, Baldwin wrote, "I shall be very happy to remain with the *Times*," adding "I shall continue to try to make myself of more and more service to the paper," in response to which the publisher expressed delight at Baldwin's decision and said he looked "forward to many years of happy association."[53] A modest salary increase was also granted.

A singular glimpse into Baldwin's political views came in an October 1939 letter he wrote to the *New York Daily News*, in which he stated that "the vital interests of this nation are not affected by the war in Europe, even—in my opinion—if England and France face defeat."[54] He scoffed at the idea that America had a mission to make the world safe for democracy, for he had seen the "folly" of that "thankless task." The only exception would be if America "could know that U.S. participation in another war would insure the triumph of principle." But history, he wrote, had shown no evidence that wars advance the principle of democracy. He agreed with the isolationist views of Colonel Charles A. Lindbergh, who was then advocating American neutrality. Baldwin also saw no need to modify the arms embargo of the 1937 Neutrality Act, at least until events dictated that a revision was needed.[55]

Sulzberger was "distressed" when he read Baldwin's letter in the *Daily News*. He pointedly reminded Baldwin that Baldwin had assured him that his writings done outside the *Times* would "not take a position, . . . [yet] I find in this letter a most firm statement of position. It is distinctly embarrassing," admonished Sulzberger.[56]

Baldwin's prompt reply to this rebuke showed the flinty side of his personality, sometimes self-righteous in the defense of his actions. He denied that the *Daily News* letter had violated the agreement, defending his right to express his personal opinions. He claimed there was a line between his views as a military analyst and his personal views as an individual, adding that "if there was something I believed in sincerely enough to express myself as an individual, it should be done publicly under my own name, or not at all."

Remaining on his soapbox, he stated that the current public issue of war or peace was so important to the future of America that he could no longer be silent: "I should have been a coward had I allowed any considerations of exigency to deter me from what I believed to be right and I therefore deliberately placed myself on record."[57] He added that if the *Times* had written an editorial on the subject as the *Daily News* had, he would have written to the *Times*. He denied that there was any cause for embarrassment, since his "objectivity" in reporting of military and naval news had not been called into question. He ended this long memorandum to the publisher by paraphrasing the latter's views that not all staff members at the *Times* had to be of one mind, nor should they agree "entirely" with the policy of the paper.[58] This was the first time that Baldwin had had to defend his actions, but it would not to be the last time.

Meanwhile, the seven-month lull on the western front, which followed Poland's defeat, popularly called "the phony war" or "*Sitzkrieg*," puzzled Baldwin. He suggested that perhaps "Herr Hitler is convinced, contrary to Allied opinion, that major offensive operations are not essential to win the war for Germany." But he acknowledged that there could be other factors, for example a time-favored Germany,[59] or a disagreement about how the submarine and the surface fleet should be used. They might be asking: Should the Luftwaffe adopt the Douhet theory and bomb European industries and cities to break civilian morale, or should the British Royal Navy bases and England's ports be the principal targets? Baldwin noted "some evidence" of jealousy between the German army and air force and the absence of a unified command.

A singular event, which captivated America's attention in December 1939, was the fate of the German raider *Admiral Graf Spee*. It had sought temporary refuge in the harbor of Montevideo, Uruguay, a neutral country, on December 13. It had been cruising in the South Atlantic and Indian oceans since September 1939, capturing and sinking nine British merchant ships. A Royal Navy force of three cruisers sent to find it was no match for the *Graf Spee*'s 11-inch guns. A brief naval engagement severely damaged the British force, but not before British guns had inflicted damage on the *Graf Spee*.

Its captain, Hans Langsdorff, had decided to enter the port at Montevideo to offload wounded sailors and to make emergency repairs within the twenty-four-hour rule for a belligerent ship in a neutral port. Local British diplomats tried to have the ship held longer to permit other Royal Navy ships to assemble at the estuary of the River Plate. The rumor mill at Montevideo operated at capacity, including the false information that the HMS *Renown,* a battle cruiser with 15-inch guns, had arrived at the estuary, as well as the aircraft carrier HMS *Ark Royal*. The Uruguayan government granted the German ship an additional time extension, set to expire on December 17. We now know that Captain Langsdorff's decision to scuttle his ship was based, in part, on a report from his gunnery officer who misidentified the heavy cruiser HMS *Cumberland* as the battle cruiser HMS *Renown*.[60] He also believed that other enemy naval forces awaited his ship at the mouth of the River Plate estuary. The internment option was not considered to be an honorable choice by the ship's captain.

Baldwin's analysis on December 18 was that the internment of the ship and its crew was preferable to the scuttling of the ship. He reported that he had boarded the *Graf Spee* two years earlier during his 1937 European tour, when the ship was in England's Portsmouth harbor for the Coronation Naval Review held to honor King George VI. He denied that the ship held any new secrets, as its diesel engines and other equipment were already well known. Its codebooks and fire-control instruments would be destroyed in any case before internment. He concluded that the scuttling of the *Graf Spee* would be "a premature concession of defeat and a recognition, perhaps for the first time, on Herr Hitler's part that public opinion in Germany might not welcome a heavy casualty list."[61] Baldwin's long narrative about this dramatic event was praised by Lester Markel, the *Times* Sunday editor, as a "beautiful job." For Markel, that was praise indeed.[62]

Before the European war overwhelmed everyone, Baldwin published his first collection of non-fiction sea stories, entitled *Admiral Death* (1939), demonstrating his continuing love of the sea and his admiration for those who assumed risks by sailing on it. In this period piece, the romantic heroes face impossible odds but all are determined to survive the hazards of the sea. It pits the primal force of the sea against the human spirit; the heroes, all victims of circumstance faced with odds beyond their control, put their own lives and those of others in harm's way. Duty is their motivation to survive, and there is no thought of quitting.

The book's twelve chapters describe some well-known sea tragedies, including the loss of the *Titanic* (1912), the *Lusitania* (1915), and the battle of Jutland (1916), as well as lesser-known mutinies and stories about persons otherwise cast adrift on the high seas. The extensive endnotes demonstrated Baldwin's careful research into the primary and secondary materials on which he based his narrative. The book was in the tradition of other adventure stories, such as Charles A. Lindbergh's *We* (1928), Admiral Richard E. Byrd's *Little America* (1930), and Anne Morrow Lindbergh's *North to the Orient* (1936). There was a market for that genre, as Baldwin was well aware. His literary agent, Willis Wing, attempted to interest Hollywood studios in Baldwin's *Titanic* story. Wing assured his client that the well-known movie producer David O. Selznick might take up that project once *Gone With the Wind* was completed, but nothing ever came of this hope.[63]

With Baldwin's apprenticeship now years behind him, his skills at reporting and analyzing the meaning of the swiftly changing events of World War II would now be fully tested.

CHAPTER **8**

Danger Ahead, Prepare Now, 1940–41

On Friday, May 10, 1940, Germany renewed its military offensive in western Europe, on the same day that Winston S. Churchill became the prime minister of Great Britain. Baldwin must have felt like a voice in the wilderness trying repeatedly, in his national magazine articles and his pieces in the daily *Times*, to alert America to the future dangers to its continued peace and tranquility and the urgent need to immediately strengthen its defenses.

Throughout the late spring and summer of 1940 Germany seemed invincible, as it conquered seven European countries. A week before Germany invaded France in May 1940, Baldwin asked the rhetorical question, "Can Germany Be Stopped?" He was all too aware that U.S. armed forces were not ready for any war. His answer was yes, if the United States adopted some of the features that made the German military so powerful a force. Grudgingly, Baldwin praised the Wehrmacht's "boldness, speed, surprise, ruthless blows, coupled with [its] willingness to assume risks and take losses, and [its] precision of planning and execution."[1] Those decisive measures, he wrote, explained why Poland fell in eighteen days and Norway and Denmark soon thereafter.

Where would Hitler strike next? In August 1940 Baldwin thought the Low Countries, and then Britain: "The cold truth is that Germany prepared for this war, France prepared for the last war, and Britain prepared for no war."[2] To stop these possible moves, the Allies needed "a leader with the capacities of a Wellington or a William Pitt, the elder."[3] He was, however, encouraged that Churchill had become prime minister, as he brought bold leadership in his determination to use Britain's air and naval power to strike at German-held targets. What was needed, eventually, was for the Allied forces to assault Germany from Italy, or perhaps from western Europe. To do so successfully would require "sufficient singleness of purpose and unlimited effort," in brief, a total war effort.[4] He observed sadly that 1940 "seem[ed] to be Germany's year," but he warned, "The Reich must win quickly, or lose slowly," which, as we know now, was true.[5]

In America, there were "vocal" pressure groups that asked, "Where is our frontier: France, or the English Channel?" President Roosevelt, ever mindful of American public opinion, which sought to avoid becoming involved in Europe's affairs, was willing to speak out in favor of the defense of the Western Hemisphere. That seemed to be a safe solution for many citizens because there was no immediate threat to that hemisphere in 1940. Baldwin was not satisfied with such safe, defensive thinking. He believed we should seek bases in the West Indies and in the Caribbean from countries such as Holland, Britain, and France, which had colonial possessions there: "We must make it worthwhile to those countries to be on our side. We must make it worth their while to maintain systems of government friendly to our own."[6]

Congress and the White House should agree to enlarge the U.S. Navy, Baldwin advised. There should be operational coordination between the Army, Navy, and Air Force. More planes should be built. He opposed a peacetime military conscription. If the international picture warranted a military draft, the president should declare a state of national emergency and Congress should declare a state of war.

He thought the U.S. Regular Army ought to protect key points, including the Panama Canal, Hawaii, and Puerto Rico and develop a roving field force of well-trained and well-equipped soldiers to act as an expeditionary force for duty anywhere in defense of the Western Hemisphere. The National Guard could provide for coastal and antiaircraft defense in the United States, while older reservists would act as a home guard in their communities.[7] Those suggestions now seem quaint, but in 1940 Baldwin tried to alert the country about the need for an integrated military and government plan for defense. He said that the United States must agree on what we must defend and against whom, and have an organization to carry out such a plan. Baldwin asked the big question: Who was America's number one enemy: Germany or Japan (the U.S. Navy's choice), or is it an ideology—Communism, Fascism, or Nazism?[8]

This August 1940 article in *Harper's* magazine was an example of Baldwin using a national magazine to attempt to educate the American public about steps to be taken in its defense. It also showed his independence from the *Times* editorials that in June 1940 favored universal military training (UMT).[9]

Baldwin gained access to the eastern foreign policy establishment with an invitation to become a member of the prestigious Council on Foreign Relations in 1939. Its quarterly magazine, *Foreign Affairs*, was one of Baldwin's better forums. His wife's uncle, Bud Cummings, who was a member, may have helped his membership path, but most likely it was his growing reputation for balanced writing on national defense issues that contributed to his being invited to become a member. At the council's closed meetings and private dinners he associated with those who had access to Washington policymakers at the State Department. Some members proved to be valuable news sources.

During the war he served on the Armaments Group that was within the council's War and Peace Project, whose job it was to investigate the effects of the war upon the interests and policies of the United States and to suggest policies for the postwar settlement. The secret deliberations of the project resulted in 868 memorandums, reports, and studies that were submitted to the office of the secretary of state.

The sixteen-member Armaments Group included Army and Navy officers who represented the three military services, a Princeton University professor (Harold Sprout), Allen W. Dulles (later to become the head of the CIA), and one journalist, Hanson Baldwin. It was well known at the time that President Roosevelt acted as his own secretary of state, so that the hundreds of reports forwarded by the council to Washington probably had less effect upon policy development than the council had anticipated; this was certainly Baldwin's assessment years later.[10]

In 1940 he wrote almost daily for the *Times* and the frequency of his writing impeded his ability to create new approaches to the war. As a result, he often repeated himself in words, phrases, and ideas. Although he tried to stand back from daily events to make sense of the military events around the world, he was not always successful. For example, his coverage of the Battle of Britain while it was being fought had a superficial quality to it and his pieces often conveyed uncertainty about what the outcome would be.

The cancellation of Operation Sea Lion by Hitler on September 17, 1940, gave Britain some relief from its invasion fears. Baldwin summarized the views of three groups in Washington on aid to Britain. There were those who favored increasing American aid because Britain would win; another group believed that only with direct American military intervention could Britain win; and a third group felt that Britain had already lost the war, regardless of America's future participation in it. He commented that Britain could win only if the United States provided ships, planes, men, and money. But, with the current lineup of "active belligerents unchanged, the odds are still upon the Axis."[11]

President Roosevelt's announcement of the Destroyers for Bases agreement in September 1940 meant that fifty of the United States' World War I destroyers would be given to Britain in exchange for rent-free leases on naval bases in the British West Indies, British Guiana, Bermuda, and Newfoundland. Not pleased with the announcement, Baldwin told James, the managing editor, that there were only 116 old destroyers left. Any ships the British received would come from a pool of ships "already in active commission" or being recommissioned. "We have no surplus of destroyers. All are in use today or being prepared for duty. The fifty ships promised by the President would be taken from our Atlantic fleet and would reduce the strength of the fleet in the Atlantic Ocean."[12] Short of American intervention in the war, President Roosevelt was determined to help Britain.

On September 16, 1940, Congress passed the Selective Service Act. A month later, all men between the ages of twenty-one and thirty-five were required to register for America's first peacetime military draft. Baldwin was not overly pleased. He had written about the Army's old equipment and its lack of ammunition stockpiles, just enough ammunition for "one big battle."[13] In 1940 he believed that any attack on the United States from Europe could only come by sea and/or by air. But if the new American Army of conscripts was to defend the Western Hemisphere, it would only produce "the shadow of strength without substance."[14]

Baldwin's sharpest criticism was leveled at unnamed senior Army officers who were still in "the citadel of the mind" and slow to accept new ideas from middle-ranking officers. Too many officers "stand too much upon pomp and prerogatives of rank," he wrote.[15] Fortunately, since General Marshall, the Army chief of staff, was not one of those in the citadel, he anticipated that changes would be made to increase and improve upon the Army's mobility, flexibility, training, and tactics, while keeping "high morale" in the ranks.

Reviewing America's defenses in 1940, Baldwin despaired. There was no unity of command or of planning. Our troops were not well trained, and their equipment dated from World War 1. The fact that the Army could not decide which new weapons were the best complicated new weapons procurement. During the August 1940 training exercises, troops acted as if air power would not play any role in modern war. Commanders plodded along at a slow pace. There was no attempt at concealment or surprise movement. In the larger picture, there were "bottlenecks" (a much-used word then) in airplane production, as well as other production delays of military equipment. Baldwin quoted William S. Knudsen, a member of the National Defense Advisory Commission, who said that the United States could not produce the equipment needed for a projected two-million-man Army until the middle of 1944.[16]

During the spring and summer of 1941, in North Africa, Field Marshal Erwin Rommel's panzer forces pushed British forces rather easily eastward from Libya toward Egypt. At sea, the U-boat campaign was devastating the convoys destined for Britain. Germany's air offensive over Britain was renewed in February 1941. In April, Yugoslavia and Greece were invaded and German paratroopers landed on Crete in May. On June 22, 1941, Germany invaded the Soviet Union, and many presumed it would result in yet another quick victory for Hitler.

U.S. air power was "virtually non-existent," Baldwin wrote in *Fortune* magazine in March 1941.[17] The Atlantic Ocean was no longer a moat that protected America's shores. No plane, currently operational, could cross that ocean with a full bomb load and expect to return to its home base in Europe. As the distance to the target increased, the bomb load should be decreased and accuracy would be sacrificed, so the United States had "nothing to fear today, or in the immediate future, from trans-Atlantic air assaults," he warned, but this would not always be so.[18]

Baldwin did not agree with President Roosevelt's decision to send 80 to 100 percent of America's new planes to Britain, in the hope that such aid would keep it in the war against Germany. If this policy was to be continued, it would far better for both countries if the United States were "in the war." He recommended that America keep all of its new long-range bombers at home and send the fighters and medium bombers to Britain. The B-17 and B-24 bombers could protect U.S. Atlantic shores while the U.S. Navy ships protected its Pacific coast. In time, when the two-ocean U.S. Navy was completed, the bombers could be withdrawn for other missions.[19] If Britain fell before the two-ocean Navy was built, then air power would be its only defense. He wondered, as did so many others, how long Britain could hold out. By aiding Britain now, Washington hoped to buy time to rearm itself with a larger Navy, thousands of planes, and a four-million-man Army. That rearmament would make the United States "the most powerful nation on earth."[20]

Baldwin opposed the creation of a separate Air Force, noting how air power advocates had long believed that airplanes had made navies and armies obsolete.[21] He felt that, at present, air power was no more than an adjunct of the surface forces, but it could not "now or in the foreseeable future supplant either armies or navies."[22] Air power, for too long, had been "a stepchild" of the other military services. Baldwin's reasons were that there were no coordinated operations in which a separate Air Force could help in a unity of forces between air and ground operations. To make such a sweeping reorganization of the U.S. armed forces would jeopardize U.S. rearmament plans, he thought.[23]

During the spring of 1941, when newspapers chronicled a series of new German victories, Baldwin cabled the New York office with some insider information he had learned during one of his visits to Washington. The Capitol, he reported, "seems full of gloom." His sources agreed that Britain "cannot defeat Germany without the actual United States' participation in a shooting war." But the American public is "not ready to support a shooting war, in fact it is not ready to support convoys to Britain."

Baldwin always believed that things were never as good or as bad as they seemed. For example, the German advance eastward in North Africa was not viewed by the U.S. Army's Intelligence (G-2) as pessimistically as it was by other observers. G-2 felt that Rommel's advance on Alexandria, Egypt, was "spent" due to the increasing length of his supply lines and the "British Eighth Army was definitely pressed for men and materiel."[24]

While in Washington, Baldwin also wrote a piece on the shortage of antiaircraft guns. The 1926 3-inch .50-caliber gun had become obsolete, as it had a slow rate of fire, a low muzzle velocity, and small projectile with a short range that could not reach high-flying bombers. The Navy had equipped its new ships and those under construction with the better 5-inch .38-caliber gun. Baldwin praised the British "pom-pom"—a fast-firing gun that was effective against low-flying planes and dive bombers. The British also used the "Bofors," a 40-mm quick-firing gun that had been very effective during the Battle of Britain. Made in the United States, the Bofors would not be available to the U.S. Army or Navy until 1942. The U.S. Navy would manufacture the "Oerlikon" 20-mm gun to replace the .50-caliber machine gun on ships. His point was that existing antiaircraft guns were "not adequate" to provide for the defense of American cities, and the new guns would not be ready for some time, concluding that America's "present deficiencies would prove to be a definite handicap if we started convoying soon or entered a 'shooting war.'"[25]

Assistant Secretary of War John J. McCoy cabled Baldwin that his piece on antiaircraft guns was "very fair . . . it may do a lot of good."[26] Most likely Baldwin, as an outsider, could and did use the *Times* to publicize information about military needs in 1941 that, given the constraint of government service, needed to be said, but could not be said by officials then in government employment.

Especially after September 1939, many readers of the *Times* were quick to spot evidence of bias in his newspaper articles. They let him and the publisher know this, but there was no agreement among his critics as to the bias of which he was guilty. For example, what Baldwin thought was an objective commentary on the European war revealed to some a pro-German bias. In general, flattering letters were sent to him, while the critical ones were sent to James, the managing editor, demanding that Baldwin be dismissed. One writer saw Baldwin's bias as favoring those "who are for totalitarian and against democratic principles." Asked to comment, Baldwin justified his admiration of German military efficiency while disclaiming the idea that he was an admirer of Germany's political philosophy or of its totalitarian principles. He told the editor that unless the British or Americans meet "the German military efficiency with equal or superior efficiency, they had no hope of defeating their machine."[27] In reply, James assured the irate writer that Baldwin, "whom I know very well, has no liking whatsoever for totalitarianism of the Nazis."[28]

He answered the word blitz in a rare whimsical article. The problem, he argued, began with the term "expert," "a loathsome word." To some he was an "armchair strategist," to others, the "typewriter general" or the "dry land admiral" were the appropriate pejorative epithets. After the European war began, Baldwin was again castigated as pro-Nazi ("Goebbel's [sic] mouthpiece"), or a war lover who was eager to sacrifice the lives of American soldiers, or even a "paid propagandist" for one side or another.

At social gatherings outside the office "the expert" was hounded by eager querists seeking immediate answers to questions both trivial and imponderable. Regardless of how carefully he tried to appraise the military strengths and weaknesses of the warring nations, their political systems, economic resources, and military potential, he learned "that thousands of Americans believe only what they want to believe."[29]

After Germany invaded Soviet Russia in June 1941, Baldwin was often criticized by readers for being pro-Nazi or anti-Russia for his comments on the early ease of the German advances. "The Commies" are after me, he told the *Times* managing editor, as they organized postal and letter-writing campaigns over his Red Army comments.[30] Later that year the *Daily Worker*, a left-wing newspaper, editorialized, "It is a disgrace that a newspaper with the enormous facilities of *The New York Times* should have such a nondescript military expert."[31]

In his defense against his perceived bias in reporting, Baldwin could only comment that war "perhaps more profoundly than any other subject, involves the passions, the pride and prejudices, the fortunes and the lives of men. . . . Modern war means all of life, and all of a society is affected by it."[32] He also took solace in President Lincoln's observation about not being able to please all of the people all of the time.[33]

On Saturday, May 24, 1941, the British battle cruiser HMS *Hood,* then on patrol in the Denmark Strait between Greenland and Iceland, sank quickly when gunfire from the German battleship *Bismarck* ignited its powder magazines. Of the 1,416 men on board, only 3 survived. Baldwin called the *Hood*'s sinking "a sea tragedy of Homeric proportions," but he also noted the cruiser's numerous deficiencies owing to its age (it was completed in 1920) and its inadequate armor protection, calling it "the last of a fast vanishing type—monster battle cruisers." The *Bismarck*, on the other hand, completed in 1940, had a high speed and heavy armor protection, extensive underwater protection, and 15-inch guns that fired new and "improved design" armor-piercing shells.

The subsequent sinking of the *Bismarck,* three days later on May 27, 1941, Baldwin noted, was "due primarily to air power which tracked it and reduced its speed by repeated assaults. . . . Air power has come of age over deep water and the aircraft carrier is now more important than ever before." Land, sea, and air power had "merged in a global power . . . with each service dependent upon the other and with air power absolutely essential to them all."[34] Even this straightforward account upset a New Jersey businessman, who wrote to the editor, "If you let [Baldwin] alone, he will have us licked before we start, as his stuff is all defeatist á la Hitler."[35]

A week before the German invasion of the Soviet Union, Baldwin wrote an article for the *Times* Sunday edition entitled "Hitler Can Be Defeated." He was optimistic, but he added many caveats. Britain must be kept in the war for future offensive operations in Europe and be aided "with more of everything."[36] At the time, the Royal Air Force (RAF) was its only offensive weapon, as the Royal Navy was spread thin protecting both the Atlantic and the Mediterranean sea-lanes. Its Eighth Army, then in North Africa, was not large enough to invade German-occupied Europe. At best, Britain could only prevent a successful German invasion, but alone it could not defeat Germany. Baldwin discounted the hope, held by some, that high-ranking Nazi officials, other than Rudolf Hess, would escape to England, which would indicate cracks within Hitler's inner circle. England's survival depended upon U.S. industry's continued shipments of supplies to Britain. Baldwin was careful not to suggest that the United States enter the shooting war against Germany, as public opinion still favored hemisphere defense and remaining as the lone "Arsenal of Democracy," as advocated by President Roosevelt.

Elmer Davis, who had just returned from London where he had visited his CBS radio colleagues, including Edward R. Murrow, told Baldwin, "I have some idea of how things look from both sides of the Atlantic. And I would agree with every line of your piece in today's *New York Times Magazine*."[37] A reader who praised the article added that Baldwin's columns were "invariably carefully balanced, keenly aware of the value involved and display a rational judgment."[38]

In August 1941, Baldwin's "Blueprint for Victory" in *Life* magazine called for a much greater effort from the United States than before. Despite Germany's military successes to date, its future would depend on its Russian campaign, and if it "[bogged] down into Napoleonic futility, Hitler himself [might] face eventual defeat."[39] However, if Hitler won in Russia, the costs might be so high as to weaken Germany in the West. The best Germany could hope for then would be "a negotiated peace," but only if the United States used its "unlimited" power to "tilt the scale." America, he wrote, "no longer had the choice of staying out of war." If the United States wanted to defeat Hitler, it would require an "all out" effort, "far more than it had yet exerted."[40] "Only offensive measures win wars," he advised.[41]

He posed the questions, "Should we continue to aid Britain, or should we enter the war in Europe in an 'all out' effort to defeat Germany? While U.S. military forces are too weak now, can it wait longer?"[42] The United States would not be ready to go on the offensive until 1943, he wrote; meanwhile, it should send two or three divisions to the Middle East to anticipate a German drive after the end of the Russian campaign.[43] If Britain could only hold out through 1941, then "the democracies [could] weather the war," the end of which might not come for another two to seven years.

Many of Baldwin's readers may have gulped at so harsh an assessment of what American "total sacrifice" would mean to achieve victory. It was not surprising that President Roosevelt was reluctant to suggest that the United States declare war on Germany during that summer, as Germany had made no hostile moves directly against the United States. The president's decision, in the autumn of 1941, to order U.S. Navy destroyers based in Iceland to escort supply convoys to Britain provoked a tense situation.

In his 1941 *Life* article, Baldwin demonstrated once again that he was not always good at predicting the future. He had been warned repeatedly by James not to do it, but he did it nonetheless. He was confident that the United States and its allies would have to invade Europe to defeat Germany, and that Norway would be a good landing site, as it would be hard for the German forces to reach the site quickly. He also dismissed Japan as not a "real enemy," but against whom economic warfare would be successful while the United States strengthened its bases in the Philippines and elsewhere in the Pacific. Also, he thought Germany was "too far along the road to victory" for America to challenge Japan directly. He warned that the invasion of Europe, by whatever route, would be costly financially and in terms of lives lost; "We cannot re-conquer a continent without wholesale death." In this future total war, the United States would have to be directly involved. Paraphrasing Churchill, Baldwin wrote that the United States faced "blood, sweat, and tears no matter what road it took." The United States faced "a hard decade" ahead, but one in which he was confident that it would develop that "calm arrogance of strength" that had made it great. He felt sure that a united America would prevail in that total war.[44]

In September 1941 the U.S. Army held the largest peacetime exercises in its history. Over 400,000 Regular Army, National Guard, and Army Reserve troops roamed over 3,400 square miles in Louisiana. Needless to say, Baldwin was embedded, filing almost daily reports about the mock battles, the first in which two armored divisions were used. The army recognized armor's new status as an independent arm, along with infantry and artillery.[45] On September 17, 127 paratroopers jumped from planes, at a height of 1,200 feet, onto a cotton field, the first use of such troops by the U.S. Army.[46]

While in Louisiana talking with the troops, Baldwin noticed a serious morale issue. Two hundred thousand of the men would be leaving the Army on December 10 when their enlistments expired. Many thought that their "time in the Army was wasted." Exacerbating their mood was the fact that there were shortages of almost all of their equipment, including radios, anti-aircraft guns, anti-tank guns, 105-mm Howitzers, and especially ammunition. Wooden guns were used on the "battlefields." General Leslie J. McNair, who directed the exercises, was critical of the leadership, especially between the National Guard and the Reserves, many of whom were primarily civilians whose military commissions were made due to political considerations, rather than leadership abilities. Baldwin concluded that the U.S. Army was "months or even a year away from readiness for combat. But it is on its way."[47] Also in Louisiana and taking great interest in the exercises was Army Chief of Staff General Marshall, looking for officers who had initiative and leadership abilities. Among those he found were Eisenhower, Patton, Clark, and others, who were later appointed to field commands.

Shortly after Baldwin returned to his New York office from Louisiana, he spoke with Sulzberger about his idea of going to the Middle East to observe British troops in Egypt, as well as other places, including Singapore. The trip would begin in January 1942 and last for three or four months. It would provide Baldwin with valuable background information for future articles, but because of the attack at Pearl Harbor on December 7 that trip was never taken.[48]

That sudden Japanese attack, called by President Roosevelt "a date which will live in infamy," was the precipitating event that drew the United States into both the Pacific and European wars. Baldwin called the attack "the most stupid action the Japanese could have taken . . . clearly [a] by-product of the military mentality that has so long been a powerful influence in Japan."[49] Just a day earlier Baldwin had written, in the *Times* Sunday edition, an article that praised the Hawaiian base as "more heavily garrisoned land, sea, and air, than ever in history," with the implication that those forces would be on alert against any Japanese attack.[50] He had also predicted that in a "full blown" war Japan would initially attack the Philippines, Singapore, and Hong Kong, but that without German aid it would "certainly lose [the war] though not quickly."[51]

Americans were shocked and angered by the attack. The fact that Japanese diplomats in Washington had talked of peaceful resolution, even as the Imperial Japanese Navy was en route to Pearl Harbor, was not lost on the American public. Reflecting and feeding upon popular feeling, the William R. Hearst–owned newspapers in California did not urge its readers to show forbearance and forgiveness toward the Japanese. Baldwin's commentary on the Pearl Harbor attack did not use popular demeaning stereotypes or epithets about Japan or the Japanese people. In fact, he praised their successful planning for a series of almost simultaneous attacks on Guam, the Philippines, Hong Kong, Malaya, Thailand, and other points in the western Pacific.

The *Times* editorial on December 8 reminded its readers that the real battle would "not be fought in the Far East . . . but on the English Channel." After Hitler had been "smashed—the situation in the Far East will take care of itself automatically." In other words, Nazi Germany, not Japan, was "the greatest threat to [U.S.] security." This point of view mirrored President Roosevelt's "Germany first" priority.[52]

However, Baldwin disagreed with this priority, believing that America as a nation had long underestimated Japan's ability to do extraordinary things. He stated that more bad news from the Pacific would come, including an attack against the Panama Canal, which had been the "target" of U.S. naval exercises in the 1930s. He said that the Pacific war was not a sideshow to the war in Europe and would have a "profound effect" on the course of events in Europe, and this time his prediction was not far from the mark.[53]

Before Baldwin left for Washington to find out the extent of the damage done by the Japanese attack, there was a fast-moving rumor that New York City was about to be bombed. He dismissed such alarms as being part of "the usual fountain of panic and hysteria that always accompanies the start of a war."[54] At the Navy Department he talked with Undersecretary of the Navy James V. Forrestal, whom he had met earlier at the Council on Foreign Relations. Whatever information he learned about the extent of the damage to the battleships and to shore installations, Baldwin did not print it, possibly due to the Navy's strict censorship of any detailed news that might alert the Japanese to the success of their attack.

He later recalled a humorous incident from that trip that illustrated how extreme were the hurried security measures in Washington. In a passageway between the U.S. Army's Munitions Building and the Navy Department's offices on Constitution Avenue, he had left the Navy building and was about to enter the Army building when he was stopped by an MP who demanded to see his pass. He had none and was refused admittance. He tried to return to the Navy building, but a Marine guard at the door refused him reentry. Eventually, he was permitted to enter the Army building; no one had told him that he needed an interbuilding pass.[55]

In spite of his many contacts, Baldwin did not know all of the details surrounding the Pearl Harbor attack. At the time, his readers thought that he did a very good job of trying to make sense out of the chaos of war in the rush of events. Two weeks after the attack, Baldwin wrote a four-part series entitled "The Events in Hawaii," his first attempt to answer a number of questions that many were asking. He praised the appointment of Admiral Chester W. Nimitz as the new commander in chief of the Pacific Fleet (CinCPac), who replaced the discredited Admiral Husband E. Kimmel. After the release of the Roberts Commission report on the attack a month later, in January 1942, Baldwin agreed that Admiral Kimmel and General Walter Short had made errors in judgment and that their actions amounted to a "dereliction of duty."[56] He also noted that while the Japanese attack succeeded tactically, it failed strategically, because many of the Navy's ships were not damaged. Either he did not know that all eight battleships had been hit, with five sunk, or Navy censorship prevented him from revealing that information.[57]

Although he himself had earlier reported on Hawaii's inviolability, he singled out the American military's complacency about any Japanese attack at Pearl Harbor and the absence of preparedness. He noted the divided command responsibilities between the Army and the Navy at Pearl Harbor. The former was to provide close-in air reconnaissance and monitor radio detection and other listening devices on the island of Oahu.[58] The Navy was to provide distant air and surface screens around the islands. There were two admirals, one who commanded the Fourteenth Naval District (Hawaii) and the other who commanded the fleet at Pearl Harbor. An Army general commanded the Hawaiian Department. Given the well-known interservice rivalry, Baldwin questioned the degree of cooperation at the highest level in Hawaii.

He also noted that too many ships were in the harbor, none protected by torpedo nets, and that the oil and gasoline storage facilities were not protected. A photograph published postwar, taken from a Japanese plane during the attack, clearly showed the white-painted fuel storage tanks, which were fortunately not hit. He also noted how the planes at Hickham and at Wheeler Airfields were out of their hangars. From this list of mistakes, Baldwin drew three lessons. He blamed Washington for trying to maintain a political status quo in the Far East, hoping to slow down the rate of Japanese moves in China and elsewhere. That policy failed. Second, he said the United States was overconfident and wrong about the quality of Japanese skills and weapons. And last, too many overlapping responsibilities and divided commands in Hawaii worked against effective cooperation between the Army and the Navy.[59]

As to how a large Japanese naval force could have crossed the North Pacific without detection, Baldwin suggested that a cold front north and west of the islands, which brought with it rain, fog, and poor visibility, could have allowed planes to elude detection by Navy patrol planes. Whether or not he knew that such a weather front actually existed is not known, but it was an accurate guess nonetheless.[60] Baldwin also noted that the anticipated arrival of a fleet of B-17 bombers from California coincided with the Japanese attack and may have confused Army personnel who dismissed the second cluster of planes.

Two months later, Baldwin downplayed the role of interservice rivalries at Pearl Harbor and focused instead upon the lack of cooperation between the War and Navy departments in Washington. He felt that the war-warning message sent from Washington on November 27, 1941, was vague, paraphrasing it as, "Be careful, look out, but don't hit the enemy first." In his opinion, that defensive tone only reinforced the defensive mode already in place. He broadened his criticism of prewar policies to include Congress and the State Department. U.S. foreign policy for years had been in direct conflict with Japan's imperial plans, yet because of the Five Power Treaty of 1922, it was not able to strengthen its defenses in its Pacific outposts.[61]

The public's denunciation of Admiral Kimmel was made personal for Baldwin when one of Kimmel's sons, then a student at Princeton University, came to his office to speak with him. He began by asking, "Do you think my father's as guilty as everybody says he is?" Baldwin tried to be as gentle and kind as he could, reminding the young man that it was the Army's job, not the Navy's, to defend the Pearl Harbor base. That was cold comfort to a son whose father's long Navy career ended abruptly because of events over which he had little control and which brought harsh public vituperation. Baldwin tried to soften his remark by adding that there was a national state of mind that refused to believe that such an attack could occur and that local commanders were solely to blame for the disaster. The interview, Baldwin recalled, was "painful."[62]

From his review of the problems inherent with divided commands, Baldwin urged that President Roosevelt appoint a single commander to coordinate the War and Navy departments, and a General Staff to give direction to the entire war effort. The president instead created the Joint Chiefs of Staff (JCS), which met for the first time on February 9, 1942. It never followed the German model that Baldwin favored, nor did it solve the Army-Navy rivalries that persisted throughout the war. President Roosevelt may have enjoyed decision making too much to give it up to another man.[63]

On the eve of the fall of Wake Island (December 23), Baldwin was on a radio panel in the Town Hall, New York City, to discuss the topic "Outlook in the Pacific." He took that opportunity to use words that would shake Americans out of their complacency about what was going to be demanded of them in the years ahead. His message was that war is uncertain. Americans could not win this one by being on the defensive. He advocated that America should "attack, smash, and destroy" the enemy. He noted that Japanese attacks, thus far, had been against U.S. outposts in the western Pacific in order to deny American bases from which to attack the Japanese home islands in the future.

Rejecting the uninformed characterizations that had underestimated the fighting capabilities of the Japanese, Baldwin further informed his radio audience, "The Japanese are skillful airmen, good seamen, intelligent offi-cers, tough foes whose fanatic devotion to duty and to their half-feudalistic . . . traditions, make then unafraid to die. . . . They have practiced war; like the Germans, they are professionals in the art of war; the Democracies are amateurs." He also warned that although they had some weaknesses, "morale [was] not one of them; they [would] yield only when they are beaten in the air, on the sea, and on the land."[64] Eight months later, U.S. Marines learned firsthand on Guadalcanal the degree to which the Japanese would fight and die. On the panel, Baldwin also stressed the need to hold Singapore. The former British naval base fell nine weeks later to a Japanese attack.

He ended his talk with a prediction that both the European and Pacific fronts would affect each other. To gain the inevitable victory he advised that the United States must do its utmost: "There can be no halfway measures, no trafficking with time, no casual complacence." America as a nation had witnessed what complacency had bought it: "We have done with it," he concluded, warning that the time for action was now.[65]

CHAPTER 9

"This Is a War We Can Lose," 1942

T he early months of 1942 were grim ones for the Allied powers. On all fronts, the Axis powers were victorious. The German forces continued to move eastward in Russia's Ukraine, and the Deutsches Afrika Korps, led by Field Marshal Rommel, continued to move eastward in Libya, despite the defensive efforts of the British Eighth Army. German U-boats operated freely off the East Coast of the United States, sinking oil tankers and other commercial ships with ease. In the Far East, British forces surrendered their key naval base in Singapore to the victorious Japanese in mid-February. At sea, Japanese naval forces destroyed an Allied squadron in the Battle of the Java Sea (February 27–29). For the Americans, Manila, the capital of the Philippines, fell to the Japanese in early January. The combined American-Filipino forces evacuated the Bataan Peninsula, on Luzon, for the island of Corregidor in April, where they held out for another month against repeated Japanese attacks. General Jonathan Wainwright surrendered his remaining forces on May 6, 1942. The former commander, General Douglas MacArthur, left Corregidor in March for Australia on direct orders from President Roosevelt. It was clear that military victories were going to take a long time for the Allied powers in the Pacific and in Europe.

To Baldwin, these depressing events were a wake-up call, not to engage in empty patriotic appeals, but to undertake a realistic assessment of the war's demands on America, a war that had been thrust upon the country. "This is a war we can lose," he wrote in early January 1942. He believed in the shock value of blunt words and hoped to use the power of the press as the nation faced dangerous times. He pointed out to his readers that complacency would never win a war; his message: "this war . . . is a war to the death, a war for life itself, a war the outcome of which is by no means certain." The country was now in a world war for which it was "inadequately prepared." The United States lives in a "predatory world," Baldwin wrote, and its carefree public attitudes of peacetime must be quickly replaced by a national attitude of mind with "one aim—victory."[1] To that end, there had to be a "mutual confidence" between Washington and the American people.

That confidence should be demonstrated by a change in Washington's public relations policy, which was only issuing overly optimistic assessments of the Philippine campaign. To Baldwin's thinking, the American public should be told "the blunt truth" that "we are losing" in the Philippines. He rejected the view that bad news would only serve to demoralize Americans. Specifically, he urged Washington to develop a "positive public relations" policy, which would effectively counter Japanese radio broadcasts exaggerating their victories and U.S. defeats. In his view, America's "raucous voice" needed to reach the "teeming millions" in the Orient. Public opinion was a powerful instrument in a total war, a war in which the United States had to go on the offensive if it was to win.[2] Later, Baldwin viewed the Allied defeats as a tonic for a home front that welcomed such words as "bold, frank, pitiless truth—the worst is yet to come." And indeed the worst did come.[3]

Doubtless some of his readers thought his January piece defeatist, but to Philip Fox LaFollette, the former governor of Wisconsin, Baldwin's piece showed "a rare quality to tell the truth," and that alone would help the country to win the war. "The country needs [truth] and you,"[4] he wrote. Edward L. Bernays, the founder of modern public relations, also praised Baldwin for calling for the need to crystallize public opinion about the war. In public relations, he noted, opinion molders who wield great influence are not always cognizant of it. "May I assure you that your words carry great weight and authority in high quarters."[5] For Baldwin, the transition from his peacetime coverage of Army maneuvers and naval fleet exercises to a shooting war had been swift. After the Japanese attack on Pearl Harbor, and the German and Italian declarations of war on America, the United States was no longer an observer but an active participant in a two-front world war.

Since the Pearl Harbor attack, Baldwin had been writing event-driven articles on almost a daily basis, a pace that he could not sustain. In early February 1942 Baldwin came to an agreement with Sulzberger, and with the senior *Times* editors, that his articles would appear only on Mondays, Wednesdays, and Fridays, with a longer article in the *Times* Sunday edition's "News of the Week in Review" section.[6] However, this schedule was often altered by the press of war news, or travel on assignment.

During the war he traveled to three different combat zones: Guadalcanal in September 1942, Tunisia in March 1943, and London and Normandy, France, from mid-May to early August 1944. In the spring of 1945 he resumed writing daily pieces as the German armies were pushed westward by the Soviet forces. His assignment at the *Times* was to analyze the rush of war news and to clear away the confusion of war, if possible, and if only for a fleeting moment. He tried to see the big picture of the progress of the world war and to make sense out of it, which meant that he often wrote with only sketchy details of a news event. "War itself," he later commented, was "the chief obstacle to accurate reporting." Unlike in peacetime, only half the story was told because the enemy's version of events would not be told until the war's end.[7]

A modern reader may well ask what value there is in reading Hanson Baldwin's old newspaper articles about World War II. Since 1945 thousands of books and articles have been written, not only with the benefit of the opening of national archives of documents of that war, but also with memoirs and biographies of the participants. We now know more about what the American public at home was reading and listening to; while radio broadcasts gave them immediate news bulletins, newspapers provided longer and fuller accounts of the war news.

First of all, Baldwin was very good at what he did. He had excellent sources and a solid public reputation for accuracy and integrity that prepared him to interpret the significance of war news. Second, he had an excellent forum, the *Times*, which was read daily by policymakers in Washington, D.C., as well as by the many intelligent, well-informed readers who were his intended audience. The tone of his writings was serious and well informed. He knew that he was not writing history and that there would be a cushion of time between the event and a reasoned assessment years later. Readers should consider his wartime writing as a kind of public diary, a narrative of war events about whose significance he was attempting to comment under deadline. He never considered World War II to be a "Good War," only a necessary one that the United States was forced to enter because of the actions of Germany, Italy, and Japan. He thought the war would last until 1946, or possibly longer. He never underestimated the determination of Berlin's and Tokyo's leaders to fight on as long as possible, while never doubting that the Axis powers would eventually be defeated.

Baldwin rarely wrote about members of the American military personnel as individuals. He was no Ernie Pyle, who wrote so eloquently about the experiences of foot soldiers, or Bill Mauldin, whose "Willie" and "Joe" cartoon characters portrayed the war as seen by ordinary GIs. While many war correspondents reported on war events of particular interest to their hometown papers, Baldwin wrote for a national audience, or at least one that was in the circulation radius of the *Times*.

One of the more unique features of Baldwin's pieces was his appreciation of the importance of geography on warfare on land. On his 1937 European trip he collected many maps, which he used frequently for reference during the war, in addition to the National Geographic Society's extensive map collection. He would describe in detail the terrain that was then in the news, paying close attention to land forms and rivers as possible obstacles to be bypassed or crossed by invading armies. On the Pacific islands, atolls, and other land forms, he would even note the existence of poisonous snakes as a possible concern to the invading troops. This close attention to geography gave his readers a real sense of the actual locations where American troops were then fighting.[8] Another valuable source for Baldwin was his collection of "pilot's guides," which gave details of all European ports; he used them in 1944 to guess the potential landing sites for the anticipated Allied invasion of Europe.[9] In addition to the importance of geography in war, Baldwin commented on the Axis powers' constant need to transport raw materials of metals and petroleum to their factories to continue their war production.

Although Baldwin had a very good general military and naval background, he actively cultivated high-ranking officers in the War and Navy departments for war news. His best Navy source was Vice Admiral Frederick Joseph Horne, the vice chief of naval operations who planned the logistics of the Pacific war. Admiral Horne worked closely with his ranking superior, Admiral Ernest J. King, the chief of naval operations.[10] Also helpful to Baldwin was Admiral King's deputy, Admiral Richard Stanislaus Edwards.

Another excellent source was James V. Forrestal, the undersecretary of the Navy, whom Baldwin had met previously through his work on the Council of Foreign Relations. It was Forrestal who persuaded Admiral Horne to speak occasionally with a few other newspapermen.[11] On his frequent trips to Washington, Baldwin always made it a point to call upon Admiral Horne as well as on Admiral William D. Leahy, who was President Roosevelt's liaison with the Joint Chiefs of Staff. Baldwin considered Leahy to be "an invaluable source," as he was very knowledgeable about all major decisions made in the White House as well as developments in the War and Navy departments.[12] Initially Admiral Horne was willing only to disclose facts about past naval actions, but as his trust in the former naval lieutenant's discretion, soundness, and integrity grew, he also revealed to him the details of future naval operations in the Pacific, which is why his pieces on invasions were so extensive and detailed. Baldwin never revealed such secret information until after the next island invasion had occurred and was in the news,[13] and this knowledge enabled him to develop the necessary background information for his readers.

Baldwin's specific sources in the Army and the Army Air Force are not known, though he had cultivated many of his Army sources before the war. He found that as his reputation grew, the Air Force sought him out and tried to persuade him of the merits of the Douhet theory of air power, explained earlier. Baldwin was never convinced that air power alone could win wars, but did believe that air, land, and sea power were a winning combination. General Henry "Hap" Arnold, commander of the U.S. Army Air Force, was "a very cheerful Irishman, a very likeable fellow," and he would ask Baldwin when they met, "Well, how is the war going?"[14] Such casual banter was characteristic of Baldwin's relationships with other military chiefs, whom he cultivated as news sources. Without doubt, his reputation as a sound and reliable military analyst opened doors for him, but not all: General Marshall and Admiral King remained distant figures to him throughout World War II. Unfortunately, Baldwin kept no notebook or diary listing his sources and what they told him. Baldwin was blessed with an excellent memory, a desire to protect his sources, and the pressure of deadlines, and this may explain the absence of a contemporary written record.

Throughout the war, Baldwin saw it as his task to discern themes amid the chaos of continuing reports of combat on land and sea. In 1942, for example, he stressed the importance of offense over defense, and wrote that a total war demanded the mobilization of American public opinion in support of the war effort. He felt strongly that Washington should not withhold war news, good or bad, from the public. He also stressed the need for a unified military command structure and the need to increase U.S. air power. Those were themes that Baldwin would emphasize many times in the months and years ahead.

During the first week of January 1942, he pointed to major problems facing both the Axis and the Allies. He argued that Hitler needed to "break the power of the Red armies, control the Mediterranean sea routes, and conquer Great Britain," while Allied supplies needed to be sent to Russia "indefinitely" via the port of Archangel, the Persian Gulf, and India. Britain was the only base from which the Allies could strike directly against Germany. The eastern Mediterranean—Egypt and the Suez Canal—had to be held, as well as the water route to the Black Sea. In the western Pacific, Singapore had to be held, China's armies needed to be supplied, and Russia's Far Eastern army must be maintained from Alaska and the Aleutian supply line. The strategy of these two theaters was interlocking and interdependent, and one theater of operations could not take permanent priority over another: a true assessment.[15]

Realizing that the country was militarily unprepared for a global war, Baldwin began to alert his readers about the need for unified war planning, unified materials procurement, and a unified command structure. To his thinking, the Axis powers had successfully employed all three. He praised Donald M. Nelson's War Production Board, which was empowered to direct and control the procurement of war materials and oversee industrial production. Still absent in Washington was a general staff to advise President Roosevelt on actual operations. "Lip service" had been given to such unity, but not a coordinated command structure that would override the clashing personalities in the War and Navy departments. There were hopeful signs of unity in the roles of General Marshall and Admiral King; the former was developing "an Army on wheels for modern war instead of an Army on foot," while the latter appreciated the future role of air power in the Navy by authorizing the construction of new aircraft carriers.[16] Although Baldwin did not name names, he felt that much more needed to be done: red tape, duplication, and confusion continued to hamper war mobilization and there were senior military officers who "ought not to be" in high command.

The absence of a coordinated government public-relations policy was one of Baldwin's primary concerns. Noting that the Axis used the "war of words" effectively, he wondered why not the United States, as well?[17] In early 1942, government confusion as to what the public should be told was reflected in conflicting statements made by the Office of Facts and Figures (OFF), headed by Archibald MacLeish, the former librarian of the Library of Congress, and from Senator Harry S. Truman's committee investigating the defense program. The MacLeish office exhibited a "roseate" optimism, not supported by current facts, on the nation's defenses, while the Truman committee's criticism of the defense program was based on outdated information. Baldwin wrote that there must be impartial facts, published by a responsible government source; instead there was only "carping criticism and complacency and no criticism at all."[18] To correct the confusion, an Office of War Information was created by an executive order of the president in June 1942. It was headed by Elmer Davis, a well-known CBS radio news commentator and former member of the *Times* staff.

President Roosevelt's call for increased production of new planes, tanks, antiaircraft guns, and ships would require "an industrial miracle," complete conversion of the automobile industry to war production, more subcontracting than before, and "a complete absence of labor trouble." Most important was public awareness of the urgent need to accomplish such huge tasks. Wishful thinking and optimism needed to be replaced by a "grim, rugged, and determined confidence" in America's ultimate victory, something that would occur only if the American public was informed. In a democracy, Baldwin contended, mistakes would be made, but they would always be corrected by an informed public that would demand solutions.[19]

Before the war, Baldwin had made only occasional radio broadcasts. Once the war began, the opportunity to make regular radio commentary again became an issue with Sulzberger, who was again reluctant to give his consent. As always, Baldwin tried hard to avoid saying anything on radio that he hadn't printed earlier. For example, on February 1, 1942, he was a panelist on the University of Chicago Round Table, discussing the topic "Are We Over Confident?" He repeated his previously printed words of a month before, that events since 1939 "forever exploded that old shibboleth that the defensive can win wars. . . . [O]nly the offensive can win wars." "It is a war we can lose. . . . [T]his is a total war, with all that implies. We are fighting for our lives."[20]

Later that week, in early February, Sulzberger wanted to reassure himself that Baldwin would not be lured by radio broadcasting with its promise of a mass audience and a higher salary, and that his first loyalty was to the *Times.* While the publisher's memo has not been located, Baldwin's lengthy reply has. It was a loyal testimonial to his place on the *Times* staff and an assumption that radio broadcasts "not only will not interfere with whatever value my articles may have but will enhance them." All stories, Baldwin assured the publisher, "naturally belong[ed] first to the *Times,*" and radio and other outside forums would not interfere with his *Times* work. Having caught Sulzberger's attention, Baldwin cited his desire to return to his pre-war schedule of three days a week, with another article in the Sunday edition. He felt that it would be beneficial for his readers to know the days when his columns would appear. He closed his memo with a statement that "I have tried to be of maximum usefulness to all around" and that included occasional editorials on military subjects.[21]

One of his continuing challenges was how to put war events into a larger context. Sometimes he was wrong. For example, in mid-February 1942, two German battle cruisers, the *Scharnorst* and the *Gneisenau,* and the heavy cruiser *Prinz Eugen,* fled from their base at Brest, France, through the English Channel, during daylight hours, to safer German ports farther north. Overestimating the importance of this escape, he speculated that it would "influence the whole course of the war." And he reported that Germany "probably" had two aircraft carriers. Neither was true.

Other predictions proved more accurate. The U.S. raids on the Marshall and Gilbert islands on February 1 set the pattern, he thought, for the kind of war America should fight in the Pacific. He also predicted that carrier-based strike groups would advance "step-by-step" through the atolls and islands of Micronesia toward the western Pacific, as called for by the prewar Rainbow plans to directly attack Japan.[22]

Wisely, Baldwin never promised easy victories for America. His readers were told bluntly, in early January 1942, that surface ships could not operate in narrow waters without air support. He warned against dividing U.S. Pacific forces between Hawaii and the Philippines, recognizing that the American-Filipino forces were "fighting a last-ditch fight" in the Philippines, and only after "hard years" of fighting would they recapture the Philippines and then "exact retribution to the full" on the Japanese.[23] Meanwhile, the Japanese seized Singapore on February 15, which Baldwin felt could open future attacks against Java and Sumatra, thus opening a Japanese passageway into the Indian Ocean.[24]

After Pearl Harbor, U.S. censorship of news loomed larger and larger. On January 15, 1942, the Office of Censorship, headed by Bryan Price, issued 50,000 copies of its codebook for radio and for print journalists.[25] The codebook relied upon self-censorship by journalists and it listed eight categories of news to avoid. One clause permitted journalists to publish anything so long as an official news source would release it, but that source would have to take full responsibility for news that was released.[26] Because the codebook did not address military censorship in combat zones, all journalists had to be accredited by the Army and the Navy and all news stories had to pass their censors. As of May 29, 1942, each correspondent was subject to censorship from the theater commander.

In 1942, when the Navy and the Marines were the only American forces fighting the Japanese, the Navy Department's communiqués were Baldwin's only source of war news, and he had to interpret them to create copy. He was able to read between the lines, as it were, and to write something logical. An early example was his commentary on the Battle of the Java Sea (February 27–29, 1942), where ships from four Allied countries, America, Britain, Holland, and Australia (ABDA), were easily defeated by the Imperial Japanese Navy. Two weeks after the battle, when the Navy Department announced the details of the defeat of the ABDA force, Baldwin made reference to the Japanese report issued shortly after the battle. The ABDA force had been hurriedly pulled together to stop the advance of the Imperial Japanese Navy. Based on this information, Baldwin assumed, correctly as it turned out, that the ABDA force was mostly a collection of ships of different types, speed, and gun power. All used different codes, communication systems, and tactics. It was not "a homogeneous" squadron and they had not previously maneuvered together. The ABDA commander, Rear Admiral Karel Doorman, was the senior Dutch naval officer of that doomed squadron. Given the Japanese naval superiority, Baldwin said, the results of the battle could "never . . . have been in doubt." The American Asiatic Squadron, formerly based at Cavite, the Philippines, was described as "a suicide squadron." It had no capital ships, no aircraft carriers, and only one heavy cruiser, the USS *Houston* (CA 30), that was sunk.[27]

On April 18, 1942, Brigadier General "Jimmy" Doolittle led sixteen B-25 medium bombers from the carrier USS *Hornet* (CV 8) to attack four Japanese cities. All the planes crash-landed in China. Though militarily insignificant for the little damage they inflicted, Baldwin conjectured as to how vulnerable the Japanese cities were to an air attack. If the United States had the "necessary bases" from which to conduct continual air raids, it would introduce the unexpected into Japanese military thinking and into Japanese domestic psychology, including Japanese radio broadcasts with their accent on public hysteria, and then the raid would have important results.[28]

On April 21 President Roosevelt commented at a press conference that the Doolittle raid had left from "Shangri-La," using a reference to the popular 1937 movie *Lost Horizon*.[29] Baldwin thought there was "a distinct possibility" that the B-25s could be launched from an aircraft carrier, assuming that the planes had landed at Chinese airfields or at Vladivostok, U.S.S.R., even though the U.S.S.R. was not at war with Japan at the time.

More important than the Doolittle raid was the first carrier versus carrier battle, in the Coral Sea (May 4–8, 1942). Baldwin's initial commentary was based on a communiqué from General MacArthur's headquarters in Australia that U.S. losses were "relatively light."[30] He speculated as to what the Japanese target was: Australia, New Caledonia, or the New Hebrides? "The Japanese intentions in the Battle of the Worlds [were] not yet clear,"[31] he commented, but he assumed that both Germany and Japan had similar goals of world conquest.

We know now that the USS *Lexington* (CV 2) had been sunk and that the Japanese lost a small carrier, *Shoho*, while another carrier, *Shokaku,* was damaged and another had lost most of its planes. Fortunately for America, none of the Japanese carriers at the Coral Sea participated at Midway a month later.

The *Times* publisher, Sulzberger, in a speech made in April, agreed with voluntary censorship, but he asked where censorship ended, pointing to the concentration of power in Washington that raised "the temptation" to soften bad war news masking "inefficiency of government bureaus and personnel." In his view, the power to censor news was "a heady wine," and the role of the press was to "support our government [only] as long as it is worthy of support." Only by constant "vigilance" could the press preserve "the liberties we defend against others," the publisher added.[32]

On Saturday, June 6, 1942, Admiral Nimitz issued a communiqué stating that "severe damage" had been done to the Japanese fleet that had retired from the Midway Island battle scene. On the following day, the *Times* reported that two or three Japanese carriers had been sunk.[33] The *Times* editorial, "A Momentous Victory," mentioned damage to three Japanese battleships and four cruisers. It assumed that America's Pacific fleet had overtaken the "wounded" ships, and there was no report of American losses.[34]

Baldwin's initial report on that battle made four points. U.S. forces were numerically inferior to those of the Japanese. No American battleships were present, owing to their slow speed and "obsolescent" design. The U.S. "surprised" the Japanese with its "radio intelligence" and reconnaissance planes. And the Japanese were attacked by planes from a single American carrier and from land-based planes from Midway Island. However, recognizing that censorship and other factors were at play, he ended his analysis on a cautionary note: "The end of the story is not yet written, and what actually happened may have differed radically from what we think happened."[35]

Six weeks later, when the Navy Department issued a communiqué and other materials on the Midway battle, Baldwin dismissed them as "not the candid documents that the great victory deserves." He found the loss table incomplete, and knew it would "certainly confuse the American people." In his view, "the Navy's lack of frankness had cost it some degree of public confidence." Reading between the lines, he assumed that Navy dive-bombers had done most of the damage, rather than high-altitude Army bombers,[36] but there was no detailed information on the types of ships and planes lost or damaged.

An editorial of the same date, which Baldwin may have written, reiterated his query as to why there was a delay of news about the battle: "The American people do not need the reminder of a June victory to nerve them to face the dark realities of July." Instead, he believed that the public needed "assurances that they are hearing the worst with the best," and that the United States would do everything necessary to "turn defeat into victory."[37] But, in keeping with the policies of censorship, it was not until mid-September that the Navy Department announced the loss of the carrier *Yorktown* (CV 5) and four Japanese carriers at Midway in June.[38]

Censorship continued to control news of the war. Two weeks after the First Marine Division had landed on the island of Guadalcanal, on August

7, 1942, the War and Navy departments had only issued 1,500 words about that operation. Much of what was released came from General MacArthur's headquarters in Australia, but very little came from U.S. Navy sources. The *Times* managing editor, Edwin L. James, was upset. He lamented that the American public was being "spoon-fed" by the military, noting that it should be the goal of the Roosevelt administration "to make each citizen feel that it is his war. The purpose is to unite the country in further effort and in a complete enthusiasm for victory." He continued to critique censorship policies by chastising generals and admirals who had to be convinced that there was a "middle road" between satisfying the public's demand for news details and keeping military secrets from the enemy.[39]

Baldwin jumped at James' suggestion that he make plans to visit the island. To smooth the way for the distant and dangerous trip, he first went to Washington to see Undersecretary of the Navy Forrestal, then left Hawaii on a Martin two-engine patrol bomber, a seaplane (PBM-3), and headed south to Nouméa, New Caledonia.

On arrival, he immediately noticed that things were not right: the harbor was clogged with ships. One of the other passengers on the plane was Admiral Roscoe Fletcher Good, Admiral Nimitz's assistant operations officer responsible for logistics. His mission was to find out why it was taking so long to unload cargo ships at Nouméa.

Granted an interview with Vice Admiral Robert Ghormley, the commander of the South Pacific forces responsible for the Guadalcanal campaign, Baldwin became concerned by the Admiral's defeatist attitude: "We're just hanging on by our teeth." There were shortages of nearly everything and Ghormley's staff reflected this defeatist thinking.[40]

Baldwin then flew north to Espiritu Santo, where "the gloom thickened," perhaps because the base was very primitive. The following day, since Rear Admiral Aubrey W. Fitch was going to Guadalcanal, Baldwin seized the opportunity: "I tagged along on his coattails, otherwise you didn't know when you'd get in there. It was hard to get in at that time."[41] The DC-3 cargo plane loaded with drums of gasoline and eight passengers flew toward Henderson Field on Guadalcanal, and as they approached the field they all put on life jackets, their parachute harnesses and helmets, and tried to be comfortable in the bucket-shaped seats along the side of the plane's cabin.

Ever alert for Japanese planes, the DC-3 skimmed over the water to escape detection from above. At 8:15 a.m. on Saturday, September 19, they landed and taxied to a stop near "the pagoda," the former Japanese control tower. After a breakfast of oatmeal and coffee, Baldwin was given a brief tour of the Marine perimeter, which a week before had been the site of "Bloody Ridge," a battle in which the Japanese troops tried repeatedly but failed to break through the Marine front lines.

Baldwin, realizing that his time there was limited, interviewed Lieutenant General Alexander Vandergrift, the U.S. Marine Corps commander, and his staff, and was briefed on the battle statistics. He was surprised at how small the Marine-held area was on a map of the base.[42]

Baldwin then spoke with F. Tillman Durdin, the *Times* correspondent on the island, and with other journalists. From them he learned that reporting from the only American battle zone in the Pacific Ocean was complicated by the long distance to Hawaii, the lack of available communication facilities, and the U.S. Navy's hostile attitude toward the press. In Baldwin's view, the real obstacle was not the Navy's fleet censor at Pearl Harbor, but Admiral Ernest J. King, the chief of naval operations in Washington. Baldwin was very familiar with the Navy's anti-press views, which he first encountered in the 1930s.

Admiral Nimitz's public information officer was Waldo Drake, the former Marine editor of the *Los Angeles Times* and a commander in the U.S. Naval Reserve. Baldwin learned that other correspondents disliked him for playing favorites. He was rumored to keep a little "black book" of reporters he did not like, and although Drake was aware of the Navy's stringent censorship, he chose not to communicate press complaints to the admiral.[43]

Henderson Field was rough and muddy. The Marines lived in pup tents and foxholes near the field. From what Baldwin had heard at Pearl Harbor, the Marines had the situation well in hand and controlled most of Guadalcanal. This was not true. The Marines held the airfield and the close-in perimeter around it, while the Japanese surrounded the field. In fact, the Marines held the airfield only by "the skin of our teeth."[44] He quickly realized that he had been misinformed about the situation when he learned that the night before he arrived, a few Japanese soldiers had penetrated the perimeter and had even entered General Vandergrift's headquarters area before being beaten off. Everyone was nervous and jittery, and supplies were intermittent in arriving.

In his interview with General Vandergrift, Baldwin asked whether the Marines could continue to hold the airfield in light of repeated Japanese attacks. The General retorted, "Hell, yes," an optimism in sharp contrast to Admiral Ghormley's defeatism.[45] But Baldwin continued to talk with others and to gather new information, and he used his information to good effect a month later.

As Admiral Fitch was leaving the following day, September 20, for Espiritu Santo to set up his command of the Air Force in the South Pacific, Baldwin could have remained on the island, but there was no assurance of when he could leave. Correspondents had a low priority for space on outgoing cargo planes. Fitch had been sent by Nimitz to get the logistics of the air war organized. He was "astounded" by the chaos at New Caledonia.[46]

On his flight back to Hawaii, Baldwin spoke with Admiral Good, one of the passengers, who provided him with information. With all this information, Baldwin would have to get Commander Drake at Pearl Harbor to pass on his copy if it were to be filed from Pearl. It would be a futile exercise, he thought. Other press people advised Baldwin to take his new information directly to Washington, which was what he did. He realized that it would not be easy. It was not only Admiral King who disliked the press, but his prejudice was reflected by other naval officers, including Admiral Nimitz and Admiral Spruance. According to Baldwin, the fleet intelligence officer, Commander Leighton, was "obsessed, and I mean obsessed, and I have known him for years, with the mania for secrecy of all sorts." If possible, Baldwin knew that the Navy would have liked to "wage the war completely" without any press coverage.[47]

In those early months of the Pacific war, all press copy from Guadalcanal was first sent to Pearl Harbor to be reviewed by a censor, and then passed on to the States. Delays were considerable. No radio transmissions were permitted, so Tillman Durdin's reports went either by ship or by plane, addressed to Commander Drake at Pearl Harbor. Since war needs always took precedence, press reports could take many days or weeks to arrive. In a memo to the *Times* editors on his return, Baldwin offered no easy answers to the twin obstacles of Guadalcanal's remoteness and the Navy's censorship.

Shortly after Baldwin's return from the South Pacific, Brigadier General Albert C. Wedemeyer asked him to come to Washington to brief a group of Army colonels and Navy captains. He was to tell no one at the *Times* of this visit. Wedemeyer was a member of the Joint Strategic Survey Committee of the JCS, which had arranged for the meeting.

Thirty officers sat around a long table, and General Wedemeyer asked Baldwin to tell the group what he had observed at Guadalcanal. He told of ship losses, constant supply problems, and the tenuous hold by the Marines of their perimeter around the airfield, which the Japanese were determined to seize or to destroy. He also told the group how one of the U.S. battleships, the USS *Washington* (BB 36), was almost torpedoed after the battle of the Santa Cruz Islands. Fortunately, the Japanese torpedo self-destructed before hitting the ship. The United States had only two battleships in the area, and the carrier *Hornet* had been sunk in that battle. That left only the carrier *Enterprise* (CV 6).[48]

And that was not all. Baldwin named the four heavy cruisers that were sunk off Savo Island on the evening of August 9. At that revelation, Navy captain Charles R. Brown stood up and "violently" shouted that "this is top secret information. Admiral King has given the strictest orders that no one is to know about this."[49] Brown continued to berate Baldwin in an offensive manner; the group was shocked into silence by his verbal outburst. The Army officers present knew nothing of the Navy's ship losses or how tenuous was the Marine position on that island. General Wedemeyer defused the situation by asking Baldwin to comment on the importance of air power in the South Pacific.[50] A few days later, columnist Drew Pearson printed a distorted version of the meeting in his newspaper column. Captain Brown "flew into a rage by mail" and accused Baldwin of leaking it to Pearson, but Baldwin "quickly set him straight," clarifying that he himself despised that kind of journalism.[51]

What concerned Baldwin at the time was that those Army and Navy officers were all involved in planning for the war. "That, I think," he later recalled, "is a hell of a way to run a war."[52] He knew that Admiral King had been pushing for the Guadalcanal invasion for some time, and that it had been a shoestring operation from the beginning. The early series of U.S. naval losses, if publicly known, would have reflected badly on the Navy, which was trying to recover its lost prestige after the Pearl Harbor fiasco. The

Savo Island losses seemed to demonstrate the ineptitude of the Navy, and to call Admiral King's judgment and leadership into question.[53] That meeting led Baldwin to wonder privately about the quality of America's strategic planning for the war, especially if information had been withheld from planning committees in the War Department in order to save the reputation of a senior officer.

On his return to New York, he told Sulzberger about the meeting. In those days, Baldwin could and did go directly to him and reveal information that he told no one else at the *Times*. His confidences were never broken and Baldwin continued to value this confidential relationship for many years to come.[54]

Baldwin's eight-part series was passed by the Washington censors, with the help of Elmer Davis, the director of the Office of War Information (OWI). That agency was authorized to use the media to "facilitate the development of an informed and intelligent understanding" of the war's progress.[55] Accompanying the executive order, President Roosevelt issued a statement that Davis was authorized "to issue directions to all departments and agencies of the government" regarding their information services.[56] Since Pearl Harbor, the U.S. Navy had hidden the extent of its losses, especially the loss of its three heavy cruisers off Savo Island. On October 9, Elmer Davis had had an "acrimonious" conversation with Admiral King over the Navy's refusal to release information on the Guadalcanal operations thus far. This was just prior to the review of Baldwin's eight articles by the Office of Censorship in Washington.[57]

Baldwin's reputation as America's foremost military analyst was solidified by his series on Guadalcanal, which began on October 24, 1942, and ran for the next seven days. On one level, the articles were written to inform the American public of the precarious hold of the Marines on Guadalcanal. On another level, he pointed sharply to the weaknesses of the Navy's command and logistical situation there. Reiterating one of his ongoing concerns, he wrote that many Americans, who love personal liberty and its "casual, easy, carefree ways of life in peacetime," had not learned yet the brutal lesson that "war is a hard taskmaster" and that the ways of peace are not the ways of war. He added that Americans were jealous of their prerogatives and forgot that further Axis conquests were a "terrible peril to all liberty."[58]

According to Baldwin, the Japanese possessed "a will to win and a belief in Japan's invincibility." The Japanese soldiers' and sailors' determination to "win or die" was a firm and literal commitment. Collectively they were "the best jungle fighters in the world," and they were more experienced in amphibious operations than any other power.[59] He felt that it was important to recognize that the real enemy bore no resemblance to the popular negative stereotype that dismissed the Japanese as being people of no consequence.

He was also critical of the Roosevelt administration's acceptance of the "Germany First" strategy that was reaffirmed by Roosevelt and Churchill at their Arcadia conference in December 1941. Given this policy decision, he felt it was a "dangerous fallacy" for American public opinion to hold that once Germany was defeated, Japan would be a pushover. If the United States waited until Hitler's Germany was defeated, Japan would be able to consolidate its territorial gains and become "so strong and so secure, that its defeat . . . may require years." He emphasized that the United States could not fight a protracted delaying action in the Pacific, but that it must hit the Japanese forces continuously to prevent any consolidation of their possessions.[60] On Guadalcanal, the Marines were fighting a major campaign "on a shoe string." They faced the main Japanese strength. America had a one-ocean Navy, now divided between two oceans, that was not big enough for the tasks in either ocean.[61]

Not mentioned by Baldwin was the fact that the United States entered the war with only seven aircraft carriers, six of which were in the Pacific. Between May and October 1942, four had been sunk.[62] That left only the USS *Enterprise* (CV 6) operational in the South Pacific. The first of the larger *Essex*-class carriers did not join the fleet until mid-1943.

Without naming anyone, Baldwin also asserted that one of the greatest problems was leadership. Many errors of judgment made by American naval leaders developed from their being over-cautious and too much on the defensive, which resulted in unnecessary losses. For example, he cited for the first time publicly information withheld from the American public until then: the loss of four Allied heavy cruisers (one of which was Australian) off Savo Island on August 9 from Japanese gunfire and torpedoes. He cited specific mistakes made by the American naval forces that night. All of the crews were not at their battle stations when the Japanese opened fire, the ships were patrolling back and forth on a fixed course, and the American admiral, in charge of the cruiser screen, had left the area on his flagship so that no one was in "actual tactical command." That battle "almost lost us our foothold" in the Solomon Islands, where the Marines had landed only two days before.[63]

While the Japanese naval force sailed from Rabaul, on New Britain island, to shell Henderson Field on Guadalcanal at night, the U.S. Navy made "no similar raids against" the Japanese bases on Bougainville or on Truk. Also, the Navy did not intercept the Japanese landing of reinforcements beyond the Marine perimeter on Guadalcanal.[64] Those early mistakes were being corrected, he assured his readers, as the Navy was conducting more offensive operations against Japanese resupply attempts. He noted that American forces had been on the defensive since early August, as the Marines "grimly" held on to defending Henderson Field, surrounded on three sides by the Japanese.

Since Baldwin's return to stateside, Admiral Nimitz had begun offensive operations against Rabaul and against the Japanese destroyers that were being used as supply and troop ships. In reviewing the situation, Baldwin noted that the U.S. Navy had not yet learned how to integrate the use of the naval gun (a primary naval weapon) with the bomb and the torpedo. Excessive caution by American naval commanders as to how best to use surface ships meant that there was "little of the Nelson touch," which stressed "audacity, audacity, always audacity," the touchstone of naval success in any war.[65] The Japanese had more airplanes, more ships, and shorter lines of supply than did the Americans. Truk, a major Japanese base, was 1,300 miles from Guadalcanal, while Pearl Harbor was 3,500 miles away.

He warned that if the United States continued to make mistakes and to be over-cautious and too much on the defensive, they could "defeat [them]selves."[66] He urged that more troops and more supplies be sent to Guadalcanal to build new airfields and docks so that the U.S. Navy could seize naval superiority in the waters around the island. "Until these problems are solved, our foothold in the southern Solomons cannot be termed completely secure," he wrote, urging that "a smashing offensive spirit" by land, sea, and air forces be used to defeat the Japanese.[67]

Just prior to the appearance of Baldwin's eight-part series, the Navy Department announced the relief of Vice Admiral Ghormley by Vice Admiral William F. Halsey. Some thought that Baldwin's articles played a part in the change of command, but he knew that Nimitz and King had been dissatisfied with the logistics bottleneck for many weeks, and that his articles (which did not name Ghormley) had no role in that decision.

Looking at the big picture, Baldwin noted that the outcome of this and all future Pacific battles would depend primarily upon ships that would bring needed supplies, planes, and troops. He argued that ships were needed to protect convoys and to form task forces to "help secure domination of the seas,"[68] and once America's wartime production operated at full capacity, then it could replace all of its sunken ships faster than the Japanese could theirs.[69]

A controversial part of this series dealt with his comments on Australia. America's goal was not to protect its supply line to that country, but it was part of a long-range strategy to diminish Japan's power in the Pacific by moving northwestward to Rabaul, Truk, and other Japanese island bases in the western Pacific.[70] Though General MacArthur was the commander of the Southwest Pacific, Baldwin contended that "in some ways [he was] a supreme commander in name only."[71] Baldwin continued: "his fine sense of the dramatic may at times hurt him" and his presidential hopes, which unknown sources had told Baldwin he no longer held.

As for Australia, he noted critically how it was concerned with its own defense and not with events in New Guinea. His previously mentioned dislike of labor unions was made apparent in his remarks about Australia's stevedores' unwillingness to work "after the whistle blew."[72]

In October 1942, many in Washington were concerned with the slow and partial release of information by the Navy about Guadalcanal, which Baldwin called the "unknown" battle. Elmer Davis, the director of the OWI, Secretary of the Navy Frank Knox, and Baldwin together concluded what Baldwin had always contended: the American public deserved to be kept informed of war news, good and bad. At the center of the problem, as has already been mentioned, was Admiral King, the Navy's CNO. As a member of the Joint Chiefs of Staff, he was aware that President Roosevelt was insistent that American troops fight German forces in North Africa in 1942, which would mean the diversion of troops, equipment, and supplies from the Pacific theater to the European theater. Adding to the admiral's unease was the fact that the Guadalcanal campaign was not going well. The Marines there were too few in number, poorly supplied, and on the defensive in August and September. It is understandable why the admiral did not want such information released to the American public. It was convenient for him to use the argument that the Japanese may not have known how successful their offensives were.

Baldwin's series on Guadalcanal spilled the beans, as it were, about the real conditions there, including American ship losses. When Elmer Davis spoke with Baldwin about finding someone in the Navy Department who might be less hostile to the release of information, Baldwin suggested Admiral Horne, on King's staff, and James V. Forrestal, the assistant secretary of the navy.

In early November the Navy began to release American ship losses by the name of the ship and not by the class or type of ship, a new policy Baldwin welcomed, as he had been critical of listing ship losses by class because they only "spread anguish and suspense" among families. The new Navy policy preserved the "military's need for security, the public's right to know, and the press's duty to inform."[73] He favored the national publication of all war casualties rather than the local release of casualties by the states, rejecting the view that such releases would only depress home front morale. He contended that "the American people's attitude toward the war was far tougher" than it was in January 1942. "They can take it," he wrote, "but they want to be fully informed."[74]

In November 1942, American naval victories in the Pacific were proof that it had more troops and supplies to go on the offensive in Guadalcanal. On that island the 10,000-Marine force in August was increased to 23,000 by mid-October, and to 29,000 in November. The successful landings in North Africa on November 8 were sufficient proof that the United States could fight a two-front war.

Baldwin could feel pride and satisfaction that his reports about the Guadalcanal campaign had provoked a change in the Navy Department's censorship policy. He, along with Elmer Davis and others, believed that the timely release of accurate war information was the best defense against those in the military who would restrict war news to the public, and that the role of a free press meant that the public had a right to know of war news, good and bad. War was too important a public issue to be left to the arbitrary decisions of a few bureaucrats.

The *Times* management was grateful and pleased at the widespread popular approval for Baldwin's series. He was considered a rising star on the paper's roster of very talented journalists, and he would not disappoint his editors in the coming months and years of World War II.

CHAPTER 10

War and the 1943 Prize

Beginning in mid-March 1943, Baldwin traveled to Tunisia, and later to England. It was his second trip to the front lines and it lasted for almost eight weeks. He arrived a few weeks after the American defeat at the Kasserine Pass in February that led to the quick replacement of the U.S. II Corps commander, Major General Lloyd Fredendall, by General Eisenhower, who appointed Lieutenant General George S. Patton to instill discipline and the fighting spirit in the troops. On his return to New York, Baldwin wrote a twelve-part series that analyzed the strengths and weaknesses of the U.S. Army in its first combat with the battle-hardened German troops, finding more weaknesses than strengths.

The first attempt by Anglo-American forces to engage the Germans was in North Africa on November 8, 1942. Operation Torch landed Allied troops at three points, Casablanca, Oran, and Algiers, where they met varying degrees of resistance from local French units. It was hoped that the forces at Algiers would move quickly eastward to capture the Tunisian ports of Bone and Bizerte, but heavy rains on the only coast road and the swift arrival of German and Italian reinforcements pushed the Allied units westward toward Algiers.

Always complicated was the French political-military situation, which involved the collaborative Vichy government in France and the divided loyalties of French military leaders in North Africa. Prominent and controversial was Admiral Francois Darlan, the commander in chief of the armed forces of France. After intense negotiations with General Eisenhower and his staff, Admiral Darlan issued an armistice on November 10 that urged all French citizens in North Africa to aid the Anglo-American forces. Baldwin did not criticize the Darlan deal as others did. He urged Americans to bring about "a fusion" of the various French factions in order to "bring back the clarity of purpose to rid France—and eventually Europe of the 'fuehrer concept.'"[1]

Between November 1942 and January 1943 there was indecisive fighting. In late January 1943 General Rommel's panzer forces had reached the Mareth Line in southern Tunisia, a prewar defensive line built by the French to stop any Italian moves from Libya. In mid-February Rommel decided to split the Allied forces by moving against the green American II Corps at Faid, through the Kasserine Pass en route to Tebessa, the American supply depot. The attack, which began on February 19, was initially successful but British armor and American artillery reinforcements forced Rommel to withdraw to the Mareth Line.

During the German advance, an American battalion commanded by Lieutenant Colonel John Waters (the son-in-law of General George Patton) was overrun. When Baldwin interviewed Patton at his field headquarters of the II Corps, the fate of Waters was still in doubt. No one knew if he had been killed, wounded, or captured by the Germans. Baldwin had met Patton on previous occasions and had found him to be a "dynamic figure," but on this occasion, the general was "very down" and very emotional. He was concerned about how his daughter Beatrice would take the news: "There were tears in his eyes when he talked about Johnny [Waters] and I saw an entirely different side to the man than I'd seen before."[2] It was later learned that Colonel Waters had been taken prisoner.

While in North Africa, Baldwin took every opportunity to tour recent battle sites. With a jeep and driver, he visited El Guettar, Sbeitla, and the Kasserine Pass, where he looked down upon "the great gap in the hills" to observe the "flotsam and jetsam" of that battle. At Sbeitla, a town "blasted, ruined, smashed, fought over, lost and re-won, even the Arabs have gone," only the swollen bodies of dogs and cats remained, shot to prevent the spread of typhus.[3]

The only instance where he came under direct enemy mortar fire was at Beja, in the British sector, while traveling north to the U.S. II Corps area. Baldwin was traveling with a South African captain, who "first heard the faint rising whine" of incoming fire. They jumped into a roadside ditch, "noses in the earth, the hair faintly rising on the backs of our necks," looking back to see "the geysered earth behind," then another shell hit in front of them. The captain tried to be reassuring in remarking that "the whines you hear won't hurt you." They crawled down the ditch toward a culvert that was filled with "stinking water" and swarming with gnats and flies. The concrete culvert looked "like paradise" and there they sat until the shelling had stopped.[4]

To reach General Montgomery's headquarters near the southern Tunisian border with Libya, Baldwin flew in a small, British twin-engine plane, originally designed as a corporate plane. He arrived shortly after the Battle of the Mareth Line (March 20–26), which the British Eighth Army had just won, forcing the Germans to move north. On his first day in the British camp, a desert sandstorm arose. "I finally got to Monty's caravan, as he called it," Baldwin wrote, where a large picture of Rommel in full dress uniform adorned a wall. "The old boy deigned to see me," Baldwin wrote, but he started on the wrong foot by asking about Montgomery's tactics. "'My tactics? I won't divulge my tactics to anyone,'" he blustered, and the interview went downhill from there. According to Baldwin, Monty personalized everything; it was "my men," "my Army," and "my" everything else. He was not alone in his assessment of Monty as "an insufferable bore" with an "arrogant egocentrism."[5] His staff officers concurred. The outcome of the recent battle was not certain.

Baldwin then flew north to Algiers to interview General Eisenhower at his headquarters. By the time Baldwin saw Eisenhower, there was talk of his being relieved in light of the poor showing of American units at the Kasserine Pass, the Darlan deal, and his failure to agree on strategy with the British. Fortunately for him, he had strong backing from the key decision-makers in Washington, including President Roosevelt and General Marshall. Out of frustration Eisenhower told Baldwin that "he was the best damned lieutenant-colonel in the U.S. Army," which was his permanent rank. When British general Sir Harold R. L. Alexander was made commander of the newly created 18th Army Group that included American, British, and French units to fight the Axis in Tunisia, some thought it a slap at Eisenhower, but what set his temper off that day was the mention of Montgomery. As Baldwin described it, "I brought up the name of Monty and Eisenhower burst out with anger, 'Goddamit, I can deal with anybody except that son of a bitch.'"[6] At the time, Montgomery was pushing "as hard as he could to see how far he could get" with Churchill.[7] The issue of who was in charge, Eisenhower or Montgomery, finally came to a head in the autumn of 1944 when Churchill backed Eisenhower, as did Roosevelt.

Baldwin was very careful about keeping notes. The fewer the better, he thought, not only for security reasons, but for his reportorial pieces; once the notes had been used, they were discarded. For longer analytical articles, he kept only those notes from his field interviews needed to write a series of topical articles once he had returned to New York. He had an excellent memory that served him well throughout his career, so that extensive notes from an interview were not needed. There were times when what an interviewee said was less important than Baldwin's assessment of the person's personality and thinking.[8]

In typical style, Baldwin never attempted to gloss over the U.S. Army's difficulties in Tunisia in its first encounters with the more experienced German forces. He believed that mistakes made in combat were more instructive than victories, as the former taught what changes were needed immediately. Starting at the highest levels, he believed that coalition warfare was complicated by the differing strategies, national pride, and strong egos of senior officers. For example, once the Anglo-American forces landed at Algiers in November 1942, the commander of the British First Army wanted to move quickly eastward to Tunisia. To do this he asked (and Eisenhower agreed) to detach some elements of the American II Corps to enlarge the attacking force. At the time, Baldwin thought that Eisenhower had done "the right thing—the only thing, for the need was for speed—to Tunis and Bizerte." But upon reflection, he thought that Eisenhower had ignored the lesson of 1917 when General John J. Pershing demanded that American troops fight as a separate command and not as replacements in French and British units.[9] Aside from this early decision, Baldwin praised Eisenhower for his "two-fisted leadership" that solved many difficult problems.

According to Baldwin, the untested American troops suffered setbacks and hardships in spite of lessons that "should have been learned long ago."[10] For him, the sudden creation of a new Army by "a peace-loving nation that has never much bothered nor much cared about military knowledge" was the crux of the immediate problem of leadership.[11] Age was also an issue; junior officers and sergeants needed to develop into aggressive and competent leaders, and too many middle-ranking officers were "too old" and

On wartime assignment
Courtesy of the Baldwin Estate

overly cautious, making serious mistakes. Baldwin cited an incident where an entire antiaircraft gun crew had been killed because no one told them to dig in. In another incident, a small infantry unit awoke to find that the natives in the area had stolen their equipment during the night. The sergeant explained that his men were tired and needed their sleep, and no sentry was thought to be necessary.[12] It was complacency that really bothered Baldwin. While soldiers knew why they were fighting the Japanese, they did not know "what the shooting's all about" in Tunisia, and just wanted "to get this over with and get home quickly," lacking a political awareness that he noted in the British troops. He believed that Americans were quick learners and would not repeat their past mistakes, but they needed to learn discipline and develop a toughness of mind and spirit to face the future battles in Europe.

He also felt that specific problems needed to be corrected. Soldiers needed better recognition of airplanes and how to protect themselves against strafing planes and dive-bombers. They needed to know how to consolidate a position once taken to prepare for a counterattack by the enemy. Frontal assaults were used too often when attacks from the flanks in defilade position could have been more effective.[13] There seemed to be no end to his suggestions of what needed to be done, and done quickly.

Field commanders wanted an umbrella of American planes to protect their troops from German air attacks, as used early in the campaign, and they largely controlled the use of American air power. But with the hundreds of miles of front lines and thousands of troops to protect, there were not enough planes. The result was a dispersion of U.S. air forces, while the Luftwaffe could concentrate its attacks on American positions. On February 18 the American air arm was reorganized into the Tactical Air Force, whose mission was to attack the enemy's airfields, lines of supply, and ports, as well as enemy planes on the ground and in the air. U.S. planes were then concentrated over a specific battle area, rather than dispersed over the entire front, and Baldwin applauded this change.[14]

In summary, the Tunisian campaign was "a college in which none of the Allies made perfect marks," in hindsight, "a dress rehearsal" for future operations in Europe. American casualties were high in relation to the number of troops involved. The U.S. Army learned quickly from that bitter and "bloody" experience; they had used all green troops in the previous November but by May 1943, when German and Italian forces surrendered in Tunisia, the GIs had learned some valuable survival lessons.[15]

During his 22,000-mile trip, Baldwin talked with the commanders of the Allied forces, warning his readers that while Germany was badly hurt, it was not beaten: "She has lost the war, but we have not won it"[16] was a phrase that he would use again. Never giving his readers false hope, he stressed that the United States is "our own worst enemy" if it does not anticipate more bad news and discipline itself as a nation to acknowledge that the war was far from over. Citing unnamed sources, he predicted that the earliest date for victory in Europe would be the summer or fall of 1945, not 1944 as some had hoped.[17]

Baldwin flew later to London to interview Eighth Air Force officers on the air campaign against Germany, many of whom he had met previously on his trips to Washington. There he met with Major General James H.

Doolittle, who was soon to command the North Africa Strategic Air Force that became the Fifteenth Air Force in November 1943, and also he became friends with Air Vice Marshall John C. Slessor, the head of the RAF's Coastal Command. Baldwin also made it a point to talk with Admiral Harold Stark, the former CNO, who was sent to England in 1942 as a high-level liaison between British government leaders, the Royal Navy, and Washington.[18]

From this 1943 trip, Baldwin made a number of observations about the air war. He noted the need for long-range fighter escorts for the B-17 bombers that were increasingly vulnerable to Luftwaffe fighter attacks, for with their thirteen machine guns, the B-17s were not the "flying fortresses" many thought them to be. The P-51 Mustangs, with their Rolls Royce Merlin engines, became operational in December 1943 but did not begin to escort bombers to Berlin until March 1944.[19]

He thought the controversy about the relative merits of day and night bombing a "tempest in a teapot,"[20] and that strategic bombing was a war of attrition that would take time to be effective. It required many man-hours to repair factories or to relocate them, to build coastal fortifications, to repair the transportation network, all of which would put Germany's economy on "a descending and vicious spiral," with the civilian population suffering in many ways. Baldwin concluded correctly that there seemed, at the moment, "very little likelihood of German morale or economic collapse short of much greater Allied offensive victories than have yet occurred."[21] A cross-channel invasion of Europe would be a "tremendous" undertaking and require a "prodigious amount of preparation." Such a realistic and blunt assessment dashed the hopes of many Americans who hoped for an early end to the war.[22]

Shortly after his return to New York in late May 1943, Baldwin was awarded a Pulitzer Prize for his Guadalcanal series. The citation read, "For distinguished correspondence . . . the test being clearness and terseness of style, preference being given to fair, judicious, well-balanced and well informed interpretative writing."[23] Baldwin thought his Tunisian series was better written, with more detail than he had gained in his one-day visit to Guadalcanal. He later remarked that the problem with Pulitzer Prizes was that they were "geared to topical opinion and the sensational . . . and these series from the South Pacific came as a thunderclap to the American people. That's the only reason I got the prize really."[24]

As a result of this recognition, he was made a permanent member of the *Times* editorial board. He was also appointed the *Times* military editor, the first such editor for the paper, and a post he kept for the next twenty-five years. For the previous few years, he had been writing editorials on specific military topics. With this new appointment, he could and did write on broader political-military subjects. A year later, he was given a new office (a corner room, number 1024) on the tenth floor of the Times Building on West Forty-Third Street, where all the other editors had their offices.[25]

In the wake of publicity about his Pulitzer Prize, Baldwin was also hired by the Blue radio network to make fifteen-minute weekly broadcasts on Sunday afternoons. His first broadcast was on July 2, 1943. In reviewing his radio debut, *Time* magazine praised his coverage of military events for having "a clarity and detachment that contrasted with the bombast and theatrics of scores of commentators."[26] *Variety*, the trade paper for the entertainment industry, remarked that his voice, so important in radio broadcasting, was considered to be believable.[27] Those radio broadcasts greatly enlarged Baldwin's audience.[28]

The Blue network had a more "high brow" image than the Red network. It sponsored the Metropolitan Opera broadcasts and the NBC Symphony, conducted by the famed Arturo Toscanini, as well as public affairs programs such as the Town Hall Meeting of the Air. There, Baldwin was paid very well, better than his *Times* salary.[29]

After his successful Blue network radio broadcasts, the newsreel company Paramount News hired Baldwin for a special war review newsreel to be shown in seven hundred movie theaters on January 1, 1944, before a movie audience estimated to be 17 million.[30] With this exposure to a national audience, Baldwin only added to his already large readership and reputation, which he had always tried to convince the *Times* management would benefit the paper in the long run.

During the last six months of 1943, Sicily was invaded in July and Italy in September. The strategic bombing campaign by the U.S. Eighth Air Force and the RAF began in earnest, and there were great hopes for its ability to weaken Germany's ability to produce weapons. The RAF bombing of Hamburg, in late July, created a firestorm that devastated that ancient Baltic city. The American raid over Schweinfurt in October resulted in unacceptably high loss rates among the B-17s. In Russia, the huge tank battle at

Kurst in July did not bring the victory that Hitler had desired. From bases in North Africa, the American Twelfth Air Force's B-24 bombers made their first attempt, in early August, to hit the oil refineries at Ploesti, with Rumania supplying the needed fuel to all German forces.[31]

Writing copy about such varied events was not easy, and Baldwin's pieces on raids were sometimes thin. For example, he noted that while the Ploesti raid (August 1, 1943) was an excellent demonstration of strategic bombing of a key oil refinery needed by Germany, he did not reveal how many B-24 bombers took part, where their bases were located, how far from the target they had to travel, the size of their bomb loads, the strength of the German air defenses, and how many bombers failed to return (28 percent) to their home bases. It was perhaps too much to ask for such detailed military information to have been released to the public during the war, given the level of wartime censorship.[32] Baldwin's strength was to focus on the big strategic issues, such as the roles of air and sea power, the significance of the Italian invasion, the Central Pacific campaign, and the basis of the mutual suspicion between Russia and the West.

World War II gave the U.S. Army Air Corps a perfect opportunity to prove that air power could win the war, but Baldwin was not so sure that it could. As noted earlier, in a five-part series in late August 1943, he asserted that the strategic bombing campaigns of the U.S. Eighth Air Force and the RAF Bomber Command would not bring a quick victory, that the war of attrition would take time to be effective.[33] Air power might shorten the war and save lives, but, Baldwin asked, by how many months and how many lives would be saved?[34] The popular Douhet theory during the interwar years was that the bombing of war factories and cities would weaken the will of the civilian population. However, Baldwin thought it impossible to measure the public's morale in wartime. He raised the question about how many bombs would be needed to achieve victory. "The waging of war is not an exact science; it is an art," he wrote.[35]

Baldwin rejected the boast of Air Marshal Arthur Harris, the head of the RAF Bomber Command, that with one thousand bombers every night, the war would be over by the autumn of 1943. The RAF flew night missions with entire cities as targets, while the Americans bombed specific targets in the daytime, and he noted that in the U.S. Eighth Air Force bombing campaign, only in one raid out of three did the bombs hit the intended target.[36]

To Baldwin's thinking, the American bombing campaign could only be periodic and cyclical because of the winter weather conditions in northern Europe and the endurance of the bomber crews and the flying condition of their bombers.[37] He saw no evidence that the Wehrmacht had a shortage of weapons, or that the Luftwaffe was short of fighter planes, concluding that the "quickest and most immediate results against Germany . . . are being achieved at the fighting front—in the air and on the ground—not by the strategic bombardment of the home front."[38] He often spoke of the team effort necessary among all the armed services, not one service declaring that it would bring a final victory.

The invasion of Italy in September 1943 was slow going due to the German resistance, the mountainous terrain, supply problems, and the winter weather. The fall of Mussolini's government in July 1943 and the reinforcements of German troops into northern Italy meant that the Italian campaign would be drawn out. In November 1943 the plans for an invasion of western Europe being discussed in the press meant that Italy would become a secondary front. The Italian campaign permitted Allied airfields to be constructed closer to Germany, as well as allowing German divisions that could be deployed elsewhere to be held in Italy, and those were reasons to continue that slogging campaign.[39]

At the Quebec Conference in mid-August 1943, Roosevelt and Churchill were aware of Stalin's growing suspicions of the reasons for the repeated postponements of the opening of a second front in western Europe in 1943. The subsequent Moscow Conference in October 1943 relieved many of Stalin's suspicions. Baldwin, who was no admirer of Stalin and his regime, noted that Russia's postwar plans were to annex the Baltic states, including eastern Poland, parts of Finland, and possibly northern Iran. He reviewed the continuing difficulties of the American efforts to communicate with the Soviets and Soviet unwillingness to appreciate what the United States had done to help them, especially with the bombing campaign over Germany, citing the Ploesti raid and how it would have shortened the flight time and increased the bomb load over the target had those bombers been based in Russia.

Baldwin concluded that Russia was a land power that considered the sea and air to be of subsidiary importance, while the Allies considered them to be of major importance. According to him, Russia had "no conception of sea warfare, nor of the immense meaning, in term of logistics, or sheer effort of the war in the Pacific."[40] He commented that there was no mutual understanding at present.

To Baldwin the "big reason" for Russian suspicion was "the Communist credo itself, and the record of double-dealing that the credo expressed in practical politics, has written in history."[41] While the Soviets did not forget American intervention in their civil war in 1919, the United States now could not forget the Nazi-Soviet Pact of August 1939 that permitted Hitler to move east.

As an alumnus of the U.S. Naval Academy, Baldwin was well schooled in the importance of sea power. For him, the lesson of the war was that the ship-plane team gave that combined force the mobility to choose the point of attack.[42] The surface ship remained the most important means of transport of needed materials. The bombing of Germany depended upon the surface ships for its fuel, bombs, armaments, construction equipment to build airfields, and many other needed supplies. "In other words," he summarized, "the 300 mile-an-hour plane is still tied strategically to the 14-knot ship."[43] Modern sea power, the ship-plane team, had the asset of mobility, and the ability to choose the place of attack. Confidently he wrote that the war had "proved the validity of sea power beyond a doubt."[44]

In October 1943 Baldwin reviewed U.S. victories in the Pacific since 1942, when the United States had been on the defensive (Midway, Coral Sea, and the Aleutians), and outpost victories in the Solomons and New Guinea. He speculated that a major offensive in the Pacific would occur, reviewing various approaches to Japan. He rejected General MacArthur's plan to bypass some Japanese-held bases to invade Mindanao, in the Philippines, as being "a grave risk" from enemy forces on our flanks. The overland move from India, Burma, and Malaya to China would have had the same problems of jungle, disease, terrain, and supply. He rejected the idea of those who thought that Japan could be bombed from China, because a bombing campaign alone would not defeat Japan; only a land invasion would bring victory. He thought that if Russia permitted our bombers to be based near Vladivostok it would "materially hasten victory," but he dismissed the idea as being "unlikely."[45]

To Baldwin's thinking, the Central Pacific route would be the shortest and the most direct route to the Japanese home islands. It would give the United States maximum advantage of its air-sea "superiority" in the Pacific and be quicker than slogging through the jungles of the southwest Pacific. An astute reader may have detected Baldwin's pro-Navy bias in his comments on that campaign.

On the eve of the U.S. Marine assault on Tarawa, an atoll in the Gilbert island chain, Baldwin wrote about four atolls in the Central Pacific and noted the strategic importance of each. They were all low, sandy islands with little vegetation, fringing coral reefs, and land crabs.[46] Whether or not he had been tipped off by Admiral Horne on the Navy's next invasion is not known, but his piece gave considerable information, including maps of the islands, their geographic location, their description, and the level of Japanese defenses on each, calling them the "outer shield" of Japan's "vast empire."

The Central Pacific campaign began on November 20, 1943, with the invasion of Tarawa, and it taught many harsh lessons. Baldwin was short on the details of the invasion, but he urged his readers to be prepared "to pay the price in blood, as land armies swarm ashore to take the soil we must have if we are to win this war."[47] As always, he was eager to prepare his readers for future sacrifices, when what they preferred to read about was an easy victory for U.S. Marines.

A *Times* editorial, most likely written by Baldwin, rejected the once-popular view of the late British naval affairs writer, Hector C. Bywater, that the next war in the Pacific would end quickly in one big naval battle. Baldwin commented that the current war was a total war for unconditional surrender of the enemy, not a limited war for limited ends. Given the view that the Japanese army saw its navy as an auxiliary force to maintain the lines of communication within its empire, Baldwin did not think a big naval battle would occur.[48]

Never afraid to state his views, Baldwin considered them a means to make his readers think about popular assumptions. For example, in August 1943, he challenged the popular belief that once Germany had been defeated China could be transformed into an unsinkable aircraft carrier from which to bomb Japan into submission. That notion assumed that the Chinese army, under the leadership of Chiang Kai-shek, would be able to secure such air bases. Baldwin thought that China's military strengths had been oversold to America during the war by extolling its presumed victories against the Japanese and omitting its serious military weaknesses. To his thinking, China was not a country but a "geographic expression." Its forces had been losing battles. It had no real army; its troops were poorly lead, and poorly equipped. Discipline was lax. It had few artillery pieces and fewer tanks. Its ammunition stocks were low. Keeping China supplied would prove an enormous problem, as the Burma Road alone could not support a ground army.[49]

Baldwin concluded that the Japanese "citadel" had to be attacked from many directions on land and sea, and that "the chief burden of victory in the Pacific rests upon [America] alone."[50] When this harsh yet realistic assessment of China's value to the Allies was brought to the attention of Cordell Hull, the secretary of state, he contacted Henry L. Stimson, the secretary of war. He thought that Baldwin's sources were "high-ranking officers in Washington" and he promised to investigate the matter. Stimson was concerned about the effect of Baldwin's words on U.S.-Chinese relations. He wanted criticism to be directed at Baldwin and away from the War Department, "whose policy of mutual respect and cooperation is too well known to responsible Chinese leaders to be placed in jeopardy" by the "disturbing" statements of a "single commentator."[51] Baldwin's words also upset the powers-that-be at the *Times*. On three different occasions in 1943, a flurry of interoffice memoranda brought a rebuke from the publisher, but he suffered no serious consequences.

The Cairo Declaration (December 1943) summarized the agreements reached between Roosevelt, Churchill, and Chiang Kai-shek on the future of Japan. The terms stated that it would be stripped of all its islands in the Pacific seized after August 1914, as well as all territories stolen from China, including Manchuria, Formosa, and the Pecadores. Korea would be free, and eventually it would be an independent country. Those goals would be met only after Japan's unconditional surrender.

In his analysis, Baldwin questioned the wisdom of telegraphing the Allies' intentions at that time, since Japan now knew "the drastic fate" that would ensue if it lost the war, and that, furthermore, the Declaration would make the Japanese "angry and [would] increase their will to fight [if] they can see no possible 'out' in surrender." He added that the agreements reached at Cairo were "likely to be more of a handicap than help to [the U.S.] Pacific war."[52]

Charles Merz, the *Times* editorial page editor, complained to the publisher about Baldwin's comment that the leaders at Cairo "pulled a boner in the field of political decision."[53] The managing editor, E. L. James, felt that Baldwin should stick to military events and not broaden his analysis to include political opinion more suited for the editorial page. Sulzberger advised James to warn Baldwin about his "blunders" into political matters and to advise him that he "watch out in the future" for such forays.[54]

But, as in the past, Baldwin would not listen. In an article on Russia's wartime intentions, he announced that its army was an "armed hoard" and that Russia's "territorial ambitions would include parts of Finland, the Baltic States, eastern Poland, and Bessarabia," prompting Merz to alert the publisher that Baldwin was again making political judgments that ought to be on the editorial page.[55]

The theme of unnecessary secrecy in government continued to rouse Baldwin's ire. The communiqué from the Teheran Conference (November 28–December 1, 1943) displeased Baldwin for its secrecy, which could only help Germany to spread rumors about what was agreed to by Roosevelt, Churchill, and Stalin. "The policy of secret agreements secretly arrived at bodes no good for the future hopes of the world," he wrote.[56] In what sounded like a paraphrase of Woodrow Wilson's 1919 comments, Baldwin declared that the government's public relations policy ought "to be based on swift truth" and be "ahead of the enemy, not behind him." This was Baldwin's old contention that information that the enemy already had should not be withheld from the American people.[57]

The managing editor's tolerance for Baldwin's political commentary was wearing thin. He strongly advised him to avoid political subjects and, speaking for others at the *Times*, he said: "you ought to stick to military and naval matters."[58] Sulzberger admitted in a note to Baldwin that there was "a border line" between the editorial pages and the military editor's purview that is "difficult to determine." That said, the publisher took issue with Baldwin's opinion about secrecy in wartime, expressing the belief that "a certain amount of secrecy has to be maintained in times like these."[59]

In his own defense, Baldwin pointed to his earlier articles on Tunisia and Yugoslavia, which clearly dealt with the political context of the military situation in those countries. No one had objected then, he said, assuming that some at the *Times* had chosen to criticize him anonymously. As if to prove his point about how indivisible military and political aspects of the war were, he informed James that during a recent trip to Washington he had learned from "a prominent man" how Stalin had "dominated" the Teheran discussions. Baldwin's source had read the minutes of the conference and told him of Stalin's "ruthless realism [that] so punctured some of Churchill's oratorical phrases as to make it almost humiliating."[60] To Baldwin, this brief report only reinforced his long-held view that political and economic factors could and did influence military events, despite what the *Times* management might think. It was an issue that was never resolved in the years ahead.[61]

Complicating the issue of the content of Baldwin's *New York Times* articles was an attractive offer he received from *Newsweek* magazine's publisher, Malcolm Muir. The offer would double Baldwin's *Times* salary, reduce the number and frequency of articles, and give him the option to either write under his own name or use a pseudonym. *Newsweek* wanted to enlarge its coverage of international affairs, and this change would give Baldwin an opportunity to expand his military focus to encompass broader political and economic issues. Sulzberger was kept informed of these negotiations.[62] Baldwin was of two minds. The *Newsweek* offer was very attractive; in fact the magazine courted him for eleven months.[63] Yet he felt grateful to the Sulzberger family, whose paper had given him a first-rate forum. While other military commentators, such as Major George Fielding Eliot, cited political and economic issues in their columns, Baldwin could not forget that his readers admired him for being a "temperate and conservative writer" whose frank assessment of the military situation enhanced his growing public reputation.[64] The December flap ended when he turned down the *Newsweek* offer in the hope that his *Times* salary would be increased. It was.[65]

CHAPTER 11

Total War, 1944

Six months before D-day in 1944, Baldwin lamented that after two years of combat operations, there was still "abundant evidence that U.S. fighting services [had] not . . . shaken off the dead hand of traditionalism."[1] He deplored the red tape and the conservatism that had delayed the development of new weapons. He also considered American land tactics unimaginative, and that only successful German use of rockets on the battlefield had changed former U.S. reluctance to use that weapon. Tactically, Americans swung back and forth. After the German blitzkrieg in 1940, the United States had emphasized tanks and mechanized equipment at the expense of the artillery-infantry-engineer team. In 1943 the lessons of North Africa, Sicily, and Italy led to de-emphasizing the importance of the tank while the infantry-artillery team was praised.

He suggested that the United States study the "greatest military laboratory of all history—the Russian front." Both the Germans and the Russians used a large number of tanks, mobile guns, infantry, combat engineers, and massed artillery. Defensive positions were in depth, not linear. In sharp contrast to the Germans and Russians, American troops received no such training. U.S. tactics were "primarily" those of infantry backed by artillery, and U.S. defenses were linear. Baldwin felt we should develop self-propelled guns and larger tanks to match the German "Tiger" tank. There was still time to correct those deficiencies before the invasion of western Europe began. "There is still a war to be won," he reminded his readers; "We must plan to fight the battles of tomorrow with new tactics and new techniques."[2]

A letter he received from an army corporal, who had not been overseas, enlightened Baldwin about the "lack of conviction" in the U.S. Army that resulted in the U.S. soldiers doing "as little as he possibly [could]." Officers relied on sergeants to get their work done, and their prevailing concern was to win extra stripes and bars. Army orientation programs focused more on how evil the enemy was than on what combat experience was really like, and what soldiers needed to know to survive.[3]

In response to his earlier piece on army weapons and tactics, some suggested that armored units needed infantry and artillery support and that until now those units had not been trained to work together. In other words, Baldwin concluded, "It is still the fighting team that wins battles." The U.S. Army had not yet developed the tactical flexibility or coordinated power that American mechanical ingenuity could make possible, he commented.[4]

Getting to the bottom of the Army's personnel problems, Baldwin commented that poor leadership was "the major cause" of its low morale and ineffective training and tactics.[5] While there were some effective officers, there were also "far too many without the professional or moral qualifications of leadership."[6] Junior officers, especially, were too focused on their personal advancement, as measured by decorations and service ribbons. They were "yes-men" who curried favor with those who could favor them, rather than demonstrating initiative and leadership. To Baldwin, the "one absolutely indispensable requirement of leadership [was the] care of their men."[7] Morale created a desire to defeat the enemy that represents "the forces of evil."[8] With the invasion of western Europe in the offing, Baldwin urged that the unfit and inefficient officers be replaced."[9]

Prior to his leaving for England in early May 1944, Baldwin wrote a series of ten pieces for the *Times* that detailed many of the real problems to a cross-channel invasion, which, he wrote, was "as certain as anything human can be."[10] He assumed that the Luftwaffe would be a serious problem to the invasion forces. It wasn't. He dismissed the effectiveness of local civilian resistance groups as being of little value: "It is easy in war time," he noted, "to exaggerate the effects of sabotage and of guerrilla warfare."[11] He also dismissed the value of local police forces to aid any resistance effort, as they were filled with Nazi collaborators at all levels.[12] We know now that the French resistance was well organized and was effective in many ways to delay German reinforcements from reaching the invasion beaches. Baldwin also assumed correctly that the Germans would have strewn all possible landing beaches with pillboxes, beach obstructions, and mines.

He cited a number of coastlines from Scandinavia south to France, but very few had beaches that would be suitable because of natural barriers. He also described the suitability of many ports from Denmark to France, their port facilities, tidal currents, and water depths at both low and high tides. It is difficult to believe that he thought that the Allied forces would be able to offload troops and their supplies at dockside.[13] Without meaning to, Baldwin's assessment of the formidable natural and manmade obstacles to any cross-channel invasion made his readers assume the whole operation to be a mission impossible. Allied success could not be guaranteed.

General Eisenhower's headquarters, as well as the Allied command, had been studying all those obstacles for months and had devised a number of deceptions and stratagems to convince Hitler and his generals that the invasion would be at the Pas de Calais, a point only twenty miles from England. So successful were those plans that many of Hitler's generals believed that the Pas de Calais would be the landing site.[14]

Not wishing to miss anything for the long-anticipated cross-channel invasion, Baldwin left New York Harbor on Wednesday, May 3, 1944, on board a new escort carrier.[15] The ship sailed alone, at reasonably high speed, and did not encounter any U-boats, that menace having been reduced a year before. Discipline on board was lax. Baldwin was appalled that on one occasion the officer of the deck downed six whiskies, while flirting with one of the women passengers, just before going on duty. "By guess and by God" the ship reached Liverpool on May 15.[16]

Once ashore, he dealt with the red tape of getting his accreditation as a war correspondent, drawing a gas mask, protective clothing, helmet, and a correspondent's uniform that consisted of an officer's pink trousers, olive tunic with the letter "C" on the shoulder, and a brassard (insignia) on the sleeve.[17] In 1944 the *Times* offices in London were temporarily located in the Savoy Hotel, just off The Strand, as their Fleet Street offices had been bombed earlier in the war.[18] Baldwin got right to work. He interviewed Lieutenant General Omar N. Bradley, the commander of the U.S. First Army, at his office in London, and later he traveled to Bristol to speak with Bradley's First Army staff. He also met Lieutenant John Mason Brown, USNR, who was the public relations officer for Rear Admiral Alan G. Kirk, the commander of all U.S. naval forces in the invasion fleet. Brown was better known before the war as a New York theater critic and essayist.

Baldwin requested accreditation to the USS *Augusta* (CA 31), a heavy cruiser that was to be Admiral Kirk's flagship and General Bradley's headquarters when the invasion began. Only three reporters received that coveted assignment, a magazine writer and photographer, a radio correspondent, and Baldwin.[19] It seemed to Baldwin that he had received an ideal assignment for a newspaper reporter: to be on the flagship during the major invasion of western Europe, but it did not work out as he had hoped.

On Monday, May 22, the press representatives in London were told to report at the Admiralty Arch on the Mall, with all their gear ready to go to their assigned ports of embarkation. They soon learned that it was to be a dry run to test the facilities to transport such a large number of the press to their assigned ports along the southern coast of England. Baldwin's group was sent to Fowey in Cornwall. In happier days, it was a popular vacation destination, but now the port was filled with American-made landing crafts (LCI). In the afternoon Baldwin and his group visited the home of the famed novelist Daphne du Maurier, the author of the popular gothic romance *Rebecca* that had been made into a well-received movie in 1939. Her husband was Lieutenant General Frederick Arthur Montague Browning, who commanded Britain's paratroops during the war.[20] The author's seventy-room mansion, Menabilly, served as the model for "Manderley," the great brooding house for the novel that overlooked the sea. The setting gave Baldwin a "sense of hidden dread, prayerful hope and controlled suspense" that characterized Britain before D-day. After tea with the young and charming author, her three children, and her mother, the guests headed back to London to await the real alert.

On Saturday, June 3, 1944, Baldwin arrived in the late afternoon at Plymouth Harbor and boarded the flagship USS *Augusta* (CA 31). At 5:30 p.m., the cruiser moved to the outer anchorage of the harbor to await further orders. During the twilight hours, he recalled the beauty of the almost-full moon over the harbor, the hills "gleaming golden in the daylight," and the many barrage balloons overhead.[21]

That evening, General Bradley and other senior commanders on board the flagship briefed Baldwin and the other two journalists about the invasion plans, the sites for the landings, and the German targets once the beaches had been secured. Bradley told Baldwin that he expected heavy American casualties on Utah and Omaha beaches and that the American airborne troops, who would land behind German lines hours before the beaches were invaded, were "sacrificial troops."[22] D-day was planned for Monday, June 5. On the previous day, when much of the invasion fleet was already at sea, those on the *Augusta* learned after breakfast that poor weather had forced the postponement of the invasion to the following day, June 6.

On the eve of the largest amphibious operation in history, the singular most important event in the long European war, Hanson Baldwin found the means to send a cable to his wife, Helen, reminding her that he had not forgotten their thirteenth wedding anniversary. Most likely, he had made prior arrangements with Ray Daniell at the *New York Times* London office. The cable read: "for Baldwin's anniversary wishes wife know she unforgotten. He leaves it to you (the New York office)." He did have a romantic aspect to his normally formal personality, and he never forgot what was really important in his life, despite momentary distractions.[23]

During June 5 Baldwin spoke with others on board, including John Mason Brown and Lieutenant McGeorge Bundy, then an Army liaison officer to General Bradley and his staff. The First Army command post was on the ship's main deck.[24] That night, shortly after dinner, a radio Teletype message announced that the invasion of France had started. It was a false message that had originated in New York, not in Europe. Years later, Baldwin recalled the "awful outrage" this false report made on the *Augusta*. It was an outrage that months of planning and long weeks of tension and the prevailing "sense of ominous dread and foreboding" that underlay all their thinking was for naught.[25] German propaganda, for months, had been stressing how well fortified the Atlantic Wall was, with all sorts of obstacles and devices to make a Normandy landing seem to be impregnable to any attack.[26] On June 5 the *Augusta*, together with hundreds of ships, left Plymouth Harbor heading south, then east.[27]

Early on the morning of June 6, Baldwin heard the sound of aircraft engines high above them as bombers and troop carriers were en route to France. At 3:35 a.m. the ship's crew was ordered to their battle stations. Steel helmets were put on as well as Mae West life belts, which when inflated, assumed the shape of that famous movie star. The ship was "buttoned up"—all watertight doors and hatches closed. At 5:35 a.m., Baldwin's notes recorded, the *Augusta's* main battery of nine 8-inch guns opened fire on the Normandy shore, 12,000 yards distant. It was the signal for the other 359 ships in the huge invasion fleet to begin their general barrage on German shore installations.

Baldwin climbed the ladder that led to a portion of the bridge where Lieutenant Brown was giving his running commentary over the loudspeakers to the ship's company belowdecks. As the flagship the *Augusta* had no permanent anchorage, but moved about the fleet. Occasionally the wreckage of landing craft floated by as well as the flotsam and jetsam of the invasion, including an occasional corpse.

The main worry of the commanders on the flagship was the absence of current information from Utah and Omaha beaches. General Bradley was heard by Baldwin to remark often, "What's going on?" Baldwin later wrote that there was "a sort of ordered chaos, if indeed it was ordered."[28] By midafternoon on June 6, rumors of tough going were all that Bradley had heard.[29]

Knowing that this event was of great importance to many people, and that he was the only print journalist on the flagship, Baldwin filed many reports as information came in. Much to his dismay, he learned on June 7 that all of his dispatches had been lost. The overall naval commander of the Allied invasion fleet was Admiral Sir Bertram S. Ramsey, RN. That naval service had the responsibility for all press arrangements, including arrangements for naval correspondents. In practice, this meant that all news copy was put on board many small steam boats, pinnaces, which would go among the ships of the fleet, collect their mail, then cross the Channel to England. There the messages would be transmitted by wire to London, and later distributed to individual newspapers or cabled to the United States.[30]

The storm that began on June 7 proved too strong for those little boats, and many were sunk. Baldwin learned that his dispatches were never received in New York, or were garbled, or arrived too late to be of any news value. "My grandstand seat proved to be up in the bleachers, far in left field," he later recalled.[31] His dispatches had been given the "Nelson touch," a phrase that referred to the outmoded and outdated system of news distribution still practiced by the Royal Navy since the days of Lord Nelson in the eighteenth century. A week after D-day the problem eased somewhat, but while he was on board the *Augusta* all his dispatches were delayed by at least two days.

He desperately wanted to go ashore to see for himself what had happened. Rear Admiral Arthur Dewey Struble, Kirk's chief of staff, made it very clear to Baldwin that his credentials were only for the Navy, not the Army. He protested in vain but the Navy bureaucracy won the argument. However, on D-day plus three, Admiral Kirk, General Bradley, and Admiral John Leslie Hall (in charge of supplies) went ashore on Omaha beach to find out for themselves why the Army was complaining that the Navy was not delivering the needed supplies, and Baldwin hitched a ride with them.

On Omaha beach, Baldwin remembered "the stench of oil, burnt rubber, and of dead men."[32] He heard Bradley say, "God damn it! I don't care what the reasons are, I want those supplies." Baldwin never forgot that scene. The contrast between the loud demanding words of those officers, and the rows of dead GI's, whose boots stuck out from beneath their ponchos, was an image that Baldwin could not rid himself of. On June 18, after eleven days on board the *Augusta*, he returned to London to be accredited to the British and American armies, then located in France. He was very disappointed to learn that so few of his invasion pieces had been received in New York, but knew that it was just another inconvenience of war.

The publicity that he had enjoyed from his two previous overseas trips, Guadalcanal in 1942 and Tunisia in 1943, would not be repeated in 1944. By then, a large number of war correspondents in print journalism and in radio broadcasting made the field a crowded one. He could take comfort from his excellent news sources and his extensive knowledge that gave him the confidence to try to make sense out of the confusion of war. Baldwin's early positive assessment of General Eisenhower was based on his decision to postpone the invasion of the Normandy coast by twenty-four hours; to Baldwin, it took "moral courage and decisiveness." It was not to be Eisenhower's only major decision in the months ahead.[33]

Baldwin's return to London coincided with Germany's V-1 "buzz bomb" attacks on the city. The loud droning sound of that flying bomb was unmistakable, and when the noise stopped it fell quickly to earth and exploded. His room at the Savoy Hotel was on the top floor, which was very unnerving as his description shows: "The things sounded like they were flying right in my window and I used to pull the covers over my head at night and try to forget them."[34]

The V-1 could be shot down by ground fire and from airplanes. However, the V-2 rocket was too fast in its plummet to earth to be destroyed in the air. He wrote about those two new weapons only after he had returned to New York in August 1944. He concluded that they would not win the war for Germany or alter its duration or course, though the bombs did make a psychological impression on everyone. They were an early example of the "mechanistic" warfare of the future. He called it a "Wellsian" form of modern war, after the well-known science fiction writer of the time, H. G. Wells.[35] He was also able to inspect one of the captured launch sites on the Cotentin peninsula in France. The V-1 was controlled internally by two gyrocompasses, but otherwise where it hit was more or less up to chance. His comments on the V-2 rocket touched a "live nerve" in British intelligence because of his ballistic details. They wanted no information released that would alert the Germans as to its accuracy or the damage it had inflicted.[36] As usual, this polite advice did not stop him from writing other articles on the V-2.[37]

After a brief time in London, Baldwin, now accredited to both the British and American armies, returned to France on a PT boat. One of the more interesting anecdotes he collected was about a fellow passenger, Ernie Pyle, the well-known, popular American war correspondent, who was very short. The boat landed near Omaha beach in shallow water. When Pyle jumped overboard with his Army duffle bag he was almost submerged, but the six-foot-two-inch Baldwin came to his immediate rescue and carried both of their bags ashore without further incident.[38]

Baldwin then visited the British sector at Bayeux. The British were supposed to have taken Caen in June, but stiff German resistance postponed the inevitable until July 13. While in the British sector, Baldwin was assigned a British lord to escort him. On one occasion, all correspondents in the British sector were called to a press conference held by Field Marshall Bernard L. Montgomery. At the time, he was the commander of all Allied ground forces, until General Eisenhower moved his headquarters and assumed direct command of those forces on September 1. After all had been assembled (Baldwin was the only American present), the stage was set. Monty's bull pups, called "Rommel" and "Rundstedt," appeared, and they were soon followed by Monty himself, "His Most High Majesty," who emerged from his tent wearing a black beret, a turtleneck sweater, and slacks. Baldwin took no notes, as the great man said nothing that was noteworthy. He personalized the campaign as his own. Members of the British press were respectful in his presence but made less than flattering comments among themselves. Baldwin's sarcastic opinion of Montgomery reflected an American view at the time about his failure to take Caen, as promised, while the Americans were bogged down in the hedgerow country near St.-Lô.

Accompanied by his escort, Baldwin visited the American lines near St.-Lô and spoke with General Bradley and with Major General J. Lawton Collins, who commanded the V11 Corps. As Baldwin approached Bradley shouted, "Hey, Baldwin," and motioned for him to join them. After a rather long conversation on the military situation, Baldwin's British escort commented later to Baldwin's amusement, "I say, your chaps are frightfully informal, aren't they?"[39]

Baldwin also observed the beginning of Operation Cobra (July 25), the carpet bombing west of St.-Lô. He went to a high point to better observe it. "We saw the bombing start out. At first, we just heard a rumble and saw some flashes in the distance . . . and pretty soon the whole scene was absolutely obscured."[40] Soon the bombs began to approach the American front lines, and one of the Air Force generals present stopped the bombing before it hit U.S. troops.

Continuing his tour of the American units in France in June and July 1944, Baldwin met General Manton Sprague Eddy, then in command of the 9th Infantry Division, whom he had known before the war. While the general spoke to the group of correspondents, there was a burst of gunfire in a nearby field. As Manton excused himself, he suggested that they have a martini while he was gone. As Baldwin described it, "He had his batman bring out the most perfectly chilled martinis in a silver pitcher with little silver glasses."[41] The general soon returned, remarking that the nearby Germans had tried to make a counterattack but had failed. Baldwin used the incident as an example of the general's "imperturbable" manner.

A week before he returned to New York, he summarized the Normandy campaign to date. Weather, terrain (hedgerows), and German resistance were mitigating factors to explain the slowness of the American advances after the D-day landings. The hedgerows were easy to defend, but very difficult to attack. The sunken roads made the embankments twelve feet high. Visibility was limited to 75 to 150 yards. In the two weeks during which Baldwin visited the U.S. First Army on the Cotentin peninsula, it was sunny for only two days. He acknowledged the German Tiger and Panther tanks, as well as their 88-mm gun, so effective against the American Sherman and the British Cromwell tanks. He found fault with the "slogging footpace" of the American advance in Normandy. He found no evidence that Germany's leaders were ready to quit, as the SS units would stop that. Baldwin optimistically and presciently anticipated the eventual breakthrough in Normandy that would begin in late July 1944, but he concluded wearily, "We are a long way from Paris."[42]

General Bradley, who commanded the U.S. 12th Army Group, told General Patton, who commanded the U.S. Third Army, to "let her rip" after Coutances fell on July 28, and to pursue the retreating German forces. To Baldwin, Patton was a "hard riding, hard-swearing cavalryman" whose personality was in complete contrast to that of Bradley, a "quiet, simple, common-sense American," but he felt that together they were "a good team, and they [had] given [the U.S.] victory."[43]

After almost three months in Europe, Baldwin returned to New York in early August to catch up with the war in the Pacific. That was to be the last of his three trips to the front lines. Those trips helped to blunt any criticism that he was just another armchair commentator, isolated and safe from the horrors of war in his New York office, and gave him firsthand background information for future articles.

The liberation of Paris on August 25, 1944, gave rise to the hope that the war's end was in sight. Baldwin was momentarily caught up in such hopes, but cautioned that to date no German army had been routed or shown any signs of a lack of willingness to fight. The V-1 and V-2 rockets indicated that Hitler might have other secret weapons to use against the Allies, including an "atomic explosive or something of a similar order of frightfulness." While the Third Reich was doomed, he wrote, "the rout and destruction of Hitler's armies must be completed."[44]

He wrote of the successful use by the American First Army of mobile loudspeaker trucks at Cherbourg to broadcast to German front line troops that they were cut off from their main army in France and should surrender. This combat propaganda also distributed leaflets from planes and artillery shells. Almost 40 percent of German prisoners taken at Cherbourg had one or more of these leaflets in their pockets, although German military regulations forbad keeping them. While this psychological warfare program was promising, Baldwin cautioned, "You cannot win victories with words unless you also win victories with guns."[45]

More important was the need to take and clear the German–held ports in France and in Belgium. As the Allied armies moved north and east, their supply lines lengthened from the Normandy beaches. Baldwin analyzed thirteen ports in France, Holland, and Belgium as to their capacity and whether they were still in German hands, or if not, what repairs were needed to put them back in use. Antwerp, a major port city, was captured by the British in early September 1944, but its approaches were still in German hands. The port was not cleared and opened for Allied use until late November. While the Germans wanted to lengthen the war, they needed time, and time is what the Allies' repeated attacks did not give them.[46]

The British attempt, in mid-September, failed to take and to hold Arnhem, Holland. Had it been successful, the way would have been opened for a major Allied drive across the "slightly rolling north German plain" that would lead eventually to Berlin. Baldwin's initial account of Operation Market Garden was light on operations, using such phrases as "the issue is in doubt," or that news was "sparse."[47] His main source was the British Information Service in New York City. In hindsight, he praised the British paratroopers' ability to "punch" a forty-five-mile salient into the German line and to cross three important rivers guarding the German northern flank. Baldwin concluded that the German victory at Arnhem had only "won a delay in the Battle of Time."[48]

The Italian campaign was a "shoestring" operation, Baldwin declared. As the Allied plans to invade southern France and western Europe developed in 1943, American units were withdrawn from Italy with the result that some infantry units had no relief, and when they were relieved, "weary men [were] relieved by other weary men."[49]

The siege of Monte Cassino, in March 1944, proved that air power alone could not dislodge the German defenders. Baldwin thought the bombing campaign could have been better directed against German communications lines, their supply routes, and their artillery positions, rather than destroying a historic mountain abbey. American tanks, with infantry and mobile self-propelled guns, could have targeted the German anti-tank and machine-gun positions, rather than the area bombardment that often blocked the roads to the Liri valley with rubble.[50]

The big picture was that the Italian campaign was of secondary importance to the invasion plans of western Europe. The slow progress of the Italian campaign was because of the strategy of trying to win battles "with the smallest possible number of ground troops." There were other factors: poor leadership and the weak liaison among the many Allied units that included British, American, French, and Polish forces that "required much improvement." However, those forces in Italy forced the Germans to keep twenty to twenty-one divisions in southern Italy, with perhaps another three to eight divisions in the north. The fact that Germany could not stop the Anzio landing (January 1944) showed Baldwin that its forces were spread thin, and those German reinforcements were needed in western Europe.[51]

Six months after the Normandy landing, Baldwin called Italy the "Forgotten Front." The liberation of Rome in June 1944 was followed by the slow march northwest to the Po River Valley. He reviewed critically the British plan (Churchill's) to invade the Balkans to force a back-door entry into Austria. He rejected the idea that Italy was a pointless campaign. "Strategy in modern war," he commented, "sometimes is influenced by 'pressure groups' just as legislation in Congress is similarly affected."

Allied victories in Italy had been won the hard way, "by a foot-slogging advance up the unending range of the Apennines instead of a series of out-flanking amphibious advances by sea."[52] But as a result of this effort Italy left the war, Rome was liberated, the Italian navy joined the Allied side, and American air bases were now closer to German-occupied Europe. Also, local guerrilla forces were able to provide "a spring board" for small-scale political-military operations by the British in Greece and in Yugoslavia.[53]

Two weeks before Germany's second Ardennes offensive began on December 16, 1944 (the first was in 1940), Baldwin observed in his frank way that thus far in the war, there had been no "breakthrough" or "smashing" victories in Europe or in the Pacific. "In other words, there is still a war to be won; battles of decision still to be fought, and a bloody and, probably, a long road [that] still lies ahead."[54]

However, in spite of Baldwin's cautions, the American public, buoyed up by the summer successes in Europe and by the early reports of the U.S. Philippine campaign, came to believe that the war's end was near. The public must "settle back into the rough groove of war," he wrote. This tide of optimism was fueled, in part, by newspaper reports that used "action verbs" like "smash" and "lunge" and "rip" that gave a false impression of battle-field victories. Also to blame were the optimistic statements by military and naval leaders such as Admiral Halsey, who commented about the end of the Japanese war, and General Arnold, who boasted how the U.S. Eighth Air Force had "destroyed" the German economy many times over. General MacArthur's public statements, Baldwin thought, were always overly optimistic. General Eisenhower hoped to end the war by the end of 1944, and General Marshall, in an article written weeks before, felt the European war might end before the article appeared in December 1944.[55]

There were temporary shortages of military equipment.[56] The fundamental reason for those shortages, Baldwin felt, was that the War and Navy departments in Washington did not act upon warnings by those who saw these problems firsthand, but who failed to persuade their superiors in the Washington bureaucracies to do something. Specifically, he cited the need for better tanks with a lower profile, diesel engines, and a more powerful gun. The extensive use of heavy artillery in Normandy meant that there was the continuing need for more guns and additional ammunition.

Aside from the material needs of the military, Baldwin noted the human cost in lives lost thus far in the war whose end was not in sight. The American casualty rate was 15,000 a week. The Army and Navy lost more than 121,000 men during the past three years of war, and about 430,000 others had been listed as wounded, missing, or captured.[57] The German reserves had yet to be used in battle, he noted.

The U.S. Army had improved considerably, he thought, departing from his previous critical assessment in January 1944. After D-day the Army had generally performed magnificently, but the infantry was still lacking in "dash and aggressiveness and was too dependent upon massed artillery and air support."[58] He praised the antiaircraft guns that had better fire control, the self-propelled guns, the jeep, and the two-and-one-half-ton truck as being "the best in the world." He admired the specialized landing craft for troops and heavy equipment.

While he praised the leadership of General Eisenhower, his "consummate skill," a "major" fault among junior officers was their general "lack of a sense of responsibility down"; in other words, they did not look after the needs of their men. Too many had a "highly developed sense of privilege, but not a comparable sense of responsibility."[59] While staff work was "generally good," G-2 (Intelligence) was often pessimistic at first.

What really bothered Baldwin was the Army's red tape bureaucracy behind the front lines. Too many officers assigned to rear areas created empires for themselves. Baldwin suggested a 10 to 25 percent reduction of officers and men in non-combat areas. In a few weeks' time, during the Battle of the Bulge, many would see combat firsthand, much to their surprise. He was appalled to learn that the U.S. Army command and headquarters personnel occupied 150 hotels in Paris.

As for the GIs on the front lines, Baldwin wrote that their lack of conviction about the war's aims did not prevent them from being good soldiers, but their morale was dependent upon the quality of junior officer leadership at the company and battalion level. The assistant managing editor at *Life* magazine praised this Baldwin article as "the best piece of military analysis we have ever seen."[60] His reputation had grown considerably during the war, earned through a lot of hard work on his part.

On December 16, 1944, two panzer armies, the Fifth and Sixth, which included ten armored divisions, attacked American units near the Ardennes forest by a route that the Germans had used successfully in 1940 to invade France. The attack came when winter weather had grounded all Allied airplanes, and heavy snow and fog blanketed the region, making road travel difficult. The American sector was only lightly defended by units, some of which had never seen combat before. It was thought to be a quiet sector, and Allied intelligence had not detected any prior German movement in the area.

The scene was ripe to make a real shock to the Americans. The German panzer units moved swiftly westward with their objective to cross the Meuse River and use the flat Belgium countryside to reach the seaport of Antwerp. If successful, that offensive would have divided the American and British forces. At its farthest point, the "bulge" in the American front line was sixty-five miles deep and forty-five miles wide. Two key transportation centers, St. Vith and Bastogne, were attacked, with the former surrendering on December 22. On Christmas Eve, the German offensive had lost its momentum and some panzer units had run out of fuel. Bastogne held out until Patton's Third Army was able to relieve the garrison on December 26, and the weather also cleared, which permitted Allied air power to repeatedly attack the German forces.[61]

Hanson Baldwin was as shocked, as many were, by the sudden German offensive on December 16. Two *Times* editorials, written in his no-holds-barred style, used such phrases as, this is "the worst week since the United States entered the war," and, the German attack has "set us back on our heels," and, "that no war is won until the last shot has been fired." The editorialist advised that Americans at home make further sacrifices to bring victory and an end to the war.[62]

After two weeks of trying to determine why the German counteroffensive of December 16 was initially so successful, Baldwin posed a series of questions to which there were no answers while the war was being fought, questions that only General Eisenhower and the War Department could answer. Why were we surprised? Were there no American patrols, minefields, or road blocks in the area? How widespread was the "it can't happen here" mentality among the American field commanders? Why couldn't the Allies, with more tanks, guns, transport, airplanes, and troops, punch through the German front lines on a narrow front? Why could the Germans move a greater distance in a week than we could after three months? Was there no surprise factor built into the American strategy? With sixteen Allied armored divisions on the western front, why were they dispersed so widely with no more than two or three armored divisions in any one area? Implicitly, Baldwin seems to have been critical of General Eisenhower's broad-front strategy. On the other hand, it is not clear if he approved of General Montgomery's narrow-front strategy in September 1944, which, if successful, would have opened the north German plain to Berlin.[63] As the *Times* military editor, he saw his job as provoking inquiry, raising questions, even though in the midst of a war answers would, most likely, not be forthcoming.

A good example of Baldwin using his words to provoke was his piece on the superiority of German tanks. "This has been denied, explained away and hushed up," he wrote. It is a situation that Congress should investigate. He described the new versions of the German Panther and Tiger tanks that were heavier—equipped with the new 88-mm guns that gave them more hitting power, and heavy frontal armor—than the outclassed American M-4 Sherman tank.

He contemptuously dismissed the apologists who claimed that our lighter tanks were more maneuverable, that America did not favor tank-to-tank battles, and that we could knock out German tanks with the Sherman tank's short 75-mm gun at close range. While we had 90-mm anti-tank destroyers, we did not have a tank that mounted a 90-mm gun. And while better American tanks may have been in development, the Germans had been, according to Baldwin, "ahead of us on the battlefield. And it is battlefield service that counts."

He blamed the time lag for new weapons on the "conservatism and traditionalism in the Army mind." Also at fault were the bureaucracies in the War Department, long a bane to Baldwin. The ordnance department blamed the armor center, and vice versa. The fact that procurement agencies were numerous only delayed getting new tanks on the battlefields of Europe, and when they did arrive they could outmatch "the German tank of yesterday, [but] not the German tanks of today." In short, why can't Americans be on the cutting edge of military technological change rather than behind the technology of the Germans? To Baldwin's thinking, the simple and oft repeated answer was bureaucratic red tape that contributed to the delays in developing new weapons together with U.S. "boastful self-deceit."[64]

Continuing with this diatribe, he next focused on why the Germans had operational jet-powered planes, while the United States did not, describing, in considerable detail, the characteristics of the ME 163 and the ME 262. While the British and the Americans had experimental models under development, the United States had no jet planes then in action. He warned that if the war should be protracted, Germany's technological advantage in jet-powered planes could have serious consequences.[65]

In the Pacific, the Japanese were just as determined to win or to die trying. Baldwin's pieces on the many hard-fought island campaigns, or island stepping, as he called it, demonstrated Japan's determination to fight. He was always concerned to find the quickest route to the Japanese home islands and end the war. Once the Marianas were taken in August 1944, the talk of moving farther westward to the Philippines was "in reality a diversion from the straightest course toward Japan." "The real strategic issue," he wrote, "is whether Japan shall be defeated by . . . a continental strategy (the Formosa-China route) or by the maritime route (the Volcano-Bonin Island route)." Either route would involve ground troops. "We cannot count upon air power and sea power to defeat the enemy without invasion," he said, then asked rhetorically, "Can Japan be defeated without engaging the Japanese forces in China?"[66]

President Roosevelt, Congress, and the American public viewed China with a combination of wishful thinking and a lack of realism. The United States wanted to believe that General Chiang Kai-shek was China's best hope for the future, rather than the corrupt politician he was. He thought the Communists led by Mao Tse-tung were a greater enemy than the Japanese who occupied much of his country.[67]

What changed Baldwin's earlier view that China would be a base from which to bomb Japan was the successful five-month Japanese offensive in 1944 that captured seven airfields used by the U.S. Fourteenth Air Force.[68] He thought that recent Japanese victories had so disorganized the Chinese political, economic, and military position that China's role was no longer an option. "We are apparently bypassing China . . . and are substituting amphibious strategy for continental strategy," he wrote in December 1944.[69] President Roosevelt had once dallied with the Four Policemen idea (the United States, Britain, Russia, and China) that would maintain world order once the war had ended. In 1944 that idea was no longer mentioned. Disregarding for a moment China's military weakness, Baldwin saw the need, once Japan was defeated, for China to fill the power vacuum in the Far East so as to stabilize Asia. The events after 1945 proved that China was unable to stabilize anything.[70]

The key to the air war over Japan was the B-29 Super Fortress. With the capture of the Marianas Islands after June 1944, the China route became less important. One month after the first B-29s left from Saipan, the Marianas, on October 28, 1944, Baldwin wrote two pieces that described the bomber in considerable detail, except for its range, bomb load, and altitude. Anticipating that new air bases closer to Japan would be needed, he suggested Iwo Jima in the Bonin island group and Okinawa in the Ryukyu group as possible forward bases, close enough to Japanese targets to have long-range fighter escort. He cited a number of specific target cities where steelmaking factories were known to be located, but he discounted the popular view that the Japanese were inclined "to panic and that severe bombing will break their will to resist." He reminded his readers that massive bombing of German cities only "stiffened" the Germans' will to continue the war, and that the London blitz did not result in the British public demanding an early end to the war.

Baldwin's article, which was sharply critical of President Roosevelt for withholding news of the Cairo and Teheran Conferences, and for holding few press conferences, provoked a favorable response from Oswald Garrison Villard, Baldwin's appreciative pacifist correspondent. He praised Baldwin's piece on the conferences, and added his criticism of President Roosevelt treating the war as "his private affair."[71]

Villard blamed the American press for not challenging secrecy about the war and for allowing the Army and the Navy to dominate the news about the war and the war's progress. The public's optimism about the war reflected the positive views of radio commentators who claimed that the United States was always winning: "Minor skirmishes become major victories."[72] The public did not know, he continued, "how horrible and bestial this war [was]."[73] Few American newspapers gave citizens informative war news or "any comment on military operations worth reading." Reporters did not understand the military point of view. To Villard's thinking, only Baldwin wrote "expertly, honestly and objectively" on the military and naval situation by giving "the whole picture."[74]

Villard concluded his article by warning that journalism that continues to give an entirely misleading impression does a "great disservice to itself, to the profession and to the nation."[75] Like Baldwin, he was of the fearless school of journalism, believing that a reporter must always tell the public the truth of the matter no matter what the effects might be. In reply to this unexpected fulsome praise, Baldwin could only thank him for his "very, very fine tribute to me . . . I wish I could truly live up to your praise."[76]

Baldwin's most persistent domestic critics focused on his comments on the Nazi-Soviet war. Those readers were convinced that he was consistently pro-German and anti-Soviet. This situation developed as Moscow did not permit foreign journalists on their front lines and Baldwin considered the official Russian war communiqués to be almost useless in their exaggerated claims of victory. The Berlin communiqués were not that truthful, either, after 1942, and it was difficult for him to determine where the truth about the eastern front lay.

Baldwin's perceived anti-Soviet bias was noted in *Pravda* in April 1944. A Soviet writer, David Zaslavsky, attacked Baldwin for making repeated incorrect appraisals and forecasts about the Red Army's progress. The writer charged that Baldwin repeated the German lies about its repeated victories and denigrated all Red Army advances. He said Baldwin relied upon German sources of information that was designed to "deceive everybody," including their enemies and their own people. By using such biased information, Baldwin had put "himself and his newspaper in a ridiculous position." Zaslavsky quoted an Old Russian song, "Here, in militant zeal, Mister Baldwin defeats Russia on a map by his forefinger." The writer also attacked Wendell Willkie, the Republican candidate for president in 1940 and William Randolph Hearst, the media empire publisher.[77] The *Pravda* piece revealed that Moscow considered Baldwin to be an important enough American journalist to criticize his perceived slant, and this was not the only time he would be singled out for censure by Moscow.

An American, writing to the *Times* editor, came to Baldwin's defense. He wrote that many leaders in the West had been wrong, too, including Roosevelt, Churchill, and General Marshall, and that in 1941 "Russia gave us many causes to dislike her." This writer also dismissed as being untrue Zaslavsky's claim that Baldwin only used German information. He added, "The real trouble with Zaslavsky is that he understood America as little as we understand the Soviet Union. He doesn't realize that under our code he can call Baldwin a fool . . . but [not] a knave because he disagrees with him."[78]

Like all journalists, Baldwin could at times be embarrassingly wrong. In analyzing the eastern front in the Crimea in April 1944, he was convinced that the Germans would hold the port of Odessa and the Crimean peninsula by supplying their troops from the Black Sea, forestalling the Red Army's move into the Danube River estuary.[79] Two days later, Field Marshall Paul von Kleist withdrew his forces from Odessa. The *Times* editorial noted the significance of this recapture of the last of Russia's major cities to be liberated from the Germans. Four days later, the German withdrawal made it possible for the Soviet forces to drive to the Rumanian oil fields.[80]

At home, Baldwin's local critics had a field day in their letters to E. L James, the managing editor. One wrote how his respect for the paper would "increase immeasurably" if Baldwin were dismissed.[81] Another accused him of being "consistently wrong" about Russia since 1941, his "blatant nonsense" was an irritant, "a case of stupidity and incompetence."[82] Another felt he should be kept on at the paper for the amusement value that his writing gave to many people.[83] Another referred to Baldwin as the "Reichswer [*sic*] Pepper-upper." What a sense of personal injury your "military Poo-Bah must feel for the Master Race" for letting him down by their evacuation of Odessa.[84]

An anonymous writer chastised Baldwin for always underestimating Russia's ability to fight and dismissing its war communiqués. Baldwin, the writer commented, "never saw [Russian] victories. All he found was that the Germans were skillfully executing a movement and the Russians had done nothing conclusive."[85] Another writer used sarcasm, noting how in 1941 Baldwin predicted the German invasion to end with their victory in three months. The Red Army could not stand up to the professional German army. The Stalingrad defeat in February 1943 was because of the long "Nazi lines of communication" and not because of the Red Army's encirclement of the German Sixth Army. The Kursk tank battle in July 1943, Baldwin viewed as "a defensive operation by the German High Command." In summary, the writer, a lawyer, questioned if Baldwin was "attempting to use the *Times* to minimize a Russian success and put the best possible face on Nazi defeats."[86]

Sulzberger responded that he did not think Baldwin was biased but warned him on the Odessa evacuation that it was unwise to go "out on the end of a limb unnecessarily like this" and to "prophesy on things that can so quickly be proved to be untrue."[87] After this flap receded from the public's attention, Baldwin remained focused upon Soviet territorial plans in 1944. "It is well to emphasize again that the [European] political factors in the war today are more important than the purely military factors . . . literally anything might happen."[88]

Before the Teheran Conference (November 1943), he thought that Roosevelt and Stalin would be at odds, with Churchill being in the middle, over a postwar political settlement in Europe. In the months following the conference, Baldwin thought the power arrangement had changed, with Churchill and Stalin taking the lead and FDR being the middle.[89] Baldwin remained suspicious that Russia had territorial ambitions that were advanced by its military operations. In 1947 at Fulton, Missouri, Churchill called the new borders of the Soviet sphere of influence in Central Europe that extended from East Prussia to the Adriatic an "iron curtain."

In March 1944, Baldwin noted Moscow's determination to establish friendly governments in "contiguous" territories, including Tito in Yugoslavia, and to recognize the Polish National Council (later to be called the Lublin government) rather than the Polish government then in exile in London. Moscow favored multilateral settlements in western Europe but insisted upon unilateral settlements, "her own," in eastern Europe. According to Baldwin,

Russia's "great cards [were its] military power," then being used to advance Russia's national ends under the guise of international Communism.[90]

Pointing with alarm at current trends, Baldwin alerted his readers to the political changes in Europe that the war had wrought. Though a well-respected and controversial journalist, Baldwin had little time to savor his enviable reputation with so many major military and political events demanding his attention.

1945: The Road's End

The long-awaited Soviet offensive on the eastern front began on January 12, 1945. From the Baltic Sea to the Carpathian Mountains the Red Army attacked and the German forces retreated slowly. Baldwin was moved to write a meditative piece on that horrendous struggle between the Slavs and the Teutons: "The war on the Eastern Front, gigantic and bloody, pitiless and somber, has returned again to its beginnings. Like some implacable fate the Russian tide moves on—now racing through a gap in a shattered rampart, now rising with slow but inexorable finality to overtop the dying armies of the Reich." He used the imagery of a long road now at a dead end. "It was once a fair, broad highway for the German hordes, arrogant in their might." Now, it was a straight road back that had no turning since 1943 with the German defeat at Stalingrad. It was a road whose "signposts of retreat—[were] crosses topped with German helmets buried in Russian graves." Baldwin concluded that the "surging tides of opposing national and racial ambitions, ages old . . . are meeting in [an] ultimate conflict . . . and the tide-rips and across-currents will sweep across our world for generations to come."[1]

This piece was written in a style that departed from his normal straightforward prose, and his readers were appreciative. One called his phrases "Churchillian," another felt it was "most polished and dramatic," and a third reader called it "a masterpiece of writing" whose author was "without doubt the finest military writer in the country, because events of the future always confirm the observations you have made in the past."[2] Baldwin made no public reply, as was his custom, but no doubt he was pleased that it was well received. As always, he sought to put the battle on the eastern front into a wider perspective.

Though the end of the Third Reich was inevitable in February 1945, and V-E day was little over three months away, Baldwin feared a return of the over-optimism of the previous autumn, when many were predicting a quick end of the war with Germany. The surprise German offensive that began in December 1944 shocked many home front optimists.

In February and March 1945, Baldwin wrote seven articles in the *Times* about the quality of American arms compared with those of Germany. His sources readily admitted the superiority of the M-1 Garand rifle to the German Mauser bolt-action rifle model 1898. The German light machine gun and machine pistol were outstanding, while the U.S. Army's Colt .45 automatic pistol was an "unwieldy anachronism" and the .30-caliber carbine was of limited value.[3] The problem, as Baldwin saw it, was not that America did not have the ability to produce first-class weapons, but that it underestimated German ingenuity and know-how. America had a self-delusion that its weapons were the best in the world, a view pushed by advertisers and by publicity writers.[4]

Baldwin repeatedly wrote about the known weaknesses of our M-4 Sherman tank, with its 75-mm gun, its high profile, and its tendency to catch fire.[5] Citing the *Stars and Stripes,* a GI newspaper, Baldwin reprinted comments from U.S. tankers who observed that our 75-mm or 76-mm shells just bounced off the heavily armored German tanks, which could be knocked out only if a number of Sherman tanks would concentrate all their fire power on one panzer.[6] In March 1945 a new American tank, the T-26, or Pershing, was distributed to the American 3rd and 9th Armored Divisions of the U.S. Army's 12th Army Group.[7]

Baldwin wrote that the Pershing did not look ahead in tank design to outstrip future German tank designers. It was lighter than the panzers and had thinner frontal armor, but it was an improvement. He revealed that the Pershing tank was designed in 1942 but was not put into production until much later. The limited number of Pershing tanks available meant that for the rest of the war the Sherman tank would remain the main American battle tank. "Which means, he wrote, "that our tankers are still fighting with second-best weapons."[8]

In the early evening of March 7, a platoon of the 9th Armored Division discovered a still-standing railroad bridge over the Rhine River at Remagen. Baldwin wrote that the discovery had a "profound effect on the quick German collapse." All the other Rhine River bridges had been destroyed by the Germans to slow down the advancing Allied armies from the west. Despite enemy fire, the platoon crossed the Ludendorff Bridge and prevented the main explosive charge from going off. Within twenty-four hours, eight thousand American troops, tanks, and other equipment had crossed the bridge to establish a bridgehead on the other side. Soon, Allied engineers constructed a number of other pontoon bridges across the Rhine.[9]

In April 1945 the Allied armies moved closer to Berlin from the west and from the east, with the Oder River as the informal line between the Soviet and Western armies. On April 16 Soviet forces began a massive artillery and rocket barrage against Berlin, which they entered ten days later. Baldwin wrote what amounted to an epitaph of the city. "Berlin is dying," he observed, "smoke cloaks what might have been grandeur and glory, but now is justly reduced to dust and ashes in expiration of ten thousand crimes."[10]

The always-cautious Baldwin went so far as to remark, "It is not inconceivable that V-E Day may not be far off, and there is always the possibility that it may be more clear-cut than anyone had dared hope."[11] Four days later, on April 29, Adolf Hitler married his mistress Eva Braun inside the führer bunker, and on April 30 they committed suicide. The Third Reich that Hitler boasted would last for a thousand years ended after only twelve.

On May 14, one week after V-E day was declared, Baldwin wrote what was probably the first assessment of wartime decisions. While people would say that the war against Germany ended according to plan—that is, it ended with an Allied victory—the *Times* military editor said no war has ever or will ever be fought according to a plan. Had the Tunisian campaign gone according to plan the Allied armies would have taken Tunis and Bizerte by Christmas 1942, a month after Operation Torch began. Rome would have been taken by Christmas 1943 and the cross-channel invasion of France would have occurred also in 1943. The European war would end in October 1944, said the War Department in Washington, D.C. None of these plans worked according to schedule. There were always unexpected delays brought on in part by unexpected German counteroffensives, such as the second Ardennes offensive in December 1944 (the Battle of the Bulge) that upset hopes of a quick Allied victory. Even the German collapse did not go according to plan, which anticipated continued pockets of Nazi resistance in Bavaria and elsewhere to last through the summer of 1945.[12]

According to Baldwin one of the greatest German strategic mistakes was the failure to reinforce Rommel's Afrika Korps in 1941–42 which, if successful, would have led to the German control of the Suez Canal and parts of the Middle East. Another strategic mistake was the German declaration of war against the United States after Pearl Harbor. Had Hitler issued a conciliatory statement that he had no quarrel with Washington, the American public would have focused its revenge against Japan. American public opinion, at the time, was against a war with Germany. Hitler also underestimated America's industrial potential; it could and did outproduce Germany's. Another strategic mistake by Hitler was that he should have invaded England in 1940 when the British had less than one division available after the Dunkirk evacuation in June 1940. The hurdle was the Channel, and the failure of the Luftwaffe to gain supremacy over that island. The invasion of Russia in June 1941 opened a second front for Germany without it having previously won in North Africa and knocked Britain out of the war. Had those victories been won, the German forces could have brought the full weight of the Wehrmacht against the Red Army and taken Moscow in December 1941. Hitler underestimated Russia's ability to rebuild a new army after the defeats of 1941–42, and to produce excellent weapons during the war. Baldwin concluded that Hitler's fundamental mistake was starting the war in 1939, before new secret weapons and the V-1 and V-2 rockets were in production and operational. Seen late in the war the weapons were introduced "too late and too little" to change the war's outcome. With relief, Baldwin remarked, "It is well for us that the enemy made mistakes."[13]

In the Pacific war, on February 19, 1945, two Marine divisions invaded a long-held Japanese island, Iwo Jima, that was in the Volcano island group. Those who fought on that inhospitable island would never forget the incredible fierceness of that nearly six-week battle. The Japanese defenses had been very well constructed to withstand the three-day preliminary bombardment from the U.S. Navy's big guns off shore. The Marine 4th and 5th Divisions made the initial assault, while the Marine 1st Division was, for the moment, kept in reserve. The soft volcanic ash made movement on foot very slow. The enfilade fire from the 21,000 Japanese defenders, all hidden from view, caused

American casualties to soar. By one account, 6,000 American Marines were killed while another 17,200 were wounded during that campaign.[14] Fewer than 200 Japanese defenders were taken prisoner.

The large number of U.S. Marine casualties shocked Baldwin. Three days after the initial landing he informed his readers, "Our first waves . . . were almost wiped out; 3,650 marines were dead, wounded or missing." This number, he wrote, was more than the Tarawa losses in November 1943 and "about as many as all the Marine casualties on Guadalcanal in five months of jungle combat."[15]

In early March 1945 he wrote a five-part series on the Iwo Jima campaign, in which he tried to deflect the negative civilian reaction to the number of American losses. Many Americans have "an unwillingness to meet and squarely face the inevitable fact that wars . . . can only be won by blood and death and large casualties."[16] He informed his readers that the Japanese had twenty-five years to construct elaborate defenses on Iwo, while other islands in the Pacific the Japanese had occupied for only a few years prior to an American attack. The American public had become used to the devastation of bombing and shelling in Europe where there were many aboveground buildings. On Iwo there were very few such targets, as the defenses were all underground. He tried to explain that military intelligence could make mistakes on enemy strength. On the Pacific islands, "espionage is impossible" and to get an accurate number was "practically insurmountable."[17]

The cave positions created many tactical problems. To fire directly into the caves, the curved trajectory of Howitzers was less effective than the flat trajectory of 75-mm tank guns. Other effective weapons against cave emplacements were bazookas, bulldozers, and flamethrowers. He discounted the use of poison gas on that island, though. Weather, atmospheric conditions and wind must be ideal, or else the gas fumes might not penetrate caves or pillboxes.[18]

Aside from the tactics of the campaign, the value of Iwo Jima was to use the two airfields on the island from which long-range fighters could accompany the B-29 bombers from the Marianas en route to Japanese cities. Iwo could also serve as an emergency landing field for damaged B-29 planes that could not make it back to their base on the Marianas.

In March 1945 Major General Curtis LeMay, the commander of the 21st Bomber Command, stationed on the Marianas, changed the bombing tactics from high-level bombing with high explosive bombs, to low-level bombing using incendiary bombs on Japanese cities. This change in tactics proved to be very successful. To increase the planes' bomb load, he ordered all guns and ammunition removed from the bombers. The bombers flew night missions so that no fighter escort was needed from Iwo Jima. Thus, the reasons for the invasion of that island were less valid than before.

Within weeks of the end of the Iwo Jima campaign, American planners decided upon the next target, Okinawa, in the Ryukyu group of islands that was just over three hundred miles from the Japanese homeland. As was his pattern, Baldwin's first piece on Okinawa was a detailed description of the topography, climate, population, settlements, airfields, and harbors. Okinawa had long been a Japanese naval and air base that was heavily defended.[19] We know now that the initial landings by Army and Marine Corps units on April 1 were not vigorously resisted. Japanese forces had moved to the southern part of the island, where they put up a determined resistance. That hard-fought campaign lasted for almost three months.

On April 7 American carrier-based planes spotted the battleship *Yamato*, together with one cruiser and eight destroyers, headed for Okinawa. Soon, more than three hundred American planes joined the attack, and after hits from ten torpedoes and five heavy bombs the largest battleship in the world sank. Baldwin thought the *Yamato*'s sortie was "inexplicable" and an example of Japanese "fanaticism or stupidity." If that great ship's mission was to attack the American naval forces around Okinawa, "the plan was so impossibly foolhardy as to be silly." To him, "it almost seems as if the remnants of the Japanese Navy were trying to commit hara-kiri."[20]

Of immediate concern were the repeated kamikaze attacks on American ships. In summary, Baldwin concluded that "the inflexibility of the Japanese military mind, the enemy's sea and air weaknesses, and the overpowering American might, have already decided the battle of Okinawa and have doomed the Empire of Japan."[21]

Baldwin focused his April pieces on the anticipated American attack on the Japanese home islands. Would it be a siege or an assault? An assault now, he wrote, would catch the immediate Japanese defenses off guard for a time and, with luck, end the war quickly. A long siege, including a tight naval blockade around Japan and the continued American air attacks on ground targets, would prolong the war but reduce the level of American casualties.

He suggested that a siege strategy would give us time to transfer thousands of American troops from Europe to Asia, and when accomplished an invasion would have a better chance of success. The drawback to this option was that Japan would have ample opportunity to mobilize its ground forces for a prolonged defense of its homeland. He did not forget the effective Japanese defenses on Iwo Jima and the current slow campaign on Okinawa. Baldwin thought that Japan had already lost the war by the late spring of 1945, but that its military leaders were not prepared to admit defeat.[22]

On August 6, 1945, the first atomic bomb was dropped on Hiroshima, Japan, destroying 60 percent of the city and killing almost 100,000 people. On August 9 a second atomic bomb fell on Nagasaki, with 35,000 casualties. The Japanese government accepted the terms of the Potsdam Conference and also agreed to the American terms to keep the emperor, who would be subject to the authority of the Allied supreme commander of the occupation forces. On August 14, 1945, Americans joyfully celebrated V-J day. The war in the Pacific was over.

Baldwin had been aware that something big would happen soon in Japan, but he had no idea that it would be a nuclear bomb. On the day following the Hiroshima bombing, instead of gloating over the event, he suggested that, in the short run, the bomb would save American lives, shorten the war, and compel the Japanese to surrender, but taking a longer view of things, as always, he wrote about it with dismay: "We have sowed the whirlwind. . . . Because our bombing has been more effective and hence more devastating, Americans have become a synonym for destruction." The atomic bomb, he continued, "will sow the seeds of hate more widely that ever. We may yet reap the whirlwind." As a warning to future policymakers in Washington, he observed, "With such God-like power under man's imperfect control, we face a frightful responsibility. Atomic energy may well lead to a bright new world in which man shares a common brotherhood, or we shall become beneath the bombs and rockets—a world of troglodytes."[23]

In the history of warfare, the pendulum swings between offensive and defensive weapons. In light of the atomic bomb's demonstrated power, if coupled with the German V-2 rocket technology Baldwin thought it might be "the ultimate triumph of the offensive over the defensive." There was, as yet, no defense against "rockets with cosmic warheads" raining down on helpless cities. He raised rhetorical questions for which there were no answers. Will atomic bombs reduce the frequency of wars? Will mass armies of conscripts, large navies, and piloted planes be weapons of the past? Will future wars substitute "push buttons for cannons?" Baldwin felt that atomic bombs had limited battlefield use, especially over natural terrain such as mountains, forests, and jungles. Only a large massed army would be a human target. Until these and other questions were answered, he advocated that U.S. postwar military planning should make it "A-1 priority" to continue with research, development, and production of technologies to defeat new atomic weapons.[24]

There were other issues caused by the "unexpected peace," and all were large issues. Baldwin saw the need for a civilian commission of "leading minds" to formulate modernized defense policies that would support postwar foreign policies. There must, he said, be a smooth reconversion from a wartime economy to a peacetime economy to avoid large-scale unemployment. There would be the need for occupation and garrison forces in Germany and in Japan. To meet the manpower needs for such forces would require the continuation of the wartime draft for twelve months to three years. He suggested a combination of the draft and volunteer enlistments, with many incentives for the troops. He questioned the need for a new Defense Department, or whether it would be better to continue the traditional military service departments that only perpetuated the interservice rivalries that he so often deplored.[25]

On Japanese issues, Baldwin did not favor keeping the emperor in power, though he recognized the validity of arguments that Hirohito could stabilize a postwar Japan. He argued that Hirohito was "certainly the symbolic incarnation of a system . . . that bears a major responsibility" for almost four years of war in the Pacific. "Probably many Americans," he wrote, "would like to see Admiral William F. Halsey Jr. ride Hirohito's white horse" as a public demonstration of America's victory and Japan's defeat.[26]

He also rejected any softening of the unconditional surrender policy that the U.S. had imposed on Germany. Baldwin was piqued by the Japanese delaying tactics over the terms of its surrender. "Our temporizing with the Emperor, and . . . our rushing pell-mell into peace and beginning reconversion and demobilization before the Japanese were even disarmed, must have caused delight in Tokyo."[27] While the Japanese air force and navy were destroyed, the Japanese army was "virtually intact." He feared the renewal of the stab-in-the-back myth perpetuated for twenty years by right-wing German politicians that exonerated the German army from the onus of defeat in World War I. Emperor Hirohito's national radio broadcast on August 15 accepted peace that forestalled any Japanese version of the stab in the back. Baldwin called for the immediate disarmament of all Japanese troops at home and on the islands, the American control of the national government, and the "punishment or elimination of the Japanese militarists who are fully as dangerous as the Nazis ever were."[28] He thought General Douglas MacArthur was too patient with the Japanese leaders in the days following, and if they were allowed to continue their lingering tactics, "we shall be . . . the world's greatest fools."[29] On September 2, 1945, the formal surrender document was signed on the battleship *Missouri* in Tokyo Bay, and the Americans later established a war crimes commission that tried forty of the Japanese leaders, both civilian and military.

In retrospect, Baldwin was convinced that the United States won the war against Japan for one major reason: superior U.S. industrial strength. The United States could produce more weapons, of all types and sizes. Many of the war's new techniques entailed sea power—the control of the seas by U.S. ships and planes defeated the Japanese. Among those techniques were the carrier task forces and the fleet train of auxiliary ships that permitted the task forces to operate far from fleet bases. Floating mobile dry docks, tankers, floating machine shops, store ships, water-distilling ships, and many others kept the forward task forces supplied with everything from 16-inch shells, oil, and gasoline, to movies and cigarettes. To support over 150 amphibious landings in the Pacific, special ships and landing techniques were developed. The key lesson that Baldwin loved to emphasize was that air, sea, and land forces had to work together to demonstrate the "essential indivisibility of military force." But it was the U.S. industrial base that permitted the mass production of the tools that won the war.

As for Japanese military mistakes, he listed the initial raid on Pearl Harbor as a major mistake, since the enemy saw it as a raid only on our capital ships, rather than an invasion of the Hawaiian Islands, which could have fallen to the Japanese in December 1941. The attacking carrier planes did not bomb the oil storage tanks, the machine shops, and the naval dockyards at Pearl Harbor, and the U.S. carriers were at sea during the attack. The Japanese also did not seize Port Darwin, located in northwestern Australia and lightly defended in 1942. At Guadalcanal, in September and in early

October 1942, U.S. naval forces were limited. Had the Japanese sent a large naval force during those months, they could have dislodged U.S. Marine forces on the island. In November 1943, at Tarawa, the enemy did not counterattack during that first night when our Marines were still on the beachhead. In October 1944, at the Battle for Leyte Gulf, the Japanese admiral did not press home his attack on lightly defended U.S. ships off Leyte Island. In general, Baldwin noted that the Japanese leaders were "strangely lacking in resolution when that quality would have brought them victory"[30] For the United States, the key battles of the Pacific war were at Midway Island, Guadalcanal, the Marianas, Leyte Gulf, and the successful invasions of Iwo Jima and Okinawa. The island-hopping strategy was a necessary "highroad to victory."[31]

The war was over but the problems of peace were just ahead. In 1945 the United States was the world's only military power that possessed the secrets of the atomic bomb, an advantage that Baldwin correctly predicted would last for at least the next three years, but not longer than five years. The Russians exploded their first atomic bomb four years after the war. Baldwin quietly observed, in mid-August 1945, that "the battle of men's minds is just beginning. The inexorable economic conflict resumes. The political conflict continues. The unity that found us in defeat is less powerful in victory. The problems of peace are a thousand times more complex—but not less compelling—than those of war."[32]

In October 1945, just before he took a well-deserved two-month vacation from his almost daily writing during the war, Baldwin wrote a four-part series on the military and the political effects of the atomic bomb. The "secret" of the bomb was not in the laboratory or in nuclear physics; it was in the engineering and industrial processes used to manufacture an atomic bomb. Anticipating the Cold War, he discounted the current belief that our present monopoly of the bomb would translate into political leverage with the Soviet Union, because the "Russians are realists" and know that the United States would never use the bomb unless it was first attacked by Moscow.[33]

From 1920 on, the technology of war that began with poison gas, the tank, and the airplane, had produced, by 1945, the atomic bomb, long-range rockets, radar, the long-range bomber, and many other new weapons. How could the United States defend itself, since Baldwin believed that some nuclear-tipped intercontinental rockets would "always get through?"[34] He proposed a "master" government agency, independent of the Army and the Navy, to collect foreign intelligence to avoid a future atomic Pearl Harbor. The creation of the Central Intelligence Agency (CIA) in 1947 was the answer. Baldwin thought we should develop rockets, pilotless bombers that would give the United States an offensive capability. There should be, also, a civilian commission to review the nation's entire military program and its relation to U.S. foreign policy. An atomic energy commission was needed to foster further research and to remove the extreme secrecy now prevailing that could only hinder the openness of scientific research.[35]

How should the United States defend itself in the atomic age, Baldwin asked? The greatest deterrent to an atomic attack would be the fear of retaliation in kind. But, he warned, had Hitler and Tojo had the bomb, they would have had no scruples about using it. If other nations would agree to retaliate, that might be a deterrent. However, he also noted that the idea of collective security, so popular in the 1930s, had failed to prevent World War II. He suggested that the new United Nations organization establish an arms limitation and inspection plan, whereby a "visit and search" program would permit American and Soviet inspectors to visit each other's nuclear plants.[36]

In 1945, Baldwin felt that Washington should make the suggestion anyway, knowing that Moscow would reject it. But it would enable the United States to take the high moral ground "in the eyes of the world."[37] A divided postwar world, two power blocs, was unacceptable to Baldwin. In his view, the bloc idea had to be broken and both nations had to work to do it. If the blocs continued, then the United States would have to decentralize its cities and industries, spend more money for bigger and more effective atomic bombs, boost the funding for the Army, Navy, and Air Force, and develop better rockets and place them on our forward bases closer to the Soviet Union. We would become a garrison state, a theme he would cite later on. In brief, he advised America to "keep our defenses strong [and] our guard up."[38] That was not an optimistic view of the world after six years of a world war, but he always considered himself to be a realist, not an idealist. He preferred to see and report on the world as it was, not as it ought to be.

CHAPTER **13**

The World of Tomorrow, 1946–49

In the immediate postwar years, millions of veterans enjoyed being civilians again, and they tried to make up for the time lost in their lives because of the war. Their war skills no longer had any relevance, but Baldwin's skills were still needed. There was no rest from the new national security and defense problems created by the war. He outlined them in a commencement address given in 1946 at Hollins College, a school in Virginia where his wife, Helen, and his younger sister, Dorothy, were alumnae. Instead of pleasant platitudes about a future of hope and personal fulfillment, he shocked them with a rather grim picture of the near future of international power politics, competing ideologies, the economic clash between Marxism and capitalism, and the impact of a technological revolution of new weapons based on the atomic bomb and long-range rockets. Americans were an impatient and optimistic people noted for their wishful thinking, but Americans must be realistic, he said. Atomic energy need not be destructive but could be put to peaceful purposes in medicine, transportation, and space exploration. The "world of tomorrow" (the title of his address) will be one of "struggle and threat," but do not despair, he advised the graduates; "keep your feet in the mud of the world you live in . . . but your eyes on the stars of tomorrow." He loved this phrase because he used it, with variations, on other occasions where hope and idealism were called for.[1]

While most Americans wanted to put the war and all military matters behind them, Hanson Baldwin found sufficient subjects on which to write, including the appointment of World War II military officers to civilian government jobs, the issue of universal military training (UMT), the unification of the armed services, the expansion of Soviet Communism in Europe, and the impact of the atomic bomb on future wars. Those serious topics did not cause the furor that Baldwin's words about the maritime workers strike in New York City did.

The year 1946 was characterized by widespread labor strikes that involved major industries such as the railroads, coal, and steel. In New York, the maritime workers strike lasted for eight days and was the fourth maritime strike in that year. Baldwin, never a friend of organized labor since his brief membership in the newspaper guild in 1934, wrote a scathing attack on how the union had destroyed the merchant marine service. "Where are the hard-hearted, hard-fisted, leather-lunged 'sun-downers' who could spit into the teeth of a gale?" he asked. With nostalgia, he noted how the skippers of yesteryear were masters of their ship, but not today. A ship cannot be run by grievance committees or by "sea lawyers." The war created "much drivel" about the wartime services of the merchant sailor, who enjoyed a soft berth, large salaries, and exemption from the military draft. Baldwin scoffed at Congress for establishing the Merchant Marine Academy and putting it on the same level as West Point and Annapolis. The granting of a BS degree was ludicrous, he thought. The presence of Communist leaders in some unions was another mark against the maritime unions. The "vital" issue was who would command the ship, the captain or the union organizer?[2]

The union response was immediate. On the following day, three thousand seamen staged a two-hour mass demonstration around the Times Building on West Forty-Third Street, carrying "Down with Baldwin" and "Baldwin Distorts the Truth" signs. A fifteen-member delegation was granted a rare personal interview with the *Times* managing editor, E. L. James, to present their demands. The outcome was that the paper agreed to print a letter from the seamen and to disavow Baldwin's piece. In their presence, James pointed to a number of favorable *Times* articles and editorials about the wartime services of the merchant sailors.

Within the *Times*, there was clear annoyance that Baldwin had again caused the paper embarrassment. The senior bullpen editor in the newsroom told the managing editor that he had better "keep his nose out of current labor troubles," about which he knows nothing. He later added, "Personally, I don't think he [Baldwin] ever wrote anything that was worth a God-damn." Sulzberger was very annoyed and asked rhetorically if the status of Mr.

Baldwin's column should be reconsidered. With the war over, he might again go further afield and provoke other public demonstrations. Sulzberger suggested that Baldwin be advised that the *Times* could not continue to allow a column that is "devoted to personal expression," and he must stick to military subjects. While Baldwin's status and value to the paper was being questioned by management, there were definite strains between the two superpowers.[3]

In the five years between the end of World War II and the beginning of the Korean War, the wartime alliance with the Soviet Union quickly collapsed as Moscow showed its determination to dominate all of Central Europe. Some thought that this was based on its need for security from future invasions from western Europe, but later the view was that Soviet expansion was based upon the ideology of Communism. There was never an agreement as to what motivated the Soviet Union, ideology or national security. Its determination to deny Americans access to a divided Berlin in 1948 and the increased strength of the Communist parties in France and in Italy seemed to be proof enough of Moscow's imperial designs in western Europe. Great Britain was a spent force to some observers and could do little to stop this expansion of Communism in Europe. After six years of war, its ability to quickly recover without outside economic help was in doubt. Its once vaunted empire had its own problems as its colonies sought their independence, especially India. The civil war in China between Chiang Kai-shek and Mao Tse-tung, that Washington tried to mediate, continued unabated until October 1949, when Mao's forces entered Beijing and Chiang's defeated followers fled to Taiwan. In August 1949 the Soviet Union exploded its first atomic bomb, which shocked many Americans who believed that our monopoly of the bomb would last for a number of years. Such was the full plate of issues on which Baldwin commented in those five years.

The big issues that he wrote about were the unification of the armed services and UMT. The two weapons of war that initiated a major reassessment of America's postwar military strategy were the atomic bomb and the German V-2 rocket. Both weapons changed many ideas of what a future war would be. Complicating the debate was President Harry S. Truman's determination to reduce the size of the military budget, putting the armed services under great pressure to get along with less. This fiscal restraint exasperated the long-standing interservice rivalries between the Army and the Navy so often noted by Baldwin.

The Air Force made it clear, even during the war, that it wanted to be independent of both the Army and the Navy and to be considered as an equal branch in the postwar military establishment. The Air Force was adept at public relations and Congress in demonstrating how it was the future key to American security in an atomic age. Did it not drop two atomic bombs on Hiroshima and Nagasaki that ended World War II and cancelled the planned November land invasion of the Japanese home islands? No one disputed the view that heavy American losses would have resulted from that invasion and that the Pacific war possibly could have lasted until 1946.

In this immediate postwar period, Baldwin developed a strong bond with James V. Forrestal, the secretary of the Navy since 1944, previously the undersecretary of the Navy in the early 1940s when Baldwin first began to interview him as a Navy contact for war news. Forrestal probably saw in Baldwin a sympathetic person, one in whom he could confide without fear that his confidences would be revealed in the *Times*. For Baldwin, this was the perfect news source: high enough to know what was going on in the Truman administration, but outside the inner Missouri circle that surrounded the president with comfortable people engaged in the "Washington knifing game"[4]

As an Annapolis graduate with technical naval knowledge, Baldwin's background was attractive to Forrestal, judging from the numerous memos and correspondence between them that either praised specific Baldwin *Times* pieces or solicited his input on a current issue. The relationship developed into a personal friendship. Between 1947, when Forrestal became the first secretary of defense under the National Security Act of 1947, and 1949, when he committed suicide, Baldwin watched his friend's mind slowly deteriorate under the political pressures from the Truman crowd and the increasing menace of Soviet Communism.

In his obituary column, Baldwin noted what an "extremely sensitive, very shy, and thoroughly conscientious [a] person" Forrestal was. A man who "built around his inner soul, a wall of toughness and reserve, that seemed to some to amount to brusqueness." A man who sought nothing for himself "save the knowledge of a job well done." Baldwin felt that he should have resigned after the 1947 act went into effect that established the model for the Defense Department. The dirty infighting in which the "corrosive personal abuse" of Louis Johnson, the Truman insider who got his job, and the columnists Drew Pearson and Walter Winchell, who "maligned and traduced and attacked him," were also to blame for the "Forrestal tragedy."[5] The uncharacteristic sharpness of Baldwin's words were an indication of how well he knew and wanted to speak out in the secretary's defense against those who had slandered him for years. In spite of the forceful words, Sulzberger praised Baldwin's piece as "good strong meat, [that] tastes mighty good to me."[6]

One of the popular ideas during the immediate postwar years was UMT, driven by politicians and the U.S. Army to provide for trained manpower to be mobilized in the advent of another war. Its proponents viewed the six-month training of all eighteen-year old males to be character building, improving their physical and mental health and instilling discipline into their undirected civilian lives.

In 1945 Baldwin, not afraid to take an unpopular stand, once again upset his *Times* bosses, who strongly favored UMT, by sharply criticizing the program as being expensive, unworkable, and militarily useless. The Army was not a trade school, nor an educational institution. Neither would it improve America's youth's physical or mental health. He questioned whether military discipline had any relationship to one's moral fiber, citing Dr. Leonard W. Mayo's comment that the goal of military training was "to teach men to fight and kill."[7] After six months of training, the citizen trainee would be "trained privates" and nothing more.

Baldwin was particularly upset with the specious argument that military conscription would reduce postwar unemployment, an argument used by Adolf Hitler in 1933. The U.S. Army could not be used as an institution to improve the nation's economy. In brief, the United States did not need a mass army, as in the last war, but a small, well-trained, skilled force.

Two years later, when the UMT campaign was well under way, Baldwin renewed his criticism. He belittled the view that "absolute preparedness" in peacetime was vital to America's security."[8] The "pushbutton" war of the future was not here yet. The atomic bomb must be carried in piloted bombers to their targets. He presciently anticipated a time when rockets—he called them "inter-continental robots"—with atomic warheads would hit enemy targets thousands of miles from the United States. Today, we know them as intercontinental ballistic missiles, or ICBMs.

The key threat in 1947, he wrote, was from rockets and not from mass armies. Falling rockets would signal the beginning of the next war, which could be over in days. Since there was no effective defense against rockets, the United States would have to retaliate with ship-launched missiles immediately or else "have lost the war."[9] What the country needed, he argued, was not a mass standing army but a professional force trained to use rockets, long-range piloted bombers, missile-launching submarines, and airborne and amphibious troops ready to seize advance bases or to capture enemy missile-launching sites.

He observed that the atomic bombs of 1945 might never be used again because of the devastation inflicted on two Japanese cities. However, if used in the first assault, then a war of attrition would follow. American foreign policy must be neither provocative nor appeasing, backed up strongly, but not dominated by, modern military strength.[10] America's first line of defense would have to be diplomacy. The second line of defense would be a global intelligence service, and the third line a well-funded research and development program for the military.

Amid all the uncertainties of European developments in 1947, Baldwin remained convinced that in the United States, elected civilian government leaders should always dominate the military establishment. What concerned him was the number of military officers of the late war being appointed to top civilian government posts. The most obvious were General Marshall, secretary of state, and General MacArthur, head of the American occupation government in Japan, posts that ought to have been given to professional diplomats, Baldwin thought.

What bothered him were the military's plans for "absolute security" to prepare America for total war, even an atomic war. To achieve this, the military, especially the U.S. Army, used the advertising tools of public relations to convince the American public and members of Congress that the United States needed the UMT program because it was weak. The Army produced a film, "Plan for Peace," that was widely distributed and favored UMT. He cited a House subcommittee report that was critical of the Army's efforts, which went beyond providing factual information to the public about UMT to engaging in propaganda to influence legislation before Congress. Baldwin cited a passage from that report that stated how the film made "the individual believe that he is thinking for himself."[11]

The problem was far deeper than just a film. The structure of the military establishment, in the recently passed National Security Act, provided for the creation of a joint staff of one hundred officers to serve under the Joint Chiefs of Staff that would resemble the disbanded German General Staff. A current idea was a "unified command," which had been approved by the Army and the Air Force, but not the Navy, where a single officer would command all American armed forces in the continental United States. The officer would be under the civilian branch of the government, but answerable only to the Joint Chiefs of Staff. In a national emergency, the power would be enormous.[12] The military's influence was evident in the Reserve Officers' Training Corps (ROTC) programs on college campuses, where the military paid the college administration to establish the programs. Much of university research in the sciences was funded by the military, which could censor publication of the research results. The Air Force contracts kept the airplane industry alive after the war.

Again Baldwin challenged censorship. He cited other disturbing examples of undue military influence, the most egregious being censorship at the source, a practice whereby news of interest and importance to the American public was classified as being "confidential" or "secret."[13] The hiding of military facts of value to the Soviet Union was one thing, but the deliberate efforts of the military services to influence Congress and the public was another matter altogether. In his words, the problem was "older than the atomic bomb; it is the age-old conflict between security and liberty—a conflict in which nations that have endured have usually ended in a compromise between a degree of relative security and guarantees of basic liberties." The military, he observed, should be "honored but not extolled, allowed to influence, but not to propagandize, have their place in government but a place [that was] strictly circumscribed."[14]

Baldwin felt compelled to alert his readers in his 1947 *Harper's* magazine article that he was not a Communist, nor a fellow traveler, because of his critical comments on the military's influence in American public life. He despised totalitarian police states, such as the Soviet Union. He felt the need to speak out against what he saw as the growing influence of the military as being dangerous to American democratic liberties.

The New York City paper *PM*, a left-wing newspaper, considered Baldwin's article to be "so brave and honest and important as to be almost sensational." His credentials were so well known as to be above reproach. The editorial writer noted that Baldwin's conservative reputation would

enhance his views to a wide audience.[15] Even the conservative and anti–
New Deal *Chicago Tribune* picked up on Baldwin's view that criticizing the
military resulted in a smear campaign against the accuser. It agreed that
UMT would only create "an ill-trained, obsolete, mass Army. The brass hats
are for it because it will provide jobs for thousands of brass hats." It concluded that our military leaders must be "curbed and punished."[16] Even the
chief of naval operations, Admiral Louis Denfeld, a professional and social
friend of Baldwin, commented that while he did not agree with the thrust
of the article entirely, he thought his "approach was excellent." Denfeld discounted the Navy Department's criticisms, saying, "I have not [a] too high
a regard for those who made it."[17] The longtime correspondent Oswald
Villard, who admired Baldwin's writings, was sure that the article would do
"an enormous amount of good." He cited U.S. senator Robert A. Taft, who
told Villard that he would hold out against UMT to the last.[18]

The 1947 *Harper's* article was not the norm for Baldwin's writings of the
period, but it certainly expressed his deeply held beliefs that the role of the
press in a democracy was to expose any threats to American liberties, regardless of the source. In spite of the opposition, the Universal Military Training
Act was passed in 1951. Draftees, eighteen and one-half years old or older,
served for a minimum of twenty-four months. The Korean War was a factor
in the passage of UMT.

Another major domestic issue that concerned the military and its role
in the country's defenses in the atomic age was that President Harry S.
Truman was determined to cut the military budgets from the high levels
of the war years.[19] With these force reductions came the budget cutbacks.
All the services tried to persuade Congress that their service was best suited
to the needs of a future war, and the bureaucratic infighting was fierce.
Further complicating service competition for specific military missions
were the plans to merge or unify the armed forces to reduce the costs of
the military establishment to Congress. The Air Force demanded complete
autonomy from the Army and the Navy so as to be a co-equal service with
the other two. It wanted complete control of the Navy and Marine Corps
air groups. The Army plan wanted all ground forces, including those of the
Marine Corps, to be under the new Army organization. Since the Soviet
Union had no Navy to speak of, there was little need for U.S. capital ships.

Forrestal quickly realized that if these plans were implemented the Navy would be reduced to a transport service and the Marines to embassy guards.

Ferdinand Eberstadt was commissioned by Forrestal to develop a Navy plan for the unification of the armed services. He was a New York investment banker, a close friend of Forrestal, and, incidentally, an acquaintance of Baldwin. The Eberstadt plan was far reaching. Based on his wartime experiences in Washington, he saw the need for interagency coordination in the executive branch, an interest of Baldwin's for many years. He favored new agencies to centralize defense plans, to collect and to analyze intelligence from overseas, to oversee the mobilization of resource planning, and to sponsor research and development for the military. This plan was quickly adopted by Navy partisans in Congress and, for a time, checkmated the Army and Air Force schemes.[20]

In 1947 President Truman and Congress, tired of the endless debates over the roles of the military services, passed the National Security Act. However, it did not unify the services.[21] The act created the National Security Council to advise the president and to coordinate all national security policies. The amended act of 1949 created a new executive department, the Defense Department. The first secretary of defense was Forrestal, until then the secretary of the Navy. He realized quickly that he had no power to enforce cooperation and coordination among the military services, a job that was formerly done by the service secretaries. The secretary of defense now had cabinet rank, while the service secretaries were subordinate to him, and the Joint Chiefs of Staff were kept in an advisory capacity. Its chairman became the president's chief military adviser. While the new structure laid out clear lines of responsibility, it still did not do away with interservice rivalries.[22]

As long as Forrestal remained as the secretary of defense, the Navy felt reasonably protected from the deprecations from the Army and the Air Force. Congress had approved the Navy's new 65,000-ton supercarrier, *United States* (CVA 58), in 1948, from which nuclear-equipped bombers could be launched. The Air Force had widely advertised its new long-range bomber, the B-36, the first of which was delivered in 1948. That bomber was designed to be able to fly nonstop to Soviet targets.

In 1949, all this changed. President Truman had long surrounded himself with men who openly favored the Air Force's view of national security. The two most prominent were Stuart Symington, the secretary of the Air Force, and Louis A. Johnson, a very politically ambitious lawyer-politician and the chief fund-raiser for the Democratic Party. On March 1, Truman pressured Forrestal to resign.[23]

Johnson was sworn in as the second secretary of defense a few weeks later. With the president's approval, he cancelled the contract for the Navy's new carrier five days after its keel had been laid. The secretary of the Navy was not told of his decision beforehand and resigned in protest. Johnson also reduced the number of aircraft carriers in service from eight to four and made other reductions that tried to merge the Marines' air groups with those of the Air Force to save money and to further service unification.[24] The new secretary of the Navy dismissed Admiral Denfeld as the chief of naval operations.[25] Needless to say, the Navy brass was appalled at these decisions and could not understand how rapidly the political atmosphere in Washington had undercut it. Its once-secure allies on the Hill seemed to have joined the Air Force camp. What followed were months of charges and countercharges, in which the press was utilized for partisan ends. It was a period that has been called the "revolt of the admirals."[26]

In August 1949, President Truman signed a law that made significant changes to the 1947 National Security Act, which differed from the plan that Forrestal favored to one that favored the Army. The structure of the new Defense Department established control over, but not cooperation among, the services. The secretary of defense now had far more power than previously. A new position, chairman of the Joint Chiefs of Staff, was created, and he had direct access to the president. The civilian secretaries of the three services were denied access to the president and were now subordinate to the chairman of the JCS. This act seemed to have sunk the Navy's hopes.[27]

During most of 1949 the American public was alerted to what had been discussed previously behind closed doors in Washington about the direction of America's national defense. It was an often ill-tempered debate that was characterized by frequent and nasty public comments by Navy and Air Force officers and their supporters in Congress. The basic issue was the budget cuts imposed on the military services by President Truman and Secretary of Defense Johnson. The cuts were not uniformly applied, as the Air Force suffered fewer. To many, the personality and the political ambitions of Johnson were to blame for the ruckus. Baldwin considered him to be completely "Truman's creature," who took his boss' wishes to reduce military spending as a command to use a meat-ax approach.[28]

Johnson was driven by political ambitions that also included the White House. He approached defense issues with an eye on political expedience. Baldwin recalled that Johnson was not popular with the military, especially the Navy, but he had many political friends in Washington who supported him. He was also a poker-playing buddy of the president, along with Stuart Symington, the secretary of the Air Force, thus Baldwin was surprised when Johnson once greeted him publicly as a long-lost brother by putting his arms around him, even though he had written critical articles about him. To Baldwin, he was a politician with "a hard shell."[29] "He was such a complete politician that he would sacrifice any defense effectiveness or combat effectiveness in the interests of political achievement," Baldwin later observed.[30]

The forum for the Navy's attack on the Air Force was the House Armed Services Committee, chaired by Carl Vinson, a formidable congressman from Georgia who was generally sympathetic to the Navy's viewpoint. The first salvo was in the form of an anonymous document circulated in May and June 1949 that charged fraud and other improprieties by senior Air Force officers and the secretary of defense on the awarding of the contract for the B-36 bomber to the Convair Corporation of Ft. Worth, Texas. At the end of the July hearings, the committee found that all charges made against the Air Force and the secretary of defense were unfounded. The author of the anonymous document was identified as a civilian who worked in the office of the undersecretary of the Navy. He was fired. It was hard for Baldwin not to be involved in the Navy's salvos, as he knew all of the participants and was sympathetic to their views. He was once accused of being the source of the anti-B-36 bomber articles. His reportorial independence was certainly challenged by the issues.

Six propellers and four jet engines powered the B-36 bomber, on which the Air Force put its hopes for strategic bombing of the Soviet Union. Introduced in 1948, it was the largest plane ever to be mass-produced, and there were very few hangers large enough to house it.[31] The main source of the anti-B-36 data was Glenn L. Martin, whose company lost out in the bidding to Convair.

It was no secret that Baldwin did not like Secretary of the Air Force Symington. His Air Force sources, whom Baldwin respected, did not like the "dirty pool" he played in the Washington scene.[32] Baldwin considered Symington to be "a slippery politician," and the Forrestal family felt Symington had contributed to their father's death in May 1949. He was the only service secretary not invited to be a pallbearer at the funeral. Also in Baldwin's pantheon of undesirables was Air Force general Hoyt Vandenburg, whose uncle was the influential U.S. senator Arthur H. Vandenburg.

Symington didn't care for Baldwin either. Once, while Baldwin was having a drink in Washington at the Statler-Hilton Hotel with General Pete Quesada, who once commanded the Fifteenth Air Force in the war, Symington walked into the bar and saw them together. The following morning, Symington called Quesada into his Pentagon office and said, "You don't pick your friends very carefully do you?" The general, who had a quick temper, shot back, "I pick my friends," and walked out.[33]

In September, Captain John G. Crommelin fired off the second Navy salvo. In 1949 he had become obsessed with the fear that naval aviation was about to be taken over by the Air Force. He also felt that the new post of chairman of the JCS was akin to the German General Staff concept, which he felt was foreign to Navy principles. The immediate problem was the membership of the current JCS, who favored the Air Force views and who had "a landlocked concept" of national defense. He thought the new JCS chairman, General Omar N. Bradley, "wielded tremendous power."[34] Crommelin's letter to Francis P. Matthews, the secretary of the Navy, included covering letters of endorsement from several admirals in operational commands.[35] When in Washington, which was frequent during that autumn, he would telephone Baldwin and ramble on for an hour or so, making all sorts of charges and innuendos about many subjects and people. Baldwin thought him to be "almost psychotic."[36]

In October, Congressman Vinson reconvened his committee to hear from interested service personnel on unification issues. Admiral Arthur Radford, the Navy's senior aviator, stated that the B-36 was "a billion dollar blunder" that promised the American people "an atomic blitz," which would bring "a cheap easy victory."[37] Retired admiral Chester Nimitz challenged the view that high-level area bombing or strategic bombing would win wars.

The man on the spot was Admiral Louis Denfeld, the CNO. It was impossible for him to be neutral between the Truman administration's position that air power was America's only deterrence to the next war, and his Navy colleagues' view that naval aviation must be kept and enlarged. These hearings were a no-holds-barred event, with sharp views vigorously expressed. The Navy's big guns fired their broadsides at the "enemy," the U.S. Air Force. Admiral Denfeld solidly supported Radford's views against those of Secretary Matthews and the secretary of defense. It was a very risky career move but one he told Baldwin he had to take. In fact, on the night before his testimony, Baldwin had dinner with the admiral at his quarters, where he was shown Denfeld's written testimony. Baldwin made a few editorial changes but left the wording intact.[38] Denfeld admired Baldwin and occasionally he would ask him for advice on various issues. It was a relationship that was built on trust and the knowledge that there would be no leaks to the press. They were also friends and Baldwin was a dinner guest at the Denfelds' on occasion. On the day following his testimony, General Omar Bradley fired a verbal barrage at the Navy admirals. "This is no time," he said, "for fancy dans who won't hit the line with all they have on every play unless they can call the signals." He continued to say that the Navy had never been behind unification and never accepted that civilians now managed the Defense Department.

For having taken that position, President Truman removed Admiral Denfeld as CNO on October 27, 1949, shortly after the president had reappointed him. Editorially, the *Times* supported this dismissal because the admiral did not accept "civilian authority . . . [that] must always be superior to professional military authority."[39] Baldwin was furious, writing that the curt manner of Denfeld's dismissal "suggests deliberate intent to humiliate . . . so flagrant that the men who committed it are scarcely qualified to lead other men."[40] It was a criticism leveled at Secretary Matthews, and at Johnson, and indirectly at President Truman. The revolt of the admirals ended with this decision and both Denfeld and Crommelin resigned from the Navy in 1950.

In August 1949, after the Soviet Union exploded its first atomic bomb, Baldwin saw no immediate threat that the Soviet government would attack the West, but he speculated that within a few years their nuclear stockpile could increase rapidly. Somehow both nations had to realize that there must be "a mutual restraint, bred by fear," to prevent the use of atomic bombs in the future.[41] He urged that the Soviet Union be persuaded that "the game of aggressive war is not worth the candle . . . that even her possession of the atomic bomb would not insure her a blitzkrieg victory."[42]

The Truman administration was so concerned about the end of the American atomic monopoly that the president ordered the development of the hydrogen bomb. Not all American scientists favored such a bomb, one of whom was Dr. Hans Bethe, who taught at Cornell University's Laboratory of Nuclear Studies. He had written in April 1950 that the H-bomb would have little military use, but it would be devastating on civilian populations in large cities. In response to Baldwin's letter asking him for further elaboration, Dr. Bethe wrote a carefully worded response reminding Baldwin of the extreme security regulations about the entire project and that no attribution of any information in the letter could ever be revealed. Baldwin always kept such confidences.

He then told Baldwin that the H-bomb probably could be developed but that there were many technical and engineering obstacles to be overcome over several years' time. To produce liquid hydrogen in large quantities in order to extract deuterium would be "a great task." If the core of the bomb were encased in cobalt, "tremendous amounts of radioactivity" from gamma rays would be produced. The particles from the explosion would "settle as dust." Radioactive cobalt has a half-life of five years, but by that time everyone on earth would be dead from either radiation poisoning or from starvation. There would be no protection and "the attacker's country would be just as much poisoned by the radioactivity as the country [being] attacked." In conclusion, Dr. Bethe said, the H-bomb would be "a frightful weapon" with little military value beyond the existing atomic bombs.[43] Dr. Leo Szilard, who also publicly opposed the development of the H-bomb, called it a "doomsday device." He was a professor of biophysics at the University of Chicago and was directly responsible for the Manhattan Project during World War II.

This warning about the H-bomb, from Baldwin's "un-impeachable" source, reinforced his skeptical views on the limits of science to develop new weapons, and the military application of atomic bombs on the battlefield. This caution was evident in his remarks before New York City schoolteachers in April 1950. He concluded his presentation with the following advice: "we must be strong, but not too strong; our strength must be flexible and relative to the world situation. We must never become the garrison state or the bankrupt state. Military security is only one element . . . of our strength. We must be strong politically, economically, and psychologically. We must never lose at home what we are trying to defend abroad."[44] His statement was to presage a threat to American values.

Building upon Cold War tensions and finding domestic partisan political advantage, the junior senator from Wisconsin, Joseph R. McCarthy, made an accusation in the spring of 1950 against the State Department, listing a number of its employees as either Communists or Communist sympathizers. It was his charge that there were traitors in the government who had enabled the Russians to develop an atomic bomb. There was just enough hard evidence about real spies in the U.S. atomic program to give credence to McCarthy's accusations. Baldwin castigated "the Sir Galahads of security," who tilted their lances with our freedoms.[45] He regarded the notoriety of the senator as just "one manifestation of Congressional and public concern with security in the atomic age,"[46] and pointed with alarm at the tactics of guilt by association, the smear technique, and the increased level of government secrecy.

Baldwin's education about the dangers of Communist expansion was influenced by his friend and news source, Secretary of Defense Forrestal. Initially, Baldwin pondered whether Communism was the driving ideology behind Stalin's territorial expansion after 1945, or merely a cover to renew the traditional czarist imperial ambitions. He came to believe that the post–World War II years were directly influenced by decisions made during the war by President Roosevelt.

In 1949 he was asked by the Claremont Colleges in Pomona, California, to give a series of public lectures on the war. This opportunity gave him the forum to speak out on current political realities of the immediate postwar years. Those lectures received national circulation when two articles based on them appeared in the *Atlantic Monthly* magazine in January and February 1950. Entitled "Our Worst Blunders in the War," Baldwin pulled no punches itemizing FDR's poor wartime decisions.

In his view, major American wartime errors were part of "our political immaturity." The United States fought the war to win a military victory but failed to realize that the purpose of any war was a more stable peace. Paraphrasing Carl von Clausewitz, the early nineteenth-century Prussian general and war theorist, Baldwin noted that wars were "an extension of politics by other means." He felt that American judgment was "emotionally clouded" by our hopes that the war would usher in a brave new world, where the Brotherhood of Man would emerge from the carnage of war.

The United States had no peace aims other than the vague ideas found in the Atlantic Charter and in President Roosevelt's "Four Freedoms" speech of 1941. Americans were idealists but not pragmatists. We fought to win the war but did not know "what [we] were fighting for."[47] Washington made fundamental errors about the Soviet Union. It wanted to believe that the politburo leadership was more nationalist than Communist, that Stalin was a good leader with whom we could work, that if the United States did not aid him he might make a separate peace treaty with Hitler's Germany, and that the Soviet Union's entry into the Asian war against Japan in the summer of 1945 was essential to the Allied victory.

The key to the American war effort was President Roosevelt. He had great confidence in his political skills at home and believed that those skills of personal diplomacy could be used at the wartime conferences. He had great personal charm and considerable persuasive powers and he acted frequently as his own State Department. Baldwin noted that the president's foreign policy was marked more by "idealism and altruism than by realism."[48] There was still no one in Washington to integrate military and political policy.

Baldwin wrote that it would have been in the interest of Britain and the Unites States had the United States "encouraged—the world's two great dictatorships to fight each other to a frazzle." The result would have weakened both Nazism and Communism and have placed "the democracies in supreme power in the world."[49] He rejected the separate peace idea between Stalin and Hitler. "A man being strangled to death struggles with all that's in him; Russia could not quit," he opined.[50] As for Russia's entry in the war against Japan in August 1945, the United States should have tried to keep it out of that war, rather than pleading with it to enter with territorial inducements made at China's expense.

Turning to other decisions, the Unconditional Surrender Policy, reached at the January 1943 Casablanca Conference between Churchill and Roosevelt, was "the biggest political mistake of the war," as it "probably lengthened the war, cost us lives and helped to lead to the present abortive peace."[51] Stalin chose to soften the inevitable defeat of Germany with attempts to encourage anti-Hitler opposition. The policy demonstrated "political bankruptcy" and, to Baldwin, "confirmed our lack of a reasoned program for peace." For a war in Europe to end in Germany's complete destruction would create a political vacuum and leave the Soviet Union "the top dog" in Europe.[52]

Baldwin noted that the loss of Central Europe to the Russians reflected the divergent plans of Churchill, who favored a Balkan invasion, and Roosevelt, who favored the cross-channel invasion of Normandy. At the 1943 Teheran Conference and the 1945 Yalta Conference, Stalin favored the Normandy invasion as the second front, since it would leave Central Europe open to Russian influence after the war. While Baldwin did not criticize General Eisenhower's plan for the cross-channel invasion, which was sound militarily, it did allow for Russia's domination of Central Europe.

The Berlin decision to let the Russians take the capital city was, to Baldwin, a result of "our lack of politico-military realism during the war."[53] Another issue was the Allied corridor to Berlin after the war, which was not made clear on the matter of access. He blamed the War Department, which did not cooperate with the State Department. The former had strong leaders in 1945, while the latter was weak. The European war ended with boundaries that had been established by the European Advisory Commission and approved at the Quebec and Yalta Conferences.[54] He concluded, "We could have moved further eastward. But the political die had been cast; there was not much point in military sacrifice for a political lost cause." That was why Berlin became an island "in a Russian sea" and Central Europe remained under Russian control for decades to come.[55]

In the Pacific war, the loss of the Philippines in 1942 was because of "high-level errors," many of which were made by General Douglas MacArthur.[56] There was no cooperation between the Army and the Navy leaders in the nine hours after the Pearl Harbor attack. Baldwin referred obliquely to a "secret" press conference in Washington on November 15, 1941, in which "a top-ranking Army official" stated that war with Japan was imminent. Once begun, B-17 bombers already in the Philippines would fly off to bomb Japanese cities and continue to fly on to Vladivostok, Russia. This Army official assumed that the Pacific war would be an air war with little need for the Navy. Not named in those 1950 articles, that officer was General George C. Marshall, the Army's chief of staff. When queried by Baldwin after the war, the general declined to have his name publicized but confirmed his views of 1941.[57]

The prewar Rainbow Five plan called for American forces to be on the defensive after a Japanese invasion. Just before the Pearl Harbor attack the plan was revised to include an air offensive against enemy forces. In Washington, air enthusiasts were able to sell the potential of air power to policymakers. In hindsight, General MacArthur's estimates of his ability to defend the islands were "wildly over-optimistic." As a result, the Army and Navy units did not anticipate the speed of the Japanese invasion. MacArthur's communiqués on the war in 1942 "bore so little resemblance to actual events that when the gist of them that were cast in a cheerful mood of utter unreality, were broadcast, via U.S. radio, to our suffering troops on Bataan, they aroused actual resentment."[58] The unkindest cut of all was that MacArthur assured his troops, on January 15, 1942, that help was on the way from the United States. It was not.

Baldwin moved on to what he called "appeasement in Asia," which involved America urging a Russian commitment in 1945 to enter the Japanese war by offering Chinese territory in Manchuria as an inducement. This urgency was based upon conflicting intelligence information on the size and strength of the Japanese Kwantung Army in Manchuria. This was a factor in the American plans for the invasion of the Japanese home islands in the fall of 1945. General Marshall favored the invasion and the Russian entry into the war.[59] Baldwin commented how "our military men underrated Japan in 1941 and overrated it in 1945."[60] At Yalta, Stalin drove a hard bargain for Russia's entry, within ninety days of V-E day, in the Asian war for territorial concessions that were willingly granted by President Roosevelt. Baldwin quoted former secretary of war Henry Stimson's observation that, at Yalta, there was "a good deal of altruism and idealism instead of stark realities."[61] The dropping of two atomic bombs in August 1945 may have shortened the war "by a day, a week, or a month—but not more." The United States dropped the bombs to end the war quickly, but in so doing lost its role as the world's moral leader. It was no longer an idealistic nation, but one in which unrestricted warfare on enemy civilians defeated any peace aims it might have had. As he said, "We cannot hasten military victory by slaughtering" the innocent. Unrestricted warfare, which the United States practiced, could "never lay the groundwork for a more stable peace." In summary, the *Times* military editor concluded that "we have embarked upon total war with a vengeance; we have done our best to make it far more total. If we do not soon reverse this trend . . . to limit and control war . . . we shall some day ourselves become the victims of our own theories and practices."[62]

One of the benefits of having a national reputation as a journalist was correspondence with others of equal stature in the profession. Walter Lippmann, the celebrated columnist with the *New York Herald-Tribune*, took issue with some of Baldwin's points, namely his view that President Roosevelt relied too much on personal diplomacy. Baldwin's reply was that while Churchill had the rhetoric, Roosevelt had the power that became the "fundamental" basis of U.S.-Soviet relations during the war.[63] In commenting upon Churchill's often-stated plan to attack the so-called soft underbelly of Europe to prevent the Russian armies from entering western Europe, Baldwin told Lippmann, "I think there was a real chance strategically and militarily ... that the southern invasion could have pushed through the Adriatic into Czechoslovakia and perhaps into eastern Germany before the Russians reached there." He admitted that this subject required "a great deal more spade work" before any conclusions could be reached.[64] World War II had ended but the world of tomorrow had begun.

There were perquisites to his job, some of which were from his outside associations and some from his being on the *Times* staff. During the war he met King Peter II of Yugoslavia at a black-tie reception, because he was a member of the Council on Foreign Relations. In October 1947 he and Helen met the Duke and Duchess of Windsor at a private reception at the Waldorf Astoria Hotel in New York City, an invitation extended by the New York director of the British Information Service that Baldwin used extensively during the war for their war communiqués.[65] Perhaps the most memorable event (which, in Baldwin's words, "fully lived up to all [of] my expectations") was when former British prime minister Winston Churchill dined at the *Times* on Monday evening, March 28, 1949. He was on a speaking tour in America and was invited by Sulzberger to a private dinner to meet the senior staff in the news and editorial departments. At the time, the paper was serializing Churchill's war memoirs.

In attendance, in the publisher's private dining room on the fourteenth floor of the Times Building, were thirteen staff members, together with six invited guests that included Bernard Baruch, Captain Christopher Soames (Churchill's son-in-law), and Randolph Churchill. Accompanying the party was General Walter Bedell Smith, the former U.S. ambassador to the Soviet Union. The ground rules were that no one was to take notes, though some did covertly.

The evening started with Churchill holding a glass of tomato juice, rather uncomfortably, someone observed. He switched quickly to champagne when it was offered during dinner. The 1934 Pol Roger champagne flowed without interruption and mellowed the great man. After dinner, when cigars were distributed, he enjoyed several snifters of brandy. So fortified, he fielded questions for almost an hour on the concessions made at Yalta, how to deal with the Russians, Roosevelt's comments on Pearl Harbor, the Balkan issue, and other topics. Baldwin recalled how Churchill thought that the American atomic bomb served as a deterrent to Russian aggression; this was six months before the Russians exploded their first atomic device.

It was a unique experience for all present to be in the company of such a famous man, who, by all accounts, was enjoying himself immensely. Did he like writing? "I do not write, I dictate," he replied. "I hate calligraphy," which is what he called writing one word at a time on a page. On the day following the dinner, Sulzberger asked all staff members present to write a memorandum, addressed to him, of their recollections of the previous evening.[66]

On a less lofty plane, but just as enjoyable, were the Sunday sit-down luncheons at the Sulzberger home, Hillandale, a thirty-two-room mansion on a fifty-seven-acre estate in White Plains, New York, to which the Baldwin family was often invited, together with other staff families and other guests. "Everybody who was anybody" was there, Barbara, Hanson's older daughter, recalled. For the children there were all sorts of outdoor activities, including tennis, croquet, swimming, and baseball. Elizabeth, Hanson's younger daughter, recalled running down the long second-floor corridor with other children. Arthur Sulzberger later sold that house, which had belonged to his father-in-law, Adoph Ochs, and bought a smaller home of sixteen rooms on eleven acres near Stamford, Connecticut. He renamed it Hillandale as well.

The summer luncheons continued at the new location. Occasionally, a mystery guest would attend, someone prominent in the news at the time. The reproving blue memos from the publisher to Baldwin when the content of his *Times* pieces strayed outside military coverage did not create a breach between the men. What happened in the office stayed there, and did not spill over to spoil their social relationship.[67]

Korea, 1950–53

The sudden beginning of the Korean War in 1950 caught Baldwin by surprise, as it did many others. The conventional wisdom in the post-war years was that the Soviet armies would attack in Western Europe. It was also believed in Washington that Joseph Stalin controlled a worldwide Communist conspiracy that would eventually try to make the world safe for Communism, Soviet style. The Korean War was viewed by some as a test of the determination and ability of Washington to fight. The concern within the Truman administration was that Stalin would use the Korean War to engage American forces, thus permitting Russia to move elsewhere in Europe.

Beginning on June 25, 1950, the North Korean forces moved swiftly south across the 38th parallel, decimating the poorly equipped and trained South Korean army (ROK). American occupation troops in Japan were sent over to bolster the ROK, but to little effect. By the end of July 1950, Lieutenant General Walton H. Walker, who commanded the UN forces in South Korea, had established the Pusan perimeter, a 130-mile barrier of contact with the enemy. The harbor at Pusan, on the southeast coast of the Korean peninsula, was the only link to all supplies arriving from Japan and from the United States. For the next six weeks, until September 15, the defenses of the perimeter were tested repeatedly. General Walker did not have enough troops to defend the entire line, and was forced to move his troops about to repel the North Korean attacks at various points.[1]

In mid-July Baldwin became concerned about the loose talk in Congress that favored the use of the atomic bomb, America's ultimate weapon. Since 1945 he had been writing that the bomb was a weapon of limited military value. In the context of the current war situation, he observed that as the going gets tough, "expediency replaces ethics." Proponents for the bomb's use were the "voice of doom," he wrote. Our strategy ought to be to "avoid an atomic strategy . . . in any war," citing military reasons against the bomb's use: our limited stockpiles, no large targets in North Korea, and the inability of the bomb to stop the war.

There were larger issues. "If we want to lose what friends and what influence we have left in Asia, a good way to do it is to drop the atomic bomb on North Korea."[2] World public opinion would label us as being warmongers. A Communist-sponsored petition, currently being circulated throughout the world, called for the outlawing of atomic warfare. We would fall into that Communist propaganda trap if we went ahead and used the bomb on Korea. Baldwin thought that the existing arsenal of World War II's non-atomic weapons would be adequate for the current war.

To break the stalemate around the Pusan perimeter, General Douglas MacArthur proposed an invasion of the port of Inchon, on the west coast of the Korean peninsula and close to the South Korean capital of Seoul. In his mind, this invasion would relieve the UN forces near Pusan and force the North Korean forces to move north, where the U.S. Eighth Army would be moving south to engage them. The breakout from the perimeter would trap the enemy and lead to their destruction.[3]

While this bold move by MacArthur was a sound strategy, its implementation would be very difficult. The JCS had many doubts and told MacArthur so. He persisted over several weeks' time and was able to get their reluctant approval by arguing that the North Korean commanders most likely thought that such an invasion would be so difficult as to be almost impossible. Thus, the element of surprise by the UN-U.S.-ROK forces would contribute to the success of the operation.[4]

The invasion took place on September 15, 1950, to the surprise of the enemy troops in the area. Its success raised new questions, such as where to go from there: to the 38th parallel or on to the Yalu River that divided Manchuria from North Korea? MacArthur wanted to unify the peninsula under Syngman Rhee's anti-Communist government.

Baldwin was just as surprised and pleased as anyone that the Inchon landing came off as well as it did. By late September 1950, the city of Seoul was occupied and the nearby Kimpo airport was seized as well. MacArthur's forces moved north to the 38th parallel with the ROK forces crossing it on October 1 and the U.S. Eighth Army on October 9. The North Korean capital, Pyongyang, was overrun on October 20. ROK units reached the Yalu River at Chosan, which divided Manchuria from the Korean peninsula.

In late June, Baldwin complained at the paucity of communication between General MacArthur's headquarters in Tokyo and the Pentagon. Richard Whalen has observed that "one of the roots of the tragedy of the Korean War" was Washington's dependence upon MacArthur's headquarters for information. Once President Truman made the political decision to send in American troops, the military decisions were "based almost entirely on MacArthur's reports, evaluations, recommendations—and demands."[5] To find out for himself what was going on, Baldwin spent October and November 1950 visiting Japan, Korea, Taiwan, Hong Kong, and French Indochina.

His first stop was Tokyo, where an article of his published in *The Saturday Evening Post* detailed his visit. The volume of mail generated by "We're Not the Best in the World," much of it hostile, surprised Baldwin. The article was based largely on his evidence that most American weapons of the late war made during the war were not created by American know-how, with the exception of the proximity fuse and improved radar. Even the atomic bomb was developed from scientific steps previously worked out by expatriate scientists from Europe. However, it was built by American industrial and engineering skills, which solved the many problems in its manufacture.[6]

The blunt tone, as in many of his articles, challenged American self-worth and pride of country. Despite Baldwin's assertion that he did not intend to "slur" the American military, a number of readers came to that conclusion. It may have been his comments that the United States was not a disciplined or a militaristic society, and that the current values of "work less and make more" were weakening our country's former stiff societal fiber. His closing words were: "The America of tomorrow can no longer rely solely on mass production. Quantity without quality could be catastrophic." Those words were like a jeremiad, alerting America to wake up and be aware of the dangers ahead.[7]

Baldwin's critique was not well received. The following vulgar and hostile letter, though not typical, represented the feelings of one U.S. Marine in Korea. He and his buddies thought Baldwin was "full of shit" to suggest that America was not the best in the world. If Baldwin doubted how brave the

Marines were then he ought to put any "God damn Red or Japs" against us and see "if we walk away." Once the writer left "the rock" he was going to "punch you [Baldwin] right in that big fat face of [his]. Drop dead."[8]

On his arrival in Tokyo, Baldwin sought to renew his acquaintance with Major General Willoughby, MacArthur's G-2 chief. They had first met before the war when he was an infantry instructor at Fort Benning, Georgia, but Baldwin quickly learned that his recent *Saturday Evening Post* article had been circulated among the general's senior staff, and he was on the do-not-see list of reporters. Fortunately, Baldwin was not without other resources.

The American ambassador to Japan, William J. Sebald, was General Willoughby's brother-in-law. A Naval Academy graduate, class of 1922, Sebald had been Ensign Baldwin's senior when they both served on the old USS *Texas* battleship in 1924. They became lifelong friends and corresponded with each other over the years, and although Sebald could not help his friend overcome the barriers erected by MacArthur's staff, he could brief him on some little points.[9] For example, his wife, Edith Sebald, who was a friend of Jean MacArthur, acted as an official cohost at the many social functions given by the MacArthurs. She told Baldwin one story that illustrated what it was like to be in his presence. On that occasion, Jean MacArthur greeted their guests and offered them cocktails or other libations. After a time, the curtains at the end of the living room parted and the general entered the room, greeting his guests warmly. The whole staged appearance confirmed the growing perception that he had a sense of the dramatic.[10]

As Washington's official representative to MacArthur in his role as the supreme commander of the Allied occupation forces in Japan, Sebald later recalled that MacArthur was very sensitive and also very self-sufficient. In his role, Sebald had to be very low-keyed. He avoided the temptation to draw the general out for fear that he would think that Sebald was being critical of him and his decisions. On the positive side, he felt that it was an education just to listen to the general's pronouncements on any number of subjects: "There were very few subjects that he didn't know more about, either actually or he thought he knew more about, than I did."[11]

Baldwin observed that MacArthur's entourage in Tokyo was "really a can of worms," with feuds among members of the senior staff who had been with the general before and during the war. Baldwin later observed that having these "satrapies, each one vying for power . . . was MacArthur's way to administer his staff. Generally, he was so aloof that his chief of staff took care of much of the office business."[12] He was surprised that the staff included so many mediocrities. Baldwin later commented that the staff was "ingrown," and that those close to the general had "an almost idolatrous worship for their chief," overcome as they were by his personal charm and magnetism. In the eyes of his staff, what was good for Douglas MacArthur and what was good for the United States were "synonymous." His judgments were always correct, they thought.[13]

In his eagerness to contact the general, Baldwin dutifully went through channels. This meant making his request known to the chief of staff, General Edward Mallory Almond. After what seemed to be a long time in his waiting room, he finally saw Almond, who told Baldwin that because of things he had written the general could not see him, but that if he mended his ways an interview might be arranged. *The Saturday Evening Post* article was specifically mentioned, confirming Baldwin's fears.[14]

Baldwin then asked if he could see MacArthur's intelligence reports, so as to determine whether the United States was prepared or unprepared for the North Korean invasion on June 25, 1950. He was able to see only partial reports, which he thought were almost useless for his purposes. Later, he did read the entire set of the intelligence reports that showed there was no sense of urgency in MacArthur's headquarters that the North Koreans were about to attack in June 1950.[15]

Leaving Tokyo, Baldwin hitched a ride on an Air Force plane, his usual method of getting around in a combat zone. As always, his aim on these trips was to "cover the waterfront," making it his business to talk with battalion and regimental commanders, as well as to anyone else he could find. He was particularly interested in enemy weapons and tactics. A. J. Liebling commented upon this attention to detail in a *New Yorker* profile of Baldwin, noting that unlike other military experts, Baldwin supplied his readers with a considerable amount of information, including weapons characteristics.[16] In another report, Baldwin attributed the collapse of the North Korean units fleeing north as illustrating the volatility of the enemy's morale; savage and aggressive in victory, depressed and sullen in defeat.[17]

The Korean War emphasized to Baldwin the need to relearn one of the lessons of World War II, that military and foreign policies had to support each other. Specifically, Korea did not play an important role in the American strategy after 1945; U.S. occupation troops left in 1948. The National Security Council advised President Truman in 1949 that if South Korea were invaded from the north, Washington should aid President Syngman Rhee with weapons only, no troops. After June 1950, the president changed U.S.-Korean policy once again and committed U.S. forces "to an area of the world strategically unimportant."[18] He advised that the United States could not be strong everywhere and added "we cannot stand a series of Koreas." He stressed that the United States must not be overcommitted, saying, "We must not promise what we cannot fulfill."[19] While there may have been warnings of a North Korean attack, such intelligence was not taken seriously in Washington.

On the tactical level, Baldwin learned that there were no accurate maps of the peninsula, with no roads or railroads, because after 1945 the high level of photo reconnaissance and photo mapping done during World War II had not been maintained. There was, therefore, a need for counterintelligence to screen refugees to sift out spies behind U.S. lines. It is not surprising that the United States knew far less of what the North Koreans were doing than they did of U.S. movements. He noted that the Americans hired Koreans to work on the airfields during the day, and these same Koreans, at night, took to the surrounding hills to shoot at them. Another bothersome aspect of the war was that Americans "look[ed] down" on the Koreans "as an inferior race." GIs used the derogatory term "gook," which Baldwin heard often about the South Koreans. With proper training, they proved to be very tough soldiers. The future destiny of the United States, he felt, depended upon a better knowledge of the Far East. Unfortunately, few American civilian and military personnel understood the diverse peoples and culture.[20]

Baldwin was on the island of Taiwan when Chinese forces entered the war in support of North Korea in November 1950. General MacArthur was taken by surprise, having previously denied that China would commit to the war, although China had warned Washington in October that crossing the 38th parallel would trigger the entry of its troops. One of Baldwin's sources on Taiwan was Colonel David D. Barrett, U.S. Army. He was one of the "old China hands," having been there since 1927. In 1944 he headed the Dixie mission to Yenan to talk with Mao Tse-tung. Their favorable reports praised Mao's forces in fighting the Japanese. After the war, those reports from the U.S. foreign service officers were used to force their resignation from the State Department for having praised the Chinese Communist leader. Colonel Barrett was not fired but was denied a promotion to brigadier general.

The prevailing popular view was that the UN forces crossing the 38th parallel and moving north to the Yalu River was the trigger for China to enter the war. What Baldwin later reported was that in early 1950, at a meeting in Beijing, Russia, Communist China, and North Korea had agreed on the invasion of South Korea. Also agreed upon were the specific roles each nation would play. China would send in troops if the North Korean army was collapsing, and Russia would supply weapons and military advice. From this information, Baldwin concluded that MacArthur's decision to cross the 38th parallel did not cause the Chinese to enter the war; it was instead the collapse of the North Korean forces that forced China's decision. He was almost certain that Colonel Barrett was his source for this information. He was serving at the time as a military attaché to the Nationalist government of Chiang Kai-shek, and given his long background as a China observer, his contacts, and his fluency in the language, he could have been aware of such a meeting. Unfortunately, Baldwin's notes did not include the name of his source, as he talked with several others while in Taiwan.[21]

One of the major political developments after World War II was the decline and fall of European empires in Africa and in Asia. In some instances the colonial power left, as the British left India in 1947. The French, however, chose to remain in Indochina, an area that included Vietnam, Laos, and Cambodia, as well as the three Vietnamese colonies of Annam, Tonkin (bordering on China), and Cochin China in the south around Saigon.[22]

When Baldwin arrived in Saigon in November 1950, a civil war had been going on for four years. In Hanoi, the largest party in the National Assembly was the Vietminh, led by Ho Chi Minh. With no possible agreement with Paris, the Vietminh's forces openly clashed with French colonial troops, beginning in December 1946.[23] At the time of Baldwin's visit, the French feared that China would intervene on the side of the Vietminh as it had in Korea to help the North Korean army.

Baldwin thought that Saigon deserved the appellation of the Paris of the Orient, with its shaded boulevards and sidewalk cafes. In reality, it was "a French-held island in a Vietminh sea."[24] The Truman administration had begun to send American planes and other equipment to aid the French, and within a few years, Washington was paying for 78 percent of the total French military expenses in Indochina.[25] French officers, with whom Baldwin spoke, did not underestimate the fighting abilities of the Vietminh, whom they said used the "wiles of stealth, cunning, and ruthlessness." An ambush was often "the shot from the dark and the tossed grenade."[26]

Within the U.S. legation in Saigon, Baldwin noted a major disagreement on what policy the United States should adapt. Donald R. Heath, the envoy extraordinary and minister plenipotentiary believed that Washington should support the French in Indochina with no independent policy of its own. He passed on French reports of their progress against the Vietminh to Washington that were not very accurate. The larger picture was that the Truman administration felt that to encourage France to join the North Atlantic Treaty Organization (NATO) in Europe, it had to support France's attempts to preserve its empire in the Far East. Opposing Minister Heath was Edmund L. Gullion, the chargé d'affaires at the legation, who believed that the United States should recognize the Vietnamese desire for independence from France and encourage the French authorities to take the necessary political steps.[27] The American military mission in Saigon was divided as well on what U.S. policy ought to be.

Baldwin traveled with a French unit into the Delta region, south of Saigon. There he saw mud huts and watchtowers manned by colonial troops and commanded by French officers. Fields of fire had been constructed behind barbed wire enclosures. He took an Air France plane north to Hanoi where most of the fighting had occurred. He recalled an elaborate meal served on board the plane as it flew over dense jungle that was infested with Vietminh troops.[28] The French perimeter was 375 miles around Hanoi and the port of Haiphong. Within that area, however, the French commanders lived very well, and Baldwin enjoyed the privilege of eating a seven-course dinner, with the appropriate wines. It began with the most junior officer present offering the traditional French army toast that the next officer to die would bring the opportunity for rapid promotion for others.[29]

Baldwin was critical of the French static defenses in forts that reminded him of the popular 1924 adventure novel by Percival Wren, *Beau Geste*, set in French Morocco. In Vietnam the French Foreign Legion, with its multinational troops from Europe and Africa, all fought there in the best tradition of the beau geste, or gallant gesture.

The war in the North Vietnam had changed from pacification of anti-guerrilla attacks to mobile operations. The Vietminh army, under Ho Chi Minh and with Chinese help, made coordinated attacks against French positions. "When the sun goes down the Vietminh is king," he reported. At night, loudspeakers blared over the rice paddies telling the people where to bring their rice and warned those who aided the French that they would suffer reprisals. Baldwin noted that, ironically, the peasants who blew up roads at night were hired by the French in the morning to repair the damage. Baldwin also noted the excellent quality of Vietminh weapons supplied by Communist countries.

The increasing number of enemy coordinated attacks did not, he noted, "seem to disturb the French too much. Here one lives with guile, stealth and fear, and learns to treat them as brothers. It takes a fatalistic philosophy, and the French in Indochina have acquired it," he concluded after his visit.[30] He would not return to Vietnam for another fifteen years, but he would note the declining French military position over the next few years.

On his return to New York, he wrote a well-received summary of his Far Eastern visit. The two greatest dangers now facing the United States were the military power of China and the "identical policy" aims of Russia and "Red China." The United States was in an "impossible" position in Korea and must end its involvement there, "lest [it] be bled white." He tied the Chinese role in Korea with its role in French Indochina. Based on what he learned on his visit to Taiwan, he cited the aforementioned meeting in Beijing in early 1950, where Kim Il Sung was given the go-ahead to invade South Korea by Mao and Stalin. Baldwin did not know what conditions China had been promised for its help in Korea and in Indochina, but he surmised that this aid would expand the Chinese "zone of influence" in both areas.

In a worst-case scenario, he warned that if the United States abandoned Chiang Kai-shek on Taiwan to the Communists as a condition to end the Korean War, or granted the Beijing government a seat on the United Nations Security Council, then "much of Asia will fall like a house of cards to Communism." It was an early description of the domino theory that President Eisenhower and later presidents cited.

Baldwin listed the errors in General MacArthur's assessment of the Chinese intention to enter the Korean war, and his decision to move U.S. troops north to the Yalu River, which made the American position untenable, warning: "We can never win a land struggle on the Asiatic continent . . . against the hoards of Asia . . . but we can lose the world in Asia if we are not wise and strong."[31] This piece was a far cry from his normal focus on military equipment and strategy, an early sign of his alarm at the changing political forces in the world and their effect on the United States. Interestingly, Sulzberger, his publisher, who often criticized Baldwin for writing on political issues, praised this piece.[32]

On Wednesday, April 11, 1951, when President Truman dismissed General MacArthur as the UN commander in Korea, the American public was shocked. Previously the House minority leader, Representative Joseph Martin, a Republican from Massachusetts, had read to the House a telegram from the general that clearly stated his beliefs that the Manchurian bases for the Chinese army must be bombed, that Chiang Kai-shek's forces on Taiwan must raid the Chinese coast, and that U.S. naval forces ought to blockade the Chinese coastline. The general continued, "In Asia we fight Europe's war. Lose the war in Asia, Europe is doomed." A win in Asia and Europe would probably avoid a future war. In a later, frequently quoted phrase, the general said that in war "there is no substitute for victory."[33]

What the American public did not know was that there was growing hostility between the Pentagon and the general over strategy. Truman wanted to keep it limited, to keep the Russians out and negotiate a peaceful solution. The general was convinced that China was not militarily strong, and he demanded that no limitations be placed on what he thought best to win the war. He went ahead, on his own authority, and informed the Chinese commander in the field that the time had come for a ceasefire, in other words, that the Chinese should surrender when its forces occupied half of Korea.[34]

What followed Truman's decision was, in Baldwin's words, the "biggest emotional binge" in America for many years.[35] The public was outraged that such a genuine American military hero should be sacked in the middle of the war. There was talk of impeachment. The president's popularity polls showed that his ratings were low, even before his announcement.

Baldwin wrote extensively before and after the general's dismissal on the war's progress, or the lack thereof. In one of his better descriptions, he characterized MacArthur as a "man armored in his own omniscience."[36] Baldwin felt the general ought to have resigned earlier because, as a civilian, he could have expressed his views on America's foreign and military policies. Baldwin felt that it was wrong for him to remain in uniform while he protested openly his disagreement with Washington's military policies.

Baldwin agreed that President Truman had the right, in the U.S. democratic system, to dismiss MacArthur, because elected government officials should always be dominant. He thought there was a "fine line" as to what was proper, or improper, for a military commander to say about political subjects.[37] Dissent by the military should go through the proper chain of command, rather than be conducted in the public media.[38]

Douglas MacArthur had made a career of speaking his mind on many subjects over the years. No one denied his intelligence, his considerable knowledge of military history, or his willingness to take military risks, as was demonstrated in the Inchon landing on September 15, 1950. He liked to speak in generalities, rather than in the specifics of how he would implement his views. His ingrown staff never challenged his ego and his "granite self-assurance."[39] What he did to provoke his dismissal was to "deliberately set out to swing American public opinion to his concepts and to use his domestic and international political prestige to force a change in Government policies."[40]

There was a larger issue to consider, beyond MacArthur's charisma. The American public had had nothing to cheer about since V-J day in 1945, and his one-liner about the need for a victory in war rather than prolonged indecision cut through the public miasma about the Cold War. After the dismissal, Baldwin received a number of readers' letters that were sharply critical of the president and the JCS. One writer from Massachusetts asked why didn't the "Big Brass" in the Pentagon support the general and "defy the bankrupt haberdasher?"[41] Another admirer of the general from New Jersey compared MacArthur favorably with George Washington, Abraham Lincoln, and Winston Churchill.[42] Baldwin considered these and letters in a similar vein to be emotional and hysterical.

The "great debate," as Baldwin called it, was how to end the Korean War. He sensed America's war weariness, especially in response to increasing monthly casualties. When the United States as a nation understood why it was fighting, then we will understand its losses, he wrote. But the United States had no clear-cut objectives in Korea. It had "the bull by the tail and [didn't] know how to let up." Normally in war, the objective was to destroy the enemy's forces or its will to fight. According to Baldwin, "Neither [was] possible in Korea," a war limited by geography—the Yalu River frontier with

Manchuria—and by how many forces it was willing to commit. Baldwin saw the dilemma clearly.[43]

He dismissed as "fatuous" President Truman's view that increased enemy losses would lead to peace negotiations. He thought it would be a "miracle" if the Communists accepted the 38th parallel as the starting point for peace negotiations, which they did in July 1951. In Baldwin's view, Korea was "a strategically unprofitable area of the world [where] a definite victory seems impossible."[44] The 38th parallel would not guarantee peace on that peninsula, but it would permit the withdrawal of American troops.[45]

The armistice negotiations with the North Koreans and the Chinese did not lead smoothly to a swift conclusion but dragged on for almost two years. The most controversial issue was the repatriation of the prisoners of war. Over this and other issues the talks went through a series of suspensions, recesses, and adjournments, while both sides continued to reinforce their front lines and the death rate continued to climb. To one observer the opposing trench lines resembled the western front during World War I, replete with sharp, small unit actions. As President Eisenhower observed, "Small attacks on small hills would not end the war."[46]

The seemingly endless delays in the truce talks bothered Baldwin as well as many other observers. As the months dragged on, his military sources advocated an offensive action against the Communists, but that action would play into the enemy's propaganda labeling the United States an aggressor. An offensive action would increase U.S. casualties during an American presidential election year; but to do nothing would increase the American public's demand to get out of Korea, as French citizens were saying about Indochina. Baldwin concluded that it was up to the enemy to decide whether or not the limited war in Korea would expand into an unlimited war in Asia.[47] The longer the UN forces waited for the truce talks to end, the more opportunity it gave both sides to reinforce their defenses to a point where any offensive would be at a considerable cost. He estimated that the enemy's forces in Korea in March 1952 numbered 900,000 troops.[48]

In a piece that was killed by assistant managing editor Ted Bernstein, the chief of the bullpen editors in the *Times* newsroom, as being too political, Baldwin laid out his views on Soviet motivation and long-range goals. The Communist goal was world domination, its tactics to divide and conquer its enemies by using the "velvet glove" that enclosed "a mailed fist" to give them whatever advantage they desired. In his view, "Communism believed in one moral law, that the end justified any means."[49]

The death of Stalin in March 1953 led to Russia's willingness to moderate its position on the Korean War. Georgi Malenkov, the momentary successor to Stalin, wanted to improve relations with the West, and the best way to do that was to influence China and North Korea to end the stalemated war. A month later, the Communists agreed to settle the always-difficult issue of the repatriation of prisoners.[50] Baldwin was suspicious of any Communist proposal. While a cease-fire in Korea was popular with Americans at home, in military terms it saved the enemies' forces from American air attacks on their supply lines, ceased U.S. air surveillance over enemy lines, and last, provided a respite that would give the enemy the time to rebuild its defenses should the war resume. Baldwin reminded his readers that "we must keep our vision clear and must remember that the Communist ends never change, only the means."[51]

After the armistice was signed on July 27, 1953, at Panmunjom, Baldwin assessed the lessons that had been learned from that war, from the perspective of the world struggle between Communism and democracy: "We fought the battle for Asia in Korea, hampered and delayed the Communist timetable of conquest in the Orient . . . and increased greatly the strength of the anti-communist front."[52]

He was not sure if the United States had won or lost the Korean War, as it was "a battle, rather than a campaign, in the struggle for the world."[53] From a military point of view, he felt that the United States had to relearn some lessons of World War II, especially the need for a closer liaison between military and foreign policy. The National Security Council was designed to act as a coordinating body that provided civilian advice to the JCS. Baldwin advocated improved psychological warfare, better intelligence gathering and assessment, rethinking strategic bombing beliefs that were not tested in Korea, while close air–ground tactical support forced a cooperation between the air and ground forces. There were limits to what air power could and could not do in that mountainous terrain against an enemy that moved largely on foot at night. Baldwin stressed the continuing need for ground troops and naval support, a not-too-subtle jab at the Air Force proponents who designated big bombers as the key to victory in future wars.[54]

The deplorable physical and mental condition of the returning American prisoners of war angered Baldwin and enhanced his anti-Communist stance. He wrote, "The vicious ordeals in North Korean camps reaffirms once again the ruthless nature of the enemy and emphasizes his unlimited aims. The Communists are trying to recreate man after their own image. Conformist man—robot man . . . cowed by fear or blindness—this is the objective of a world-wide conspiracy implacable in its ruthlessness." With confidence, he predicted that human beings would always resist being reduced to a "common denominator,"[55] and advocated that America teach its troops how to meet the rigors of imprisonment. A few years later, the U.S. Army printed a booklet advising prisoners of war about what to expect.

Months later, Baldwin returned to the idea of a neutralized Korea that would permanently keep the country divided and stable. The United States would save money by the withdrawal of its troops, and the reduction of the size of its army, and he warned that most military men felt that "a ground war in Asia could waste the nation's substance without achieving any decisive success," a lesson that was forgotten a decade later.[56]

CHAPTER 15

The Dean of American Military Analysts, 1950s

In 1953, the new Eisenhower administration realized that it could not continue the high level of military spending reached during the Korean War. The new defense policy, the "New Look," called for a reduction of Defense Department spending, and in fiscal year 1954 the department's budget was cut by $5 billion. In the following year the proposal called for a reduced military budget of $3 billion less than the JCS's desired budget of $42 billion. During the two Eisenhower administrations, the defense budget fell from 64 percent of federal spending to 47 percent.[1]

Reduced spending was coupled with a new strategic defense policy called "massive retaliation," which was announced in January 1954 by John Foster Dulles, the secretary of state, before a meeting of the Council on Foreign Relations. Dulles said that any Communist aggression in the world would be met by U.S. retaliation, at places and with methods of its own choosing. Many assumed that would be an atomic war. Baldwin was in attendance and Allen Dulles, the head of the CIA and the secretary's brother, asked for his opinion. Baldwin replied, "Well, I don't think it's realistic." According to Baldwin, "Allen didn't like that too much because they thought it was going to impress the Russians a great deal," but it wasn't realistic, because "we just wouldn't use it [the atomic bomb] when the time came."[2]

Dulles' massive retaliation speech, a new military budget that placed increased reliance upon the U.S. Air Force delivering atomic bombs to Soviet targets, the implied escalation to an unlimited atomic war, and the prospect of bypassing diplomacy and other limited military responses was upsetting to Baldwin. Elevating the Air Force as the primary service was, to his thinking, a "reversion to the one-weapon, one-service, one-type of war concept,"[3] and unlimited atomic war would "bleed us white far more rapidly than mass land warfare." Dulles' policy had increased our calculated military risk, he commented, "in order to decrease our calculated economic risk,"[4] a risk that could be justified only if it were accompanied by a lessening of world tensions.

The Cold War years of the 1950s were characterized by the threat of a U.S.-Soviet nuclear war, and the sensational charges by U.S. senator Joseph R. McCarthy that there were Communists, or Communist sympathizers in the U.S. government. The infamous Army-McCarthy hearings in the spring of 1954, which were televised nationally, gave the senator a platform from which to make baseless charges that ruined the lives and careers of many government employees and military personnel.

Such fears did nothing to help Americans think clearly and rationally about their national goals. Baldwin deplored dangerous and fuzzy talk about how easy it would be just to drop atomic bombs on Russia. In one of his more memorable phrases, Baldwin told an audience at the National War College, "Ideological crusades, gentlemen, tend to end in unlimited wars of unlimited means with unlimited aims which usually end in unlimited devastation and despair."[5]

To put an end to what he thought was popular nonsense about the Cold War, he used words that were a virtual slap in the face for Americans. In a *Saturday Evening Post* article he listed several painless phrases that had become truisms to many Americans, saying they "probably do as much damage to any rational solution of our cold-war problems as communist propaganda."[6] Among the phrases were: "War with Russia is inevitable," "Russia can only be licked with the atom bomb," "There is no defense against the atomic bomb," "America does not need the rest of the world," and, "We must have a final showdown with Russia." Those phrases illustrated America's tendency to oversimplify and to overstate issues. For example, those who said that World War III was inevitable were not thinking of it as a general recurring human event in history, but as a specific war against Russia. In Baldwin's view, if the majority of Americans thought that such a war was inevitable, then it would be. Moscow sought world domination but it was in no hurry to achieve it. The best defense for the United States was to remain strong and undivided. Russia would not start a general war, Baldwin correctly concluded, and if the United States won the Cold War, then "there will be no major hot war with Russia."[7]

Secretary of State John Foster Dulles' massive retaliation policy assumed that any war with Russia would be a nuclear one. In fact, American war plans called for the use of atomic weapons. Baldwin favored an alternative plan for a limited war with limited political aims that would not result in "the complete destruction of Soviet Russia and a Carthaginian peace." He thought Russia could be defeated by a limited war on its periphery that would encourage people in the area to rise up against Soviet domination.[8]

As for the statement that there was no defense against an atom bomb attack, Baldwin was not reassuring: some of the piloted bombers and submarines that fired missiles would get through to their targets. He could only suggest the decentralization of the population from cities and the dispersal of industries. He suggested that the major shift of population would take, among other decisions, a "fearless political leadership."[9]

In any event, he believed that the United States must never retreat into a new isolationism, a policy that had not served it well in the 1920s and 1930s. Planes and missiles could now penetrate U.S. frontiers easily. Overseas forward bases could give the United States time and warning of hostile action and could also be used to disperse enemy attacks. U.S. allies would give the United States a collective strength in the event of attack.

The "greatest myth" to Baldwin, was the shortsighted view that the final showdown with Russia would solve all the world's problems. He recounted a story that occurred shortly after World War II, when he had been writing about the danger of future wars. A young woman wrote to deplore his cynicism after six years of that terrible war, adding that if she knew another war was coming, she would commit suicide. Baldwin commented that it is "not cynical to be realistic." He recalled Woodrow Wilson's phrase about how America's entry into World War I would be "the war to end all wars." In Baldwin's view, "History shows there is never a final solution" to the world's problems. A showdown with Russia, in the form of an ultimatum, would only bring what the United States wanted to avoid: World War III. The United States must have patience, a sense of history, and the knowledge that there were "no permanent solutions to global problems in the world of man." As he had noted in the past, he advised his readers to keep their ideals grounded in political reality, using his "feet in the mud" quote.[10]

A transitory thaw in the Cold War that followed the "Spirit of Geneva Conference" in 1955 was the Moscow Air Show on June 24, 1956. An annual event, this particular one was different, as delegates from twenty-eight Communist and non-Communist nations were invited to attend. General Nathan F. Twining, the chief of staff of the U.S. Air Force, and six other Air Force officers headed the American delegation. Although Baldwin doubted that "the Soviets would grant him a visa,"[11] to his surprise the Soviet Embassy in Washington issued a tourist visa (good for only one month) to Baldwin six days before the air show began. New York cabled the *Times* Moscow office and alerted them to Baldwin's arrival in Moscow on Friday, June 22, advising them to give "every assistance" to him during his stay, as "this is a rare opportunity for him to get [an] insight into [the] Soviet setup" and to gather "considerable background material."[12]

The air show began in less-than-perfect flying weather (there were thunderstorms in the area). The ground observers had only a fleeting glimpse of the fly-bys, and there were more fighters than bombers. Baldwin reported that the "most spectacular" were the four jet-engine Bison bombers, which he said were similar to the new U.S. B-52s. There were also three experimental delta-winged fighters.[13] To better appreciate what he saw, Baldwin relied exclusively upon the American air and military attachés' accounts to identify which planes were which. Everyone was permitted to take pictures.

In the days that followed, there was a lot of entertainment and many opportunities for drinking. At the Soviet Officers' Club in Moscow, Nikolai Bulganin and Nikita Khrushchev, Twining, and U.S. ambassador Charles E. Bohlen sat at the head table, while the other guests were seated at smaller tables in front. After many toasts, and more glasses of vodka, the remarks from the Soviet hosts became more pointed, but since there were no American translators, only Russian, General Twining did not fully understand many of the remarks. Ambassador Bohlen, who understood the language, tried to meet the Soviet jabs point by point.[14]

Baldwin spoke with a number of foreign diplomats who were divided on how long committee rule by Khrushchev and Bulganin would last. Only the Italian ambassador thought that Khrushchev would be the top man. On asking why the Italian ambassador was so well informed, Baldwin was told he was a bachelor whose earlier liaisons were now the wives of senior Soviet officials.

The Dean of American military analysts in his *New York Times* office, ca. 1950s

Courtesy of photographer Arnold Newman and the Baldwin Estate

One thing that bothered the normally abstemious Baldwin was the need to drink after each toast. A general seated next to him kept saying, "Bottoms up," which could be from any bottle of alcohol on the table. "I couldn't go for that kind of thing," Baldwin said, and eventually, after much prodding by his table companion, Baldwin said, "Nyet ... Americans can say no, too."[15]

When he returned to New York in mid-July, he wrote a twelve-page report for Turner Catledge, the managing editor, and three other senior editors. He noted the contrast between his 1937 visit, when fear was so apparent during the Stalin purges, and the current "relatively freer air and atmosphere."[16] Gone was the "oppression and the terror which was almost physically sickening in 1937." Another of his impressions was that the Soviet government had "borrowed heavily from, and perfected, the trappings of Hitlerism," by which he meant the banners, the propaganda, the mass meetings, and the broadcasting from public loud speakers.

While the question of the duration of the collective leadership by Khrushchev and Bulganin divided its outside observers, all agreed that the army's political influence was not what it once was and that Khrushchev's influence over army appointments was a means to stop the Zhukov faction. The army was still very large and well equipped for a defensive or offensive war. The air force was becoming stronger because of the emphasis on air power. The navy was not well respected, especially by Khrushchev, whose patronizing and contemptuous remarks belittled that service's value to the state. On seeing a sailor rowing a boat in a small lake, he remarked to General Twining, "There's our navy."[17]

In conclusion, Baldwin believed that Soviet Russia was strong, but not as strong as the United States. He had his doubts about the exchange of delegations, especially on the technical level, unless on a strict quid pro quo basis. Even then, he thought the Russians would benefit from learning about the West's technological advances. He concluded that the United States had a considerable amount to lose and little to gain by an exchange of technical personnel and, as we know now, the spirit of Geneva did not last very long.

Though he traveled often for the *Times*, at home he loved the seashore. While the family vacationed at various times on Cape Cod, the Maine coast, and Long Island, their favorite spot was at Little Compton, Rhode Island, in a rented cottage near Sakonnet Point. By water, it was six miles due east of Newport but over twenty miles by land from the Naval War College. He did not play golf, but he thoroughly enjoyed using the eighteen-foot Alden-class sailboat that came with the cottage. His sailing skills, however, left something to be desired; family lore held that his daughter Elizabeth once called him the "Captain of the Lobster Pots" because of his ability to entangle the boat's centerboard with the lobster pot lines. If there were no military crises in the offing, he took most of August for his annual vacation.[18]

One of his neighbors at Chappaqua, New York, was Charles A. Lindbergh, the famous "Lindy" who flew solo across the Atlantic in 1927. In the early 1940s his isolationist political comments seriously tarnished his earlier public image with many Americans, including President Roosevelt. Helen enjoyed having dinner parties, but when the Lindberghs were guests, it was necessary to find other guests who would not take offense at his presence. One of his sons, Jon, was interested in Barbara Baldwin and would drop in at the Baldwin house not only to see her, but also to enjoy one of Helen's famous chocolate cakes. Barbara remembered him as being "so sweet and nice." Their friendship ended when she married Mark Potter in 1952.[19]

Hanson's daughter Elizabeth, called "Libby" by the family, recalled how her father compartmentalized his life, never discussing office matters at home. She was proud that he wrote all of his books and magazine articles in his third floor study and not in his *Times* office, and she recalled that he judged people by their character and not by their job title or social position.

Since he was often traveling while Libby and Bobbie were growing up, he would make up for his absence with quality time with them on his return. He loved to tell them stories about imaginary people or creatures that lived in the woods that surrounded their Chappaqua house. He would occasionally take them to New York City to have lunch at the *Times* and to meet some of his colleagues. Warm and loving to his family and loyal to his close friends, he would lose his temper if he felt someone had insulted Helen, the light of his life. He lived a self-disciplined life, one of the lessons he had learned from his Naval Academy training.[20]

Baldwin's correspondence files contain many letters from appreciative readers. One group in particular that held him in high esteem was his Naval Academy classmates of 1924. In 1954 *Shipmate*, the alumni magazine, published the results of its survey in which decennial classes between 1894 and 1934 were asked to select one member of their class, living or dead, who had brought the most credit to the Academy and to the naval service. Baldwin was the only non-career officer to be nominated by any class surveyed. It was a good choice. He had written about Annapolis over the years, as well as the important role of the U.S. Navy in peace and in war. His excellent forums meant that his words were read by a wide audience.[21]

Baldwin had self-imposed views about his profession that included the proscription never to violate a confidence given and never to sacrifice truth for a clever phrase. To some he was rather rigid and self-assured. One staff member at the Council on Foreign Relations thought him to be "straight as a string and scared of no one alive."[22]

The year 1957 raised the fear in the United States that the Soviet Union was ahead of them in the arms race. In August it launched its first ICBM. The United States tried and failed twice to launch its Atlas ICBM. On October 4 the Soviet Union sent *Sputnik 1*, the first man-made satellite, into space. A month later, *Sputnik II* was launched with a dog inside. In December, the United States failed to launch another missile.

On November 7 President Eisenhower received the secret H. Rowan Gaither Report on U.S. defenses. When portions were leaked to the press, they revealed that the report called for a massive increase in the U.S. military budget, and an acceleration of its ICBM development. The report noted that the United States was falling behind in its missile program, relative to the Soviet Union. Unknown to the public, but known to President Eisenhower, the very-secret CIA U-2 overflights of Russian missile sites showed that the United States had nothing to fear from their ICBM program for the time being. That successful spy program was revealed two years later, in May 1960, when one of the planes was shot down.

It was in this context that Baldwin's six-part series on the U.S.-USSR arms race appeared in the *Times*, beginning in February 1958. In the panic-charged political atmosphere in Washington at the time, the Democrats discovered that there was "missile gap." Baldwin did not panic. He noted that since 1949, when the Soviets exploded their first atomic bomb, the balance of military power had changed. Each country could now mutually destroy the other with nuclear weapons. He reported that the USSR was twelve to eighteen months ahead of the United States, and that it had "enough nuclear weapons to devastate" us, but he added the cautionary words, "if the weapons can be delivered."[23] The United States had four thousand to five thousand piloted planes, both land based and carrier based, many of which could carry nuclear weapons. As Russia had only sixty to one hundred "prime targets," the United States could "wipe out" those targets forty to fifty times over and had the "tremendous capability for massive retaliation."[24]

But he did not consider a general war likely. He thought that all nations would "shrink" from deliberately initiating a major war because of the global devastation that would result. Baldwin thought it "unlikely" that Moscow would suddenly launch "a nuclear Pearl Harbor," unless U.S. defenses were so weak so as to prevent retaliation in kind. No Soviet ICBM in 1958 was capable of traveling the 5,500 miles to hit the continental United States, though by 1961 perhaps they could.

The United States had NATO missile sites and air bases in Western Europe and in Morocco, Malta, Cyprus, and Crete, all of which would have to be taken out by Soviet air forces "simultaneously" to prevent quick retaliation by U.S. defenses. Being a Cold Warrior, he did note that small-scale wars would occur, as well as "the creeping infiltration of communism on the unstable flanks of Asia, the Middle East and Africa."[25] He believed the Boy Scout adage of his youth, "Be Prepared," was a good guideline for the present and the future.

Walter Lippmann, whose column "Today and Tomorrow" appeared in the *New York Herald-Tribune*, wrote a note to Baldwin on reading this article. "I would like to congratulate you on the series of articles you are now writing. . . . More power to you." Baldwin replied that "Praise from you is praise indeed and I value it highly."[26] The six articles were edited, modified, and shortened for a book entitled *The Great Arms Race: A Comparison of U.S. and Soviet Power Today*. On reading this 116-page book, Samuel P. Huntington, an important scholar of military affairs, praised the author for being "informative, balanced and comprehensive" and for pointing out the strengths and weaknesses of American defenses that "seldom receive attention."[27]

In the late 1950s the belief was that an unlimited war, much like World War II, though fought with nuclear weapons, would result in the mutual devastation and destruction of both the United States and the Soviet Union. The subject attracted many commentators and concerned Baldwin deeply, and he challenged "the comfortable thesis" that limited wars could be fought and won by using small, or battlefield, nuclear weapons.[28] He thought that there always would be the temptation to escalate to an unlimited use.

What the debate on limited war called for was "a cold-blooded, dispassionate, objective analysis and discussion," which he felt he was qualified to give to help the American public to "avoid the catastrophe of nuclear war."[29] His answer was that limited wars must be "fought for well-defined political objectives, with limited military force, and generally in a limited geographic area."[30] Baldwin praised Henry Kissinger, then a professor at Harvard, for correctly stressing that the "primary requirement for keeping a war limited was the limitation of the political and military objectives" of the war.[31]

To keep a war limited, Baldwin believed, was "to know what you are fighting for" and to define what price you are willing to pay for that objective. The Korean War was fought for limited objectives and was "for the first time in [U.S.] history [fought] for something besides victory unlimited."[32] He rejected General MacArthur's popular quote that the "object of war is victory." Future wars had to be limited to tangible political goals, or else become a senseless slaughter.

Citing the Prussian military theorist von Clausewitz, Baldwin concluded that "war is not an end in itself; war is justifiable only if it is a servant of policy, if it is invoked to achieve a definite political aim, if it is fought for the vital interest of the nation, and if it results in increased security for the nation and a more stable world."[33] He realized that, at the beginning of a war, national fear, hysteria, and emotional patriotism push for a war's extension, but that the national leadership must rein in such feelings or else the end would be chaos.

In the atomic age, Baldwin felt restraint must be the first requirement, since the temptation to use nuclear weapons would always be present. To limit war, he said, "we clearly cannot use unlimited means to attain limited ends," urging that there must be restraint on the political objective desired and restraint as to the weapons used.

One of the many military exercises Baldwin witnessed over the years was called Sage Brush in Fort Polk, Louisiana. It was the largest field exercise since 1946, and it involved almost 150,000 ground and air forces. Its purpose was to simulate an atomic war. The attempt by the commanders of the opposing forces to limit that "war" failed as both sought to destroy the other's airfields, missile sites, and troop concentrations by using ever-larger weapons. Before the exercises were concluded, much of Louisiana was in "theoretical shambles."[34] That six-week exercise in 1955 led Baldwin to conclude that although a war may start with limited goals to be achieved with non-nuclear weapons, it would soon escalate to the use of nuclear weapons. In Western Europe a limited nuclear war was "impossible," as the area was relatively small, heavily populated, and nations not directly involved in the war could not escape the radiation from the bombs and shells.[35] This would result in a nuclear stalemate in Europe.

Baldwin concluded that "the greatest problem" for our military planners was to maintain our forces capable of fighting "any kind of war anywhere."[36] But he advised that our armed forces must not be maintained at peak levels ready for war, as that would not only bankrupt the United States, it would lead us to become a garrison state, which he opposed. Rather, the United States must maintain a small cadre of forces capable of expansion in case of war. He wanted to avoid the "one-weapon, one-concept mold" that would rigidly tie us to an inflexible strategic concept, allowing no freedom of action. Mr. Dulles' massive retaliation policy of 1954 was exactly this kind of rigid policy. In diplomacy, as in politics, Baldwin contended, "the art of strategy and war is the art of choice. We risk defeat in peace or war if we limit our military capabilities to nukes and thermo-nukes."[37]

As the recipient of privileged, if not classified, information during his long career, Baldwin developed some definite views on the subject of the ultimate loyalty of a reporter in a democracy. For some, the journalist's credo "publish and be damned" was a license for a muckraking reporter or crusading editor to expose the malefactors of great wealth or the paid lobbyists in the state legislature, all justified on the basis of the need to serve the public's right to know. To Baldwin, that was irresponsible journalism.

He felt that there was a higher loyalty that ought to claim the allegiance of each and every reporter, and that was a loyalty to the nation. To him, reporters were citizens first and newspapermen second, and there were times when this higher loyalty superseded a reporter's instinct to tell all and to let the chips fall where they may. There must be restraint on the reporter's part as to when to withhold information from the public in the national interest.[38] There was a recognizable tension in all this that responsible journalists like Baldwin recognized, for when the government attempted to silence or delay the release of information about what it was doing, then a reporter must carefully weigh the merits of publication against those of remaining silent. For Baldwin, the Argus Project was one such episode.

On Thursday, March 19, 1959, the *Times* headline read: "US Atom Blasts 300 Miles Up Mar Radar, Snag Missile Plan: Called 'Greatest Experiment.'" The two articles that followed, written by Walter Sullivan, the *Times* science editor, and Baldwin, told of a process by which the U.S. government sought to test a theory put forth by Nicholas C. Christofilos, a largely self-taught, lone-wolf type of physicist whose research into high energy physics led him to believe that high-energy electrons released in the earth's lines of magnetic field would envelop the globe in a shell. The effect might be to disrupt radio and radar waves. After this theory was brought to Dr. James A. Van Allen, who had discovered the existence of a natural radiation belt in the earth's outer atmosphere, the Pentagon began developing a top-secret project.

In late August and in mid-September 1958, in the South Atlantic, the U.S. Navy ship *The Norton Sound,* a former seaplane tender, launched three nuclear rockets into outer space, where they were detonated. The Christofilos Effect, as it came to be known, occurred when the electrons were trapped within the earth's magnetic field and encircled the globe, thus creating, at various points, an aurora borealis–like sight that disrupted some radio and radar communications for a time. An Explorer IV satellite monitored the level of radiation intensities in the atmosphere.[39]

Baldwin's March 19 story pointed to the military and to the international political implications of this once-secret experiment, including the possibility of the Soviets setting off a series of high-altitude nuclear explosions to blank out America's early-warning and tracking radar prior to launching their own missiles, the temporary disruption of some radio frequencies, and the premature detonation of incoming enemy missiles. The scientists he interviewed all said that further testing was needed and they did not all agree at to what were the effects of the experiment.[40]

The story behind the story was that Baldwin, and later Sullivan, knew of the plans for the experiment as early as June 1958—nine months prior to the release of the story. Their sources within the Pentagon repeatedly warned them of the international implications should there be prior publicity about the project. During the autumn months of 1958, both authors were told that the key question was whether or not the Soviets had detected any disruptions in their radar reception, and, therefore, knew that something was afoot.

As the months dragged on, the reporters faced a difficult dilemma, between the public's right to know about what their government had done and their desire not to harm the national interest. Ironically, seven years later in the context of the Vietnam War, Baldwin confidently told a correspondent that "no newspaper and no commentator can regard a classified stamp as a bar to publication, or virtually no newspapers could be published [if they did]."[41]

However, in 1958 and in early 1959 he had agonized over which course to follow. Both reporters decided to work within the system to "play the game," as Baldwin described it, to persuade the nervous Pentagon bureaucrats, especially Dr. Herbert F. York, the Defense Department's director of research and engineering, that Soviet scientists most likely already knew about the effects of the Argus Project, and that Dr. Van Allen had already announced in January 1959 that the Explorer IV satellite had detected huge increases in radiation. Walter Sullivan spoke with Dr. James Killian, President Eisenhower's science adviser, and the Christofilos Effect had been discussed publicly at scientific conferences.

It finally dawned upon both Baldwin and Sullivan that Washington's reluctance to permit the story's release was based on a fear of the embarrassment of disclosure that the United States had secretly exploded atomic weapons far from its shores and far from its normal proving grounds, which would only raise "doubts abroad as to [the United States'] good faith" concerning a nuclear test ban treaty and our participation in the International Geophysical Year program. In anger, Sullivan told Baldwin that further delay in releasing the story only "postpones the day of diplomatic reckoning." He advised his colleague to go for early publication without giving prior notice to Washington, "other than a last minute phone call."[42] Still, the Naval Academy graduate hesitated for almost another two months. His dilemma was acute. What finally ended his hesitation, in mid-March, was that he learned during one of his visits to Washington that the Pentagon was preparing to release the results of the Argus Project at a scientific meeting in April.[43]

A week following the story's release, he felt obligated to write to his old friend and valuable news source, Admiral Arleigh A. Burke, the chief of naval operations. He confessed that he had "played the game completely and in fact bent over backwards to avoid injury to the country which all of us serve."[44] He was very upset that the Navy had been blamed for leaking the story, since the missile was launched from a U.S. Navy ship, a lie that he wanted to set right with Admiral Burke.

In retrospect, it is clear that Baldwin felt a responsibility of the *Times* to the public, as well as to the country and the freedom of the press. His military contacts thought that Baldwin, as a newspaper writer, had had no right to determine what the public should read on military-political subjects, but he would reply that that was what a free press was all about. In his words, "Your sense of responsibility to the public good and to the country must be balanced against your responsibility to a free press and to your paper."[45]

Though he experienced discomfort over the length of time that he had voluntarily withheld an important news story, his colleagues were quick to praise him when the Argus story did appear. The assistant managing editor telegraphed from Washington that the story "hit the Pentagon and surrounding areas like an H-bomb."[46] Harrison Salisbury congratulated him on his "brilliant scoop. It is tremendous."[47] The city desk editor called the piece "one of the great exclusives of newspaper history. I am delighted that you got it for *The Times*."[48]

While praise from colleagues was gratifying, there was a larger issue at stake. The Argus Project was to Baldwin just another example of the developing "attitude of the government that the public must know only what the government thinks it is good for it to know"—a kind of father-knows-best patronizing attitude, or possibly a more sinister Orwellian scenario.[49] He noted the acceleration of a trend, evident after 1945, first to keep atomic secrets from the Soviets, and then to justify American rearmament with new weapons, beginning with the Truman administration. Baldwin often had been concerned with the danger of the United States becoming a garrison state in its seemingly never-ending goal to achieve permanent national security. To his way of thinking this could only be done by directly sacrificing all of the democratic principles and practices that he held to be dear and precious.

Reflecting upon this episode, Baldwin was forced to reassess his views on the Washington bureaucracy. The press corps and government officials no longer shared the belief that they were both on the same side, as was the case during World War II. Formerly, there had been a working trust that reporters would not reveal state secrets if asked not to, and if a legitimate issue of national interest could be proven. After the Argus Project, this trust was broken. With considerable passion, Baldwin told Admiral Burke that the real issue in all this was neither the security of information nor the denial of data to the Soviets; instead it was the issue of "controlling information and . . .

issuing it when the government wanted to and under the terms it wished."[50] In his view, in Washington's concern to maintain secrecy it had exhibited a "fundamental failure to understand the first principle of good public relations and of democratic government."[51]

As the Eisenhower years drew to a close and the difficulties reaching a mutually binding agreement on arms limitation with the Soviet leaders continued, Baldwin reminisced about that "hopeful era" after World War II when the United States offered to share its atomic secrets with the world in the 1946 Baruch Plan. Those were the days "when mankind expected the 'brave new world'—had faded into the mists of history. The quest for disarmament—the political Holy Grail of generation after generation—has got lost in the trackless forests of power politics and has confronted squarely the mountainous obstacles of Communist expansionism."[52]

In Baldwin's writing there was a sense of longing for times past that were far better, in his mind, than the present. He admired the values of his post-Navy years of the 1920s, in which the personal attributes of self-reliance, personal initiative, and drive were popular. In contemporary society, he wrote in a 1959 *Saturday Evening Post* article, the popular view was "Work less, make more," and "It's all right, if you can get away with it." The article was a jeremiad in which Baldwin deplored current attitudes and values that reflected the social and economic legislation passed during and after the 1930s that made the country soft, in his view. Baldwin had always been a social and political conservative, views that became more pronounced as he aged. He criticized the conformity of modern American life so well portrayed in the popular 1956 book *The Organization Man*, written by William H. Whyte, an editor of *Fortune* magazine.

Baldwin also blamed the many deficiencies in the military for the misguided values of American society. In the age of the military draft, discipline was lax, the number of courts-martial was high, and 40 percent of America's youth were deemed unqualified for any kind of military service because of mental, physical, or moral characteristics. Since 1956 the U.S. Army had weeded out 70,000 draftees and categorized them as Group IV, those having low intellectual levels. Citing these and other statistics, he concluded that the picture of an Army draftee was of "a slow-witted, vacuous adolescent," whose intellectual interests were confined to comic books.[53]

After the racial integration of the armed services by President Truman in 1948, Baldwin exhibited regrettable racial bias. While he admitted that racial integration was "here to stay," he also identified what he considered morale and combat effectiveness problems.[54] "Negros," he wrote, present "the most difficult problems," due in part to their limited education that contributed to high AWOL numbers and courts-martial proceedings. He offered no numbers to support his conclusions, and in keeping with insensitive racial attitudes, none was asked of him.[55]

An important theme of Baldwin's writings was the "civilianization" of the Defense Department, a trend that he opposed, since it downgraded the role and contribution of the career military officer. There were too many civilians, political appointees, and "dead beats" who had the authority to tell the line officers what to do, but who did not have to take the responsibility for their policies or judgments.[56]

As Baldwin noted, the CNO, Admiral Arleigh Burke, "no longer command[ed] the fleet." The Army's chief of staff had to deal with thirty civilians in the Defense Department who could give orders or directives. The result was a diffusion of authority and responsibility. The career officer could become "the goat" when incorrect decisions were made by civilians. Baldwin criticized the cost-accounting and functional-budget schemes of civilian budget watchers that "distract[ed]" the military services from their job, which was primarily "to win battles." Always an important factor in the military was the quality of leadership in the officer corps. The ROTC and Officer Candidates School (OCS) officers, who were the junior officers, usually lieutenants, showed little incentive to make a military career. Too many were time-servers during their three years on active duty.

This article received a reaction. One general, who declined to be quoted, agreed that civilians in the Pentagon had the authority "to screen or influence [what] their civilian boss sees and hears." Promotion called for "obsequiousness" and an ability of the officer to get along with the civilians, rather than his military experience and "personal integrity characteristic of the old Army's 'Duty, Honor, Country' credo."[57]

Perhaps the most important response to this article came from Congressman Carl Vinson, the very powerful and influential chairman of the House Armed Services Committee. He wondered what should be done to remedy the many defects in manpower that Baldwin cited. As for racial integration of the military, Vinson agreed with Baldwin that it has "probably reduced overall combat effectiveness and it has posed some major morale problems," adding, "Never were truer words expressed." He wrote, "I do congratulate you on an excellent and thought-provoking article." Baldwin met with the congressman, but only rarely, as his Washington visits were confined to the Pentagon and the CIA and not to Capitol Hill.[58]

As his reputation grew, Baldwin was often asked for advice on how to become a newspaper military writer and analyst. Most often those inquiries began with, "How did you 'get' your job?" To which he would reply sharply, "You don't get it, you make it."[59] Most military writers had previous military service or, as in Baldwin's case, had graduated from one of the military service academies. He advised the inquirers to start at the bottom as a spot news reporter, as that was what papers required, not a military writer. He would remind them that he had been a general assignment reporter for eight years before being assigned to focus on military and naval topics. During those apprenticeship years, he advised, "seek out, make and develop" contacts that will help your writing and reputation. In short, "you don't spring full born from the brow of Jove in any profession." Writing is "on-the-job-training—the art of applying the seat of the pants to the seat of a chair," he advised. There was a lot of hard work involved. There were no short cuts. He advised his correspondents that to better understand the role of the military in society, the writer would "greatly benefit" from knowledge of military history and politics, as well as a humanist understanding of history.[60] The opportunities for the military analyst on a newspaper staff were small. In the early 1970s there were only five military analysts on American newspapers, and the prospects for further expansion for such analysts were bleak.

Given Baldwin's own limited encounters with television interviewers, he did not mention that media as a possible employment option. His main objection to television journalism was that, in his unhappy and brief experience, his words were either edited or omitted, which changed the meaning or eliminated the qualifying words Baldwin knew he had used. A decade later, he cited the late Frank McGee of NBC's *Today* program, whom he thought had distorted his taped views on the Vietnam War.

Baldwin was very generous with advice to other authors who, on occasion, would send him samples of their literary efforts. He vetted a few books for friends. He had an editor's eye to sharpen an author's phrasing in order to avoid the passive voice, redundancy, and inconsistencies, advice that illustrated the old adage that to write clearly, one must think clearly.

All journalists have their confidential sources, and Baldwin was no exception. Like other print journalists, he protected their anonymity, unless they permitted him to quote their words for attribution. He was no kiss-and-tell reporter. To Baldwin, a confidence given was a confidence kept. Near the end of his life he still refused to reveal his sources on some of his scoops, citing a faulty memory for stories that were based on multiple sources, and for others the need to have a release from his source to reveal the name to a third party.[61] When in doubt, he would delay using the information until corroboration had been secured. There were exceptions. When his single source was "absolutely impeccable" and the piece of information deemed to be very important, he would go with it.

There were those military sources whom Baldwin "knew so well" that he could use "what they were saying, without their names," allowing the words themselves to give authority to the piece. He assumed that his sources "did not wish [their names] used, unless they said [so]." If a source knew he was going to be quoted, Baldwin would tell him that what he was saying was for attribution. He was so familiar with his Pentagon sources, and they with him, that "the interviewee took it for granted that his name would not be used."[62]

An excellent example of a single-sourced article about which Baldwin had no doubt occurred in May 1960. The U-2 incident had begun on May 1 when an American photo-reconnaissance plane was shot down over Central Russia near Sverdlovsk in the Ural Mountains, 1,200 miles inside the border of the Soviet Union. On learning of this event, the National Aeronautics and Space Administration (NASA) stated that the plane was on a weather observation mission that had flown off course. The CIA was confident that neither the plane nor the pilot had survived the crash, as the pilot had the means to destroy his plane and to kill himself before being captured by Soviet authorities.

That make of U-2 spy plane, developed in 1954, had the ability to fly at 65,000–70,000 feet, which was then above the range of Soviet planes and missiles. In Washington, Democrats had criticized President Eisenhower for there being a missile gap after Russia's *Sputnik* rocket was launched in October 1957. The president knew, from U-2 photographs, that there was no missile gap. The photographs showed that Moscow was not ahead of the United States in missile development. Moscow had complained formally about the overflights but could do nothing about them. For Moscow to admit publicly that their air defenses were inadequate would have had political and military repercussions at home for Premier Khrushchev.

Baldwin had learned of the U-2 flights two years earlier but chose to keep quiet following his CIA informant's plea, much as he had remained silent about the Argus Project a year earlier. Argus was to protect Washington from embarrassment over what the United States had done, while the U-2 flights were clearly vital to U.S. national security. Two of his colleagues at the *Times*, James Reston and Arthur Krock, also knew of the U-2 flights but kept quiet, as did two other correspondents.[63]

On May 5, two days after the NASA cover story, Premier Khrushchev held a press conference in Moscow to announce that a U-2 plane had been shot down over Russia for its violation of Soviet air space. The following day he displayed photographs of the plane and its uninjured pilot, together with high-powered cameras, reconnaissance instruments, and photographs of Soviet military installations. In Washington, the State Department acknowledged that the plane was "probably" on a spying mission. President Eisenhower then broke his silence and admitted publicly that the purpose of the flights had been to break the Soviet wall of secrecy surrounding its missile program and to prevent a future nuclear "Pearl Harbor."

In his initial commentary on the event, Baldwin expressed reservations about the pilot Francis Gary Powers' choice to save his life, which seriously compromised the very successful five-year CIA espionage program. As he expressed it, Powers "may spend the rest of his life trying to answer the question of why he survived."[64] To Baldwin's thinking, while there was the strong taboo in the Judeo-Christian culture against suicide, there is another "unwritten law" that required that a spy be willing to kill himself to avoid capture. Since Powers was not willing to do that, "It is safe to guess," Baldwin observed, "that all that Mr. Powers knew about the U-2 operations is now known to the Russians."[65]

He rejected the rumor that the timing of the flight, just prior to the Paris Summit meeting between Eisenhower and Khrushchev, was the work of a rogue U.S. Air Force base commander, the supposition upon which the popular 1964 movie *Dr. Strangelove* was based. Baldwin praised the U-2 program as vital to U.S. national survival, and he supported the view that the risk of a surprise attack in the age of the hydrogen bomb was so great that the government was justified to have all possible information about the Soviet Union's missile program.

A *Times* editorial, written two weeks after the story broke, criticized "naïve" Americans who were shocked that the U.S. government would send spy planes over Soviet territory. The editorial reminded its readers that it was "a matter of necessity" that the U.S. learn as much as possible about its potential enemies. In words that suggested Baldwin's authorship, the article cited that the free world had a justifiable "Pearl Harbor" complex, the fear of a sudden attack. That fear would last until international disarmament and inspection systems were in place. In the meantime, the U-2 flights over Russia were justified.[66]

Two weeks after the U-2 incident, Baldwin scored a worldwide scoop with his full disclosure about the extent of America's growing espionage program.[67] Written in a question–and–answer format, Baldwin provided details of the extent to which Washington was willing to go to penetrate Moscow's secrecy about its defenses, including its nuclear and missile programs, noting that the U-2 planes were only a part of a global intelligence-gathering operation controlled jointly by NASA, the CIA, and the U.S. Air Force. Knowledge about the program was limited to the president, the National Security Council, and the CIA, and Baldwin considered the program to be "one of the most successful intelligence operations in history."[68]

Baldwin speculated that Powers' plane may have had a "flame out," and that he may have descended to a lower altitude to denser air in order to restart the engine. At that altitude, a Soviet missile had then come within range and exploded, damaging Powers' plane. Eventually, Baldwin softened his earlier opinion that Powers should have committed suicide to avoid capture, since Powers identified himself as "a pilot first, an agent second; and pilots do not have a 'self-destruct' philosophy."[69] Hinting at a probable Air Force source for this article, Baldwin praised the Strategic Air Command (SAC) as being "a major deterrent to nuclear war," with its ability to break through all Soviet defenses in an all-out U.S. attack. Many SAC bombers might be lost, but some would get through.[70]

In summary, as a veteran military analyst, Baldwin concluded that the faults in the U-2 incident were not intelligence faults but rather a lack of coordination in the multi-government-agency program. The lack of internal communication resulted in NASA's initial story about the plane being on a weather observation mission. When the White House issued a statement about the purpose of that flight, Washington's credibility was damaged, as was the credibility of the American press, which had believed in the truthfulness of official government statements. The press now realized that the age of managed news had arrived. As for the piloted overflights, Baldwin speculated that this incident would probably end such flights, as new reconnaissance satellites, being developed then, would provide photographs of Soviet defenses.

In my last interview with him, shortly before his death, Baldwin told me that his primary source was General Thomas D. White, chief of staff, U.S. Air Force. Their friendship began in Rome in 1937 when he was the military attaché for air, and it continued over the years and developed into a mutual respect. It is not surprising that General White would feel confident enough to tell Baldwin about the U-2 program in detail, with the understanding that this information was secret and not for publication or attribution. Baldwin was a Cold Warrior and could quickly understand the importance and significance of this intelligence-gathering operation and the need to keep it from the public's attention. Once the U-2 incident was news, and Washington's cover was blown, there was no reason to keep the program a secret from the American public.[71]

The Eisenhower years gave Americans what they wanted: a popular president who encouraged consumer spending and pro-business growth at home, while trying to contain the spread of Communism abroad and avoiding World War III. In January 1961, that older generation of American leaders, born in the late nineteenth century, was replaced by a younger generation, born in the twentieth century, who were eager to make their own bright futures for themselves and for the nation.

CHAPTER 16

The Winds of Change: The *Times* and Washington, 1961–66

The 1960s began with high hopes and expectations of the young Kennedy administration, and they ended in despair and disillusionment about the Vietnam War. Three developments during that decade affected Baldwin's professional life in various ways. The first was the retirement, in 1961, of his patron and *Times* publisher, Arthur Hays Sulzberger, which prompted changes in the management of the *Times* and its editorial policies. The second development was the change in Pentagon policies initiated by Robert Strange McNamara, the secretary of defense from 1961–68. Those changes authorized civilians in the office of the secretary of defense to oversee and to implement a systems-analysis approach to all military matters. The third development was the war in Vietnam and the policy of gradual escalation implemented by President Lyndon B. Johnson (1963–69), and the centralization of control of all military operations by the White House and the Pentagon.

The two pillars of support for Baldwin's career at the *Times* were Julius Ochs Adler and Sulzberger. General Adler, a brigadier general in the U.S. Army Reserve, who liked to be addressed by his military rank, was the number-two man in the *Times* organization, responsible for the financial aspects of the business. He was also a cousin of Adolph Ochs, who had bought the paper in 1896. Baldwin recalled fondly how Adler had "eased [his] way often" over the years.[1] Adler always favored a strong national defense, which was reflected in the paper's favorable treatment of military subjects for many years and, coincidentally, aided Baldwin's career in unspecified ways. The two men did not always agree on every issue; for example, Adler favored a peacetime military draft, while Baldwin opposed UMT, as it was then called. At Adler's funeral in 1955, at the Arlington National Cemetery, Baldwin gave the eulogy at the family's request. His death started a series of changes in senior management and new policies that eventually eroded Baldwin's privileged position at the *Times*. A few years later, Sulzberger's declining health led Baldwin to sense that the paper was less sympathetic to the military and the need for a strong national defense than before.[2]

Other changes were not reassuring. To counter the popular perception of the *Times* as being dull, in 1956 Sulzberger invited Bruce Barton, the founder of the famous advertising agency Batten, Barton, Durstine and Osborn (BBD&O), and his executives to meet with the publisher and senior *Times* editors (of whom Baldwin was one) in his fourteenth-floor office in the Times Building. The purpose of the meeting was to find ways to increase the paper's circulation, advertising revenue, and readability.[3] Each editor addressed the advertising executives on his function and his role at the paper. One of Barton's people used a phrase that Baldwin clearly remembered years later: "News is a commodity that must be sold."[4] He was appalled by this remark. He believed that the paper was a public trust, a view that was endorsed originally by Adolph Ochs, who had stressed accuracy and completeness of news coverage. The paper had a public duty to perform every day of the year. One result of this meeting was a new advertising slogan, "It's so much more interesting." One editor who was irritated by this phrase was Lester Markel, the autocrat of the Sunday edition. He thought the new slogan ought to be, "It's so much more accurate." Baldwin and others were upset also because BBD&O had recently been hired to represent the Republican National Committee, and senior staffers did not like the idea of the paper being linked with a political organization.[5] The management's desire to make money led some editors to question whether that aim would undermine the paper's reputation of being a public trust, a newspaper of record.[6]

Another a sign of the changing times was when Turner Catledge, the managing editor, told Baldwin not to use any Shakespearean quotations in his pieces, as the paper was written for readers with a high school level of education, and not college graduates. Needless to say, the military editor objected initially, but accepted the copyeditors' deletions of quotations from famous writers.[7]

Arthur Hays Sulzberger retired on April 25, 1961. At the age of seventy, he was in poor health and was confined to a wheelchair. With Sulzberger's departure from the active management of the paper, Baldwin lost his boss and friend, patron and critic. Sulzberger never fully agreed that the boundaries of military journalism should be expanded to include related political and economic developments, as Baldwin always stressed. Nonetheless, the warm friendship between them endured over the years despite Arthur's numerous blue memoranda to Hanson rebuking him on what he thought was the political tone of that day's piece.

With Sulzberger's departure, Baldwin came to appreciate the legacy of Adolph Ochs and that of his son-in-law, Sulzberger. Together they were, in Baldwin's mind, "great editor-publishers" who viewed the *Times* as a public trust with a responsibility to edit the news of the day and to present it "without fear or favor." Under their leadership, accuracy, fairness, and completeness were the bedrock of the paper, and advertising and promotion did not influence the news columns or the editorial page. During the 1960s those goals were replaced by readability, entertainment, and profitability.

The Sulzberger family selected Orvil Dryfoos to succeed Arthur. Almost from the time of his marriage to Marian Sulzberger in 1941, he had been consciously groomed to be his father-in-law's successor. He served as his assistant for twelve years until 1954, when he was made vice president of the New York Times Company. He learned all of the required duties of a publisher from Arthur Sulzberger, his mentor.[8] Baldwin liked the new publisher, as did many others. "He was a very nice person," he later recalled, "just a plain, decent, nice guy."[9] Once, when Orvil was asked what factors determined his career, he replied in a self-deprecating manner that he had married the daughter of the publisher of the *Times*.[10]

Within *Times* management, there were two continuing concerns about Baldwin: the boundaries of his writing, and the publisher's approval to exempt his pieces from copyediting without Baldwin's approval. Orvil Dryfoos, then the assistant to the publisher, had asked about Baldwin's right to editorialize in his pieces in 1953 and another editor, Ted Bernstein, had told him "he is allowed to be."[11]

In March 1962 E. Clifton Daniel, an assistant managing editor, complained to his boss, Turner Catledge, the managing editor, that Baldwin "gets away with things that are not permitted to any other correspondent on this paper of whatever status." Specifically, he "dumps" stories of great length onto the national news desk without alerting it as to subject matter, length, or timing. Frequently, the pieces "imping[ed]" on foreign subjects that the foreign news editor was unaware of until it was printed in the paper. For example, Baldwin "dropped" a 1,300-word piece on the end of the Algerian War and its effect on the French army that required the foreign desk to add two additional pages in its coverage of that event. The national news desk knew nothing of this piece from Baldwin. Fortunately, both desk editors spoke with each other and the copyeditors made sure that Baldwin's piece did not duplicate anything previously printed. Clifton Daniel asked rhetorically why Baldwin could not show the third-floor national desk "the simple courtesy of prior consultation." The recently appointed editor of the national news desk, Harrison E. Salisbury, suggested that a "rule of reason" be adapted with regard to Baldwin's pieces to allow foreign news material from him to be handled by the foreign desk.[12]

Four days later, Baldwin told Salisbury that "he had been told by the former publisher that he had the right to write what he felt should be written, when he felt it should be written, at whatever length he deemed appropriate, and [to] express whatever editorial opinion he felt was required." Salisbury reminded Baldwin that he had the editorial responsibility for national news, and he would not hesitate to exercise his editorial judgment. Baldwin was told that, in the future, he would advise the national desk in advance of what he had written.[13]

Turner Catledge apologized to Orvil Dryfoos for "the Baldwin situation" that needed to be spelled out better so that "everyone down here" [at the national desk] knows what is what "when dealing with Baldwin."[14] He added, after reading Salisbury's memorandum, that "we simply cannot have Mr. Baldwin walking promiscuously" over the national desk. He warned the publisher that Baldwin might well take up this issue with him, and he did.

Unfortunately, the issue did not fade away. Catledge was put in a difficult position as he and Baldwin were friends and colleagues for many years and he respected his proven talents and achievements. But, Turner had a responsibility to the third-floor national desk for an orderly presentation of the news without duplication or conflict. Recently there were several times when Baldwin would surprise copyeditors with an unanticipated long article, covering subjects already received from other reporters. The solution,

Catledge thought, would be for him to "accept the simple procedures that are followed by everyone else on this paper."[15]

On the following day, Harrison Salisbury "killed" Baldwin's piece that dealt with Congress' vote on the B-70 bomber issue. The 1,300-word piece, which arrived at the national desk in mid-afternoon from Ed Mossien, Baldwin's office manager and assistant, covered many of the same points as Washington bureau's Jack Raymond's piece did. Baldwin's article also made editorial observations about the Kennedy White House's relations with Congress. Salisbury concluded that in the future, Baldwin should confine his comments to military matters and avoid political issues in Washington, D.C.[16]

Faced with these encroachments on the prerogatives he had so long enjoyed, Baldwin appealed directly to the *Times* publisher, Orvil Dryfoos, a practice he had used successfully during the Sulzberger years. In a four-page memorandum to the publisher, Baldwin noted with alarm that his pieces had been shelved or postponed so long that they lost any news value they may have once contained. He complained how hard it had become for him to get interpretative or background pieces into the paper "as I write them," adding, "I still have the feeling—in fact more than ever—that someone is looking over my shoulder while I work."[17]

To bolster his case, Hanson cited his Q-head (an analytical piece, short of an editorial, that was given a byline and a special headline) on Secretary McNamara's relations with Congress. The piece was delayed for a month until Jack Raymond, the *Times* Pentagon reporter, wrote a news story on the same subject. He cited other examples, and asked just what his future role was on the paper as its military editor and analyst.

His solution to the problem was to funnel all his pieces to a few persons knowledgeable about military matters on the national desk. For reportorial pieces, he wanted to continue to select his assignments as he had been permitted to with Sulzberger's approval. Baldwin also wanted to return to a regular schedule (begun in 1942) for his Q-heads. He suggested that they appear once a week, placed opposite the editorial page. He thought that increasing the frequency of his Q-heads, and having a better location in the paper, would be attractive and useful to his readers.

As to his tendency to editorialize in his pieces, he reiterated his long held position: "I have the right to *criticize* and *interpret,* regardless of whether or not my point of view agrees with the Times editorial policy."[18] He linked his freedom of expression and criticism with his continuing value to the paper.

In trying to smooth many ruffled feathers, Clifton Daniel spoke with Baldwin after Dryfoos had read Baldwin's long memorandum, picking up on Baldwin's suggestion that copyeditors be experts in military affairs. Daniel rejected that suggestion, claiming that Baldwin's copy could be handled by "any one of a number of qualified copy readers."[19]

This whole matter clearly put Baldwin on notice that his former privileges with regard to his professional relations with others on the paper were now a thing of the past. From now on, he would submit his pieces "through normal channels and in the normal way," which meant that he would have to deal primarily with Harrison E. Salisbury, who considered Baldwin "a loner" who "worked for himself."[20]

To outsiders who knew nothing of the office politics and clashing egos, Baldwin was to be admired greatly. He had many irons in the fire. In 1960 the Lippincott Company of Philadelphia asked him to be the general editor of a new series, Great Battles of History. His job was to select the authors and to assign a specific battle for a book-length manuscript. Early books in the series sold well, but by the late 1960s, the publisher's interest had waned as sales declined. Also, some authors clearly disappointed Baldwin in the lack of quality in their work. In six years, nineteen books were published in that series. As the general editor he asked Harvard historian Frank Friedel to write a book on the 1898 Battle of Manila. Friedel declined the offer but added that he had long admired Baldwin, "the dean of American military writers."[21]

In addition to his difficulties with Baldwin, one event that certainly aggravated Dryfoos (who had a heart condition) was a labor strike by the local typographic union that forced the Times and three other New York City papers to cease publication for 114 days (December 8, 1962–March 30, 1963). A month into the strike, the publisher ordered a four-day work week and salary reductions for all employees, and Baldwin's $25,000 salary as the military editor was reduced to $17,000.[22]

But Baldwin's personal inconvenience did not begin to match the strain that the strike placed on Dryfoos as publisher. "It just ate at him in a most destructive way," recalled Arthur Ochs "Punch" Sulzberger.[23] The strike settlement was costly to the Times, and Sulzberger family members thought that it contributed to Dryfoos' death on May 25, 1963, at only fifty years old.

His passing was a definite shock to the Sulzberger family, who had expected that he would serve for many years as the publisher. A strong desire to keep the *Times* in the family overcame their reluctance to select the thirty-seven-year-old Punch. His father, Arthur, felt his son was "awfully young and immature,"[24] but his mother, Iphigene, a force to be reckoned with, overruled his reservations. She thought that Punch had the instincts— if not the experience—to be the next publisher,[25] and other family members concurred. On Thursday, June 30, 1963, the board of directors chose Arthur Ochs Sulzberger as the next *Times* publisher,[26] although his reputation before 1963 had been that of a "reckless and irresponsible" young man. Later on, Baldwin came to praise him as "a pretty ruthless businessman" who became "an extremely able publisher," although he was less interested in the content of the paper than his father had been.[27]

While the paper was able to financially weather the storm of the strike, the publisher quickly realized that the *Times* would have to make more money than it had in the past. In short, it had to increase its circulation, raise its advertising rates, and enter the computer age. The latter decision would reduce the number of clerks and bookkeepers on the staff, but not to be skimped on was the breadth of its famed news coverage and the hiring of top talent.[28]

Inevitably, there were senior personnel changes, as members of the old guard were either kicked upstairs, reassigned, or gracefully retired. Baldwin was quick to note the implication of these changes and their effect upon his assignments. Within six months of the new management, he complained to one of his military correspondents, "I have been finding it more and more difficult, under the changed management here, to get what I consider important military news into the paper . . . without undue cutting and editing." He did not think this antimilitary attitude would change. It did not.[29]

In March 1966 Punch Sulzberger became worried about employee morale. He hired the research firm of Daniel Yankelovich to develop a questionnaire to be sent to all five thousand *Times* employees. One of the sixty-three questions asked respondents to point out "the major shortcomings in your job" at the *Times*. Baldwin seized the opportunity and replied "with great frankness" that clearly indicated the basis of his growing controversy with the paper. His long answers showed him to be unwilling to change his set views about the importance, that "sense of professional identity and pride," of newspapers and the newspaper business. He clearly idealized the values of a golden age when Adolph Ochs and Arthur Hays Sulzberger considered the *Times* to be "a public institution and public trust," where nonpartisan, objective, and accurate news reporting were the key elements to maintaining that trust. It was an age in which advertising revenues and circulation enhancement did not influence the news columns or the editorials.

In 1966 Baldwin pointed with alarm to the number of news columns that focused on entertainment and society issues. The management had been successful in making money, but at a high cost: the *Times* was "sloppy, inaccurate, and partisan." The anti-Vietnam editorials were reflected in the news columns. In summary, the paper was "less authoritative" in its foreign news coverage, "less thorough" in its national news, and simply "frivolous" in its metropolitan news coverage.

A very important event, to Baldwin's thinking, was the demise in March 1966 of the *New York Herald-Tribune*, the *Times'* only serious competitor in the New York City newspaper market. Those at the paper always read the first edition of the *Herald-Tribune* to see whether the *Times* had missed a story that the *Tribune* carried. In addition, it kept the *Times* on its toes from both the point of view of comprehensive news coverage and also accuracy and good writing.[30] In Baldwin's opinion, without the daily competition of the *Tribune*, the *Times* would drift for a long time on its past record unless, in his words, "substance is stressed, instead of form."[31] It is doubtful that Punch Sulzberger ever read those pointed comments, as the questionnaire was anonymous and returned directly to the research organization, where the results were transferred directly to IBM cards to be statistically analyzed.[32] In the venting of his spleen, Baldwin was also lashing out at his reduced status on the paper. His comments were a good reflection of his state of mind in the year before he informed the publisher of his intention to retire in 1968.

One of Dryfoos' personnel changes in 1961 was the appointment of John Bertram Oakes as the new editorial page editor, to replace the retiring Charles Merz. Gone was the latter's trademark phrase, "on the other hand," for a more assertive and lively editorial voice. Oakes was a political liberal whose opinions favored all environmental causes, civil rights, abortion rights, and divorce rights. He strongly favored negotiations to end the war in Vietnam rather than the escalation of the number of American ground forces there, a stand that continually annoyed Baldwin.[33] Following the death of Dryfoos, Punch Sulzberger continued to show confidence in John Oakes, with whom he shared many liberal views.[34] Baldwin once referred to Oakes as "a knee jerk flaming liberal," but he quickly added that he could never fault Oakes personally.[35]

With the decline of his former favored status among senior staff, Baldwin thought of early retirement. At the age of sixty he enjoyed a very good salary, and he made between $10,000 and $12,000 annually from his outside writings in addition to his *Times* salary. What persuaded him against retirement was his recent participation in the company's plan whereby credit units that represented shares of common stock of the New York Times Company were given to selected employees at the discretion of the management. Baldwin was honored to be included in the plan, which began five years earlier. If he remained for another five years, when he would be sixty-five, the plan would pay him $200 a year, paid out in ten annual installments. Since the financial cost of the 1963 strike settlement was high, he did not think the credit units would be voted upon. So, retiring at age sixty was not a good option. And there was always his wife Helen's continued welfare for him to consider.[36] In 1963 America's involvement in South Vietnam was deepening, which was an obvious inducement for him to stay on as the *Times* military editor to observe and report upon the unfolding events of the unhappy and divisive war.[37]

The 1960s started off with high hopes for America's future and great expectations for the new youthful administration of John F. Kennedy. For Baldwin, who was at the top of his form, prestige, and influence, the shakeup at the top management level of the *Times* was upsetting, but the new Kennedy administration brought changes to how the U.S. military was managed in the Pentagon, and it showed a sensitivity to press criticism that he thought alarming.

In hindsight, 1961 was the high noon of the American century. The youngest president and his new frontiersmen had a world to conquer. They went in search of foreign monsters to destroy. Their quest was to make the world safe for democracy and safe from the spread of Communism. In the Third World, the new Kennedy administration wanted to change the lives of those people for the better so that Communism would not take root in poverty, misery, and deprivation. To achieve these lofty goals, President Kennedy attracted young men in their forties, like himself, to apply rational solutions to solve the world's problems. They were the technocrats, the "can do" fast talkers, who had enormous self-confidence in their ability to do good in the world.

On the national security level, President John F. Kennedy appointed the Ford Motor Company president Robert S. McNamara to be his secretary of defense.[38] Baldwin first met the new secretary on Tuesday, February 7, 1961, at a small cocktail party in his Pentagon office, a day after McNamara had met with the Washington press corps. Present at the small gathering was Deputy Secretary for Defense Roswell Gilpatric and a few other reporters.

During the 1960 presidential campaign, the Democrats had made much of the "missile gap" with the Soviet Union. Since their dramatic *Sputnik* rocket launching in 1957 and, more recently, their successful long-range ballistic missile tests in 1960, they had put Washington on the defensive in the missile race.

It was at this cocktail party that Baldwin posed the question, "Well, Mr. Secretary, have you discovered anything about the missile gap? Have you found there isn't a missile gap, or what?"[39] McNamara replied, in an off-handed way, that there was nothing to worry on that issue. The ground rule for this gathering was that what was said would be off the record. An Associated Press reporter who was present later asked the public affairs officer (PAO) at the Pentagon for permission to use the secretary's words on a not-for-attribution basis. Permission was given on that basis, and the report appeared in the press three days later on February 10, 1961.

Baldwin looked forward to his appointment with McNamara that afternoon to discuss his policies on national defense, but the interview was terminated after only a few minutes because of a sharp White House reaction once McNamara's remarks about the absence of a missile gap became public knowledge. McNamara told Baldwin that he could not talk to "any member of the press now [that] his confidences had been revealed." He explained that as the head of the Ford Motor Company he had been able to call in reporters and tell them things off the record. Baldwin told him that in Washington "anything you say privately or otherwise is news." McNamara replied, "I've got to get used to that."[40] The veteran *Times* man later expressed surprise that Roswell Gilpatric, an old hand at Washington politics, and who was present at the February 7 cocktail party, had not advised Secretary McNamara of the power of words, using them with caution when dealing with the Washington press corps.[41]

Despite this awkward beginning, Baldwin reported on a number of McNamara's new policies, which had the effect of centralizing procedures that had been formerly handled separately by the military services, for example, intelligence gathering. Before McNamara, each service had had its own intelligence division. His plans were to merge all of the military services' intelligence-gathering roles. Baldwin saw this move as part of a general centralization of power in the Defense Department, reducing the influence of the individual service departments.[42] He called attention to a few dangers inherent in this merger: "Intelligence," Baldwin noted, "has always been a function of command."[43] Field commanders and ship captains relied upon the background and strategic information supplied by their service's intelligence branch. Removing these sources would make intelligence officers in the field "military orphans, a body without a head."[44] Another danger would be that specialized and detailed intelligence data could be neglected or downgraded "by a higher level agency."[45]

The "most dangerous aspect" of a merged intelligence service would be the need for "agreed [upon] or collective estimates." Elaborating on this point, Baldwin continued, "Intelligence data, by their very nature, cannot be precise, except in a few instances. There are bound to be varying estimates of the details of enemy strengths, and when these are projected into the future, as intelligence attempts to do, the uncertainties and hence the differences are even greater . . . differences would be suppressed, or so far downgraded that minority views would never reach the eyes of the Secretary of Defense or of the President."[46]

Baldwin advised that "intelligence collection and evaluation must never be confused with policy making."[47] He contended that "agreed upon collective military estimates" by "[a] monolithic agency so close to the throne of policy-making power in the Pentagon might well be susceptible to policy influence [and] the facts might subconsciously be distorted to suit the policy." It is human nature, he continued, to interpret facts to fit preconceived prejudices, a tendency that "must be guarded against to the utmost in intelligence work."[48] The old checks-and-balances principle in American politics was also applicable to intelligence collection and evaluation, he concluded.

After Secretary McNamara had been in office two and one-half months, Baldwin noted the following trends: the phasing out of massive nuclear retaliation as a deterrent force to Soviet moves, the creation of mobile limited war and unconventional forces, the elevation of civilians to decisionmaking levels in the office of the secretary of defense, the diminished authority of the military within the Pentagon bureaucracy, and finally, increasing pressure on the military to conform and to eliminate the interservice rivalries of the past.[49]

These and other changes were spurred on by McNamara "a man in a hurry [who] . . . wants answers to his questions—now."[50] The difficulty, Baldwin observed, was that his questions dealt with "the life and death" of the nation and some of his questions were unanswerable. McNamara's directed studies covered all military affairs. The Navy was trying to answer questions about the future of the aircraft carrier. Others were to compare Army with Navy and Air Force units and the personnel needed to support those units. The Joint Chiefs of Staff was given only a month to answer the question, "What is America's overall strategy?" Other projects included creating a unified command for research and development, as well as for construction projects and operations. In all of these projects the JCS might or might not participate, as "the decisions are being made by the Secretary and his civilian assistants, with the approval of the President."[51]

The civilians, who were recruited from the Rand Corporation and from the groves of academe, brought with them their baggage of operational analysis, a statistical and scientific tool designed to bring rational thought to bear on military problems. In Baldwin's view, operational analysis was "almost trying to pre-guess history, to plot the course of future battles, to tell the commander what to do, when and how."[52] It would change war from an art to a science. It bothered him that such a mechanistic and mathematical approach to military operations would destroy his deeply held belief that men, not machines, were at the heart of battle. Baldwin was a humanist at heart who fully understood the intangibles of war, of leadership, and of decisionmaking in war—all of which could not be "calculated, predicted or charted" by a mathematical equation.[53] War, he wrote, was "waged by human beings, and subject to all the emotions and the irrationalities and illogicalities of which human beings are capable."[54]

He did not, however, completely reject operational analysis, so long as it was only used as a tool to aid in problem solving. It was fallible when applied to the "stupendous uncertainties of the battlefield. The danger is that it may assume ... the aura of infallibility" and would lead to analyses "that smell[ed] heavily of the ivory academic tower and that bore little relation to reality."[55] To bolster his view, Baldwin cited Robert A. Lovett, the former secretary of defense, who once described a statistician as a "fellow who drew a straight line from an unwarranted assumption to a foregone conclusion."[56]

Nevertheless, McNamara recruited civilians from the "same school of graphs and formulas and quantitative and qualitative analysis,"[57] and they were no longer simply technicians or analysts, but they had the authority to review all military programs and procedures in light of the new evaluation criteria. During the Eisenhower administration the military services used major research universities to study specialized problems. Under McNamara, operational analysis became "the hottest subject" in the military.[58] To Baldwin's thinking, its application directly challenged the military's ability to know what was best for each particular service. Another annoying feature, to Baldwin, was that McNamara's civilian deputies, who worked out of the office of the secretary of defense, had the authority to tell the military services what to do, and how to do it.

In a six-month review of McNamara's regime, Baldwin could still say of him that he had an "incisive manner and [a] commanding intellect," but he also noted that McNamara would rather make "a quick wrong decision than none at all."[59] One of the secretary's major difficulties continued to be public relations. After the missile gap controversy in February 1961, he required that a third person be present whenever he met with a member of the press.

Like Baldwin, the senior officers in the Pentagon felt that McNamara's "major weakness" was "a tendency to think in terms of things rather than of people." His emphasis upon theoretical analyses of weapons systems convinced them that "man, as the heart of battle, is not being sufficiently emphasized." The secretary denied this characterization, but "the image of the slide rule and the graph, which hung over the Pentagon, had been hard to dispel," Baldwin observed.[60]

At year's end he wrote a three-part series that summarized the centralizing changes in the Pentagon, how policymaking, administrative, operational, and strategy-forming power in the office of the secretary of defense had been placed in the hands of civilians, rather than, as before, with the military.[61] The effect of these changes could be the merging of all military services into a single service headed by a single chief of staff, a shift that would directly threaten the current Joint Chiefs of Staff, which could become just a "council of senior military advisors" without any administrative or operational responsibilities. Their vice chiefs would handle the day-to-day duties.[62]

The big defense picture, as Baldwin saw it, included ever-increasing power and authority for civilians in the Pentagon and the diminution of the military services. Formerly, the secretary of defense had been a policymaker whose policies were carried out by the military services. With McNamara assuming more of the administrative details, assistant secretaries of defense, of whom all were civilians, now assumed the operational responsibilities that were formerly controlled by the JCS. Where would these super agencies and civilian hierarchies end? Baldwin could not answer this question, but he could and did point to his growing concern about the effects of the new centralization schemes then being implemented.[63]

On July 26, 1962, the *Times* ran the front-page headline over Baldwin's piece: "Soviet Missiles Protected in 'Hardened' Positions." The main point of the piece was that the Soviets were "hardening" (reinforcing) some of their ICBM missile sites that were of the "coffin" type, in which missiles lay horizontally in large concrete boxes flush with, or slightly above, the ground, where one large nuclear blast would destroy eight or more missile sites. When launched, the missiles would be raised to a vertical position from an opened coffin lid.[64] The swift negative reaction to this piece by the Kennedy administration not only challenged Baldwin's role as a military analyst, but the subsequent investigation of him hardened his hostility to the Kennedys over the issue of news management.

President Kennedy found it "incomprehensible . . . that someone of Baldwin's experience and stature and the status of the *Times* would do . . . a story which was not of particular interest to anyone but the Soviet Union."[65] Attorney General Robert Kennedy said "it was the worst leak that we had during . . . President Kennedy's administration," because as a result of Baldwin's piece, the Russians began to put their ICBM missiles into reinforced "concrete" sites and started "hiding" them, which caused "tremendous difficulty for our intelligence."[66] Baldwin viewed all the fuss as a demonstration of how freedom of the press operates in a democracy, in spite of Kennedy administration attempts to limit that freedom by ordering the FBI to find the leak and, by extension, to chill reporter–government news source relations for the future.

When Baldwin's piece appeared, the United States had "close to 100" land-based Atlas and Titan missiles (with 200 to be ready by the end of 1962); its nine Polaris submarines (with forty-one still to be built) gave America the edge over Soviet Russia "in the strength and diversity of its launching sites."[67] Baldwin cited the new science of "image interpretation," which included composite interpretation of photographs, infrared and radar images, and electronic "emanations," all of which gave the United States a qualitative and technological lead over the Soviet Union in ICBMs. Such technological advances could help ease world tensions and could be a deterrent, as each side would find it impossible to "knock out the other's nuclear capability by a surprise first strike."[68]

President Kennedy and his brother Robert quickly determined that Baldwin's piece was a major security breach that alerted Soviet Russia to what Washington knew about its ICBM placement. Attorney General Robert Kennedy was the force behind the FBI's investigation, and he persuaded a reluctant J. Edgar Hoover, the head of the FBI, to find the leak. His use of the FBI caused Baldwin to dub them "Mr. Bobby's Storm Troopers."[69]

In the ensuing monthlong investigation, 20 FBI agents interviewed 238 people in the Defense Department, Congress, and the State Department, producing a 970-page FBI file on Baldwin.[70] Baldwin's home phone was tapped on Saturday, July 28. In Washington Arthur Krock's secretary, Laura Walz, who made all the appointments for visiting reporters, was called upon at her apartment by agents who wanted to know the names of all persons who Baldwin had seen during his recent July 16–19 visit.[71]

On Monday, July 30, two agents from the New York office arrived at Baldwin's home at Chappaqua, New York, at about 7 p.m. He informed them that he would see them at his office the following morning at 10:30, closing his front door in their faces.[72] Hoover advised Robert Kennedy that given Baldwin's "resentment and arrogance," no further attempt would be made to interview him.[73]

Later that same evening, Scotty Reston, chief of the *Times* Washington bureau, called Baldwin at his home. The FBI telephone wiretap made a verbatim transcript of that conversation. Reston had just been told by Laura Walz of her experience with the FBI agents, and he was "so goddam mad about it" that he called Hanson to see "if you could calm me down or be mad with me."[74] Baldwin told Scotty about his experience with the FBI agents earlier that evening. "It is a goddam outrage," Reston replied, "and we ought to print the whole thing." Hanson advised caution until Orvil Dryfoos, the *Times* publisher, had been informed: "What they're coming to me for is to know the sources of my information—of course I won't tell them."

Reston and Baldwin agreed that the implications of the investigation were "extremely dangerous." Baldwin had been interviewed by the FBI years before in his *Times* office about a few of his pieces, but the agents had been "very polite and very nice." This current aggressive tactic by the FBI was new.

He saw the current FBI investigation as part of a growing need of the White House to manage the news, a pattern that had been evident in the 1961 Berlin Wall crisis when Lloyd Norman's story in *Newsweek* revealed various administration plans to meet the Russian challenge. President Kennedy "blew his top" and told his brother to send the FBI into the Pentagon to find the person who had spoken with Norman.[75] Reston suggested that the *Times* print an account of this current investigation, since President Kennedy was "essentially a politician, rather than a cop." A news story about this latest incident would be "more damaging to him than the information he would gain by talking to everybody you [Baldwin] saw." The bureau chief advised that he or Baldwin write a story about the issue and let Turner Catledge, the *Times* managing editor in New York, decide whether or not to kill it.[76]

The next day, Tuesday, July 31, Baldwin met with Dryfoos and Catledge to decide whether or not the *Times* should print an account of the FBI's recent evening visits to staff members. The upshot was that Reston (who was on a speakerphone during the discussion) would call McGeorge Bundy, a special assistant to the president for national security affairs, to find out the details behind this FBI investigation. Reston believed that the decision to use the FBI was made at the highest level and that perhaps the National Security Council had initiated it.[77]

Later that same evening, Secretary McNamara paid a visit to Scotty Reston at his home, a visit that lasted for almost two and one-half hours. The gist of his comments was that he knew nothing about the FBI's aggressive questioning of suspects and apologized for such tactics. He was concerned, however, about the "leak" of information to Baldwin about the Soviet

ICBMs, and he thought it to be a "clear violation of the law"—but which law he did not say. He assured Reston that the investigation was not directed against the *Times* or Baldwin, and that only three people in the government knew of the clustering of Soviet coffin-type missile sites. He ruled out General Lyman Lemnitzer, Dean Rusk, Adlai Stevenson, or Arthur Dean, the U.S. ambassador to the nuclear test ban treaty talks, as being Baldwin's source.[78] He did not suggest other persons.

In hindsight, the secretary of defense's evening visit to the home of the *Times* Washington bureau chief does suggest the importance of the paper among Washington policymakers and the importance of preventing publicity about the FBI investigation from being released to the general public. Indeed, talks between senior editors and Dryfoos at the *Times* resulted in a decision to print nothing about this episode. On Wednesday morning, August 8, the UPI news service did carry a story that was based on a Drew Pearson column about the incident.[79]

The reluctance of the *Times* to print this story did not mean that the publisher dismissed it. Reston called on McGeorge Bundy, who showed him the letter that was to be hand delivered to Dryfoos by Captain Tazewell T. Shepherd Jr. (USN), the president's naval aide. According to Reston, the confidential letter contained information that showed just how serious was Baldwin's leak. Bundy wanted to know Baldwin's source, but Reston assured him that Baldwin would never reveal it. Bundy seemed "puzzled" by this remark and quietly suggested that he did not want the FBI investigation to include all the leaders of the armed services to a point that they "might not want to talk to Baldwin anymore."[80] Reston thought that Bundy's statement "sound[ed] like tacit pressure."[81]

At 12:30 p.m., August 9, Captain Shepherd met privately with Dryfoos in his office in the Times Building and handed him the president's confidential letter. Later that day, the publisher spoke with Baldwin to assure him that the letter made no reference to him or to the need to know his source. Included with the letter was a secret intelligence report about the Soviet ICBMs. Bundy had assured Reston that the FBI's role was to plug the leak and not to go after Baldwin or the *Times*.[82] Reston viewed this incident as a freedom of the press issue. To his thinking, the pattern of the Kennedy administration was to use "tacit threats and pressure" against journalists. Despite assurances from Bundy and McNamara, Baldwin was convinced that for the previous eight months of 1962, President Kennedy had complained to Lester Markel, the *Times* Sunday editor, and to other *Times* men, about its editorials. In January 1962, Ted Sorenson, who was one of the president's aides, threatened to bar the *Times* from the White House and to use White House power to keep the *Times* from its news sources. Baldwin's subsequent requests to interview the president withered on the vine, the work of Pierre Salinger, he thought.

Another of Baldwin's concerns was the content of the president's letter to Dryfoos. If he was being accused, then he wanted to see that letter. He never did. The publisher tried to downplay Baldwin's paranoia by recalling previous FBI secret documents about *Times* men during the Joe McCarthy era of the early 1950s that accused some of being Communists. Dryfoos reiterated his belief that Baldwin's work was of continuing value to the paper.

While he wondered what was going to happen, twenty FBI agents spent August 1962 interviewing 238 military and civilian personnel in the government to find Baldwin's source. No one was exempted, from the secretary of defense to the CIA to the JCS and on down through their bureaucracies. In the words of one in-house FBI memorandum, the investigation was going to be "exhaustive, detailed, penetrative and complete."[83] One FBI progress report suggested that Baldwin should be called before a grand jury and be forced to name his sources, but that option was not pursued.

The urgency of this investigation was demonstrated by J. Edgar Hoover's frequent progress reports to both the attorney general and to Kenneth P. O'Donnell, a special assistant to the president. The investigation was given "the highest priority and [was] handled as special," one internal FBI memorandum stated.[84]

Baldwin was at the peak of his long career and the FBI interviews revealed what his peers thought of him. This information touched upon whether his source was a single, well-placed individual, or whether there were multiple sources from which he pieced together his July 26 piece. Or, perhaps it was a deliberate leak. The military services, which were interviewed, all denied being Baldwin's source. The president's military aide commented that Baldwin's contacts were only with senior officials in the government, and it would be "beneath his dignity" to see any lesser officials.[85] Others concurred with this assessment of the type of persons Baldwin would interview.[86]

Three weeks into the investigation, Hoover reported to Robert Kennedy that Baldwin had "unlimited access to sources on a high echelon [level] within the Government [who were] either friends or acquaintances of many years . . . [who] talked to him quite freely." During Baldwin's brief visit to Washington in mid-July 1962, his ability to contact "so many persons knowledgeable of highly classified data created a presumption that information of value was imparted to him."[87]

The FBI focused on his Washington visit, July 16–19, and the twenty-two persons he interviewed then; the list was obtained from the *Times* Washington bureau staff. All agreed that Baldwin dealt only with "high statured" persons. Admiral George Anderson, the chief of naval operations and a longtime friend, described his skill as an interviewer. He said that Baldwin was "a skilled individual in interviewing [who was able to] draw a knowledgeable person into a seemingly innocuous discussion and obtain meaningful answers to leading questions without giving an indication he was seeking that particular data."[88]

In a private telephone conversation with Mark Potter, one of Baldwin's sons-in-law, married to his daughter Barbara, the FBI recorded Baldwin venting his anger at recent events. He was still smoldering over the Miss Walz incident, which violated his somewhat Victorian sense of propriety toward women. Aside from this, he saw a pattern of intimidation by the White House in its use of the FBI to plug news leaks in the Pentagon. "The thing that makes me maddest," he told Potter, "is that they go into the Pentagon—with officers who have sworn oaths of fidelity, loyalty and obedience and they threaten them with lie detector tests—and this is incredible as compared with the kind of country which I was brought up in," noting that this had happened on two previous occasions. He also noted that although President Eisenhower "blew his top" about news leaks during his administration, he never sent the FBI into the Pentagon.

He ended his near-monologue of a telephone call by observing that the Kennedy brothers had "a Boston Irish inferiority complex—undoubtedly he [Jack] was snubbed when he went to Harvard . . . when the President blows his top—if there were someone else there instead of his brother, they might say—now wait a minute—take it easy—these things [leaks] happen. But I think Bobby goes off half-cocked and says 'God dammit let's get those SOBs.'"[89]

Baldwin's source (revealed only in 2005) was Roswell Leavitt Gilpatric, the deputy secretary of defense (1961–64). He had known Baldwin for ten years and had met with him alone in his office on July 17 for forty-five minutes. According to the interview report, Baldwin was interested in the status of the National Guard Reserve, changes in command in NATO with the retirement of General Lauris Norstad, and the possible candidate to be the next chairman of the JCS after the scheduled retirement of General Lyman L. Lemnitzer. Gilpatric denied that the conversation touched upon classified information or on intelligence subjects. In fact, he said that he had only read Baldwin's piece of July 26 for the first time while en route to New York City for a private lunch with eight members of the *Times* editorial board. Such luncheons were a routine function of the board as a means to collect background information from important people in the news. Baldwin, as a member of the board, was present and dominated the conversation, Gilpatric later recalled. After the luncheon, Gilpatric spoke with Dryfoos, the publisher, and openly criticized Baldwin for his "insensitivity" to national security issues. He told Dryfoos that Baldwin's source came from someone in the military.[90]

If Gilpatric was Baldwin's source, why did he reveal what he knew was classified information about the Soviet ICBMs? Some government officials, interviewed by the FBI, suggested that the leak was deliberate; others opined that Baldwin had picked up bits and pieces of information and had drawn his own conclusions. If Gilpatric was Baldwin's single source, then why did he tell him? Since their conversation was private, we will never know what was said. Both men kept their silence until their deaths decades later. Gilpatric denied to FBI agents that he was the source, and he continued to protest his innocence to Dryfoos by publicly criticizing Baldwin. I reject the possibility that Baldwin forgot to ask Gilpatric for permission to use the information without attribution. Neither was naive and both knew the political ramifications of this information with the Kennedy administration.

Baldwin was not the only reporter singled out for censure by the Kennedy White House. On August 28, 1962, the day that the FBI removed its telephone tap from Baldwin's home, a *Look* magazine article cited eleven instances where the president, or his family, or the White House staff contacted specific reporters to complain about what they had written. That was one of the first articles in a mass-circulation magazine that documented specific examples about how sensitive the administration was about its press image. As the author bluntly concluded, "Never before have so few bawled out so many so often for so little."[91]

For Baldwin, the issue was far more significant than press imaging; it was news management, not an academic matter to him. The FBI investigation had brought the *Times'* reputation into question on the issue of national security and the reputation of one of its big guns, Baldwin, on the basis of his having revealed classified information. Despite Dryfoos' assurances to the contrary, Baldwin felt the need to justify his position by writing an in-house memorandum in early September 1962.

The issue as he saw it was freedom versus security. For the free press to exist it could "never be . . . the mirror of government, or its spokesman." It must instead be the "monitor and watchdog of government." Without this function, democratic government could not exist in this country.[92] The secrecy mania that was so prevalent in Washington during the Cold War years meant that much information was classified, too much in Baldwin's view. He argued that if the press only printed non-classified information, "much of our major news would never be published."[93] However, a "patriotic" news-paperman would never quote verbatim from a classified document, since encrypting codes and ciphers could be revealed. The final responsibility as to whether or not to print lay with the newspaper, and not with the govern-ment, otherwise "the government controls the press."[94]

As to how to exercise this judgment, there could be no agreement between Washington and the press. The matter of leaks was complicated. The news source might want certain information printed, even though oth-ers in government might not. The source might not know the full story, only part of it. However, if the information were highly classified and it was given to the reporter in confidence, or for background only and not for publica-tion, the "reputable" reporter would not print it.[95] A government official's suggestions that a story be killed should be taken into consideration by a reporter, but Baldwin warned against the growing influence in Washington of the "intelligence mentality—the kind of mind-set that holds that the less information [that is printed] the better."[96]

Baldwin rejected the "intelligence mind-set," including the view that any published information about the Soviet Union's defenses only alerted Moscow to the need for improvements. He rejected the White House argu-ment that his July 26 piece led the Russians to alter their missile sites, saying,

"This kind of reasoning is a good example of the 'intelligence mind' at its worst and is nonsensical." He noted that the American popular and technical press had, for years, printed photographs and full descriptions of U.S. missile sites, often using U.S. government information: "The Russians can read, they can also think." He added that they did not need a *New York Times* piece to tell them that their early missile sites needed improvements, and they were already building new and better-protected sites.[97]

In retrospect, Baldwin believed that there would never be "complete agreement" between official Washington and the press corps as to what should or should not be printed. As he saw it, the day when the government ceased to complain about what the press printed, would be "the day when press freedom ends."[98]

But the decision about what to print was a continuing problem. To Baldwin's thinking, a newspaper reporter had to have a "sense of responsibility [that] should be [his or her] North Star.[99] In his personal experience, he could single out three instances in World War II in which he felt that the "general good" outweighed a momentary embarrassment. The stories he cited were the deplorable conditions in the U.S. Army's replacement depots in Italy in 1944, the superiority of German tanks to U.S. tanks, and the loss of four Allied cruisers in August 1942 near Savo Island in the Solomon Islands.

In the past Baldwin had been interviewed by FBI agents, but he cited nine examples from the 1950s where the paper withheld his stories or delayed publication at his urging. He drew the line against publication of military information about specific future operations, data about sources of intelligence information, or printing technical specifications of new weapons systems. As an aside, he said he thought the *Times* ought to have printed much more in the spring of 1961 about the preparations to invade Cuba.[100]

In his view, the recent attempt by the Kennedy White House to plug news leaks was worthy of "a police state—not a democracy,"[101] The aggressive methods used by the FBI against the *Times* employees and their threats to impose lie detector tests on officers in the Pentagon had to be challenged by the press.

To ameliorate the situation and challenge the trend, Baldwin suggested that President Kennedy and members of his administration host an informal session with the Washington press corps to explain the reasons why a particular story should be withheld, without having to call upon the FBI.

Lest he be misunderstood, he strongly rejected the idea that the government had to determine what news it wanted to release, calling it "the fundamental responsibility of the newspaper [to make] final determination [about] what it prints."[102] He emphasized that government friendships, favors, or "frowns" should never be "the decisive factor in determining what news is fit to print."[103]

As Baldwin well knew, President Kennedy did not invent managed news. It had developed after 1945 when it was felt that secrecy was needed in the global context of atomic weapons research and Communist political expansion, strengthening the influence of the FBI and the CIA bureaucracies that enshrined "secrecy as an abstract good."[104] President Kennedy's desire to maintain his popular public image as a strong leader led his administration to react swiftly to any press criticism.

Baldwin singled out for special criticism Arthur Sylvester, the assistant secretary of defense for public affairs, whose words and actions were carefully chosen to represent the Kennedy administration and White House policy. That policy was best summarized in his speech to the New York chapter of Sigma Delta Chi, the journalism fraternity, in December 1962. Referring to the Cuban missile crisis, Sylvester said, "It is the government's inherent right to lie, if necessary, to save itself when faced with nuclear disaster, this is basic." He continued, saying that "information is power" used to further the aims of our foreign policy.[105] Baldwin was shocked that Sylvester had used those words.

Sylvester had over twenty years of newspaper experience, sixteen of which were in Washington, D.C. To Baldwin, the comment was a direct reflection of the "intelligence mentality" that he decried as being so pervasive in Washington. It was a mind-set that all news must be surrounded with secrecy and safeguards. This mania for secrecy led to the compartmentalization of information, which to his thinking only protected "inefficiency" and hid "corruption."[106] The morale of government employees would suffer, and such secrecy chilled the "channels of cooperation" between the press and the government.

The World War II belief that "the press is on our side" had given way to centralization by government authorities who alone would determine what news would be released to the public. In short, news management, restriction, control, and censorship directly undercut the constitutional right of a free press to let the public know what its government was doing.[107] In his view, news leaks would always occur in a democracy. "When no leaks occur," Baldwin wrote, "I shall really begin to worry."[108] Baldwin concluded that honesty was the best policy for the government and censorship was wrong. Press access to officials was to be encouraged, not monitored or limited. The press alone must decide what to print and what to withhold, because news was "not a commodity, but an inherent democratic right and a public trust."[109]

Relating this general concern about secrecy to national security matters, Baldwin commented that if the American armed forces ever "spoke with one unanimous voice" and came to represent "a monolithic military-political point of view, democracy will be in danger."[110] The danger would come from "undue military influence in policy-making and in decisions of the government; the danger of swollen military budgets, and of a long step forward towards the true 'garrison state.'"[111] This was the very thing President Eisenhower had warned the nation against in his farewell speech in January 1961.

Baldwin was also very upset that he, of all people, had been singled out by the Kennedy administration for an FBI investigation. It implied that the *Times* military editor did not know which of the government's secrets to keep secret. He later commented that there was too much classification in Washington, and that it was done more to save personal reputations than to conceal information vital to America's national security during the Cold War. In hindsight, this whole episode with the FBI and the Kennedys revealed an issue of security and press freedom. It was not the first or the last time the issue would be raised. In hindsight, it faded with the real crisis of the discovery of Russian missiles in Cuba in October 1962.

Baldwin's hostility toward Secretary McNamara and his deputy, Arthur Sylvester, only increased as the United States became involved in Vietnam. The latter once dismissed Baldwin as being "one of his favorite fiction writers," and Baldwin later dismissed Sylvester as a "stooge" for McNamara.[112] As the Vietnam War continued and Baldwin's critical comments about how the war was being managed from Washington multiplied, McNamara bluntly told Baldwin, "You're the most inaccurate reporter I've ever known," to which he replied, "Mr. Secretary, I think you're the most dishonest secretary" I've known.[113] It is not surprising, considering the tone of this verbal exchange, that McNamara remained "very cool, very hostile, and never newsworthy."[114]

In "The McNamara Monarchy" in the March 1963 issue of *The Saturday Evening Post*, Baldwin exposed the myth of the Pentagon as a businesslike efficient machine, whose leader, McNamara, effectively reined in the disputatious military service chiefs. He expressed the fear that the McNamara reforms would lead to a "monolithic military-political point of view [in which] both freedom and security would be in jeopardy through the slow erosion of democracy into a garrison state and [would result in] stagnant conformity that leads to combat ineffectiveness."[115]

Behind McNamara's unification moves, he saw "subtle and insidious dangers": to make the Pentagon speak with "one voice," to discourage dissent, and to mold military intelligence to fit "preconceived policies." In his view, those centralization moves could lead to the "top political and policy control of military intelligence that would be politically dangerous." He cited how the JCS had been "pressured" to sign off on an agreement as to the adequacy of the Defense Department budget, part of a pattern whereby McNamara had overruled and otherwise bypassed the JCS, and generally ignored its advice.

Since the secretary of defense had decided that he alone would determine what was best for the nation's security, one result was the concentration of power into the hands of "a few men" in the executive branch, which had helped the military-industrial complex to grow. The multi-billion-dollar contracts awarded by the office of the secretary of defense could make the companies lucky enough to receive one, and break those companies that were overlooked.

These trends could develop into a military "party-line," where the secretary of defense would permit no deviation from the established policies set, and where future military officers would be urged to become "yes-men" and be schooled in the new techniques of operational analyses. In conclusion, Baldwin warned that a "garrison state" might emerge in Washington. In a parting shot, Baldwin noted that even Mr. McNamara and his "strange new breed of computer experts . . . [could not] run the world."[116]

The reaction to the magazine article was swift in coming. A brief notice in a military trade journal noted that newspaper and magazine editors were advised by the Pentagon to "kill" Baldwin's article. His longtime friend, William J. Sebald , then the U.S. ambassador to Burma, praised the article and commented that "there is entirely too much empire being set up in the administration . . . and it is about time that something be done about it."[117]

Though Baldwin was quite capable of making his own independent assessment of the McNamara administration, his views did mirror those of many Navy admirals who worked in the office of the chief of naval operations at the time. None of them had a high opinion of the civilians who worked out of the office of the secretary of defense, one expressing the view that Secretary McNamara had a "mania" about being "right all the time," even if that meant changing the parameters of a study to alter the results.[118]

Given the FBI investigation of Baldwin in 1962 and his concerns about the alarmingly autocratic and cost-effective guidelines of the McNamara administration in 1963, it is not surprising that he later blamed the mistakes of the Vietnam War directly on the policies and the mismanagement of Robert S. McNamara.

CHAPTER 17

Duty and Despair:
The Vietnam War, 1962–68

Baldwin's approach to the Vietnam War was that of a Cold Warrior. He favored a foreign policy that was based upon a realistic balance of power, "the American way" that was between isolationism and imperialism. The weakness of this middle way, he thought, was that Americans were an impatient people who had a tendency to go off on ideological crusades to extend the arena of freedom, or to otherwise make the world safe for democracy. In 1945, on the occasion of the founding of the United Nations Organization, Baldwin (as cited earlier) wrote, "we must keep our eyes on the stars but our feet planted firmly in the mud of the world we live in."[1]

He accepted the fact that limited wars would continue to occur, but insisted that America's involvement be based upon realistic and clear political goals. Such wars, he said, must never be allowed to degenerate into wars of passion, their ends hazy and their prosecution ruthless, for the resulting chaos would only further the expansion of Communism.[2] To his thinking, the best policy for containing the spread of Communism was to keep non-Communist states politically stable and economically prosperous. Communism could be contained not by military threats of a nuclear war, but by denying to it the chaotic political, economic, and social conditions that fostered it.[3]

Reviewing the world situation in 1962, Baldwin regretted that U.S. leaders had not, in the recent past, used America's power to curtail the "creeping encroachment" of Communism in various parts of the world. In Southeast Asia, the United States did not use its political, military, economic, or psychological power to stop Ho Chi Minh in the early 1950s. The 1954 Geneva settlement, which gave the Communists control of Vietnam north of the 17th parallel, had resulted in the United States "reaping the whirlwind" in South Vietnam. To his thinking, "the world respects strength and we gave it weakness. We didn't lack power, we lacked the will to use it."[4]

During the brief Kennedy presidency, Baldwin was less concerned about the events in South Vietnam than he was about the managed news policies of the administration. He was "deeply concerned" about the growing autocracy and centralization of government, and "a confirmed believer . . . in the fact that Congress must have the right to determine the size, the policies, and even the details about the armed forces."[5]

In 1963 Baldwin received two important letters that alerted him to the fact that all was not well in Saigon, despite Kennedy's claims to the contrary. First, Bernard B. Fall, a recognized authority on Vietnam, warned Baldwin that the reports from General Paul D. Harkins and U.S. ambassador Frederick E. Nolting were overly optimistic about the progress of the antiguerrilla campaign. In Fall's words, the "cynicism and misstatement of fact, and blind over-optimism" of the official reports outstripped anything he had encountered before. He urged Baldwin to check out the facts on the Vietnam story himself, adding that his comments were not for attribution.[6]

Later that year, Baldwin received a long letter from Lieutenant Colonel John Paul Vann, who had recently retired from the U.S. Army. Vann reviewed his experiences as a military adviser working with the Saigon-appointed field commanders, together with his stormy relations with General Harkins about the progress reports from the field. He advised that Secretary McNamara and General Maxwell D. Taylor, then the chairman of the Joint Chiefs of Staff, could get the unvarnished truth if they would bypass General Harkin's headquarters and talk directly with battalion, regimental, and division advisers (American) on their visits to Vietnam.

In an astute observation, Vann further advised Baldwin that the Vietnamese will "always say what they think you want to hear." Westerners, who did not understand this way of thinking, either "accept[ed] erroneous information as fact, or on finding it [wasn't] so, [thought] they [were] dealing with unscrupulous liars."[7] Commenting on the political situation in South Vietnam, Vann posed the question, "What in the hell is our objective there anyhow? To establish a democracy in a nation that isn't ready for it or, to establish a strong, anti-Communist government? I think it should be the latter!!!!!"[8]

He ridiculed the current program of having free elections in the fortified hamlets when all the higher levels of government in South Vietnam were run by appointed officials.

Those two letters alerted Baldwin to the fact that the Vietnam situation was going to be a very difficult problem for America and that there were no easy answers. The murder of President Ngo Dinh Diem on November 2, 1963, removed the Nhu family from power, but it opened the door to many other political problems, including the continuing search for a strong national leader who had the power to create a stable non-Communist government in Saigon.

During one of his regular Washington visits, in April 1964, Baldwin was told that the U.S. Army was not trained or equipped to fight jungle warfare. General Maxwell Taylor felt that it would take "at least twenty divisions." The war would be, in the words of General Harold K. Johnson, who was then on General Earle G. Wheeler's staff, "a long, hard, dirty road."[9] Baldwin considered this an example of the pessimism of the Army's "never again school," which was against committing American ground forces in Asia as it had in Korea fourteen years earlier. He learned further from Cyrus R. Vance, the deputy secretary of defense, that the United States had "to win" the war in Vietnam, and that neutralization of that country was not an acceptable solution.[10]

Reflecting upon his continuing battle about the *Times'* editorials, Baldwin told John Oakes that same April that "we must very clearly face the implications to the United States of a defeat there."[11] He was afraid that if the United States lost in South Vietnam, then Washington would be seen as a "paper tiger in Asia," and that would lead eventually to the collapse of all of Southeast Asia to Communist control. The big question for Washington, Baldwin felt, was whether or not to carry the war to North Vietnam and whether or not to send American ground troops into South Vietnam.[12] He told a military audience that since the goals of Moscow and Beijing were the "Communist domination of the world," America must never adapt a "peace at any price" policy. If it did, then "we are licked . . . we are Red or dead or both."[13]

The Pentagon's new command and control system raised the question of whether or not the centralized Washington command post could win wars. Baldwin had his doubts. With an apology to Winston Churchill, Baldwin quipped, "Never in the history of human conflict have so many been able to say no—so few to say yes." He could not resist commenting upon the recent trend by Secretary McNamara to downgrade professional military judgment with the "civilianization" at the Pentagon, adversely affecting the morale of the armed services.[14]

He also felt that President Lyndon Johnson, the former vice president until November 1963, ought to tell the American public what U.S. objectives were in Vietnam. For without a frank and comprehensive public information policy by the government, the public's frustration, apathy, and opposition to the war could develop, especially in a long war of attrition, as they did in the final stages of the Korean War.[15]

Thus, in 1964, a year before President Johnson sent U.S. ground troops to South Vietnam, Baldwin tried his best to alert the American public about what was at stake there and what the Johnson administration ought to do. In December 1964 he complained that the *Times* editorials spoke "in rather high and lofty moralistic terms about the brave new world, and about the debacle we are all trying to avoid." That attitude was similar, in his mind, to the appeasement thinking of the 1930s. He reminded John Oakes, the *Times* editorial page editor, that the "safest policy" for the United States and for the *Times* was "to speak softly and carry a big stick."[16] In other words, to use diplomacy backed by force. In Baldwin's analogy, 1964 was not 1904, when President Theodore Roosevelt was applauded for uttering such maxims.

In 1965 President Johnson and his advisers decided that American action was called for. The continuing parade of generals in Saigon was not reassuring. James Reston counted eight governments in the eighteen months after the assassination of President Diem in November 1962: "In Saigon, Prime ministers change like bus drivers at the end of the run, and unless they are numbered, like football players, it is almost impossible to know who is on the field."[17] President Johnson was equally frustrated. "I don't want to hear anything more about this coup shit! I've had enough of it, and we've got to find a way to stabilize those people out there!"[18]

Guerrilla raids by the Vietcong throughout the country continued unabated, and the thousands of American military advisers assigned to South Vietnamese units (ARVN) witnessed the repeatedly poor performance by troops in the field. Hanoi was encouraged by this political and military incompetence, and by America's continuing restraint in the limited bombing campaign ordered by President Johnson after the Gulf of Tonkin incidents a year earlier.[19]

In late January 1965 the President's military and civilian advisers urged him to escalate U.S. air strikes against North Vietnam. He hesitated. What changed his mind was the Vietcong attack on the American airbase at Pleiku and on the nearby helicopter base at Camp Holloway in the central highlands on February 7, 1965. Nine Americans were killed and 137 were wounded in the attack. Twenty-two helicopters and fixed-winged planes were destroyed or damaged.[20] Three days later, the Vietcong attacked another American base at Qui Nhon on the coast, where 23 soldiers were killed and a like number were wounded. On February 13 the president authorized Operation Rolling Thunder, an extensive bombing campaign of North Vietnam that lasted for three years and dropped more bomb tonnage than all of World War II.

Given the debate within the Johnson administration about what to do, Baldwin's long article in the *Times Sunday Magazine* on Sunday, February 21, 1965, entitled "We Must Choose—(1) Bug Out (2) Negotiate (3) Fight," provided clear if unpleasant choices. As he had at other times in his long career, Baldwin felt that the military and political situation overseas called for a loud wake-up call so that Americans would realize what was at stake in Vietnam. In 1942, a month after the Pearl Harbor attack, he suggested that the United States could lose World War II unless it stopped being so complacent about the Japanese military threat.

In this current article, Baldwin's words were uncompromising, vigorous, and forceful, suggesting that a war in Vietnam was the right war in the right place and that Communism was the right enemy. The global issue was the containment of Asian Communism, led by China's Mao Tse-tung: "We must fight a war to prevent an irreparable defeat. We must use what it takes to win."[21] The Korean War had stopped the spread of Chinese Communism in that peninsula, but now Beijing and Hanoi sought a new opportunity to expand into Southeast Asia. The time was now for the United States to act to prevent this expansion from occurring. America's "global prestige and power is intimately bound up with the outcome" in South Vietnam, he said.[22] The United States must end what Soviet premier Khrushchev called the "wars of national liberation." If it failed "the world would gradually become Red."

Baldwin ridiculed the "polite fiction" of the previous four years of the Kennedy and Johnson administrations, that the United States was not fighting a war there, merely advising a small Asian country how to be free from a Communist takeover by the Vietcong, agents of the Communist government of Ho Chi Minh. The United States had reached "a crossroads," a "point of no return," he wrote. Compromise and consensus, so useful in domestic politics, could not be guideposts in our Vietnam policy. The situation there called for a "clear-cut and courageous decision." In a sentence that must have shocked many of his readers, Baldwin wrote that "we must fight a war to prevent an irreparable defeat. We must use what it takes to defeat Communist expansion in Asia," but not by seeking to remake the Saigon government into "our own image."[23]

The issues at stake were global. American prestige and power were linked to events in Vietnam. Writing like a geopolitician, he warned that once the "rim lands" of Asia fell under Communist control, then the Philippines, Taiwan, and Okinawa would be doomed. The domino theory would be implemented. Baldwin then moved against what he called "the voices of defeat and despair, caution and fear." The United States must "arm to parley" so that the United States could speak from a position of strength by putting up a fight for Vietnam.[24]

He dismissed the popular view that a guerrilla war could not be won. He denied that that was true, citing civil wars in Greece, the Philippines, and Malaya, in which the guerrillas were defeated, though he cautioned that it would take a force "10 to 30 times larger" than that of the guerrillas to win. Such a war would result in American casualties but he said, "You cannot win a war without spilling blood."[25] The United States had to take risks, but that was the "price of power," he wrote. For America to hesitate or to appease the enemy would lead to "ultimate disaster" in South Vietnam. In one of his more strident phrases he warned, "If we are inhibited from action by Hamlet-like indecision over legalistic concepts of international law, we shall lose the world."[26]

The continuing instability of the Saigon government after the death of Diem was caused by Washington's lack of "tangible determination to win."[27] Once U.S. national leadership found that determination to win, only then would the Saigon leaders find the courage to fight the Vietcong. The American people must understand that the United States was now fighting a war, and not merely advising its friends how to fight one. The *Times* military editor observed that being on the defensive would not win the war;

"We must get more Americans and more Vietnamese out of the bistros of Saigon and into the bush."[28] Baldwin urged that the U.S. Air Force begin an "unrelenting massive" attack on North Vietnamese power plants, docks, and oil storage facilities, and that a naval blockade and naval gunfire begin a bombardment of North Vietnam's harbors and shores.

One of President Johnson's continuing fears was that if the United States escalated the war, the Chinese might intervene. Baldwin doubted that that would happen. Though its army was sizable, it had an "obsolete" air force and little sea power. He did assume that China's continuing shipment of supplies to Hanoi would increase to match U.S. escalation.[29]

The big question was how many American ground troops would the offensive require? Based on numbers given to Baldwin by General Harold Johnson, the Army's chief of staff, and by General Wallace Greene, the Marine Corps commandant, at least ten or twelve divisions would be required. But if one included all Air Force, Navy, and ground forces, then "perhaps 200,000 to 1,000,000 Americans would be fighting in Vietnam." This would mean "a major war no matter what euphemisms would be used." The U.S. economy would be put on a war footing and the public mobilized for a "long, nasty, and wearing" war.[30] His final comment was that in the struggle for freedom, "there is no good place to die." It would be far better to fight in Vietnam on China's doorstep than to fight some years hence "in Hawaii, on our own frontiers."[31]

It may be noteworthy that this article appeared not in the daily *Times,* but in the *Times Sunday Magazine*, which for years behaved as a semi-independent publication run imperiously by its editor, Lester Markel. As fellow editor Max Frankel once observed, the *Times* Sunday sections had become a "refuge for those of us who felt suffocated by the daily paper's constraints."[32]

Baldwin's article came at a time when the American public desired to limit its involvement in Vietnam. The college teach-ins had begun, in which the professoriate spoke out against war in general and Vietnam in particular. President Johnson himself had many doubts during those early months of 1965, when the Saigon leadership seemed to be a revolving door of generals and the ARVN troops were ineffective against the repeated Vietcong attacks.[33]

This article had the expected shock effect, which is what Baldwin anticipated. The *Times* lead editorial, "The Debate on Vietnam," sharply criticized

Baldwin by name for urging a sharp increase in American military commitment in Vietnam and for expanding the air war in North Vietnam. To Oakes, and to others on the editorial board, the U.S. role was "to protect" the Vietnamese people, not to begin an ideological global struggle. For if we followed Baldwin's advice, then President Johnson's Great Society social programs would end, the Moscow-Beijing-Hanoi axis would be strengthened, and possibly Communist China would send its armies to the rescue of Ho Chi Minh's government. The resulting chaos would be "an escalation of such dimensions" that would inevitably lead to a "calamitous atomic exchange." The blame for all this would be placed at the doorstep of South Vietnam, which "now shows no will to fight in its own defense." The editorial favored negotiations that would seek the neutralization of South Vietnam and lead away from "a road to global holocaust."[34]

Members of the Columbia University professoriate found Baldwin's article to be "an alarming example" of a writer preoccupied with the use of military power. One million American soldiers amid "hostile or sullen" people in Vietnam was not the answer to what was "basically a civil war" there. The professors agreed with the editorial that if America were to intervene on the scale urged by Baldwin it would lead to a nuclear war, in which the American values of freedom and democracy would be lost as it sought to win a global power struggle for its own sake.[35]

Baldwin did have a few supporters, but they were all in the military. Without doubt many people quietly dismissed his views as being too extreme a solution to the Vietnam problem.[36] Partial agreement with Baldwin's article came from Roger Hilsman, the former assistant secretary of state for Far Eastern affairs during the Kennedy administration (1963–64), a former news source for Baldwin. Commenting upon current policy, Hilsman thought that President Johnson's limited bombing campaign was a "weak response" to Communist aggression in Southeast Asia. Only American ground forces would be able to impress the Communists. However, any escalation of our troops must be coordinated with military, political, and diplomatic "instrumentalities" to persuade China to curb its imperial ambitions. The goal should be a negotiated agreement along the lines of the 1954 Geneva Accords that would result in "Southeast Asia for the Southeast Asians"; however, if Washington's ideological goal was to make South Vietnam into an anti-Communist bastion, Beijing was to do everything it could to prevent this from happening. Hilsman ended his letter with the warning, "If we do not face the possibility of fighting on the ground now … then we will surely have to face it later."[37]

Eight years later, in 1973, the *Wall Street Journal* featured an editorial at a time when all U.S. troops had been withdrawn from Vietnam, and the last of the American prisoners of war had been released. That editorial, "Vietnam: Looking Back," reflected on what had once, but incorrectly, passed as conventional wisdom in the mid-1960s. It singled out Baldwin's 1965 article "We Must Choose" as standing up very well from among the "legion of commentators and onlookers."[38]

On April 7, President Johnson gave an important speech at The Johns Hopkins University, which he hoped would satisfy both the "hawks" and the "doves" that were fluttering about in increasing numbers. On one hand, Washington would persevere in its efforts to establish a non-Communist government in South Vietnam; on the other, once that objective had been achieved, the United States would sponsor an ambitious economic development project for the Mekong River Valley region. On the following day, Hanoi proposed its four-point plan for peace, whose terms, if accepted, would mean the end of an independent South Vietnam.

In May there was another coup in Saigon, which brought to power Air Marshal Nguyen Cao Ky and General Nguyen Van Thieu. With increasing American financial and military help, that government attained a superficial stability that remained in power until 1975.

In hindsight, Baldwin told America and Washington what the United States, as a nation, ought to do if it wanted to win the war. As we know now, President Johnson was only willing to do what was necessary to keep us from losing. He took the first step toward the eventual Americanization of the war on March 8, 1965, when he ordered two battalions of Marines (3,500 men) then stationed in Okinawa to take up defensive positions around the American coastal base at Danang, South Vietnam, a decision that reflected the civilian and military advice he had been receiving for weeks.

In June 1965, as American forces slowly increased in numbers, Baldwin noted that U.S. troop reinforcements were being matched by the enemy. His military sources told him that the "gradual, piecemeal" commitment of U.S.

ground troops might be "too little, too late," whereas a rapid buildup might have a shock effect upon the Communist forces. Contributing problems were the overmanaging from Washington, the speed of rapid communications, and the tightly controlled system from the Pentagon, all of which made it possible for field commanders in Vietnam to receive detailed orders from Washington, at times during an operation in progress. Those restrictions and controls were making military operations in Vietnam "less flexible and less effective" than they could be. Also, another complicating issue was that the United States did not command the ARVN forces, nor was there a joint command to facilitate this. For example, if the ARVN troops requested American help, those American troops would be considered as "supporting troops over whom they have no control in situations of great uncertainty."[39]

Adding to Baldwin's annoyance was the Johnson administration's policy of "dissimulation . . . double-talk, and . . . lies" by senior officials, including Secretary McNamara and the president himself, whose "complex personality" led him to manage the news and release bits and pieces of it according to his own timing. As in the past, Baldwin believed that the role of the press was to monitor what the government was doing and to criticize it when necessary, despite government pressures to remain silent.[40] Closer to home, Baldwin repeatedly criticized the *Times* editorials on Vietnam as unrealistic. It was one thing to wish for peace and favor negotiations with the enemy, but the United States must be pragmatic and inform the public of what was at stake in Vietnam and the harsh demands of war upon Americans.[41]

While Baldwin saw the war in clear terms, a colleague, Max Frankel, thought the war confusing, since it was not clear what a winning U.S. strategy ought to be, or what the issues were. He told Turner Catledge, the *Times* executive editor, "the most important thing be to said about Vietnam, it has defined clear thinking. Very few people on any side of the issue were comfortable with their own state of mind about it."[42] The diversity of opinion about the war was reflected in America's newspapers and the *Times* was not omniscient, though some may have thought it was.

On July 28, 1965, President Johnson held a news conference in which he casually announced an increase of 50,000 U.S. military forces to be sent to Vietnam, a decision that reflected the views of his military sources. Baldwin regretted the president's unwillingness to call up the military reserves at that time, when some of his Pentagon sources thought it to be necessary. Two weeks later, *The Reporter* magazine featured Baldwin's analysis of the situation. The White House policy between 1961 and 1965 had been a failure. Its attempt to win the war "without fighting it ourselves" had failed. Until the military-political situation improved, "it [was] unlikely that any basis [could] be found for a negotiated peace."[43] General William C. Westmoreland, the commander of U.S. Military Assistance Command in Vietnam (MACV), was currently unable to have a unified command over ARVN troops because of the "touchiness" of Saigon's political situation, and possibly because of the perception that he would be acting as an "American pro-consul," ordering about America's colonial troops. On the other hand, public opinion at home would not accept a Vietnamese commander in chief over U.S. combat forces. There was also the problem of what type of command structure would be best to suit all American forces.

As for which military strategy would be best, Baldwin saw the merits of the "ink-blot" strategy, in which American ground forces would move out from secure bases into the surrounding areas, a process that would be slow and costly. Another strategy would be to attack the enemy's Ho Chi Minh Trail, as it was later called, along the Cambodian and Laos borders, a move that would involve political difficulties. Another equally difficult strategy would be to attack the Hanoi-Haiphong sanctuary, with its fuel storage tanks and the surface-to-air-missile (SAM) antiaircraft gun emplacements. In time, Baldwin thought, those targets would have to be hit, but at the risk of widening the war, which President Johnson did not want to do. If the United States bombed the rail lines from China into North Vietnam and imposed a naval blockade on that country, it would also result in "serious international complications."[44]

As the war continued, so did the demands for increased draft calls, additional congressional funding, and "eventually" a limited mobilization of our military reserves. The president's refusal to call up the military reserves demonstrated to Baldwin Johnson's inability "to grasp the nettle of limited mobilization . . . that will be essential if the war continues."[45]

However, "the major problem" for President Johnson, as Baldwin saw it, would be how to enlist and to hold American and Allied support for "a long and dirty war of attrition." A rapid buildup of American forces could lose American public support for the war, while a gradual increase might mollify domestic opposition to the war yet be insufficient to win it. He predicted that for the United States the long road in the Vietnam War would require "national patience and fortitude to a degree unmatched in any previous war the United States had fought."[46] This article was Baldwin's way of informing Americans about the complications of the war, while alerting them to future national requirements should it continue for years. To his way of thinking, this was what a responsible press ought to do in time of war.

Beginning in mid-October through mid-November 1965, the American First Cavalry Division (Air Mobile) encountered fierce, at times hand-to-hand, combat with regular North Vietnamese troops in the Ia Drang Valley near the Cambodian border. It was during those battles that the widespread use of helicopters to carry troops and supplies to the combat areas began. What had been merely a military theory about quickly airlifting troops over rough and inaccessible terrain quickly became standard operating procedure.

As was his custom in earlier wars, Baldwin spent over a month in Vietnam beginning in late November 1965. It was his second trip to the country, his first having been in 1950 when it was called Indochina.[47] Once in country he traveled extensively, visiting various front-line units and speaking with all ranks. General Westmoreland, accompanied him during some of his travels. He had previously cultivated Baldwin's friendship while he was the superintendent at West Point.

Shortly before he left Saigon in late December, Baldwin wrote a two-part article. The tone was cautiously optimistic about the future of the war, but he noted many continuing problems. There was the need for proper training for all U.S. troops to meet the challenges of the various kinds of terrain in the country: rice paddies, jungles, and mountains. The hit-and-run tactics of the Vietcong reminded him of the "frontier fighting against the Indians." The Army field manuals about proper infantry tactics had to be modified, as the "sound of a bullet is a greater teacher than any field manual."[48] He noted how the troops relied heavily upon fire support from artillery and from helicopters, a reliance that was excessive, said one military source, just to kill one sniper or to destroy one bunker. Those tactics may have reduced the number of American casualties, but they often increased civilian casualties in the process. Baldwin praised the use of helicopters, both to coordinate the ground units with the command of those forces and to increase the battlefield mobility of troops. The troops admired the new M-16 rifle, when it did not jam, and the promised shipment of cleaning rods had not solved that immediate problem.

As for the quality and the training of the ARVN troops, Baldwin gave a lot of numbers about the size of those units, but accurate figures were hard to come by. He noted that the "main burden of the day-to-day war" was borne by the ARVN troops and that their battlefield effectiveness in the field was improving, words that appeared to damn their performance with faint praise. In hindsight, his assessment of the ARVN troops was probably overly optimistic.

"We have stopped losing. We are not yet winning," Baldwin quoted one of his military sources as telling him. In summary, he noted that after six months of American ground operations, the war could last for at least another five years and would require the deployment of up to 500,000 American troops in country. The people of South Vietnam were "war weary," but the Vietcong were "everywhere" and owned the night. To Baldwin, this was the sort of blunt assessment that Americans back home needed to hear. What was required, he wrote, was the repeated bombing of North Vietnam's petroleum storage areas, the docks and wharfs at Haiphong, and the railroad line between Nanning, China, and Hanoi that brought many needed supplies from China. He also advocated the mining of Haiphong Harbor, which would hinder Russian supply ships from using that harbor. He thought a selective call-up of U.S. military reserves was "mandatory." Baldwin's military sources, both in Washington and in Vietnam, had been stressing such strategies and policies for months. He thought that the increasing antiwar demonstrations and the public criticism of President Johnson's war policy only encouraged the Hanoi leadership to believe that the United States was not prepared for a long war of attrition.[49]

On his return to New York, Baldwin was surprised to learn that many of his pieces, filed from Saigon and Guam, had been cut entirely, heavily edited, or combined with reports from other correspondents. Those edits made substantial cuts of information or qualifying comments that Baldwin felt were necessary for a full understanding of the situation. The heavy editing signaled again that under Punch Sulzberger's new management Baldwin was no longer a privileged staff member whose writings were protected by the no-cut-without-express-approval policy.[50] The Christmas truce of 1965, as seen by the editorialist, was "a precious thing to have. It would be even more precious to hold,"[51] a tone of supplication and hope that Baldwin thought unrealistic.

Increasingly, Baldwin stressed the important role that American public opinion would play in the war. In a long memorandum, written in early January 1966 to Clifton Daniel, the managing editor of the *Times*, he observed that public opinion might be "the dominant" factor in the kind of decision the United States got in Vietnam. Baldwin cited the lack of credibility in the press releases from the government, which he blamed on Washington's Madison Avenue policies—never kill civilians and never make mistakes— and the legacy of lies and distortions uttered by the Kennedy administration during the Harkins-Diem regime in Saigon three years earlier. That legacy made the press skeptical of all information furnished by the military spokespersons in Saigon. In addition, Baldwin did not believe in the accuracy of the official body counts: "This is the first war in which the body count has been a yardstick of victory or defeat, and it ought to be dropped."[52]

The press was not blameless in the matter of creating distortions about the war. During Baldwin's tour of Vietnam he heard lots of criticism from experienced reporters, including the *Times'* Charles Mohr, and Army commanders about the distortions, inaccuracies, sensationalism, and the generally overbearing attitude, especially of the younger members of the press corps in Saigon. Baldwin felt the young correspondents were simply unqualified to interpret and to understand the larger military picture they had observed when viewing events at the squad or platoon level. The principal fault lay in Washington, with the intense reaction of President Johnson, Secretary of Defense McNamara, and Assistant Secretary of Defense for Public Affairs Arthur Sylvester, all of whom wanted to control the release of war news that affected American public opinion about Vietnam and the public's positive image of the president.[53]

Closer to home, Baldwin protested about the editorials directly to Punch Sulzberger, predicting that the escalation of the number of American forces would occur "whether we like it or not." It was no longer a question of whether the United States had the option to leave Vietnam to its fate, or to intervene with U.S. troops. That option may have been possible twelve months before, but not in January 1966. Ho Chi Minh had no incentive to negotiate, since antiwar demonstrations and the *Times* editorials had "hardened" Hanoi's position into one in which they thought they could outlast

American patience and use American public opinion to force an end to the war on terms disadvantageous to the United States.[54]

The *Times* editorials, according to Baldwin, should try to persuade Hanoi, not President Johnson, to seek peace, and they should be against Hanoi and not against the president. "We are now in a full fledged war" and it was not to the paper's advantage to be identified with the street demonstrations that protested U.S. involvement in the war. To his thinking, the *Times*' miscalculation was in misunderstanding the nature of Communism, which, in his experience, never conceded any point "unless superior power . . . forces it to do so."[55] Appeasement did not keep the peace in the 1930s, nor would it help U.S. position today. Only the Communists and the ideological left "favor[ed] the stand taken" by the *Times*, and though he hastened to add that these positions of agreement were "coincidental," the *Times* would suffer from this coincidence. It was typical of Baldwin to state vigorously his point of view to his superiors at the paper, even though they most likely did not like what they were being told. There is no indication that his protests changed the tone of the editorials. They continued to point with concern to the fact that America's military escalation would only hinder the chances for a negotiated settlement.[56]

Baldwin kept returning to the importance of American public opinion. Unless the public "felt that the war [was] worth winning . . . we face ultimate defeat no matter how many military victories we win."[57] He urged Congress to declare a state of national emergency, to call up the National Guard and the reserves, to appropriate billions for the war, and to increase the bombing campaign of North Vietnam. Rejecting the emotional appeals of those who hated all wars, Baldwin wrote in February 1966 that in Vietnam many miscalculations had been made by past presidents, ambassadors, and generals, but those "mistakes [were] for historians."[58]

Without the call-up of the military reserves, U.S. forces in Vietnam were fighting "with one hand tied behind our backs." The result was that Hanoi believed that the United States would not stay, but if the United States mobilized its reserves, even if only partially, that decision would send a message to Hanoi that America was determined to win in Vietnam.

Baldwin feared that a gulf would develop between citizens and the military so long as there were draft exemptions for reservists and students. He was critical that the military draft weighed heavily on the "less privileged youths," and that the reservists, as a group, would be viewed as a "kind of protected elite" because they were not being called to active duty.[59]

A year later, he responded to a reader's query about the military draft by saying "the best solution to the draft problem is to eliminate as many deferments as possible—particularly college deferments." He favored a lottery system for those who had high draft numbers to be given up to one year draft notice prior to their graduation from high school, or the age of nineteen, whichever came first. Over the long term, he favored a return to a peacetime volunteer military service but opposed giving volunteers money to enlist. He did not want a mercenary military service to develop. While the war was in progress, he agreed that Congress should not make a major overhaul of the draft rules.[60]

Baldwin ridiculed President Johnson's military policy of gradualism as being too little, too late. He warned his readers that unless we change our policies from being "a no-decision, no-win war, a war of stalemate, a protracted and an indecisive—slow—blood letting," then the war will continue for many years and America will exhaust itself.[61]

In December 1966 Harrison E. Salisbury, the assistant managing editor of the *Times*, visited Hanoi and filed a series of reports that assessed the effects of American bomb damage around Hanoi. On December 27, when his first report appeared, Baldwin complained bitterly to Clifton Daniel, the managing editor, that the report placed "Mr. Salisbury and the *Times* squarely on the side of North Vietnam."[62]

He took offense at the implication that the U.S. Air Force was "deliberately and consistently" hitting civilian targets. Salisbury's report was "precise without attribution," and his report was based solely upon North Vietnamese government sources, whom the author did not reveal. Another target mentioned was the dike on the Dao River near Namdinh, which, if true, was hit by a stray bomb, Baldwin retorted. Had the dikes been primary targets, then larger bombs would have been used. In summary, the tone and content of the Salisbury article placed the United States "deliberately undertaking saturation bombing of civilians," and the *Times*, by printing such a report, "swallows the Communist line almost hook, line, and sinker."[63]

At the suggestion of Clifton Daniel, Baldwin wrote a rebuttal article in which he blamed Salisbury for not identifying his sources, but Baldwin also blamed the "distorted" and contradictory statements about the bombing campaign on the Pentagon's secrecy and the overly optimistic forecasts by the Air Force giving a false picture of air power and its effects.

That same issue of the *Times* also contained the *Ramparts* magazine advertisement that quoted Dr. Benjamin Spock, the well-known author of a popular baby care book, as saying that one million children were casualties "in the war America is carrying on in Vietnam."[64] The *Times* editorial on that Sunday stated that the bombing policy impeded negotiations because "it extend[ed] rather than end[ed] the war."[65] The Salisbury reports, the *Ramparts* advertisement, and the editorial would convince some readers, Baldwin told the managing editor, that the paper was "bitterly opposed" to President Johnson's policies, and that "we are also almost anti–United States."[66]

The year 1967 was the year of discontent for the White House, the Pentagon, and the American public. The war had dragged on for more than two years and there seemed to be little progress to show for it. Some called it a stalemate. The antiwar activists were growing in numbers. The oversimplified dichotomy of the "hawks" and the "doves" seemed to reduce a complex issue of war or peace: to send more troops to Vietnam or begin to withdraw them. Public opinion polls in the summer of 1967 were hard to read. One homemaker neatly summarized the predicament, "I want to get out, but I don't want to give up."[67] To counter public uncertainty, the White House sought to discredit the antiwar movement by trying to show that its leaders were Communists.[68]

President Johnson was a besieged man beset by problems that had no easy answers. He was determined to keep the war limited so as not to give China or Russia the pretext to enter it, even though it was well known that both nations were supplying North Vietnam with needed military supplies. President Johnson also did not want funds needed for the war to compete with the needs of his Great Society programs at home.

In August 1967 Abe Raskin, the number-two man on the *Times* editorial staff, asked Baldwin to give his assessment of the war, since the stalemate issue was in the news. He noted that the public and the military were polarizing their views to "really fight or get out." It was too late to question the general view that the United States should never have become involved in Vietnam. Since July 1965 when President Johnson sent in ground troops, the United States was committed to win somehow, a viewpoint shared by Baldwin.

Baldwin, as a Naval Academy graduate, was taught that when the commander in chief made a decision to go to war, then all should try to do their part to win it. Having said this, Baldwin carefully noted two major problems in Vietnam. The first was that the United States was not in charge, as it had been during the Korean War. Furthermore, South Vietnam was "not really a nation and its government [was] certainly inadequate, inefficient, and often corrupt." The United States could not insist that incompetent officers in the South Vietnamese army be removed. He suggested integrating ARVN troops into some American units. In time, the United States must "bring Vietnamese battalions under the *de facto* command" of some American units. To encourage this, "we have to use the power of Washington and the power of the dollar to convert the Saigon government to greater efficiency" and to place their forces under direct American command.[69]

The second problem was the policy of one-year rotation of troops and the two-year draft without the mobilization of the reserves. President Johnson's guns and butter program was "silly and foolish," since the taxes needed to support the war were being partially diverted to fund domestic social programs, with the result that the United States was fighting "a very limited war with one hand tied behind our backs" at a time when North Vietnam was fighting a total war. The United States did not have enough troops in South Vietnam to hold the areas that it had taken.[70]

The war had become a stalemate, in part because the military as well as the press understood that their civilian masters in Washington "[would] just not tell the truth much of the time about the whole war picture."[71] Some of Baldwin's military sources had become "disgusted at the spectacle of their tame service chiefs acting as Charlie McCarthy to the President's Edgar Bergen." Even if the United States bombed the docks at Haiphong, mined the Red River estuary, and sank the dredges that kept the Red River open to traffic, those actions would not win the war. The air campaign had been "episodic and senseless" because it had not put continuous pressure "against targets that count." Why hit, one cement plant and not all of them, or why hit petroleum storage facilities after the enemy had dispersed them?[72] Baldwin did not advocate an all-out bombing campaign, but he argued that the United States should hit all airfields and the all-important bridges and tunnels and other bottlenecks in North Vietnam's transportation system.

Before 1965 Americans were told that winning the war would mean creating an independent, non-Communist South Vietnamese government, which would require many years of effort. Now, in 1967, the United States was in a war of attrition with no end in sight. We are an impatient people and want immediate results, Baldwin reminded Raskin before American troops were sent in 1965. Henry Cabot Lodge, the U.S. ambassador in Saigon, felt that to build a nation from the "precinct level would require perhaps 750,000 Americans in South Vietnam and years of effort."[73] Baldwin admitted that the United States was now in a "kind of stalemate" in Vietnam.[74] He observed, in an I-told-you-so remark, that Washington should have thought about this before the United States became involved in 1965. He hoped that the war would end "in some sort of victory" before China solved its current factionalism and revived its "communist imperialist ambitions." In short, the impatience of the American people and the policies of the Johnson administration were "the principal obstacles" to victory here. The continuing "ineffectiveness" of a corrupt Saigon government and the absence of a national identity in South Vietnam were the principal obstacles to victory there.

In spite of Baldwin's continuing opposition to the paper's editorials, he suggested that the *Times* could create an atmosphere of support for U.S. troops and that the United States "should hold out the hope of ultimately better things if the American people remain steadfast and patient."[75] That hope was akin to whistling in the dark.

Always seeking a wider audience, Baldwin turned to his favorite magazine, *The Reporter*, to make points similar to those found in his August memorandum. He added that Johnson's decision to pare the Pentagon's budget request for 1968 by $3 billion must be resisted despite domestic political pressures to cut the budget. "The effects of penny pinching in war are widespread and incalculable," he warned. In the upcoming election year of 1968, the president would face "a vicious circle." He must "win the battle of the ballots to win in Vietnam, yet he must probably 'win' in Vietnam by demonstrating his capability of bringing the war to a satisfactory conclusion—if he is to win at home."[76]

In the autumn of 1967, Johnson and his policy of limited war came under increasing attack from "doves" who argued that the war was stalemated and that the United States should withdraw its forces from South Vietnam. Stung by such criticism, the president mounted a public relations offensive to discredit his critics, both in and out of Congress. The CIA was enlisted to compile files on thousands of Americans and to watch the leaders of the antiwar groups. The FBI infiltrated the peace movement to disrupt its work. The president ordered the Saigon embassy to provide statistics on the number of enemy body counts and the number of pacified South Vietnamese villages that would show that progress in the war was being made.[77] In late November President Johnson summoned General Westmoreland to Washington to make optimistic public statements on the progress of the war. The general went so far as to suggest that within two years' time Americans could begin to withdraw and to turn over their combat missions to the ARVN troops.[78]

It was in this context, but independent of it, that Baldwin made his last visit to South Vietnam prior to his announced retirement. His four-week tour, begun in mid-November 1967, was undertaken so that he could make an independent assessment of the war. This meant extensive travel around the country speaking with as many military personnel as he could, from General Westmoreland on down the chain of command to the company commanders and enlisted personnel. He even visited the windowless combined intelligence center near the Tan Son Nhut air base, a mile from the MACV headquarters.

Given Baldwin's well-known views in support of the war effort, his lengthy three-part report in the *Times*, based on his visit, contained few surprises. More progress was being made than during his previous visit in 1965. However, the effectiveness of the ARVN forces was spotty. A few of its units were extremely good, while others were "ridiculously poor," preferring to take naps during the day and skipping night patrols.[79]

In his view, the military indicators in Vietnam gave "clear-cut evidence" of progress since "the dark days" of 1965. Hanoi had "abandoned" the hope of a victory on the battlefield in South Vietnam, but its forces were "still capable of widespread and concerted attacks" there. Interviews with Ambassador Ellsworth Bunker, General Westmoreland, and military intelligence all told Baldwin that the main battleground in 1968 would be in the United States.

The American command anticipated a winter-spring offensive in 1968 by the Vietcong and North Vietnamese forces, which would be "keyed primarily to strengthening opposition to the war in the United States, and influencing American and world public opinion during a Presidential election year."[80]

Baldwin went on to report that enemy forces would try to capture district or provincial capitals and would infiltrate two divisions from the north and stockpile weapons in Laos and Cambodia. By such an offensive, the enemy could prove to the Saigon government and to the American public that it was still strong and able to strike at will.[81] Surprisingly, in hindsight, Baldwin had just outlined the plan and objectives for the January 1968 Tet Offensive. However, he also noted that his sources thought the enemy weaker "than he appears to be" and believed it to suffer from manpower shortages.

As in all of Baldwin's front-line reports, he provided considerable detailed information about many topics, including estimates of enemy strength, the effectiveness of the bombing campaign, efforts to neutralize enemy sanctuaries in Laos and Cambodia, which actions would provoke China to enter the war, and the reduction of terrorist attacks in Saigon in recent months. He never said that there was any light at the end of that proverbial tunnel, but he merely repeated his belief that the war would be long and slow, "with no clear end in sight."[82] The basic question, one officer told Baldwin, was "whether or not the American people [would] have the patience and fortitude to stay the course."[83]

During this trip, Baldwin enjoyed visiting with his godson, Joe Muse, a Marine lance corporal who was stationed at Phu Bai, near Danang in the I Corps area. He was called Joe Muse to distinguish him from his father, Joseph Muse Worthington, a retired admiral. The Baldwin and the Worthington families had socialized together for decades and shared their joys and sorrows over the years. In a letter to his father young Joe said that he did not realize, until that visit, what a VIP his godfather was. To Joe Muse he was always Hans, but to Marine Corps officers he was always Sir or Mr. Baldwin, and his arrival at Danang caused a flurry of activity. Joe's gunnery sergeant wanted to know if Baldwin was "a big wheel because the General called him telling him to get me [ready] for breakfast." He also wanted to know Baldwin's equivalent rank in the military. Joe did not know but "found out he's equivalent . . . to a Major General in the U.S. Marine Corps." However, Joe had no time to talk with his godfather at breakfast, as the brass surrounded him. Later, at Phu Bai, they had a long visit together. Afterward, Joe's commanding officer asked Joe if he had seen his godfather, and when he said yes, the officer said, "Good, then there won't be a congressional investigation."[84]

Baldwin's final tour had many of the characteristics of a royal walkabout. He was treated with great respect and admiration. With so many of the young reporters hostile to the war, it was a pleasure for the combat troops and their officers to talk with a well-respected and knowledgeable journalist who was openly on their side. He was also the oldest journalist ever to have visited them.

Baldwin's criticism of the Vietnam War was always confined to the way it was being managed by Secretary McNamara and to President Johnson's policy of the gradual escalation of a limited war. It was never about the soldiers, sailors, Marines, and airmen who put their lives in harm's way every day. In a letter, Joe Muse told his godfather that in Vietnam, "it is a seven day, all day, 24 hour job here with no time off."[85]

General Westmoreland, who appreciated Baldwin's ability to paint "as accurate and objective picture as I have yet read," also read his reports from Vietnam. In a letter to Baldwin he added that it was "our pleasure to provide you [with] an insight into the complex nature of this war, and we deeply appreciate your efforts to bring this story to the public."[86] Another letter of appreciation came from Brigadier General Winant Sidle, the head of MACV's office of information. He called Baldwin's reports "fair, factual, and objective." He added that 1968 would be a "tough one" if the Saigon government did not get off its tail and fight the war and clean out the government corruption. If it "makes an honest effort to improve," then the press here would be convinced "that we will win this war in every sense, provided we stick it out."[87]

Baldwin later told Lester Markel, the *Times* Sunday editor, that the Saigon press corps had an "inbred nature" with a tendency to "emphasize the negative."[88] Peter Braestrup and others in the *Times* Saigon bureau felt that Baldwin's reports suffered from his having "listen[ed] to the generals" too much, which they felt gave him a narrow view of the war.[89] When Sulzberger awarded Baldwin the Publisher's Merit Award with a $100 check for "well-deserved recognition of your excellent reporting," Baldwin may have had mixed feelings, since he believed that the antiwar sentiment of the paper was due, in part, to the publisher's own views.[90]

The resignation of Robert S. McNamara on November 29, 1967, when Baldwin was in Vietnam, prompted Baldwin to comment that the members of the Joint Chiefs of Staff were relieved to hear of this surprise announcement. They had many issues of disagreement during his tenure at the Pentagon, including the call-up of the reserves, the bombing pauses, and the number of U.S. troops in Vietnam. But it was his personality and his manner of working with the military bureaucracy that annoyed the service chiefs, specifically his "intellectual arrogance," his overemphasis on cost effectiveness (instead of combat effectiveness), and his "coldness to people." His civilian staff of "bright young intellectuals" won no friends with the professional military. Baldwin once told Admiral Arleigh Burke that the best secretaries of defense, in his opinion, were bankers or lawyers because they had a broader outlook than businessmen or politicians. The latter group, he feared, would likely use the armed services for social reforms instead of their primary purpose of national security.[91]

The comforting belief in late 1967 and early 1968 that the war would progress well if only the Americans did not falter was shattered on January 30, 1968, with the sudden onslaught by 80,000 Vietcong and North Vietnamese army units who attacked thirty-six of the forty-four provincial capitals, five of six major cities, and sixty-four district capitals. Eleven battalions of the enemy targeted six points in Saigon, including the American Embassy. The ancient Vietnamese capital of Hue was seized and occupied for almost a month. The Marine base at Khe Sanh, near the Laotian border, below the DMZ, had been under heavy attack for weeks in an attempt to distract General Westmoreland into believing that the main Communist thrust would be in the Central Highlands, not in the cities and towns of South Vietnam.

The real objective of North Vietnam's General Vo Nguyen Giap was to demonstrate that his forces could still attack anywhere in South Vietnam, encouraging a popular uprising against the Saigon government, which was viewed as being too dependent upon the Americans for its survival. However, the Communist offensive failed to achieve its objectives. The ARVN troops surprised the Americans by how well they fought in their counterattacks. There was no civilian uprising against the Saigon government. In early March, all the places seized by the Communists in February had been retaken, but 40,000 lives were lost, most of them Vietcong. The once-hidden enemy had exposed itself and had been killed. One result was that for the next few years the Peoples' Army of Vietnam (North Vietnamese Army, or PAVN) troops of the Hanoi government did all of the fighting.

Thus, from the American military point of view, the Tet Offensive of 1968 was a tactical victory for the American and the ARVN troops.

At home, the American public was shocked by television pictures of the battles and concluded that the Johnson administration had lied to the public about the satisfactory progress of the war. The Tet Offensive surprised the American public by illustrating how well the Communists were able to mount such a widespread and generally well-coordinated surprise offensive. Americans who were war weary, or who wanted peace negotiations to begin, were not happy about this turn of events. There seemed to be no end in sight, even after three years of American troop involvement.

A sign of public disaffection by those who had previously supported the war was reflected in a comment by the well-respected television reporter Walter Cronkite on February 27. "We are mired in stalemate," he said at the end of his nightly CBS news program: "It is increasingly clear to this reporter that the only rational way out . . . will be to negotiate, not as victors, but as an honorable people who lived up to their pledge to defend democracy, and did the best they could." He had just returned from Vietnam where he had made a report from Hue, then under siege. He later learned that President Johnson quickly turned off the television set and said to his press secretary, "If I've lost Cronkite, I've lost middle America."[92]

But Baldwin still supported the war. Now within weeks of retirement, he did not mention a stalemate in his final columns on the Tet Offensive. Rather, he doggedly focused on the need to send more troops, beyond the 525,000 promised by Secretary McNamara in July 1967. Three years earlier, Baldwin had revealed that the Army and Marine Corps generals predicted the need for 600,000 to 750,000 American ground troops to fight a long war. Without the mobilization of the reserves, U.S. forces were "spread thin" and the one-year rotation had reduced the quality of the troop replacements.[93]

Within the Johnson administration, the Tet Offensive provoked a political crisis. The president sent another 10,500 troops to Vietnam almost at once. A larger problem surfaced in February when General Earle Wheeler, the chairman of the Joint Chiefs, returned from Saigon with Westmoreland's request for 206,000 more troops, some of whom would come from the reserves that the president had always refused to mobilize. On March 10 the *New York Times* revealed General Westmoreland's troop request, which had been a closely guarded secret in the White House. The new secretary of defense,

Clark Clifford, asked a direct question of the Joint Chiefs: About how many more American troops would be needed to win? To this and to other probing questions, the Chiefs had no definite answers. There was no American plan for victory.

On March 26, a small group of retired high-ranking government and military officials, called the Wise Men, met once again at the request of the president to offer their guidance. Unlike the previous November, when they urged the president to continue his war policies, the group was divided: a number of them now favored disengagement, not escalation. Dean Acheson, President Truman's secretary of state, thought it was impossible for America to win a military victory, to which General Earle Wheeler rebutted that the United States was not seeking such a victory, it was seeking only to stop a Communist victory. Acheson sharply asked what the 500,000 troops were doing there, "chasing girls?" The group concluded that the war weakened the United States at home and abroad.[94] A few days later, President Johnson surprised the nation with his announcement that he would not seek reelection in 1968.

Away from the Washington pressure cooker that month, Baldwin was busy moving out of his *Times* office and on to other projects. He cleaned out his office and sent many, but not all, of his files to Yale University, which was close to his new home in Roxbury, Connecticut, hoping to be able to use his papers for future projects. He also wrote letters of recommendation for colleagues on the paper.

Hanson Baldwin's decision to retire from the *Times*, effective on April 1, 1968, at age sixty-five, had been announced to senior management and editors seven months earlier. As with many retirements from large corporations, he cited the usual reasons of age and a personal desire to spend more time at home with his family. However, the *Times* had no mandatory retirement age and Helen was not insisting that he spend more time tending the garden at their new home in Connecticut. The decision was his alone.

The reason he gave to the publisher, Punch Sulzberger, was that in his view, newspaper work "on a daily intensive basis" was a young person's game. It was for someone who could give "a lot more energy and oomph than a 65 year old can do," and he also mentioned that his military sources had begun to retire and he did not want to break in new ones.[95] He named a few possible successors, all of whom were on the *Times* staff, including Bill Beecher and Neil Sheehan, both of whom covered the Pentagon. He also offered to contribute occasional exclusive articles to the *Times*, if asked.

He sent his announcement to nine other editors, all of whom expressed the usual regrets and none of whom was surprised at his decision. John B. Oakes, whose editorials on the Vietnam War had enraged Baldwin, replied graciously that Baldwin's leaving would be "a very major loss" to the paper. He paid him the compliment by noting that Baldwin's "sense of what the *Times* is and ought to be" had been "an important influence around here and I truly hate to see you pull out."[96] Turner Catledge, the former managing editor, praised Baldwin for his "great job" on the paper, which must also include the grooming of his successor. After considerable discussion, the *Times* management decided not to replace Baldwin and to discontinue the title of military editor.

Baldwin first announced his intentions to the retired publisher, Arthur Hays Sulzberger, recalling how the latter had created the job of military editor in 1937, and how "[having] worked together for a long time . . . it will be a real wrench for both Helen and for me" to leave the *Times*' employ.[97] Baldwin always appreciated the fact that his once-favored position on the paper was owed in large measure to Arthur's forbearance and patronage of many years. As the many blue memoranda in Baldwin's papers at Yale demonstrate, Sulzberger was often sharply critical when Baldwin's articles dealt more with political issues than with military developments. Over time, the boundaries of his military journalism were agreed to, however reluctantly, by Sulzberger. Baldwin's depth of appreciation for Arthur's role was stated openly in his reply to the latter's brief memorandum noting his twenty-five years as military editor: "A word from you is always one of the finest rewards of working here." He noted that there had been a number of the anniversary memoranda over the years, and "needless to say, they are an intimate part of my life."[98]

Two weeks after the 1968 Tet Offensive began, Baldwin had written a long letter to Clifton Daniel, the managing editor, reiterating his determination to leave despite the urgency of war news: "As I told you, there are no end of crises in sight, and the one we are facing won't be over quickly." He listed travel and other demands as too strenuous, and kept the door open to the possibility of making future contributions: "to interpret broad trends, analyses of military consequences and lessons" that would be useful to the paper.[99]

His departure on Friday, March 29, 1968, was overshadowed by President Johnson's surprising national televised announcement on March 31. With this background, the *Times* made no public mention of Baldwin's retirement, which later caused many of his correspondents to continue to send mail to his *Times* office. Baldwin left quietly, at his expressed wish. At a private luncheon in the publisher's dining room, Punch Sulzberger gave Baldwin a Steuben glass figure of a spread-winged eagle, which was later placed on the mantle above the fireplace in his Connecticut home.

Baldwin was glad to retire, he told friends later. His age and the demands of travel were only partly true. To his thinking, the changes at the *Times* since 1963 had led to the abandonment of Adolph Ochs' standards of accuracy, fairness, and balance, to be replaced by the new standards of profitability, readability, and entertainment.

The *Times*, which he was proud to serve for thirty-nine years, had changed in ways of which he did not approve. It was time for him to leave. He left not in anger, but in sadness that so much had changed at the *Times* that it could no longer be his professional home. It was time for him to move on to other forums and to escape the tyranny of deadlines.

Years later, in a letter to his longtime friend Virginius Dabney, the former editor of the *Richmond Times-Dispatch* (VA), Baldwin confided that his continuing criticism of the Vietnam War editorials made him "quite a nuisance" with the paper's management and other senior editors, leaving him with "the distinct impression [that] many, including the publisher, were not sorry to see [him] retire."[100]

CHAPTER 18

An Old-Fashioned Fellow,
1969–80s

Freed from a lifetime of deadlines and struggles with copyeditors, Baldwin reflected upon a war that he had supported and that was tearing the country apart, driving a president from office. In one of the chapters he was writing for his next book, he used sharp words to list the lessons of the Vietnam War. It was a limited war fought for defensive ends, to persuade the Hanoi government to cease and desist from its plan to unify all of Vietnam. He recalled the words of his former mentor, Mark S. Watson of the *Baltimore Sun*, who wrote in 1950 that an industrialist, trained to keep costs down, will only use enough resources to complete the job and will avoid using excessive manpower and materials. In war, Watson wrote, that approach is not adequate, as war is both irrational and wasteful of resources. Watson believed that a military force that was just strong enough for a mission would suffer heavy casualties, while a military force that is superior to its enemy will suffer fewer casualties and have time to surprise the enemy. During peacetime, a military planner should convince civilian policymakers to accept waste in war as an ideal to be achieved. A nation that ended a war with a surplus of equipment was likely to be the nation that had won the war.[1]

Baldwin's criticism of Robert McNamara illustrated Watson's point. McNamara saw war as the rational and calculated expenditure of assets in which computers were tools to measure expenditures. The office of the secretary of defense saw the "ascendancy of the computer-minded, cost effective operational analyst and management specialist."[2] Added to this was McNamara's forceful hands-on management style that demanded statistical answers from the military to difficult questions, making life rather unpleasant for those in the Pentagon. Baldwin doubted that business-based management efficiency was synonymous with combat effectiveness.[3]

Later he commented about the mistakes made in Vietnam, including the attempts of the military to conform to McNamara's edicts and President Johnson's wishes by acting as "a messenger boy saying 'aye, aye, Sir, we'll get it done, even if it's the hard way.'" The military became "the fall guys," with the resulting steady decline of military standards and values.[4]

In Baldwin's opinion, it was McNamara and Johnson who made an American victory in Vietnam difficult to achieve. As mentioned earlier, Johnson did not sell the war to the American public. He did not mobilize public opinion to support the war, explain U.S. war aims, nor did he warn the American public that a guerrilla war was a war of attrition that would last for a long time. His "guns and butter" programs did not put American industry on a war footing. Perhaps the worst decision of all was his policy of gradualism. To Baldwin, it ignored the military principles of mass and momentum and it signaled to the Hanoi government a national weakness of will to win. President Johnson also refused to mobilize the Army Reserve and the National Guard.[5] The 1968 Tet Offensive was the last straw that convinced many Americans that the war was not winnable.[6] White House optimism notwithstanding, "the credibility gap" continued to haunt Johnson for the remainder of his presidency.

Since 1960, the secretary of defense had become the principal military adviser to the president. The chairman of the Joint Chiefs, while having "great authority, but little responsibility," had to find compromises with the other service chiefs on the JCS prior to meeting with the president. During those meetings McNamara was always present to interject or interpret for President Johnson what the JCS meant to report. It was the very strong personal leadership of McNamara that made the JCS so remote from the White House. To Baldwin, the chairman of the JCS had become the "administration's man."[7] This meant that military policies of the White House ought to be measured against the risks: military, political, and economic. The risks ought to be red-flagged to alert the President of potential dangers of the policies. Baldwin believed that too often policies were determined without emphasis placed on the risks involved. The JCS's judgment must not be downgraded, as they were charged with the defense of the nation. The president must always receive "frank and diverse" military advice.[8]

In summary, he felt that McNamara was "the most egocentric man I think I have ever met, a man who did more damage, in my opinion, to national defense than any other one man in my experience."[9] Instead of being self-analytical, McNamara "built up a hedgerow around him and became so protective and defensive."[10] Another defect, which annoyed Baldwin, was his loyalty up but not loyalty down. He did everything, including trying to anticipate what President Johnson asked of him, whereas Baldwin, trained as a naval officer, believed that an officer must always take care of his men first.

McNamara was "absolutely ruthless with anyone who said, 'We can't do it this way, Mr. Secretary.'"[11] He rigidly controlled the personnel at the Pentagon. The endless studies and analyses did much, to Baldwin's thinking, to extend lead times to produce new weapons systems and delayed the process of technological development.

The air war had an appeal with the American public, who believed that air power gave the promise of quick and relatively bloodless victories, and Baldwin had long known that the U.S. Air Force was the military service with "charisma."[12] In 1965 the Pentagon felt that a bombing campaign would convince Hanoi to cease its support for the Vietcong and force it to seek negotiations. Baldwin rejected such views, citing the lessons of the World War II bombing campaigns of German and Japanese cities, which did not weaken either government's resolve to continue the war. Communist governments were "notoriously difficult to persuade," he said.[13] U.S. air power was "so limited, hobbled, and restricted" by the White House that, to Baldwin, it was "remarkable" that the air campaign accomplished what it did in a jungle environment and the safe enemy sanctuaries in Laos and Cambodia.

Even if there were no limits to the use of U.S. air power, it would not have defeated the Vietcong. What was needed, Baldwin wrote, was the "anvil and hammer" approach, where the ground forces would be the anvil and the air force the hammer, a tactic that was successful in 1968 in the defense of Khe Sanh. But too often the gradualist policy gave Hanoi the time and the opportunity to rebuild targets and to disperse its supply depots.[14]

What he advised was a quick buildup of American air and ground forces in 1965 that would overwhelm the enemy on the ground; to bomb the sites in and around Hanoi, including its air defense installations, airfields, bridges, and petroleum storage facilities; and to mine the harbor at Haiphong, the main port in North Vietnam. Unfortunately, there is no evidence to suggest that it would have ended any sooner than it did ten years later.

Baldwin was aware of the dilemma America faced in Vietnam. If the United States withdrew, it would prove that a low-level technological war, waged by a committed native people, could defeat the world's military superpower. For America to remain in Vietnam for the foreseeable future would prove nothing and would only sharpen the public's questioning of U.S. war aims and increase the growing hostility toward the American military services. In spite of his support for the Vietnam War, he believed that the United States should not be the world's policeman, eager to invade any country that might be slipping toward Communism. The United States ought to carefully decide which geographic areas of the world were really vital to its national interests, and act accordingly.

The decade of the 1960s began with great hope and optimism about America's role in the world. It was basking in the bright light of the American Century. A decade later, those hopes and aspirations had faded. The long military campaign and the enormous human sacrifices made to contain the spread of Communism in Southeast Asia had failed to help that small country become independent of its rapacious northern neighbor. For Baldwin, his retirement years were busy but not happy ones, as he continued to reflect upon recent history.

Under the editorship of John B. Oakes, the *Times'* editorials urged negotiations with the Hanoi government to end the Vietnam War, rather than, as Baldwin frequently urged, calls for American military victory, the call-up of the Army Reserves and the National Guard, and appeals for national unity in time of war. Those trends stuck in Baldwin's craw and caused him much anxiety about the progress of the Vietnam War.

Shortly after he retired, Abe Rosenthal, the recently appointed managing editor of the *Times*, informed Baldwin that Bill Beecher, the paper's Pentagon correspondent, and Drew Middleton, a veteran *Times* foreign correspondent, would jointly hold the new title of military correspondent. Baldwin was understanding, even though he had pushed for Beecher to be his successor. Middleton was fifty-six at the time and a bit too old, to Baldwin's thinking, who felt a younger man should "grow up" with the next generation of military officers and "retain a lifetime of contacts," as he had done years before.

It is not easy to establish, he advised, the "trust and confidence . . . getting behind the scenes. . . . [It] is a problem of personal relationships and it will take a long time to do this."[15]

In 1969 he was elected president of the Naval Academy's Alumni Association, in which he had been active for many years as head of its publications committee. Prior to his retirement, he had also made a contractual commitment to be a roving editor for the *Readers' Digest* magazine, with the freedom to select his own topics.[16] He also served, for a time, on the board of visitors at the Naval War College, Newport, Rhode Island, where he had no hesitance about criticizing the curriculum from time to time, and giving advice, solicited or not, to its superintendent.

One project that he never finished was his history of World War II, which he had started in 1946. In 1976 he did publish *The Crucial Years, 1940–1941*, volume one of a projected multivolume history. Prior to that he wrote *Battles Lost and Won: Great Campaigns of World War II* (1966). His last book, *Tiger Jack* (1979), was a short tribute to Major General John S. Wood, who had commanded the Fourth Armored Division in World War II. In the mid-1970s he complained to Lester Markel, the retired editor of the *Times* Sunday edition, that he could no longer apply the seat of his pants to the seat of his chair or spend the three to five years it took to write another book, commenting, "I have about finished with my typewriter."[17]

In retirement, Baldwin was very concerned with a number of public issues, including what he perceived to be the rapid growth of permissiveness in American society, the mismanagement of the Vietnam War from Washington, the increasing intensity of antiwar activism, the public's growing distrust of government statements, the steady deterioration and demoralization of U.S. troops in Vietnam, and the rise of a general antimilitary public sentiment. He agreed with the way one soldier put it, that the war was being fought by the Woodstock generation whose antiauthoritarian bias infected the military in general. As the president of the Naval Academy's Alumni Association, he expressed his strong views on what was wrong with America. In 1970 he spoke at a few of the Academy's eastern alumni clubs, censuring much of American politics and society.

Although he was city-born and -bred, he now idealized America's rural and agricultural past as having developed the personal values that were the country's strength. He castigated the "frenetic technocrat-urban society of

Baldwin in later years
Courtesy of the U.S. Naval Institute photo archive

today," which had nurtured racial unrest, the drug culture, antiauthoritarian views, and a permissive society.[18]

He blamed all political liberals, beginning with Roosevelt and the New Deal and successive terms that had created "a lazy society with work-less and make-more beliefs." In his view, liberals facilitated those trends. As a group, Baldwin thought, they were "mal-adjusted eccentrics," "bleeding hearts," and their academic supporters were those whose "egos [were] far larger than their knowledge," whose "arrogance [was] matched only by their ignorance and whose aim [was] power."[19]

In his view, even the U.S. Navy was not insulated from these societal changes. It was no longer a "band of brothers" with shared values; now it was rife with racial tensions, with "sea lawyers" willing to counsel sailors on how to desert or how to avoid complying with orders. In a letter to a retired Marine Corps general, Baldwin commented on the current state of affairs, "And now, women at the Naval Academy: Ye Gods!"[20] He also feared that preoccupation with the Vietnam war would encourage the Soviet Union to accelerate its missile program, increasing the danger of "a nuclear Pearl Harbor."[21] With America beset by so many internal and external threats, Baldwin's answer was to take a long view of history to gain a perspective and balance.

Aware of dissent within the officer corps, he reminded his audience of naval retirees that the service was not a debating society, and that there were limits to an individual's freedom of expression. Public dissent by military professionals was "not privilege but heresy." If an officer could not accept national policy, then resignation or retirement was the only option. His best advice was for naval officers to accept the eternal values and traditions of duty, honor, and country, to which he added loyalty, endurance, and a will to win. "We must make the flowers of the past and proven values bloom again," he advised.[22] Baldwin's conservative political ideal was that of his youth:

Theodore Roosevelt's militant American patriotism, including such maxims as "my country right or wrong," and "speak softly and carry a big stick," were so out of date in 1970.

He also vented his criticism of America in his private correspondence. To retired admiral Arleigh Burke, Baldwin wrote, "There is no [racial] homogeneity any more, nor is there likely to be any in the foreseeable future. . . . And I have great worries about the service combat effectiveness."[23] To a school administrator in Darien, Connecticut, he pointed out the main weakness of modern public education: the inability of students to relate the past to the present. He added that "a study of the classics taught our forefathers a knowledge of history and a considerably better understanding of the nature of man than we seem to have today." With the explosion of scientific and technological knowledge in recent decades, he saw "the need to relate them to each other and to man himself."[24]

Baldwin had few forums in which to express his continuing outrage over the course of the Vietnam War, which is why he welcomed the opportunity to review David Halberstam's book *The Best and the Brightest* (1972), as it rekindled Baldwin's criticism of Johnson's and McNamara's mistakes. The author's views were anathema to Baldwin, including the view that the war was not winnable. The United States had turned a civil war in South Vietnam into a global crusade to contain the spread of Communism. Baldwin disagreed that Hanoi would win and thought such confident predictions "premature."[25]

Baldwin also criticized the author's selective use of *The Pentagon Papers* to show that the United States was the aggressor in South Vietnam, noting that the National Liberation Front (NLF) was not composed of indigenous freedom fighters from the south but was created by and controlled from Hanoi (which was found to be true after 1975).

As for personalities, Baldwin agreed with the author on McNamara's dominant policymaking role in and outside of the Pentagon. He relished the opportunity to characterize the former secretary of defense as "intellectually arrogant . . . [and] intellectually dishonest," for ignoring or withholding "unpalatable facts" or long-range military estimates provided by the Joint Chiefs of Staff.[26] Baldwin retold his story of how in early 1965 General Harold Johnson, the Army's chief of staff, and General Wallace Greene, the Marine Corps commandant, told him that 500,000 to 1 million U.S. troops would be needed for eight years to crush the enemy, to be followed by many years of an American army of occupation in South Vietnam. McNamara chose, with President Johnson's concurrence, to minimize those force estimates.[27]

The tragedy of Vietnam, in Baldwin's eyes, was the deterioration of the quality of our armed forces since 1965, from being well-trained professionals to becoming a force of "unwilling and hastily trained draftees" in an "army of amateurs" led by young junior officers "still wet behind the ears."[28] This disintegration reflected the decline of America's moral and ethical standards in an age where national security became ephemeral in an insecure world. Baldwin praised Halberstam's "vividly etched" portraits of the key players, who acted like "historical marionettes" in their "fatalistic dance macabre." The participants in that dance, named by Baldwin, included John Kennedy, Lyndon Johnson, Robert McNamara, Dean Rusk, George Ball, McGeorge and William Bundy, Walt Rostow, Maxwell Taylor, and William Westmoreland.[29] While Halberstam's analyses of them were perceptive, Baldwin concluded that, as a group, they were not the best nor the brightest. All shared "an over-weaning sense of self-importance." They loved power and they manipulated it with "an exaggerated sense of loyalty up to President Johnson, but little loyalty down."[30]

When compared with our leaders of World War II, the policymakers of the 1960s fell far short, in his estimation. "We have had too much Madison Avenue," he observed, "too much of the Harvardian academe, too much of the impersonal Rand Corporation computer analyses in Washington. We need to return to the men of yesterday, who gave of themselves without major concern for their own fame or fortune."[31] With those words, Baldwin said farewell to a world he believed no longer existed, where hubris blinded leaders to the generally accepted moral values and personal behavior of an earlier age.

In the context of antiwar values, Baldwin was troubled by a letter he received in 1974 from an eight-year Navy pilot who had decided to resign his officer's commission. The pilot had entered the Navy filled with idealism. He observed that the naval officers he knew were more concerned with self-serving rank advancement than with the common defense of the country. The "old military maxims of orders and commands," he continued, "had been replaced by younger sailors who acted as they pleased—an unintended result of the Zumwalt reforms to humanize the Navy.[32]

In reply, Baldwin did not dissuade the young lieutenant from leaving the Navy but reminded him that politics and self-serving behavior were rampant in civilian life too. The current Watergate scandal showed the lack of national morality and ethical behavior by President Richard Nixon and his associates. Baldwin attributed this to a weakening of the bonds of society and the end of the Naval Academy's "band of brothers." In retirement, Baldwin could only fume passively on the sidelines of American society. His letters were filled with his angst.[33] He wrote to a serving officer that "the Navy is no longer a profession [but] merely a job. And in many cases not even a job worth doing ... a good many of them regard themselves ... as not much better than messenger boys or 8 to 4 job-holders."[34]

Particularly upsetting to Baldwin were the racial incidents on board the U.S. Navy carriers *Kitty Hawk* (CV-63) and *Constellation* (CV-64) in 1972. He blamed Admiral Elmo R. Zumwalt, the Navy's CNO (1970–74), who attempted to change the Navy's traditions of racism and sexism. He did so by a series of directives that were popularly known as "Z-grams," of which there were eventually 121. They dealt with many subjects, including the permission of all sailors to grow facial hair, to wear civilian clothes while in port, and the idea that no sailor should wait in any line for more than fifteen minutes.

While Admiral Zumwalt, in his Z-gram No. 1, wanted to restore "the fun and zest of going to sea," the results were not always as intended. On a visit to the U.S. Sixth Fleet in the Mediterranean for *Reader's Digest*, Baldwin saw firsthand the effects of the Zumwalt reforms. Morale and discipline on the big ships were "deplorable," he observed. On the carrier *John F. Kennedy* (CV 67) officers were "very scared" because of the racial tensions on board, and it was almost impossible to transfer an African American sailor home for discharge. Not surprising, Baldwin favored a return to discipline and to the restoration of leadership that could hold the line against "congressional, and bureaucratic, political and sociological pressures." In short, the Navy should discharge malcontents, misfits, and troublemakers. Baldwin urged the restoration of the "pride of service and the fidelity to authority."[35] To a correspondent, he castigated the current craze for the Harvard Business School methodology that confused personnel management in a corporation with naval command, or personal leadership in the Navy that downgraded the naval officer to "a job holder."[36]

Another important issue to Baldwin was the need to safeguard military intelligence. In 1975 the *Los Angeles Times* featured a story, later to be picked up by the *New York Times*, on Howard Hughes' deep-sea mining ship, the *Glomar Explorer*. It had raised a Soviet nuclear submarine, the K–129, which had sunk near the Hawaiian Islands on April 11, 1968. Subsequent news stories linked the ship's mission to the CIA. The *Times* continued to run other stories about the mission and its real objective. The CIA tried to discourage the news media from printing additional stories but without much success.

This intelligence coup provoked Baldwin to write an op-ed piece that protested vigorously that the retrieval of the Soviet submarine in the popular press was "one of the most damaging and irresponsible leaks in United States intelligence history."[37] He sharply censured the *Times* for printing the details of how "a fantastic technological feat" was accomplished. In his view, to publicize intelligence-gathering techniques was to violate necessary secrecy, especially in a democracy, about such national security matters. The issue, he thought, was how to define "the thin line between freedom and license, security and repression, the right to know and irresponsibility." The rhetorical question was who should be the proper guardians of the good, and the answer was certainly not Congress, "noted for its blabbermouth proclivities." Baldwin argued that since intelligence gathering was a tool of government, it should be the responsibility of the FBI and the CIA. Intelligence, today and in the future, he wrote, was "the difference between the life and death of a nation." The former military editor concluded by asking, "How do you operate a democratic government without secrecy?"[38]

In 1958 Baldwin had voluntarily withheld his piece on the secret Argus Project at the request of the government, until the project was to be revealed publicly. In 1975 an older Baldwin favored keeping secrets from the American public because of national security.

The *Glomar* piece was well received. Even Lester Markel, the former *Times* Sunday editor, praised it, not because it was "good," but because Baldwin was "swinging out as vigorously as ever."[39] David Rockefeller praised the piece for saying what needed to be said about intelligence: "We still need your wise judgment and objective analysis."[40] The story behind the story was that Baldwin's op-ed piece was rejected initially by Charlotte Curtis, the op-ed page editor, because Baldwin had openly criticized the *Times* and refused to delete his reference to the paper. Curtis was overruled by Johnny Oakes, the editorial page editor, and it was printed with the offending paragraph.[41]

Hanson Baldwin's "last fight" was the ratification of the Panama Canal Treaty in 1978 that would turn over the American control of the Canal Zone to the Panamanians in the year 2000. Privately, he confided that we "own it [the canal], its title is clear; that, in effect, we ought to tell [General Omar T.] Torrijos to go to hell."[42] He felt the U.S. Senate ought to reject the treaty.[43] To Baldwin's thinking, the Panamanian issue was an emotional and a psychological one. "Without the Canal," he wrote, "that country would be nothing."[44] His views on the canal were shaped at a time, now long passed, when the United States operated on the assumption that the Caribbean Sea was an "American Lake," in which the United States was the dominant military, political, and economic power in the region after the Panama Canal had opened in 1914.

The American Enterprise Institute, a conservative think tank, asked Baldwin to write a pamphlet on the issue in 1977. The result was a long narrative that gave considerable historical background on the political, economic, and strategic issues raised by the prospect of a United States–Panama Canal treaty, then being considered by the U.S. Senate. A larger issue for Baldwin was, of course, the steady decline of America's world position since U.S. withdrawal from Vietnam in April 1975. He feared that once the United States left the canal, Panama would become a new target of opportunity for Communist influence. If the United States were to show weakness in the Caribbean, it would lead to unfortunate consequences for America in the long run.[45]

The antitreaty campaign, in which Baldwin was a minor participant, suffered a major political setback when U.S. senator Barry Goldwater decided to switch his vote on the treaty, citing the lessons of the Vietnam War. He said that, realistically, the United States would not fight to keep the Panama Canal; the Vietnam experience "taught me that we wouldn't. So we might as well hand it over."[46] The U.S. Senate ratified the Panama Canal Treaty on April 18, 1978.

While Hanson Baldwin may have felt helpless to influence national events, he took great joy in being a grandfather to his seven grandchildren. His daughter Barbara's five children lived close by in Waterbury, Connecticut, and they saw their grandparents fairly frequently. On milestone birthdays,

"Balda," as he was called in the family circle, would give a champagne toast, listing the honoree's accomplishments and his or her hopes and dreams for the future. The birthday gift would be a practical one, perhaps a sleeping bag for future camping trips. Helen (called "Boo" in the family) would make the grandchild's favorite foods, often her famous chocolate cake.

Older grandchildren fondly recalled Balda's third-floor study in the old Chappaqua house, with its elliptical bookshelves that covered two rooms and a hallway. Many of the books had slips of paper in them. One grandson, Jeff, remembered seeing the movie *Midway* with Balda in 1976, recalling how he "pointed out the Navy brass and senior Navy pilots who were in and around his [1924] class at Annapolis." The film mentioned his classmates and "re-created their deaths in living color" in the Pacific war. Jeff recalled how Balda "felt a hole in him after that film."[47] Happier memories centered around gardening chores, which seemed less important in their execution than in the importance of hard work to develop one's character.

Balda wrote many letters to his grandchildren. He also wrote limericks.[48] He had no tolerance for obscene words from the mouths of his grandsons. Those words prompted him to send a memo to "Potter, All Hands" from "Admiral Baldwin." The recipients were "hereby directed that all hands read this memorandum and signify their compliance by initialing same."[49] Such proscriptive missives were sent with love to his grandchildren, whose hits-and-misses lives occupied his thoughts and attention for the rest of his life.

As a result of a stroke in July 1978, Baldwin lost hearing in his left ear, was unstable on his feet, and could no longer drive. As the years passed, other disabilities developed, including his inability to type. "My fingers won't do what I want them to do."[50] He resigned himself reluctantly to the aging process, joking, "My doctor says I can do anything I want so long as I don't enjoy myself."[51]

Even as Baldwin despaired over the social trends of American popular culture, he enjoyed the continual companionship of six of his Annapolis classmates, who also lived in Connecticut. On occasion they would meet for lunch at Mory's, the famous Yale watering hole from the Wiffenpoof song. The group formed the "Connecticut Chowder and Marching Society," whose burgee was "a fish drinking a martini."[52]

The hardest part of aging was seeing his lifelong friends "disintegrate," as Baldwin once phrased it. As Joe Worthington's health declined seriously in 1986, Baldwin reminded Joe of the many times that he remembered his Annapolis roommate during their Academy years, when "our energy was endless."[53]

Later that year, in a condolence letter to Joe's daughter, Kathy, he wrote, "he was my best friend and that bond between men—often forged at school or college—endures past death. . . . He fitted, in the best way, that old description—so seldom heard nowadays—of an officer and a gentleman." He sought to relieve her grief over her father's death not by citing a Bible verse, but by recalling lines of poetry by Swinburne that had given Hanson comfort:[54]

> From too much love of living,
> From hope and fear set free,
> We thank with brief thanksgiving
> What ever the gods may be
> That no life lives forever;
> That dead men rise up never;
> That even the weariest river
> Winds somewhere safe to sea.

In writing Joe's epitaph, Hanson Baldwin had written his own. At his death at the age of eighty-eight, on November 14, 1991, from the effects of Parkinson's disease, the world of his youth had disappeared.[55] Those values of yesteryear, which he cherished, set the proper boundaries of personal and societal behavior. The contemporary climate of situational ethics, where there were no fixed rules for individuals or for society, contributed, he thought, to the decline of America's political and social fabric. Even the band of brothers, an ideal from his Naval Academy years that bound its graduates to a life of service to the nation and to each other, had disappeared, to be replaced by what he regarded as self-serving opportunities for promotion.

Baldwin brought considerable thought to bear on the subject of America's military, a profession little understood by the public in war and often ignored during peacetime. Over time and in spite of his limitations he developed a few maxims about war that are as relevant today as they were decades ago; do not go to war for ideological reasons, be prepared for the next war but not to the point of bankrupting the nation or becoming a garrison state, and never use military intelligence to support a political policy.

Since most of his career had spanned the Cold War years, he advised that the best way to contain the spread of Communism was not to threaten to attack the Soviet Union with atomic bombs (which would result in mutual devastation), but to support the political stability and economic growth of non-Communist countries. In other words, he advocated maintaining the balance of power among the major nations to keep the peace. His advice for future American presidents contemplating war was to convince the public first that U.S. national interests were being threatened, and that U.S. military objectives in the war were achievable.

What upset him was the increasing social and political disintegration at home brought about by the deleterious effects of the Vietnam War, which created divisions among Americans. It seriously affected military personnel and the military establishment, which began to mimic the prevailing popular culture of the 1960s that urged the country's youth to challenge all authority, to avoid the military draft, and to drop out and to tune in to easily accessible drugs. The Civil Rights and the Women's Liberation movements, which he did not understand, further contributed, he thought, to American malaise. To him, the hasty American departure from Saigon in April 1975 was not cause for a victory celebration, but a sign that the United States was no longer the bright light at midday in what had been the American Century.

Baldwin always held fast to the rules of journalism that he learned from his father: be realistic and factual in your reporting, and keep your independence safe from the influence of outside persons or groups. In war, he believed that a journalist must be a loyal citizen first and a reporter second. He did not believe that "publish and be damned" was a good guideline to follow in war. But the role of a free press in a democracy was to keep the public informed about what its government was doing, especially if it sought to exert control over the news in any way.

At the end of an interview, when he was asked what he wanted to be remembered for, he was silent for a moment and then quietly said, "fairness and integrity."[56] In those two words, he summarized the goals of his long career, which had contributed to his solid reputation for reporting on military events and to his much-admired long career in American journalism.

Disillusioned with many of the changes in American life and culture, Hanson Baldwin turned his attention and love toward his family, especially toward his grandchildren. As they grew up and became more interesting as persons and more interested in their world, he took comfort and joy in following their lives. Their optimism and enthusiasm for life served as a buoy, signaling that there was hope after all. He had found a safe harbor from the cold winds of change.

Appendix

BOOKS BY HANSON W. BALDWIN

1938: *The Caissons Roll: A Military Survey of Europe.* (New York: A. A. Knopf)

1939: *We Saw It Happen: The News Behind the News That's Fit To Print.* Edited by Hanson Baldwin and Shepard Stone. (New York: Simon & Schuster)

1939: *Admiral Death: Twelve Adventures of Men Against the Sea.* (New York: Simon & Schuster)

1941: *United We Stand: Defense of the Western Hemisphere.* (New York: Whittlesey House)

1942: *Strategy for Victory.* (New York: W. W. Norton)

1942: *What the Citizen Should Know About the Navy.* (New York: W. W. Norton)

1943: *The Navy at War: Paintings and Drawings by Combat Artists.* (New York: William Morrow)

1948: *The Price of Power.* Published for the Council on Foreign Relations. (New York: Harper & Brothers)

1950: *Great Mistakes of the War.* (New York: Harper & Brothers)

1950: *Power and Politics: The Price of Security in the Atomic Age.* (Claremont, CA: Claremont College for the Four Associated Colleges at Claremont)

1955: *Seafights and Shipwrecks: True Tales of the Seven Seas.* (Garden City, New York: Hanover House)

1958: *The Great Arms Race: A Comparison of United States and Soviet Power Today.* (New York: Praeger)

1962: *World War I: An Outline History.* (New York: Harper and Row)

1962: *World War I: An Outline History.* (New York: Grove Press)

1964: *The New Navy.* (New York: E. P. Dutton)

1966: *Battles Lost and Won: Great Campaigns of World War II.* (New York: Harper and Row)

1970: *Strategy for Tomorrow.* (New York: Harper and Row)

1976: *The Crucial Years, 1939–1941.* (New York: Harper and Row)

1979: *Tiger Jack.* (Ft. Collins, CO: Old Army Press)

Notes

INTRODUCTION

1. Frank Freidel to Baldwin, July 11, 1960, Baldwin papers, Yale University, Sterling Memorial Library, Manuscripts and Archives Division, series 1, box 232, folder 1064.

2. Baldwin to Chester M. Lewis, July 14, 1978, Baldwin papers, Yale, series 1, box 10, folder 155.

3. Needless to say, such prodigious output for almost four decades meant that he repeated himself often. I have made no attempt to read everything he wrote, but I have formed a very good idea of his views on many national defense and security topics.

Chapter 1 ⟶ A BALTIMORE YOUTH, 1903-20

1. Hanson Weightman Baldwin, *Reminiscences of Hanson Weightman Baldwin* (Annapolis: United States Naval Institute, 1976), 1–4. In 1975 Baldwin made eight taped interviews with John T. Mason Jr., director of oral history for the U.S. Naval Institute. Hereinafter *Reminiscences*. See Michael C. Emery and Edwin Emery, *The Press in America*, 6th edition (New York: Prentice Hall, 1988).

2. *New York Times,* July 18, 1878, 5. Hereinafter *NYT.* See also *Baltimore Sun,* July 18, 1878, 2. Hereinafter *Sun.*

3. National Union Catalogue, pre-1956 imprints, volume 32 (London: Mansell).

4. Robert Selph Freeman, *The Story of the Confederacy* (New York: Scribner's, 1934), II, 11, 38, and 47.

5. Douglas Southall Freeman, *Robert E. Lee: A Bibliography* (New York: Scribner's, 1934), 11, 32, 38, and 47.

6. Philip H. Sheridan, *Personal Memoirs* (New York: C. L. Webster, 1888), chapter 19.

7. Mark S. Watson, "An Appreciation," obituary for Oliver P. Baldwin Jr., *Sun*, June 21, 1932, 9. See also Maurice Matloff, ed., *American Military History* (Washington, D.C.: The Office of the Chief of Military History, 1969), 268.

8. Watson, "An Appreciation," ibid.

9. Parchment diploma, Virginia Historical Society, Richmond, Virginia, Oliver Perry Baldwin papers, folder Mss 1 B 1938a, 198.

10. Gerald W. Johnson, Frank R. Kent, Hamilton Owens, and H. L. Mencken, *The Sunpapers of Baltimore, 1837–1937* (New York: Alfred A. Knopf, 1937), 227 and 230. See also Howard W. Shank Sr. to author, October 13, 1988. Mr. Shank was the payroll manager of the *Sun*.

11. Henry M. Hyde to Baldwin, January 11, 1943, Baldwin papers, Yale, series 1, box 10, folder 140.

12. Watson, "An Appreciation," 9.

13. *NYT,* June 21, 1932, 21. In 1983 Baldwin self-recorded tape cassettes for his grandchildren that described his youth in Baltimore. He loaned the tapes to me. I have drawn upon them liberally for the details of his youth. I drew additional information on his youth from my taped interviews with him in 1985, 1986, and 1987, which are in my possession. Hereinafter Baldwin tapes.

14. Tom Buck, *Jack Willliams and Boys' Latin School, 1926–1978* (Baltimore, MD: Gateway Press, Inc., 1983), 24 and 115.

15. *Reminiscences,* 7.

16. Dyson P. Erhardt to author, December 1, 1988. He was the director of development and alumni relations and a graduate of the Latin School. The annual tuition costs when Baldwin was enrolled varied between $90 and $180 for the 120–150 students enrolled.

17. Buck, *Jack Williams,* 16. *Reminiscences,* 10.

18. Buck, *Jack Williams,* 16.

19. Ibid., 25

20. *Reminiscences,* 11.

21. Baldwin tapes.

22. *Reminiscences,* 12.

23. Harrie Irving Hancock, *Dave Darin on Asiatic Station* (Philadelphia: Henry Attemus Company, 1919), 135.

24. H. I. Hancock, *Dave Darin and Fourth Year at Annapolis* (Akron, OH: Saalfield Publishing Company, 1911), 252.

25. Ibid., 167.

26. *Reminiscences,* 13–15.

27. Ibid.

5. Baldwin to Caroline Baldwin, August 30, 1924, Baldwin papers, LC, box 1.

6. Baldwin to Captain S. S. Bunding, USN (Ret.), July 18, 1967, Baldwin papers, Yale, series 1, box 1, folder 5.

7. During World War II he was Admiral King's naval intelligence chief, based on his fluency in the Japanese language. He later became the U.S. ambassador to Japan, then to Burma, and finally to Australia.

8. "Notice to All Hands," November 20, 1924, Baldwin papers, LC, box 1.

9. Baldwin, "Death of a Dreadnought," *Shipmate*, January 1941, 2–3, Baldwin papers, LC, box 6. See also *Reminiscences*, 128–31.

10. *NYT*, October 21, 1924, 1.

11. Baldwin to Caroline Baldwin, October 21, 1924, Baldwin papers, LC, box 1.

12. Baldwin to Caroline Baldwin, November 30, 1924, Baldwin papers, LC, box 1.

13. A. Ben Clymer, "The Mechanical Analog Computers of Hannibal Ford, and William H. Newell," *IEEF: Annals of the History of Computing*, 1993, 24.

14. *Reminiscences*, 133–34.

15. Ibid., 136–37.

16. Ibid., 143–44.

17. Ibid., 146.

18. Lester Markel, *Public Opinion and Foreign Policy* (New York: Harper, 1949), 98.

19. Admiral Richard Lansing Conolly, USN (Ret.), oral history transcript. (Washington, D.C.: Operational Archives, Naval History Division, 1960), 56–57.

20. "Report on the Fitness of Officers," U.S. Navy, Baldwin papers, LC, box 1. John D. Alden, *Flush Decks and Four Pipes* (Annapolis: U.S. Naval Institute, 1965), 1. Few of those destroyers saw any combat in World War I, but they had long and useful lives. All were obsolete by 1940. They displaced between 1,215 and 1,370 tons.

21. *Reminiscences*, 159.

22. Lieutenant Commander John H. Magruder Jr., USN, *Report,* n.d., Baldwin papers, LC, box 5. Internal evidence clearly dates the report as being written between June 1926 and June 1927.

23. Baldwin to Caroline Baldwin, June 20, 1926, Baldwin papers, LC, box 1.

24. Ibid., June 28, 1926.

25. *Reminiscences*, 162.

26. Ibid., 171.

27. Ibid., 172–73.

28. Baldwin, "Marseilles, France," a travelogue, n.d., Baldwin papers, LC, box 7.

29. Lieutenant (jg) Winston Folk, USN, "How the American Navy Brought Santa Claus to France," U.S. Naval Institute *Proceedings*, December 1931, 1664–68 passim. See also Baldwin, an uncompleted typescript on two ports of call in 1927, Baldwin papers, LC, box 1, 5.

30. Baldwin, uncompleted typescript, 6–7.

31. Ibid.

32. *Sun*, January 12, 1927, 4.

33. *Reminiscences*, 184–85.

34. Taped interview with Baldwin, August 5, 1987, in author's possession.

35. *Reminiscences*, 174–75.

36. Baldwin to Caroline Baldwin, June 7, 1927, Baldwin papers, LC, box 1.

37. Ibid.

38. "Joe Starboard" to Baldwin, July 18, 1927, Baldwin papers, LC, box 1. In June 1927 Baldwin asked Lieutenant Seyfried, the former executive officer on the *Breck*, who was then in the Judge Advocate General's office in Washington, to look up his test results.

39. Report on the Fitness of Officers, April 1–September 1926, Baldwin papers, LC, box 5.

40. Lieutenant (jg) Ted Wirth, USN, to Baldwin, January 2, 1927, Baldwin papers, LC, box 1. Lieutenant Wirth was serving on the USS *Bruce* (DD 329), then at Norfolk, Virginia.

41. Frank O'Bierne to Baldwin, November 17, 1929, Baldwin papers, Yale, series 1, box 1, folder 1. He retired in 1963 as vice admiral, naval air, Atlantic.

42. Stephen R. Bedford to Baldwin, February 9, 1927, Baldwin papers, LC, box 1.

43. The articles appeared in the *Sun* on February 13 and June 5 and 12, 1927.

44. Baldwin to Caroline Baldwin, September 1, 1927, Baldwin papers, LC, box, 6.

45. USS *Breck* to Bureau of Navigation, September 28, 1927, Baldwin papers, LC, box 6.

46. *Report of the Secretary of the Navy*, for the fiscal year 1928 (Washington, D.C.: Government Printing Office, 1929), 18.

Chapter 4 ⌒ IN SEARCH OF A VOCATION, 1927-29

1. I am indebted to Barbara Baldwin Potter for sharing some of the contents of her father's scrapbooks with me that illustrated his thinking between his post-Navy years and the beginning of his newspaper career.

2. *Sun*, December 20, 1927, 12.

3. Baldwin, unpublished typescript that is partially autobiographical, n.d., LC, box 6, 8–9.

4. Ibid., 204.

5. Ibid., 205.

6. Baldwin scrapbooks, Baldwin papers, Yale, series 3, box 20, folders 276–77.

7. Baldwin, "Airship Ends Stormy Trip at Lakehurst," *Sun*, October 16, 1928, 1.

8. Baldwin, "Vestris Disaster Is Laid to Faulty Storage of Cargo," *Sun*, November 14, 1928, 1.

9. *Reminiscences*, 208. See also Baldwin's *Sun* report, November 16, 1928, 1–2.

10. Baldwin, "Along the 'Avenoo' in Baltimore's Harlem," *Sun*, May 13, 1928, 7.

11. C. B. Trusell statement, December 5, 1928, Baldwin papers, Yale, series 1, box 1, folder 1.

12. S. M. Reynolds statement, December 5, 1928, ibid.

13. *Fortune*, September 1937, pp. 62, 182, and 184.

14. Baldwin to his family, January 7, 1929, Baldwin papers, LC, box 1.

15. Ibid.

16. Baldwin, "The Navy and the Merchant Marine Service in Behalf of Amity," U.S. Naval Institute *Proceedings*, August 1930, 737–70. See also *Reminiscences*, 211–15.

17. Baldwin, fragment of an article, n.d., Baldwin papers, Yale, series 111, box 20, folder 273. See also Baldwin, "Hobos of the Ocean Highway," *Sun Magazine*, May 26, 1929, 13–14. This article dealt with the characters he had met, and not on the living conditions of the crew on board ship.

18. Baldwin to Caroline Baldwin, July 28, 1929, Baldwin papers, Yale, series 1, box 1.

19. Dr. Wilfred Grenfell to Baldwin, August 30, 1929, Baldwin papers, Yale, series 1, box 1, folder 1.

20. *Reminiscences*, 221.

21. Ibid., 222.

22. Baldwin to Caroline Baldwin, July 21, 1929, Baldwin papers, LC, box 1.

23. *Reminiscences*, 224.

Chapter 5 ⌒ ON GENERAL ASSIGNMENT, 1929–36

1. H. R. Holcome to Baldwin, September 25, 1929, Baldwin papers, Yale, series 1, box 1, folder 1. See also Stanley Walker to Baldwin, October 7, 1929, ibid.

2. Carr Van Anda to Oliver Baldwin, October 3, 1929, Baldwin papers, Yale, series 1, box 1, folder 2.

3. *Reminiscences*, 226. Baldwin later remembered Mr. Birchall as "a little Englishman with a white goatee, which always wagged like a goat." His refusal to give up his British citizenship was the reason why Adolph Ochs, the *Times* publisher, did not give him the title of managing editor. Baldwin remembered Birchall as a "delightful guy" and a "wonderful newspaperman." In 1931, he returned to Europe to head the Vienna bureau for the *Times*.

4. Baldwin to Edwin L. James, October 14, 1933, Baldwin papers, Yale, series 1, box 11, folder 567. See also Gay Talese, *The Kingdom and the Power* (New York: The World Publishing Company, 1969), 452.

5. Van Anda's knowledge of astronomy, mathematics, and Egyptology enabled him to explain the meaning of Albert Einstein's theory of relativity and the significance of opening Tutankhamen's tomb. He died in 1945 at the age of eighty.

6. *Reminiscences,* 227 and 229. See also Talese, *The Kingdom and the Power*, 206.

7. *Reminiscences*, 230.

8. Ibid., 228.

9. Robert D. Ohrenschall to Baldwin, March 23, 1930, Baldwin papers, Yale, series 1, box 10, folder 159.

10. *Reminiscences*, 229.

11. Baldwin to Caroline Baldwin, n.d., Baldwin papers, LC, box 1. From textual references it is possible to date those letters in May–June 1930. His references to the fleet's arrival appeared on May 7 and 8, 1930, in the *Times*.

12. *NYT*, May 7, 1930, 1 and 4. This was a passing reference to the 1930 London Naval Treaty, which authorized the construction of cruisers.

13. *NYT,* May 8, 1930, 1.

14. *NYT,* May 17, 1930, 2.

15. Baldwin to Caroline Baldwin, n.d., Baldwin papers, LC, box 1. The letter was addressed to "Dearest motherkins."

16. *NYT*, June 1, 1930, 1 and 24. See also *Reminiscences*, 230. The *Graf Zeppelin* was retired from service in 1937 after 144 Atlantic Ocean crossings since 1928. It was replaced by the ill-fated *Hindenburg*, which exploded at Lakehurst, New Jersey, on May 6, 1937, as it was preparing to be moored.

17. Baldwin, "Newspapers and the Navy," U.S. Naval Institute *Proceedings*, December 1930, 1086. He was identified as a lieutenant (jg) in the U.S. Naval Reserve.

18. Ibid., 1097.

19. Ibid., 1090.

20. Captain W. Baggaley, USN, to Baldwin, December 18, 1930, Baldwin papers, LC, box 1. His salutation was addressed to "My dear Lieutenant." See also David S. Ingalls, assistant secretary of the Navy, to Baldwin, December 11, 1930, ibid.

21. E. L. James to R. V. Oulahan, November 24, 1930, cablegram, *NYT* Archives, roll 58, frame 1415.

22. *Reminiscences,* 236–39.

23. Ibid., 239.

24. *NYT*, February 23, 1931, 3.

25. Ibid.

26. Baldwin to Caroline Baldwin, February 14, 1931, Baldwin papers, LC, box 1.

27. Ibid.

28. *NYT*, February 7, 1931, 6.

29. *NYT,* February 11, 1931, 8.

30. *Reminiscences*, 233. See also Baldwin to Caroline Baldwin, June 8, 1930, Baldwin papers, LC, box 1.

31. Ibid.

32. She taught at Wilson College in Chambersburg, Pennsylvania, for a year before being appointed as the history department chair at Hood College in Frederick, Maryland. After five years she resigned to accept a $2,250 Social Science Research Council fellowship in London in the summer of 1929. On her return, she wrote travel articles for the *Sun* and later worked in the American Historical Association office in New York City. Sidney J. Silverman to author, August 1, 1988. He was a professor emeritus at Hood College. See also Baldwin to Caroline Baldwin, June 8, 1930, Baldwin papers, LC, box 1; and Margie H. Luckett, ed.,

Maryland Women, II (Baltimore, 1937), 13. See *Sun*, March 23, 1930, 5–6, for one of her travel articles on London city life.

33. Baldwin to Caroline Baldwin, n.d., Baldwin papers, LC, box 1. Textual references date this letter in May 1930. The play was reviewed by Brooks Atkinson, who commented upon Tracy's "muscular" acting ability. The play was described as "an evening of nerve-racking tension." *NYT Theater Reviews*, 1920–70, IX, 21.

34. Recorded interview with Baldwin, August 5, 1987, and June 1989, in author's possession. See also *Reminiscences,* 232–33, and Baldwin to author, July 23, 1987.

35. Recorded interview with Baldwin, August 5, 1987.

36. He held over fifty patents in eight countries, the best known of which was the Bruce mercury contact cable relay system. He died suddenly while Helen was a junior in college. *The National Cyclopedia of American Biography,* XXII, 1932, 236–37. Barbara Potter told me that her father told her that Mr. Bruce took his own life at the age of fifty-one. Taped interview, April 5, 2005, in author's possession.

37. They had first met a few years before while both worked for the *Sun*. In 1937 Crowther became the movie critic for the *Times*.

38. *NYT,* June 9, 1931, 31 and 34. See also Talese, *The Kingdom and the Power,* 61; and Frank R. Weaver, USN (Ret.), to Baldwin, March 9, 1965, Baldwin papers, Yale, series 1, box 19, folder 947.

39. Recorded interview with Baldwin, June 1989. See also Geoffrey T. Hellman, "Sorting Out the Seligmans," *The New Yorker*, October 30, 1954, 62.

40. Recorded interview with Baldwin, June 1989.

41. *NYT*, March 13, 1962, 35. *NYT*, September 23, 1975, 40. See also recorded interview with Baldwin, June 1989, in which he spoke at length about his and Helen's friendship with Raes. See also Talese, *The Kingdom and the Power,* 52.

42. Dorothy Baldwin to Hanson Baldwin, December 21, 1931, Baldwin papers, Yale, series 1, box 1, folder 2. She addressed the letter to "dearest darling chubblet."

43. *Sun,* July 5, 1931, 4. Elizabeth Baldwin died at Park West Hospital, New York City. See also Luckett, *Maryland Women,* 13.

44. F. T. Birchall to Baldwin, September 7, 1931, F. T. Birchall papers, *NYT* Archives, microfilm roll 58, frame 1416 and 1418. Birchall made arrangements to provide a tent, meals, and office space for Baldwin in the local Western Union office.

45. *NYT,* August 28, 1931, 5.

46. Ibid., August 30, 1931, 16.

47. Ibid., September 1, 1931, 8.

48. F.T Birchall to Baldwin, September 7, 1931, *NYT* Archives, roll 58, frame 1423.

49. Baldwin, taped interview, August 5, 1987.

50. "Oliver Perry Baldwin," editorial, June 21, 1932, *Sun*, 28.

51. *Reminiscences*, 661.

52. Mark Skinner Watson to Baldwin, September 20, 1933, Baldwin papers, Yale, series 1, box 19, folder 957. See also Baldwin to Grafton S. Wilcox, September 23, 1933, Baldwin papers, Yale, series 1, box 19, folder 957. He was the managing editor of the *New York Herald-Tribune*.

53. Baldwin to Willis Wing, December 4, 1932, Baldwin papers, Yale, series 1, box 19, folder 979, and Baldwin to Wing, September 13, 1965, Baldwin papers, Yale, series 1, box 19, folder 979. See also Wing's obituary, *NYT*, June 27, 1985, IV, 23. His clients included Sloan Wilson, John LeCarre, and Nicholas Monsarrat.

54. Lieutenant (jg) Baldwin to the Commander, Third Naval District, January 27, 1932, Baldwin papers, LC, box 5. See also *NYT*, February 26, 1931, 6.

55. Hayne Ellis to the Commander, Third Naval District, January 4, 1933, Baldwin papers, LC, box 5.

56. Baldwin, "Our Five New Destroyers," *Sun Magazine*, December 1, 1932, 1. Baldwin's article provided a good deal of factual information about the new destroyers, including their speed (36–37 knots), the number of torpedo tubes (8), their maximum displacement (2,300 tons), and the use of welding in their construction.

57. Baldwin to Commander, Third Naval District, January 16, 1933, Baldwin papers, LC, box 6.

58. Navy to Baldwin, n.d., Baldwin papers, LC, box 6.

59. Rear Admiral F. B. Upham, USN, to Lieutenant (jg) Baldwin, January 30, 1933, ibid. See also Watson to Baldwin, February 16, 1933, ibid.

60. Chief of the Bureau of Navigation to Baldwin, March 13, 1933, ibid.

61. Baldwin to Navy, ibid.

62. Baldwin to E. L. James, July 12, 1933, Baldwin papers, LC, box 6. Mr. James became the *Times* managing editor in 1932, a post he held until his death in December 1951.

63. Rear Admiral William D. Leahy, Chief of the Bureau of Navigation to Lieutenant (jg) Baldwin, March 2, 1934, Baldwin papers, LC, box 5. See

also Baldwin to BuNav, March 24, 1934, ibid. His commission as a lieu-
tenant was dated May 14, 1934, Baldwin papers, LC, box 5. BuNav to
Baldwin, July 12, 1934, ibid. See also W. D. Spears, BuNav to Baldwin,
September 21, 1934, Baldwin papers, LC., box 6.

64. Baldwin to Secretary of the Navy, August 20, 1934, ibid.

65. Baldwin to Marshall Newton and Carl Randau, September 1, 1934,
Baldwin papers, Yale, series 1, box 1, folder 2. See also Randau to
Baldwin, September 11, 1934, ibid.

66. Baldwin, "Japan and the Future," *The North American Review*, March
1934, 204–6. Japan did not want a war with the Soviet Union and it
could never conquer China. Baldwin thought that it was more feasible
for Japan and Germany to seek a political rapprochement, as the former
was "isolated in the East" and the latter was "isolated in the West." Two
years later, in 1936, Berlin and Tokyo did sign an anti-Comintern Pact
that was nominally against international Communism but was really
against the Soviet Union. He predicted that, at the forthcoming London
Naval Conference in December 1935, Japan would demand naval parity
with the United States, which, in his view, President Roosevelt would
reject, thereby instigating a new naval arms race. In his words, 1935
would "mark the fork in the road of tomorrow for Japan, and upon the
road she takes will depend the course of world history."

67. Baldwin, "Wanted: A Naval Policy," *Current History*, November 1935,
128–30. This magazine was issued monthly by the New York Times
Company as an auxiliary publication. See also Talese, *The Kingdom and
the Power*, 264–65.

68. Admiral William H. Standley to Baldwin, November 16, 1935, Baldwin
papers, Yale, series 1, box 18, folder 901.

69. Baldwin, "Navy Blue and Gold," *Esquire*, December 1935, 72.

70. Ibid., 126.

71. Ibid., 72.

72. *Reminiscences*, 242.

73. Baldwin, "The Army Plays Its Huge Game of War," *NYT Magazine*,
August 18, 1935, 6–7.

74. *NYT*, August 21, 1935, 3.

75. *NYT*, August 26, 1935, 1.

76. Ibid.

77. *NYT*, August 28, 1935, 7.

78. "Our Military Manoeuvers," editorial, *NYT*, August 31, 1935, 12.

79. Susan E. Tifft and Alex S. Jones, *The Trust: The Private and Powerful Family Behind the New York Times* (Boston: Little, Brown and Company, 1999), 167–68. See also *Reminiscences*, 241.

80. *Reminiscences*, 241.

81. George W. Baer, *One Hundred Years of Sea Power: The U.S. Navy, 1890–1990* (Stanford, CA: Stanford University Press, 1999), 131–32.

82. Alan Bullock, *Hitler: A Study in Tyranny*, revised edition (New York: Harper Collins, 1964), 309.

Chapter 6 ⌒ A NEW ASSIGNMENT, 1937

1. Hanson W. Baldwin, *The Caissons Roll: A Military Survey of Europe* (New York: A. A. Knopf, 1938), vi.

2. E. L. James, Arthur Sulzberger, Hanson Baldwin, memoranda, December 1936, *NYT* Archives, roll 58, frames 1450–53.

3. *Reminiscences*, 244.

4. Baldwin to E. L. James, January 5, 1937, telegram, *NYT* Archives, roll 58, frame 1455.

5. Harry A. Woodring to Arthur Krock, January 16, 1937, roll 58, frame 1457.

6. E. L. James to the *Times* European offices, cablegram, February 12, 1937, roll 58, frame 1466.

7. Baldwin to E. L. James, n.d., roll 58, frames 1453–58. See also *Reminiscences*, 275.

8. Baldwin, *Caissons*, iv.

9. *Reminiscences,* 270–71.

10. Baldwin, diary entry, February 17, 1937, 3. Baldwin papers, Yale, series 3, box 7, folder "European trip 1938."

11. Ibid., box 86, folders 530 and 532.

12. Baldwin, *Caissons*, v.

13. Ibid., 4.

14. Ibid., 5 and 9.

15. Ibid., 10 and 11.

16. Ibid., 284.

17. Ibid., 286–87.

18. Ibid., 284.

19. Ibid., 287–89.

20. Ibid., 428.

21. Ibid.

22. Ibid., 71 and 72.

23. Ibid., 43.

24. Ibid., 64.

25. Ibid., 72.

26. Ibid., 312.

27. Ibid., 299–300.

28. Ibid., 305–8.

29. Ibid., 309.

30. Ibid., 314–16.

31. Ibid., 86.

32. Ibid., 88.

33. Ibid., 89–90.

34. Ibid., 98.

35. Ibid.

36. Ibid., 105.

37. Ibid., 111.

38. Ibid., 113.

39. Ibid., 118.

40. Ibid., 127.

41. Ibid., 128.

42. *Reminiscences*, 276. On May 7, 1945, he surrendered all German armed forces to the Allies.

43. Ibid., 275.

44. Robert Hessen, ed., *Berlin Alert: The Memoirs and Reports of Truman Smith* (Stanford: Hoover Institution Press, 1984), 136.

45. Lindbergh's flight in an ME 109 occurred on Friday, October 31, 1938. In hindsight, he learned nothing of Germany's experiments with jet propulsion engines and rockets.

46. Baldwin, *Caissons*, 132.

47. Ibid., 136.

48. Ibid., 144.

49. Ibid., 146.

50. Ibid., 155.

51. Ibid., 156.

52. Ibid.

53. Ibid., 230.

54. Ibid., 232.

55. Ibid.

56. Ibid., 236.

57. Ibid., 237.

58. Ibid., 159.

59. Ibid.

60. Ibid., 181.

61. Ibid., 184.

62. Ibid., 186–87.

63. Ibid., 190.

64. *Reminiscences*, 280.

65. Baldwin, *Caissons,* 205. Tukhachevsky had formed the Red Army tank corps, 1936–37, whose mission would be to make deep penetrations behind the enemies' lines. After his execution in June 1937, his tank organization was abandoned and not revived until 1942, when it became a great success.

66. Ibid., 206.

67. *Reminiscences*, 282.

68. Ibid., 281.

69. Ibid., 279.

70. Baldwin, *Caissons*, 195 and 227.

71. Ibid., 194–95.

72. Ibid., 211.

73. Ibid., 215–16.

74. Ibid., 218.

75. Ibid., 195.

76. F. T. Birchall to E. L. James, May 25, 1937, *NYT* Archives, roll 58, frame 1515.

77. *Reminiscences,* 284–85.

78. A. H. Sulzberger to E. L. James, June 7, 1937, *NYT* Archives, roll 58, frame 1516.

79. Baldwin to Sulzberger, June 9, 1937, ibid., frames 1594–95.

80. E. L. James to Sulzberger, June 11, 1937, ibid., frames 1596–97.

81. P. M. B. (?) to Sulzberger, November 5, 1937, ibid., frame 1520. The amount of Baldwin's salary raise was in Sulzberger's handwriting.

82. *NYT Book Review*, March 6, 1938, 4. The reviewer was Major General William C. Rivers, U.S. Army (Ret.). He was alarmed that, based upon the tables at the end of each chapter, the five powers could have 56,230,000 men available for military service, with 17,000 first-class airplanes available.

83. George Bernard Noble, *The American Political Science Review*, June 1938, 594. Professor Noble taught at Reed College.

84. William A. Lydgate, "Funeral March," *The New Republic*, March 30, 1938, 229.

85. *The Saturday Review of Literature*, February 5, 1938, 6.

86. Alfred A. Knopf to Baldwin, February 7 and 24, and July 19, 1938, Baldwin papers, Yale, series 1, box 8, folder 416.

87. *Reminiscences*, 291.

88. Ibid., 291–92. See also Richard F. Shepard, *The Paper's Paper: A Reporter's Journey Through the Archives of the New York Times* (New York: Times Books, 1996) 176.

89. Baldwin to Lieutenant H. S. Hansell, U.S. Army, May 16, 1938, Baldwin papers, George C. Marshall Library, Lexington, Virginia, box 7, folder 29.

90. Ibid.

91. *Reminiscences*, 285. After his retirement in 1937, Admiral Standley was recalled to active duty and served on the Roberts Commission to investigate the Pearl Harbor attack. Later he served as U.S. ambassador to the Soviet Union where, Baldwin recalled, he continued to be "useful as a newspaper source."

92. Ibid., 256.

93. Baldwin "Men-at-Arms," 16, Baldwin papers, LC, box 6, 22. This twenty-two-page partial autobiography was written in 1937, as indicated by his 1970s addenda to this manuscript.

94. Ibid., 10.

95. Ibid., 17.

96. Ibid., 20.

97. Ibid., 22.

98. Ibid. Stephen R. Bedford to Baldwin, September 20, 1937, Baldwin papers, Yale, series 1, box 2, folder 59. He was in Baldwin's wedding party in 1931.

99. Baldwin, "Shake-up in the Navy," *NYT*, November 4, 1938, 24.

100. Roosevelt, *The Complete Presidential Press Conferences*, XII, 207–8. See also Arthur Krock to James, cablegram, November 4, 1938, Baldwin papers, Yale, series 1, box 24, folder 1105. Arthur Krock quoted the president's compliment, cited above. See also Willis Wing to Baldwin, November 23, 1938, Baldwin papers, Yale, series 1, box 19, folder 979, which also noted the president's praise. Wing was Baldwin's literary agent.

101. "Steam in the Navy," editorial, *NYT*, November 9, 1938, 22.

102. *Reminiscences*, 321–22. See also Baldwin to Commander John D. Alden, USN (Ret.), November 8, 1975, George C. Marshall Library, Lexington, Virginia, Baldwin papers, box 7, folder 14.

103. *Reminiscences*, 267–68.

104. Ibid., 268.

105. Bernard L. Austin to Baldwin, November 1938, Baldwin papers, Yale, series 1, box 1, folder 40. See also Vice Admiral Bernard L. Austin, U.S. Navy (Ret.), oral history transcript, 1971, U.S. Naval Institute, Annapolis, Maryland, 67.

106. Louis Denfeld to Baldwin, December 15, 1938, Baldwin papers, Yale, series 1, box 4, folder 190.

107. Stanley Grogan to Baldwin, June 3, 1941, Baldwin papers, Yale, series 1, box 6, folder 300. See also Baldwin papers, Yale, series 1, box 17, folder 879.

108. William J. Sebald to Baldwin, January 19, 1938, Baldwin papers, Yale, series 1, box 11, folder 170.

109. Sebald to Baldwin, July 31, 1938, ibid.

110. Ibid.

111. Ibid. Sebald left Japan in 1939. With his special knowledge of Japanese affairs, he was welcomed by the office of naval intelligence in that year with the rank of lieutenant commander. At war's end he began a new career with the State Department as the chairman of the Allied Council for Japan, which brought him into almost daily contact with General Douglas MacArthur.

112. Sterling Fisher to Baldwin, March 29, 1938, Baldwin papers, Yale, series 1, box 3, folder 147. See also Baldwin to Joseph M. Worthington, March 2, 1938, ibid., box 1, folder 18. He felt that his radio broadcast of February 27, 1938, would be, most likely, his last for "the distant future." It was not.

113. *Reminiscences*, 287–88.

114. Ibid., 289–90.

115. Ibid., 289. President Truman fired Mr. Johnson after he served as the secretary of defense for only eighteen months.

116. Baldwin to John R. Wadleigh, March 2, 1974, Baldwin papers, LC, box 1. He was a 1937 graduate of the Naval Academy.

117. *Reminiscences*, 289.

Chapter 7 〜 DISTANT THUNDER, 1938–39

1. *NYT*, February 20, 1938, IV, 3.

2. Baldwin, "America Rearms," *Foreign Affairs*, April 1938, 444.

3. Ibid., 430.

4. Ibid.

5. Ibid., 441

6. Ibid., 442.

7. "Army Critic Finds Initiative Killed," *NYT*, October 9, 1938, 46. Baldwin's papers at Yale list this piece as having been summarized by him. Who else at the *Times* would read *The Infantry Journal*?

8. "America Rearms," 436.

9. Ibid., 437.

10. Ibid. For an excellent article on the U.S. Navy see "Big Navy," *Fortune*, March 1938. The magazine's staff did the research and wrote this very informative article.

11. *NYT*, October 2, 1938, IV, 3.

12. Ibid.

13. "A National Defense Program," editorial, *NYT*, December 12, 1938, 18.

14. Ibid.

15. *NYT*, December 13, 1938, 24.

16. Ibid., December 14, 1938, 24.

17. Ibid., December 16, 1938, 24.

18. Ibid.

19. Ibid., December 18, 1938, IV, 8.

20. Baldwin, "Should America Re-arm?" radio script, WEVD, February 27, 1939, 7–8, Baldwin papers, Yale, series III, box 48, folder 265.

21. Ibid., 469. See also *NYT*, February 12, 1939, E7. Section E of the paper was now called The News of the Week In Review.

22. Ibid.

23. Ibid.

24. Oswald G. Villard, "Wanted: A Sane Defense Policy," *Harper's*, April 1939, 449–56.

25. Ibid., 452.

26. Ibid.

27. Ibid.

28. Theodore Peterson, *Magazines in the Twentieth Century* (Urbana, IL: University of Illinois Press, 1964), 433. Founded by H. L. Mencken in the 1920s, the magazine had an iconoclastic attitude toward American life, which was popular with Jazz Age readers but not with 1930s readers. Under the new management of Lawrence F. Spivak it successfully solicited well-known writers to reverse its declining circulation. Sales rose to peak of 84,000 copies in 1945. See also *Current Biography* (New York: W. H. Wilson Company 1956), 597–98.

29. Baldwin, "Impregnable America," *The American Mercury*, July 1939, 257.

30. Ibid., 267.

31. Ibid., 263.

32. Ibid., 264. When completed in 1913, the locks were 110 feet wide and 1,000 feet long. The new *Iowa*-class battleships, ordered in 1939, had a beam of 108 feet. He noted how "alarmism" tended to overemphasize the canal's role in America's defense. Should the canal be blocked, more ships would be needed to reinforce the Atlantic fleet, which in 1939 was composed of old training ships.

33. Ibid.

34. Rita Potter to Baldwin, June 7, 1939, Baldwin papers, Yale, series 1, box 1, folder 19. He was paid $150 for this article.

35. Eugene Lyons to Baldwin, April 20, 1939, ibid. He was the editor of *The American Mercury*.

36. Baldwin to Lester Markel, July 1, 1939, Edwin L. James papers, *NYT* Archives, roll 58, frames 1557–58.

37. *NYT*, August 27, 1939, 1 and 33.

38. Ibid.

39. "Soul of the Army," editorial, *NYT*, August 28, 1939, 18.

40. Ibid.

41. See *NYT*, August 19, 1939, for numerous articles, as the lights of Europe went out again after twenty years of peace.

42. *NYT*, September 7, 1939, 2.

43. Ibid., September 10, 1939, E4.

44. Ibid., September 14, 1939, 3.

45. "The Russian Betrayal," editorial, *NYT*, September 18, 1939, 18.

46. Ibid., September 10, 1939, E4.

47. Ibid., September 3, 1939, E5.

48. Ibid., September 24, 1939, E5.

49. Baldwin to Sulzberger, October 3, 1939, Arthur Hays Sulzberger papers, *NYT* Archives, Hanson Baldwin file, 1–3.

50. Ibid., 4.

51. Ibid., 6.

52. Baldwin to Sulzberger, October 10, 1939, Sulzberger papers, *NYT* Archives, Baldwin file.

53. Baldwin to Sulzberger, October 17, 1939, ibid. See also Sulzberger to Baldwin, October 18, 1939, ibid.

54. Baldwin letter in the "Voice of the People" column, *New York Daily News*, October 3, 1939, Sulzberger papers, *NYT* Archives.

55. Ibid.

56. Sulzberger to Baldwin, October 9, 1939, ibid. See also Edwin I. James papers, *NYT* Archives, roll 58, frame 1582.

57. Baldwin to Sulzberger, October 10, 1939, Sulzberger papers, *NYT* Archives.

58. Ibid.

59. *NYT*, November 19, 1939, 1.

60. Dudley Pope, *Graf Spee: The Life and Death of a Raider* (New York: J. B. Lippincott Company, 1957), 212.

61. *NYT,* December 18, 1939, 2. For a large photograph of the *Graf Spee* leaving Montevideo Harbor prior to its being scuttled, see *NYT*, December 18, 1939, 3.

62. Markel to Baldwin, December 22, 1939, Baldwin papers, Yale, series 1, box 11, folder 570.

63. Willis Wing to Baldwin, July 9, 1939, ibid., box 9, folder 979.

Chapter 8 ⌐ DANGER AHEAD, PREPARE NOW, 1940-41

1. *NYT*, May 5, 1940, E4.

2. Baldwin, "Wanted: A Plan for Defense," *Harper's*, August, 1940, 227.

3. Ibid.

4. Ibid.

5. *NYT,* January 7, 1940, E1.

6. Baldwin, "Wanted: A Plan," 228.

7. Ibid., 229.

8. Ibid., 238.

9. Tifft and Jones, *The Trust,* 196. The paper endorsed the Republican candidate Wendell Willkie for president in 1940.

10. *War and Peace Studies Project: History,* October 1944, confidential, 1–5, Baldwin papers, Yale, series 4, box 115, folders 1 and 2. See also Robert D. Schulzinger, "Whatever Happened to the Council on Foreign Relations?" *Diplomatic History* (Fall 1981): 282–83. During the war he summarized the progress in fourteen quarterly articles in *Foreign Affairs* as "The World at War." They provided a narrative and analysis of the war while it was being fought. The series was never intended by Baldwin to be a history of World War II, which was a separate project that he began in 1946 but never completed. The first article appeared in April 1942, and the last in January 1946.

11. *NYT,* November 9, 1940, 10.

12. Baldwin to E. I. James, memorandum, 1940, *NYT* Archives, roll 58, frames 1590–93.

13. Baldwin, "The New American Army," *Foreign Affairs,* October 1940, 45.

14. Ibid., 53.

15. Ibid.

16. Ibid., 52.

17. Baldwin, "U.S. Air Power," *Fortune,* March 1941, 75–77. This article was reprinted in *Shipmate,* April 1941, 2, the alumni magazine of the U.S. Naval Academy.

18. Ibid., 4.

19. Ibid., 27.

20. *Fortune* magazine press release, March 3, 1941, Baldwin papers, Yale, series 3, box 28, folder 414.

21. Ibid.

22. Ibid.

23. Ibid., 27.

24. Baldwin to Ted Bernstein, cablegram, April 16, 1941, *NYT* Archives, roll 58, frames 1636–37. He was the assistant managing editor at the *Times.*

25. *NYT,* April 18, 1941, 1 and 11.

26. McCoy to Baldwin, cablegram, E. L. James papers, *NYT* Archives, roll 58, frame 1638. Baldwin told James, the managing editor, that the U.S. Army had approved of his piece. Ibid., frame 1639.

27. Baldwin to E. L. James, March 23, 1941, memorandum, *NYT* Archives, ibid.

28. Ibid., frame 1645.

29. Baldwin, "The Military Expert Faces a Word Blitz," *NYT Magazine*, November 16, 1941, 9 and 31.

30. Baldwin to E. L. James, August 18, 1941, memorandum, E. L. James papers, *NYT* Archives, roll 58, frame 1668.

31. Willis Wing to Baldwin, November 24, 1941, Baldwin papers, Yale, series 1, box 19, folder 979.

32. *NYT*, November 16, 1941, E9.

33. Ibid., 31.

34. *NYT*, May 28, 1941, 3.

35. T. G. Westcott to E. L. James, May 31, 1941, E. L. James papers, *NYT* Archives, roll 58, frame 1643.

36. Baldwin, "Hitler Can Be Defeated: But Total Effort Is Required," *NYT Magazine*, June 25, 1941, 3–5, 24.

37. Davis to Baldwin, June 15, 1941, Baldwin papers, Yale, series 1, box 4, folder 175. See also Roger Burlingame, *Don't Let Them Scare You: The Life and Times of Elmer Davis* (Philadelphia: J. B. Lippincott Company, 1961), 171.

38. Jack Benjamin to Baldwin, June 19, 1941, Baldwin papers, Yale, series 1, folder 44.

39. Baldwin, "Blueprint for Victory," *Life,* August 4, 1941, 39.

40. Ibid., 42.

41. Ibid.

42. Ibid., 47.

43. Ibid.

44. Ibid., 47.

45. *NYT*, September 27, 1941, 8.

46. *NYT*, October 1, 1941.

47. Ibid.

48. Baldwin to E. L. James, October 24, 1941, memorandum, *NYT* Archives, roll 58, frame 1693. See also Baldwin to U.S. State Department Passport Division, December 2, 1941, ibid., frame 1715.

49. *NYT*, December 8, 1941, 7.

50. *NYT*, December 7, 1941, E4.

51. Ibid.

52. "War with Japan," editorial, *NYT*, December 8, 1941, 22.

53. *NYT*, December 9, 1941, 20.

54. *Reminiscences*, 330.

55. Ibid., 314–15.

56. *NYT*, January 29, 1942, 4.

57. *NYT*, December 18, 1941, 4.

58. *NYT*, December 19, 1941, 20.

59. *NYT*, December 21, 1941, 20.

60. For confirmation of this weather front, see John Keegan, *The Second World War* (New York: Penquin Books, 1989), 254.

61. *NYT*, January 29, 1942, 4.

62. *Reminiscences*, 336–37.

63. *NYT*, January 29, 1942, 4.

64. Rough draft of a radio script, December 22, 1941, Baldwin papers, Yale, series 4, box 30, folder 446.

65. Ibid.

Chapter 9 ⌒ "THIS IS A WAR WE CAN LOSE," 1942

1. *NYT*, January 3, 1942, 13.

2. Ibid.

3. Ibid., February 15, 1942, E4.

4. Philip LaFollette to Baldwin, January 6, 1942, Baldwin papers, Yale, series 1, box 9, folder 429. The writer's father was Robert M. LaFollette (1855–1925), a Progressive party leader and a former governor of Wisconsin.

5. Edward Bernays to Baldwin, January 3 and 22, 1942, ibid., box 2, folder 65.

6. Baldwin to A. H. Sulzberger, February 5, 1942, E. L. James papers, *NYT* Archives, roll 58, frame 1766.

7. Baldwin to James R. Myers, September 14, 1971, George C. Marshall Library, Lexington, Virginia, Baldwin papers, box 8, folder 12. Mr. Myers was doing research for his honors thesis about the accuracy of news reporting during World War II.

8. *Reminiscences*, 330.

9. Ibid., 397.

10. *NYT*, October 21, 1959, 43. See also *Who's Who*, vol. 3, 416–17.

11. *Reminiscences,* 361.

12. Ibid., 285.

13. Ibid., 338 and 362.

14. Ibid., 382.

15. *NYT,* January 4, 1942, E4.

16. *NYT,* January 23, 1942, 12.

17. Ibid.

18. Ibid., January 24, 1942, 6.

19. Ibid.

20. Transcript of radio broadcast, February 1, 1942, 5 and 19, Baldwin papers, Yale, series 2, box 48, folder 265. The broadcast was made on the Red Network in New York City at 2:39 p.m.

21. Baldwin to Sulzberger, February 5, 1942, E. L. James papers, *NYT* Archives, roll 58, frames 1735–39.

22. *NYT*, February 16, 1942, 11.

23. Ibid., January 2, 1942, 4.

24. Ibid., February 15, 1942, E4.

25. Michael S. Sweeney, *Secrets of Victory: The Office of Censorship and the American Press and Radio in World War II* (Chapel Hill: University of North Carolina Press, 2001), 43.

26. Ibid., 40.

27. *NYT*, March 15, 1942, 12. The USS *Houston* (CA 30) was a *Northampton*-class heavy cruiser ordered in 1924 and commissioned in 1930.

28. *NYT,* June 1, 1942, 6.

29. Ibid., April 22, 1942, 6.

30. Ibid., May 10, 1942, 4. The Navy Department's communiqué said no report had been received about any American losses.

31. Ibid.

32. Ibid., May 4, 1942, 6.

33. Ibid., June 6, 1942, 1. Robert Trumball was the *Times* resident correspondent in Hawaii.

34. Ibid., June 8, 1942, 14.

35. Ibid., June 9, 1942, 8.

36. Ibid., July 16, 1942, 8.

37. "The Battle of Midway," editorial, *NYT*, July 16, 1942, 18.

38. "The Yorktown," editorial, *NYT*, September 17, 1942, 24.

39. E. L. James, "News is Sadly Lacking on American Fighting," August 23, 1942, *NYT*, E3.

40. *Reminiscences,* 345–46.

41. Ibid., 346. Admiral Fitch was the air commander of the U.S. naval forces in the area.

42. Baldwin, "Flight to Guadalcanal," *NYT Magazine*, November 1, 1942, VII, 3–4 and 34.

43. *Reminiscences,* 341–42.

44. Ibid., 348.

45. Ibid., 349.

46. Ibid., 351.

47. Baldwin to E. L. James (and other editors) and Sulzberger, October 12, 1942, E. L. James papers, *NYT* Archives, roll 58, frame 1754.

48. Samuel Eliot Morison, *The Struggle for Guadalcanal, August 1942–February 1943* (Boston: Little Brown and Company, 1949), 223.

49. *Reminiscences*, 357.

50. Admiral Charles J. Moore, USN (Ret.), oral history transcript, U.S. Naval Institute, June 8, 1964, 781.

51. Baldwin to Krock, January 3, 1968, Arthur Krock papers, Seeley G. Mudd Manuscript Library, Princeton University, Princeton, New Jersey, box 17.

52. *Reminiscences*, 359.

53. Ibid.

54. Ibid., 361.

55. Burlingame, *Don't Let Them Scare You*, 190.

56. Ibid., 189.

57. Ibid., 200–201.

58. *NYT*, October 26, 1942, 5.

59. Ibid., October 23, 1942, 4.

60. Ibid.

61. Ibid., October 30, 1942, 3.

62. Ibid. The USS *Saratoga* (CV 3) had been torpedoed on August 31 and was towed to Pearl Harbor. It reached Pearl on September 21 and remained there for twelve months.

63. Ibid., October 24, 1942, 3.

64. Ibid.

65. Ibid.

66. Ibid.

67. Ibid., October 25, 1942, E5.

68. Ibid.

69. Ibid., October 26, 1942, 1.

70. Ibid.

71. Ibid., October 27, 1942, 7. Australian laborers carefully observed Saturday afternoons and all holidays, with the result that U.S. troops had to unload the ships themselves. Labor, Baldwin commented, "seems primarily interested in retaining peace time privileges." Australia's foreign minister, Herbert V. Evatt, rebutted Baldwin's "labor baiting" comments by dismissing the journalist's slighting of its war effort as being both "inaccurate and intemperate." The stevedoring problems had been solved, he said, and had been taken in hand by a senior government official.

72. Lloyd Graybar, "Admiral King's Toughest Battle," *Naval War College Review,* February 1979, 39.

73. Ibid.

74. *NYT,* November 23, 1942, 10.

Chapter 10 ⌒ WAR AND THE 1943 PRIZE

1. *NYT,* May 15, 1943, 4. Baldwin wrote several articles on the complexities of French politics and their impact upon French officers, whose self-image at times seemed to be more important than whether or not to resist or to cooperate with the Allies.

2. *Reminiscences,* 371. Baldwin later recalled that Waters was a fellow alumnus of the Boys' Latin School in Baltimore.

3. Baldwin, "A Tour of the Road to Victory," *NYT Magazine,* May 23, 1943, 5.

4. Ibid., 30.

5. *Reminiscences,* 373–74.

6. Ibid., 375.

7. Ibid., 377.

8. Ibid., 379 and 381. This was especially true when he interviewed Charles DeGaulle, who was reluctant to talk very much and whose aloof manner did not encourage further questions. In that instance, Baldwin could only form an impression of the man who believed that he personified France.

9. *NYT*, May 12, 1943, 7.

10. Ibid., May 16, 1943, 35.

11. Ibid.

12. Ibid.

13. Ibid., May 19, 1943, 6. His list of improvements also included that Army trainees be able to march twenty-five miles with only a short rest and to go without sleep for long periods of time. They needed better training in camouflage. He thought the Garand rifle, the M-1, was excellent, but we needed better artillery to match the range of the German 88s.

14. Ibid., May 16, 1943, 35. In review, the tactical defeats of the first three months of the Tunisian campaign developed from a "plug-the-gap" strategy, which was replaced later by the concentration of force that brought the Allied victory in Tunisia in May 1943.

15. *NYT*, May 11, 1943, 1. In Baldwin's view, the American, British, and French forces' "time-consuming" victory over a "small Army of Germans and Italians" who held them at bay delayed for "many months" the ultimate land invasion of Europe.

16. Ibid.

17. Ibid.

18. *Reminiscences*, 384–85. President Roosevelt admired Admiral Stark, who had a direct line to the president when needed. He was a well-informed source. From him, Baldwin learned about antisubmarine tactics, and the kinds of ships needed for the future invasion of Europe, especially landing crafts.

19. *NYT*, May 11, 1943, 1. Earlier, the P-47 Thunderbolt and the P-38 Lightning, with wing tanks, did escort the bombers, but not as far as targets deep within Germany.

20. *NYT*, May 18, 1943, 7.

21. Ibid., May 21, 1943, 6.

22. Ibid., May 22, 1943, 3.

23. Columbia University, New York, commencement booklet, June 1, 1943, 67, Baldwin papers, Yale, series IV, box 30, folder 441. The award came with a $500 cash prize.

24. *Reminiscences*, 367–68.

25. One peculiar feature of that floor was the low railing around the central area where the editorial reference library was located. I am indebted to Dr. John Rothman, former *Times* archivist, who gave me a tour of the tenth floor where Baldwin spent so many of his professional years.

26. "New Voice," *Time*, August 2, 1943, 75.

27. A clipping from *Variety*, July 28, 1943, Baldwin papers, Yale, series 2, box 27, folder 259.

28. E. L. James to Baldwin, July 13, 1943, Baldwin papers, Yale, series 1, box 25, folder 9. Prior to the broadcast, the *Times* management insisted that the paper's name be used to identify Baldwin's professional connection. The management was very reluctant to permit any of its employees to use other media outlets. *Variety* pointed out this restriction, but it gave a favorable review of Baldwin's initial effort, noting that he offered no startling opinions of facts but made observations on Russia, Sicily, and the Pacific that "seemed reasonable" and made several "keen interpretations" of events.

29. Charles C. Barry to Baldwin, September 17, 1943, ibid., series 1, box 1, folder 45. Mr. Barry was eastern program manager for the Blue radio network. The contract's terms were $600 per broadcast for the first twenty-six weeks, then $850 for the following twenty-six weeks and $1,100 for fifty-two weeks.

30. National Concert and Artist Corporation to Baldwin, December 16, 1943. The newsreel was entitled, "Our Third Year at War," Baldwin papers, Yale, series 1, box 24, folder 1082.

31. *NYT*, August 5, 1943, 4.

32. Ibid.

33. Ibid., December 1, 1943, 4.

34. Ibid., August 26, 1943, 9.

35. Ibid., August 28, 1943, 3.

36. Ibid., August 25, 1943, 5.

37. Ibid., August 27, 1943, 5.

38. Ibid., August 28, 1943, 3.

39. Ibid., August 26, 1943, 9.

40. Ibid., November 12, 1943, 8. See also *NYT*, November 24, 1943, 4, for Baldwin's piece on German antipersonnel mines, which the Americans called "Bouncing Bettys."

41. Ibid., August 13, 1943, 4. "The Russians must understand what Britain and America have done and are doing in this war, just as we have understood . . . the courageous and indomitable sacrifices of the Russians."

42. Ibid., August 12, 1943, 5.

43. Ibid., August 21, 1943, 4.

44. Ibid., September 22, 1943, 8.

45. Ibid., September 24, 1943, 4.

46. Ibid., October 14, 1943, 4.

47. Ibid., November 19, 1943, 8.

48. "The Navy's Challenge," editorial, *NYT*, November 23, 1943, 24. The October 1944 Battle of Leyte Gulf was the big naval battle for which the Japanese admirals had long planned.

49. In his view, China's war communiqués were "worthless," claiming victories when there were none, and the only military value of China was its ability to hold down fifteen to twenty-two Japanese divisions that could otherwise be deployed elsewhere in the Pacific.

50. Baldwin, "Too Much Wistful Thinking About China," *Reader's Digest*, August 1943, 63–67.

51. Henry Stimson to Cordell Hull, September 19, 1943, Baldwin papers, George C. Marshall Library, Lexington, Virginia, National Archives Project, verifax 4356.

52. *NYT*, December 2, 1943, 10.

53. Merz to Sulzberger, December 2, 1943, E. L. James papers, *NYT* Archives, roll 58, frame 1755.

54. James to Sulzberger, December 2, 1943, ibid., frame 1756.

55. Sulzberger to James, December 4, 1943, ibid.

56. Merz to Sulzberger, November 17, 1943, A. H. Sulzberger papers, *NYT* Archives. See also Baldwin, "Problems in Russia," *NYT*, November 17, 1943, 5.

57. *NYT*, December 6, 1943, 8.

58. Ibid.

59. James to Baldwin, December 6, 1943, E. L. James papers, *NYT* Archives, roll 58, frame 1758.

60. Sulzberger to Baldwin, December 6, 1943, Sulzberger papers, *NYT* Archives, Baldwin file. See also Sulzberger to Baldwin, Baldwin papers, Yale, series 1, box 1, folder 8.

61. Baldwin to James, December 8, 1943, Sulzberger papers, *NYT* Archives, Baldwin file.

62. Baldwin to Sulzberger, December 8, 1943, ibid.

63. Chet Shaw to Baldwin, February 10, 1943, Baldwin papers, Yale, series 1, box 1, folder 8. Mr. Shaw was the managing editor of *Newsweek*. He told Baldwin that "the door is always open here for discussion for a full-time proposition."

64. Baldwin to Sulzberger, December 9, 1943, Sulzberger papers, *NYT* Archives, Baldwin file.

65. Baldwin to Sulzberger, December 18, 1943, ibid. In a carefully worded letter, the publisher understood the "temptation" of the *Newsweek* offer, with its "added income" incentive, and he approved of Baldwin's writing under a nom de plume for *Newsweek*. He cautioned, however, that Baldwin should be careful not to spread himself too thin by dividing his time between the paper and the magazine. He cautioned that the nom de plume should be real and not "merely an open secret." Interestingly, Sulzberger had always refused to permit Baldwin's pieces to be syndicated, despite repeated requests from other newspaper editors. See also Sulzberger to Baldwin, December 14, 1943, Baldwin papers, Yale, series 1, box 1, folder 8.

Chapter 11 〜 TOTAL WAR, 1944

1. *NYT*, January 31, 1944, 4.

2. Ibid.

3. Ibid., March 2, 1944, 4.

4. Ibid., March 13, 1944, 4.

5. Ibid., March 20, 1944, 6.

6. Ibid.

7. Ibid. Letters from enlisted men alerted him to the problems of ineffective officers. One wrote, "How many times . . . I have heard an officer say to his men, 'Your function is not to think, it is to obey.'" Poor leaders, Baldwin opined, cannot last long in battle and they put their men into harm's way, while good leaders create that "pride of outfit that is the key to morale."

8. Ibid.

9. Ibid.

10. Ibid. See also "The Unfit," *Time*, March 27, 1944, 68, which cited Baldwin's piece of March 20, 1944.

11. *NYT*, May 1, 1944, 4.

12. Ibid., May 11, 1944, 2.

13. Ibid.

14. Ibid. Field Marshall Rommel was the exception. He was convinced that Normandy would be the invasion site. Hitler wavered between both sites, though eventually he agreed with Rommel.

15. Baldwin, "D-Day Remembered: The Greatest Martial Drama in History," *Army*, June 1980, 19–20. This account was based upon his notebooks kept at the time. See also *Reminiscences*, 401. There were women and children on board who were returning home after being evacuated to America in 1940. The crew was inexperienced. The captain had been recalled from retirement and the other officers were drawn from the Royal Navy's Volunteer Reserve.

16. Ibid.

17. *Reminiscences,* 402–3. See also Baldwin, "D-Day Remembered," 20.

18. Baldwin, "D-Day Remembered," 21. Raymond Daniell was the *Times* London bureau chief.

19. *Reminiscences,* 404.

20. Baldwin, "D-Day Remembered," 22.

21. *NYT,* June 6, 1944 (delayed), 6.

22. *Reminiscences,* 406.

23. Daniell (London) to New York, cablegram, June 5, 1944, E. L. James papers, *NYT* Archives, roll 58, frame 1793.

24. Baldwin, "D-Day Remembered," 22. Seventeen years later, Lieutenant Bundy was a special assistant to President John F. Kennedy for national security affairs.

25. Ibid.

26. Ibid.

27. Ibid., 23. At a dinner of steak and mashed potatoes that evening, someone tried to make light about their "last supper" together. The remark was not well received.

28. *Reminiscences*, 409.

29. Ibid.

30. Baldwin, "D-Day Remembered," 24.

31. Ibid.

32. Ibid., 25.

33. *Reminiscences*, 412. See also Baldwin, "D-Day Remembered," 25. *NYT,* June 30, 1944, 6.

34. *Reminiscences*, 419.

35. *NYT,* August 19, 1944, 5.

36. Maj. General A. D. Surles, U.S. Army, to Baldwin, October 12, 1944, Baldwin papers, George C. Marshall Library, Lexington, Virginia, box 8, folder 24. He was in the War Department's public relations department.

37. *NYT*, November 13, 1944, 3.

38. *Reminiscences*, 421.

39. Ibid., 422–25.

40. Ibid., 425–26.

41. Ibid., 427.

42. *NYT*, July 20, 1944 (London), E4. See also, *NYT*, July 26, 1944, 6.

43. Ibid., September 3, 1944, E4.

44. Ibid., August 27, 1944. See also August 28, 1944, 6.

45. Ibid., September 10, 1944, 13.

46. Ibid., September 15, 1944, 4.

47. Ibid., September 22, 1944, 5. See also *NYT*, September 21, 1944, 11.

48. Ibid., October 1, 1944, 12.

49. Ibid., February 22, 1944, 4.

50. Ibid., March 17, 1944, 4.

51. Ibid.

52. Ibid., December 11, 1944, 6.

53. Ibid.

54. Ibid., December 6, 1944, 15.

55. Ibid.

56. *NYT*, December 8, 1944, 4. The Navy needed transport ships, rockets and spare parts, wire cable, and two new types of patrol planes. The Army needed more ammunition, guns, trucks and truck tires, and better tanks to match the German Mark V and VI panzers.

57. Baldwin, "Our Army in Western Europe," *Life*, December 4, 1944, 86–95.

58. Ibid.

59. Ibid.

60. Ibid.

61. Joseph J. Thorndike Jr. to Baldwin, November 22, 1944, Baldwin papers, Yale, series 1, box 8, folder 25.

62. Michael J. Lyons, *World War II: A Short History*, 2nd edition (Englewood Cliffs, NJ: Prentice Hall, 1994), 267–69.

63. "Lesson of War," editorial, *NYT*, December 20, 1944, 22. See also "The Critical Week," editorial, *NYT*, December 24, 1944, 8.

64. *NYT*, January 4, 1945, 4.

65. Ibid., January 5, 1945, 4.

66. Ibid., January 16, 1945, 8.

67. Ibid., September 18, 1944, 9. In October 1944 Washington dismissed General Joseph Stillwell at Chiang's insistence. He had been his chief of staff since 1942, with the mission to develop the Chinese army into an effective fighting force. See *NYT*, October 30, 1944, 4, and Lyons, *World War II*, 295–97.

68. *NYT*, October 30, 1944, 4. See also Lyons, *World War II*, 295–97.

69. *NYT*, December 5, 1944, 13.

70. Ibid.

71. Oswald G. Villard, "The Press and the War News," *Christian Century*, March 1, 1944, 267.

72. Ibid., 258.

73. Ibid., 268.

74. Ibid.

75. Ibid.

76. Baldwin to Villard, March 10, 1944, Villard papers, Houghton Library, Harvard University, Cambridge, Massachusetts, folder 121. Both men exchanged letters until Villard's death in 1949 at age seventy-seven.

77. "Pravda Ridicules Times Writer," *NYT*, April 10, 1944, 3.

78. E. M. Colby to the Editor, April 11, 1944, James papers, *NYT* Archives, roll 54, frame 1858–59.

79. *NYT*, April 9, 1944, 4. See also *NYT*, March 15, 1944, 12.

80. "Odessa Reconquered," editorial, ibid., April 11, 1944, 18.

81. Peter Godfrey to E. L. James, April 10, 1944, James papers, *NYT* Archives, roll 54, frame 1857.

82. Harry A. Johnson to the Editor, April 10, 1944, ibid., frame 1853.

83. Gerald Watson to the Editor, April 10, 1944, ibid.

84. E. Harris to the Editor, April 10, 1944, ibid., frame 1850.

85. Anonymous to the Editor, April 12, 1944, ibid., frame 1787.

86. Abram Waks to the Editor, April 13, 1944, ibid., frame 1848.

87. Sulzberger to Baldwin, April 12, 1944, Baldwin papers, Yale, series 1, box 1, folder 9.

88. *NYT,* March 9, 1944, 6.

89. Ibid.

90. Ibid., March 8, 1944, 5.

Chapter 12 ⌒ 1945: THE ROAD'S END

1. *NYT,* February 7, 1945, 4.

2. Baldwin papers, Yale, series 1, box 20, folder 1020. This folder is filled with other letters of praise for that piece.

3. *NYT,* February 6, 1945, 6.

4. Ibid.

5. By contrast, the German Panther (Mark V), Tiger (Mark VI), and King Tiger tanks had heavier armor and a larger gun (88-mm) with a very high muzzle velocity.

6. Ibid., February 20, 1945, 13.

7. The Pershing had a 90-mm gun that was effective against the Panther and the Tiger tanks, but not against the King Tiger.

8. Ibid., March 29, 1945, 5.

9. Lyons, *World War II,* 374.

10. *NYT,* April 25, 1945, 4.

11. Ibid., April 28, 1945, 4.

12. Ibid., May 14, 1945, 5.

13. Ibid.

14. Peter Young, ed., *The World Almanac Book of World War II* (New York: World Almanac Publications, 1981), 333.

15. *NYT,* February 22, 1945, 4.

16. Ibid., March 5, 1945, 8.

17. Ibid., March 8, 1945, E12.

18. Ibid., March 9, 1945, E6.

19. Ibid., March 30, 1945, 8.

20. Ibid., April 9, 1945, 12.

21. Ibid.

22. Ibid., April 11, 1945, 4.

23. Ibid., August 7, 1945, 1.

24. Ibid., August 8, 1945, 4. See also Baldwin, "The Atom Bomb and Future War," *Life*, August 20, 1945, 17–18 and 20. That article repeated many of his views of his August 8 piece.

25. Ibid., August 22, 1945, 16.

26. Ibid., August 11, 1945, 4.

27. Ibid., August 19, 1945, 12.

28. Ibid.

29. Ibid.

30. Ibid., August 20, 1945, 9.

31. Ibid.

32. Ibid., August 16, 1945, 3.

33. Ibid., October 22, 1945, 4.

34. Ibid., October 23, 1945, 4.

35. Ibid., October 25, 1945, 4. He touched upon, but did not elaborate on, the current issues of the unification of the armed services and the Universal Military Training (UMT) scheme.

36. A similar idea was raised in 1955 at the Geneva Conference with President Eisenhower and Premier Khrushchev. The idea was quickly dropped.

37. *NYT*, October 26, 1945, 4.

38. Ibid.

Chapter 13 ⌒ THE WORLD OF TOMORROW, 1946–49

1. Baldwin, "The World of Tomorrow," address, June 19, 1946, Baldwin papers, Yale, series 1, box 25, folder 1.

2. *NYT*, October 9, 1946, 6.

3. A. H. Sulzberger papers, *NYT* Archives, Baldwin file. See also "Blow the Man Down," *Time*, October 21, 1946, 57–58. George Horne, "3,000 Seamen Demonstrate. Present Protest to the Times," *NYT*, October 11, 1946, 1. The *Daily Worker* put the number of demonstrators at eight thousand.

4. Baldwin to Charles J. V. Murphy, November 30, 1980, Baldwin papers, Yale, series 1, box 10, folder 153.

5. *NYT*, May 24, 1949, 10.

6. Sulzberger to Baldwin, May 14, 1949, memorandum written in crayon, Baldwin papers, Yale, series 1, box 12, folder 581.

7. Baldwin, "Conscription for Peacetime?" *Harper's,* March 1945, 292.

8. Baldwin, "Why I Oppose Universal Military Training," typescript, 1947, Baldwin papers, Yale, series 3, box 21, folder 300. See also Baldwin, "Why I Oppose Universal Military Training," *Reader's Digest*, vol. 51, July 1947, 103–7.

9. Baldwin, "Why I Oppose Universal Military Training," 5.

10. Ibid., 9.

11. Baldwin, "The Military Move In," *Harper's*, December 1947, 488.

12. Ibid., 485.

13. Ibid., 486.

14. Ibid., 489.

15. Saul K. Padover, "The Generals Take Over," *PM*, December 22, 1947, 9–10, Baldwin papers, LC, box 8.

16. "The Military Smear at Work," *Chicago Tribune*, December 17, 1947, 18–19. Baldwin papers, Yale, series 1, box 1, folder 10.

17. Admiral Louis Denfeld, USN, to Baldwin, December 22, 1947, Baldwin papers, LC, box 1.

18. Oswald G. Villard to Baldwin, December 2, 1947, Villard papers, Houghton Library, Harvard University, folder 121.

19. James Morris, *America's Armed Forces: A History* (Englewood Cliffs, NJ: Prentice Hall, 1991), 303. At the end of 1945 the Army had 8 million troops, but in 1950 the Army was down to 591,000 men and women. Navy personnel were down 90 percent by 1950 from where they had been in 1945. The Marines numbered only 75,000 men and officers in 1950, a sharp drop from its wartime strength of 485,000 men.

20. Allan R. Millett and Peter Maslowski, *For the Common Defense: A Military History of the United States of America* (New York: The Free Press, 1984), 480.

21. Morris, *America's Armed Forces*, 304–5. The Air Force was created as a separate but equal service. It did not absorb the naval or Marine air units, nor was the Marine Corps eliminated. The Army did not get the UMT program to provide for a mass force in peacetime. The Navy's mission to protect the seaborne frontier was reaffirmed.

22. Thomas D. Boettcher, *First Call: The Making of the Modern U.S. Military, 1945–1953* (Boston: Little, Brown, and Company, 1992), 172. See also Morris, *America's Armed Forces*, 305.

23. Morris, *America's Armed Forces*, 305. His increasingly erratic behavior showed signs of mental illness. Besides, he was always on the outside of

the Truman administration and was aware that the president wanted him out of his administration. He chose not to publicly support Truman's 1948 campaign. Mr. Truman did not forget this. The president had a long distrust of the career military officers, and of those in the Navy and the Marine Corps in particular.

24. Boettcher, *First Call*, 173.

25. Ibid., 184.

26. Ibid., 180.

27. *Reminiscences,* 489.

28. Ibid.

29. Ibid., 487.

30. Ibid., 467.

31. Baldwin to Edward Woodyard, July 29, 1980, Baldwin papers, Yale, series 1, box 8, folder 106. Rear Admiral Woodyard, USN (Ret.), was in Baldwin's Naval Academy class of 1924. Using only its propeller-driven engines the B-36 cruising speed was only 230 miles per hour, but assisted by the jet engines the plane's speed could be increased to over 400 mph. It was replaced in 1957 with the B-52 bomber.

32. Captain Crommelin statement on the B-36 bomber investigation, 1949, Baldwin papers, Yale, series 1, box 4, folder 167, 5–6.

33. Crommelin to Baldwin, September 7, 1949, ibid.

34. Baldwin to Woodyard, July 29, 1980, ibid.

35. Potter, *Sea Power*, 356.

36. *Reminiscences*, 471.

37. "Admiral Denfeld Shifted," editorial, *NYT*, October 28, 1949.

38. *NYT*, October 31, 1949.

39. Baldwin, "Our Worst Blunders of the War," *Atlantic Monthly*, January 1950, 30.

40. Ibid., 31.

41. Baldwin, "Strategy for Two Atomic Worlds," *Foreign Affairs*, April 1950, 392.

42. Ibid., 397.

43. Bethe to Baldwin, April 16, 1950, Baldwin papers, Yale, series 1, box 1, folder 25.

44. Baldwin, "Conflicts to Defense Policy," *The New York Times Annual In-Service Course for Public School Teachers*, April 4, 1950, 10, ibid., box 25, folder 3.

45. *NYT*, March 30, 1950.

46. Ibid.

47. Baldwin, "Our Worst Blunders of the War," *Atlantic Monthly*, January 1950, 30.

48. Ibid., 31.

49. Ibid., 32.

50. Ibid.

51. Ibid., 32–33.

52. Ibid., 33.

53. Ibid., 37.

54. Ibid., 39.

55. Baldwin, "Our Worst Blunders of the War," *Atlantic Monthly*, February 1950, 30.

56. Ibid.

57. Ibid., 32.

58. Ibid., 34

59. Ibid., 35.

60. Ibid.

61. Ibid., 38. The two articles reappeared in a slightly expanded version with footnotes, as a small book in March 1950, with the less inflammatory title *Great Mistakes of the War*.

62. Baldwin to Walter Lippmann, January 11, 1950, Lippmann papers, Yale, group 326, series 3, box 54, folder 155.

63. Ibid.

64. Ibid.

65. Sir Gerald Campbell to Baldwin, Baldwin papers, Yale, series 4, box 30, folder 438.

66. The fifty-two pages of this file can be found at the George C. Marshall Library, Lexington, Virginia, Baldwin papers, box 3, folder 4.

67. Tifft and Jones, *The Trust*, 154, 191, 254–55. See also taped interview with Barbara Baldwin Potter, April 5, 2005, in author's possession.

Chapter 14 ⌒ KOREA, 1950-53

1. Richard Whelan, *Drawing the Line: The Korean War, 1950–1953* (Boston: Little, Brown and Company, 1990), 182–83.

2. *NYT*, July 17, 1950, 4.

3. Whelan, *Drawing the Line*, 185.

4. Ibid., 189.

5. Ibid., 121.

6. Baldwin, "We're Not the Best in the World," *Saturday Evening Post*, July 15, 1950, 29 and 107–8.

7. Baldwin to Rear Admiral R.W. Ruble, USN, September 5, 1950. He commanded the carrier division 15. Baldwin papers, Yale, series 21, box 20, folder 1023.

8. "G. I. Joe" to Baldwin, n.d., ibid. The writer made specific reference to Baldwin's *Saturday Evening Post* article.

9. *Reminiscences*, 493–94.

10. Ibid., 498–99.

11. William Joseph Sebald, oral history transcript, 1978, U.S. Naval Institute, Annapolis, Maryland, 546. He gave the general's daily schedule as follows: Arrive at the Dai Ichi building, his office, at 11 a.m., leave at 1 p.m., return at 5:30 and stay until 7 or 7:30. He did not travel about the country.

12. *Reminiscences*, 495.

13. *NYT*, March 28, 1951, 4.

14. *Reminiscences*, 497.

15. Ibid., 498.

16. Ibid., 504. See also A. J. Liebling, "The Oracles of Mars," *The New Yorker*, October 28, 1950, 88.

17. A. J. Liebling, "The Oracles of Mars," October 30, 1950, 3.

18. Ibid., October 31, 1950, 4.

19. Ibid.

20. Ibid.

21. Baldwin to Barrett, January 16, 1965, Baldwin papers, Yale, series 1, box 21, folder 51. Years later he tried in vain to find his source. Colonel Barrett, in retirement, could offer little help.

22. Ellen J. Hammer, *The Struggle for Indochina* (Stanford, CA: Stanford University Press, 1954), 179.

23. Ibid., 189.

24. Ibid., 187.

25. Hammer, *The Struggle for Indochina*, 313, note 20a.

26. *NYT*, November 22, 1950, 4.

27. *Reminiscences*, 514.

28. Ibid., 517.

29. Ibid.

30. *NYT*, November 24, 1950, 4.

31. Ibid., December 1, 1950, 4.

32. Sulzberger to Baldwin, memorandum, December 1, 1950, Baldwin papers, Yale, series 1, box 1, folder 12.

33. Burton I. Kaufman, *The Korean War: Challenges in Crisis, Credibility, and Command* (New York: Alfred A. Knopf, 1986), 161.

34. Ibid., 159.

35. *NYT*, April 23, 1951, 6.

36. Ibid., March 30, 1951, 3.

37. Ibid., March 28, 1951, 3.

38. "Truman and MacArthur," editorial, *NYT*, April 12, 1951, 32.

39. Ibid., March 28 and March 29, 1953, 3.

40. Ibid., April 12, 1951, 18.

41. Ibid., May 7, 1951, 4.

42. Ibid. The writer was T. D. Rambaut, Wyckoff, New Jersey.

43. Ibid., April 13, 1951, 7.

44. Ibid., April 16, 1951, 9.

45. Ibid.

46. Kaufman, *The Korean War*, 301.

47. *NYT*, January 23, 1952, 7.

48. Ibid., March 17, 1952, 47. Ibid., April 7, 1952, 7. Baldwin recast this piece on April 11, 1952.

49. The *Times* did print Scotty Reston's piece on the same topic on April 7, 1952. Catledge papers, Mississippi State University, Baldwin file, IIa.

50. Kaufman, *The Korean War*, 306–8.

51. *NYT*, April 21, 1953, 4.

52. Ibid., July 27, 1953, 4.

53. Ibid.

54. Ibid.

55. *NYT*, September 13, 1953, 7.

56. Ibid., October 1, 1953, 7.

Chapter 15 ⌐ THE DEAN OF AMERICAN MILITARY ANALYSTS, 1950s

1. Millett and Maslowski, *For the Common Defense*, 511–12.

2. *Reminiscences*, 454.

3. *NYT*, February 24, 1954, 7.

4. Ibid.

5. Baldwin, "The Place of War in International Relations," a speech, September 25, 1953, Baldwin papers, Yale, series 2, box 25, folder 5. He gave the same speech at the Armed Forces Staff College, June 24, 1954.

6. Baldwin, "Let's Quit Talking Nonsense About the Cold War," *Saturday Evening Post*, September 11, 1954, 25.

7. Ibid.

8. Ibid., 155.

9. Ibid.

10. Ibid., 156.

11. *Reminiscences*, 624–25.

12. Baldwin to Catledge, May 30, 1956, memorandum, Catledge papers, Mississippi State University, Baldwin file, series 11A.

13. *NYT*, June 25, 1956, 4.

14. *Reminiscences*, 630–31.

15. Ibid., 638.

16. Ibid., 635.

17. Ibid., 637.

18. Taped interview with Barbara Baldwin Potter, April 5, 2005, in author's possession.

19. Ibid.

20. Taped interview with Elizabeth Baldwin Crabtree, August 9, 1987, in author's possession.

21. Ivan Veit to A. H. Sulzberger and two others, memorandum, April 13, 1954, Catledge papers, Mississippi State University, Baldwin folder, series 11A. Mr. Veit was an executive in the business end of the paper.

22. B. D. to Hamilton Fish Armstrong, memorandum, December 22, 1949, Armstrong papers, Seeley G. Mudd Manuscript Library, Princeton University, Princeton, New Jersey, box 7.

23. *NYT*, February 2, 1958, 44, 4.

24. Ibid., February 3, 1958, 14, 9.

25. Ibid., February 4, 1958, 16, 7.

26. Walter Lippmann to Baldwin, February 4, 1958, and Baldwin to Lippmann, February 6, 1958, Baldwin papers, Yale, series 3, box 54, folder 155.

27. Samuel P. Huntington to Baldwin, July 16, 1958, ibid., box 7, folder 366.

28. Baldwin, "Limited War," *Atlantic Monthly*, May 1959, 36.

29. Ibid.

30. Ibid., 37.

31. Ibid.

32. Ibid.

33. Ibid.

34. Ibid., 40.

35. Ibid., 41.

36. Ibid., 43.

37. Ibid.

38. *Reminiscences*, 648–52.

39. *Current Biography*, 1965, 82–84.

40. *NYT*, March 19, 1959, 16.

41. Baldwin to Lt. Colonel Albert L. Kotzbue, U.S Army, May 16, 1963, Baldwin papers, Yale, series 1, box 10, folder 143.

42. Walter Sullivan to Baldwin, January 14, 1959, ibid., box 11, folder 168.

43. Baldwin's remarks at the Graduate School of Journalism, Columbia University, New York, January 4, 1960, Oral History Research Office, Butler Library, Columbia University, box 20, 13.

44. Baldwin to Arleigh Albert Burke, March 27, 1959, Baldwin papers, Yale, series 1, box 1, folder 13.

45. Baldwin's remarks, January 4, 1960, Graduate School of Journalism, 15.

46. Ted Bernstein to Baldwin, memorandum, March 19, 1959, Baldwin papers, Yale, series 1, box 1, folder 16.

47. Harrison E. Salisbury to Baldwin, memorandum, March 19, 1959, ibid.

48. Frank S. Adams to Baldwin, memorandum, ibid.

49. Ibid.

50. Ibid.

51. Ibid.

52. *NYT*, April 19, 1959, 5.

53. Baldwin, "Our Fighting Men Have Gone Soft," *Saturday Evening Post*, August 8, 1959, 82.

54. Ibid., 83.

55. Ibid., 84.

56. Ibid.

57. Major General Haydon L. Boatner, U.S. Army, to Baldwin, August 14, 1959, Baldwin papers, Yale, series 1, box 18, folder 944.

58. Carl Vinson to Baldwin, August 6, 1959, ibid. An executive with the Curtis Publishing Company, which printed the *Post*, sent a copy to Jim Hagerty, President Eisenhower's press secretary.

59. Baldwin to Robert K. Baldwin, March 7, 1958, ibid., box 7, folder 44.

60. Baldwin to Eric M. Hammel, September 9, 1968, ibid., box 4, folder 40. See also Baldwin to Arleigh Burke, February 11, 1965, ibid., box 2, folder 102, and Baldwin to R. K. Baldwin, March 7, 1968, ibid., series 1, box 7, folder 44.

61. Taped interview with Hanson Baldwin, June 8, 1989, in author's possession.

62. Ibid.

63. Michael R. Beschloss, *May Day: Eisenhower, Khruschev, and the U-2 Affair* (New York: Harper and Row, 1986), 234.

64. *NYT*, May 9, 1960, 6.

65. Ibid.

66. "The Breast Beaters," editorial, *NYT*, May 14, 1960, 22.

67. Beschloss, *May Day*, 453.

68. *NYT*, May 15, 1960, E4.

69. Ibid.

70. Ibid.

71. Ibid.

Chapter 16 ⌒ THE WINDS OF CHANGE: THE *TIMES* AND WASHINGTON, 1961–66

1. *Reminiscences*, 544.

2. Ibid., 544–55.

3. Ibid., 546.

4. Ibid.

5. Ibid., 545 and 547.

6. Ibid., 546–47.

7. Ibid., 547.

8. Tifft and Jones, *The Trust*, 287–88.

9. *Reminiscences*, 548.

10. Ibid. See also, Talese, *The Kingdom and the Power*, 285.

11. Orvil Dryfoos to Catledge, memorandum, June 12, 1953, Catledge papers, Mississippi State University, series 11A.

12. H. E. Salisbury to E. C. Daniel, memorandum, March 20, 1962, Catledge papers, Mississippi State University, Baldwin file, IIc.

13. Catledge to Dryfoos, March 20, 1962, ibid.

14. Catledge memorandum for the file, March 27, 1962, Catledge papers, ibid.

15. Salisbury to E. C. Daniel, memorandum, March 28, 1962, Catledge papers, ibid.

16. Baldwin to Dryfoos, memorandum, labeled personal, June 20, 1962, Baldwin papers, Yale, series 1, box 10, folder 154.

17. Ibid., 3.

18. E. C. Daniel, memorandum for the file, June 29, 1962, Daniel papers, *NYT* Archives, Baldwin file.

19. Ibid.

20. Interview with Harrison Salisbury, February 6, 1986. He was on the campus of Moorhead State University, Moorhead, Minnesota, for a lecture. The notes of that interview are in author's possession.

21. Frank Friedel to Baldwin, July 11, 1960, Baldwin papers, Yale, series 1, box 23, folder 1064.

22. Dryfoos to "Time Employees Now at Work," January 7, 1963, Baldwin papers, Yale, series 1, box 10, folder 154.

23. Tifft and Jones, *The Trust*, 369.

24. Ibid., 375. The quoted words are those of Arthur's daughter, Ruth Rachel Sulzberger.

25. Ibid., 376.

26. Ibid., 379–80.

27. *Reminiscences*, 549–50.

28. Talese, *The Kingdom and the Power*, 336.

29. Baldwin to Colonel Trevor N. Dupuy, U.S. Army (Ret.), December 13, 1963, Baldwin papers, Yale, series 1, box 4, folder 209.

30. *Reminiscences*, 551. See Richard Kluger, *The Paper: The Life and Death of the New York Herald Tribune* (New York: Alfred A. Knopf, 1986), 732.

31. Baldwin's comments on the Yankelovich questionnaire, September 1966, Baldwin papers, Yale, series 1, box 10, folder 154.

32. Daniel Yankelovich to the staff of the *New York Times*, September 1966, ibid.

33. Max Frankel, *The Times of My Life* (New York: Random House, 1999), 372. See also, Talese, *The Kingdom and the Power*, 318–19, and Tifft and Jones, *The Trust*, 324.

34. *Reminiscences*, 550.

35. Taped interview with Baldwin, June 22, 1985. The tape is in author's possession.

36. Baldwin to Willis Wing, April 14, 1963, Baldwin papers, Yale, series 1, box 19, folder 980.

37. Taped interview with Baldwin, July 10, 1986, in author's possession.

38. *Reminiscences*, 691. Baldwin knew nothing about him other than Robert Lovett, President Truman's last secretary of defense, had recommended McNamara to Kennedy without actually knowing much about him.

39. Ibid., 692.

40. Ibid., 693.

41. Ibid.

42. *NYT*, March 27, 1961, 6.

43. *NYT*, March 28, 1961, 9.

44. Ibid.

45. Ibid.

46. Ibid.

47. Ibid. Under the pre-1961 system, dissents from factual estimates were put in footnotes and the "nature of dissent and the reasons for it is given."

48. Ibid.

49. *NYT*, April 10, 1961, 16.

50. Ibid.

51. Ibid., 16.

52. *NYT*, March 20, 1961, 5.

53. Ibid.

54. Baldwin's review, Herman Kahn, *Thinking About the Unthinkable* (New York: Horizon Press, 1962). The review appeared in the U.S. Naval Institute *Proceedings*, November 1962, 126.

55. Ibid.

56. Ibid.

57. *NYT*, March 18, 1961, 5.

58. Ibid.

59. *NYT*, August 14, 1961, 4.

60. Ibid.

61. *NYT*, November 8, 1961, 16.

62. Ibid., 4.

63. Ibid., November 12, 1961, 45.

64. Ibid., July 26, 1962, 2.

65. President Kennedy's remarks at the President's Foreign Intelligence Advisory Board, August 1, 1962. Timothy Nafalti, ed., *John F. Kennedy's The Great Crises*, I (New York: Norton Company, 2001), 189. The United States preferred vertical underground silos for its ICBMs.

66. Edwin O. Guthman and Jeffrey Shulman, *Robert Kennedy in His Own Words* (New York: Bantam Books, 1988), 304–5. See also Robert Kennedy oral history transcript, April 1964, 154. Kennedy Archives, Columbia Point, Boston, Massachusetts. The interviewer was John B. Martin, the former U.S. ambassador to the Dominican Republic, 1962–64.

67. *NYT*, July 26, 1962, 1.

68. Ibid.

69. Baldwin to Krock, November 7, 1962, Arthur Krock papers, Seeley G. Mudd Manuscript Library, Princeton University, Princeton, New Jersey, box 17.

70. FBI file, section 1, 50.

71. *Reminiscences*, 750. See also Baldwin, "Memorandum for the Record-Confidential," August 9–14, 1962, Baldwin papers, Yale, series 1, box 10, folder 154. See same memo in the E. Clifton Daniel papers, *NYT* Archives. The lateness of their visit, their aggressive manner, and their insistent questions were a frightening experience for her, having never been interviewed by the FBI. They told her that they were conducting a private investigation for the attorney general, who did not want anything to get into the papers. When she could not recall the names offhand, she said that the list was in her office at the *Times* Washington bureau. The agents told her to get this list and to use an outside telephone coin box, not her office phone. They also wanted to know which hotel Baldwin stayed at and which telephone line he used.

72. D. E Moore to W. C. Sullivan, July 31, 1962, FBI file, section 12, 27. In 1987 Baldwin made a FOIPA request for his FBI file at my urging. In 1989 the FBI released the file. In 2000 I made another FOIPA request following the death of Baldwin and his wife Helen. The file, received in 2001, is 235 pages longer than the 1989 file. All subsequent references to Baldwin's FBI file will be to the 2001 version, which is 970 pages in length.

73. Hoover to Robert Kennedy, July 31, 1962, FBI file, section 1, 56.

74. FBI file, July 30, 1962, 1, 60.

75. FBI telephone wiretap transcript, July 30, 1962, 1, 62.

76. Ibid., 64.

77. Baldwin, "Memorandum for the Record," August 9–14, 1962, 2.

78. Ibid.

79. Ibid., 3.

80. Ibid.

81. Ibid., 4.

82. Ibid. An attachment to Baldwin's "Memorandum," 5.

83. W. R. Wannall to W. C. Sullivan, August 1, 1962, FBI file, 1, 144. Sullivan was the FBI's assistant director of domestic intelligence division. Baldwin's telephone was tapped at his home in Chappaqua, New York, for a month. His office manager and research assistant for many years, Edward Mossien, was tracked down by FBI agents at his summer vacation home at Winnesquam, New Hampshire. He provided no help to the agents, other than to say that his boss wrote his own pieces and did not discuss sources with anyone.

84. FBI file, 1, 152.

85. Major General Chester V. Clifton, U.S. Army interview, August 6, 1962, FBI file, section 1, 79.

86. August 1, 1962, interview, FBI file, section 1, 136. Arthur Sylvester, assistant secretary of defense for information, commented that Baldwin was "a loner" who remained "aloof" from other correspondents and whose bias was pro-Navy and anti-McNamara because of the centralizing policies of the secretary. As our involvement in the Vietnam War increased after 1963, the hostility between Baldwin and Sylvester increased.

87. Hoover to Robert Kennedy, August 21, 1962, FBI file, section 1, 331.

88. FBI file, section 2, 105.

89. Baldwin to Mark Potter, August 18, 1962, telephone wiretap transcript, FBI file, section 3, 31–33. Who was Baldwin's source? His voluminous

FBI file does not reveal a name. Because of privacy rules, there are many passages that are redacted. During my interviews, he always refused to name his sources other than to say that it was a high-level person in the government. In 1988 the Kennedy Library sent me a transcript of Robert Kennedy's oral history interviews made in 1964 and 1965. The name I sought was "restricted." In 2005 I asked again and received a clean transcript of the page in question.

90. Hoover to Robert Kennedy, August 3, 1962, FBI file, section 1, 165–66.
91. Fletcher Knebel, "Kennedy vs. the Press," *Look,* August 28, 1962, 18. Robert Kennedy revealed that when the FBI investigation pointed to Gilpatric. President Kennedy wanted to fire him, but McNamara was "reluctant" to do so, as he had been useful to the administration. Gilpatric intended to resign, in March 1963, but the TFX controversy delayed his leaving until January 1964. The Boeing Company's bid had been the favorite choice of many in the Pentagon.
92. Baldwin, "Notes on the Problem of Freedom vs. Security," September 6, 1962, E. Clifton Daniel papers, *NYT* Archives, 1.
93. Ibid.
94. Ibid.
95. Ibid., 1–2.
96. Ibid., 2.
97. Ibid.
98. Ibid.
99. Ibid., 4.
100. Ibid.
101. Ibid., 5.
102. Ibid., 6.
103. Ibid., 5. Robert Kennedy correctly concluded that the investigation was the reason why Baldwin became so "bitter" toward the president. Many of Baldwin's remarks to the *Times* editors in 1962 later reappeared in his long article in the *Atlantic Monthly*, where he accused the "vigorous and cocky" Kennedy administration of "astonishing" examples of "news repression and distortions, management and control, and pressures and propaganda" on newspapermen.
104. Robert Kennedy oral history transcript, 154 and 521, Kennedy Library, Boston.
105. Baldwin, "Managed News," *Atlantic Monthly,* April 1963, 53–54.
106. Ibid., 63.

107. Ibid. 57.

108. Ibid., 58.

109. Ibid.

110. Ibid., 59.

111. Ibid., 56.

112. Ibid.

113. Baldwin, "Managed News: Our Peacetime Censorship," typescript, January 1963, 10, Baldwin papers, Yale, series 3, box 21, folder 304. Those ideas were omitted from the April 1963 published article.

114. Ibid.

115. Baldwin, "Speaking Out—the McNamara Monarchy," *Saturday Evening Post*, March 9, 1963, 11. See also Baldwin, "Managed News," *Atlantic Monthly*, March 9, 1963, 53–59.

116. Baldwin, "One Voice in the Pentagon?" typescript, Baldwin papers, Yale, series 1, box 22, folder 328.

117. Sebald to Baldwin, March 6, 1963, Yale, series 1, box 14, folder 72. See also *The Army, Navy, Air Force Journal and Register*, May 11, 1963, 4. This clipping is in the Baldwin papers, Yale, series 5, box 139.

118. Admiral Charles D. Griffin, USN (Ret.), oral history transcript, 1970, U.S. Naval Institute, 542 and 531. He was the deputy chief of naval operations, 1962–63.

Chapter 17 ⌐ DUTY AND DESPAIR: THE VIETNAM WAR, 1962-68

1. *NYT*, April 20, 1945, 11.

2. Baldwin, "The Effect of Foreign Policy and Public Opinion on Military Strategy," May 6, 1954, a speech given at the Air War College, Baldwin papers, Yale, series 2, box 125 folder 6.

3. Baldwin, "Critical Tomorrows," U.S. Naval Institute *Proceedings*, December 1962, 23.

4. Baldwin, "The Proper Use of Power to Preserve Peace," *Reader's Digest*, September 1962, 119.

5. Baldwin to John Bertram. Oakes, memorandum, June 1, 1965, Baldwin papers, Yale, series 1, box 11, folder 573.

6. Bernard Fall to Baldwin, June 9, 1963, ibid., box 18, folder 1064.

7. John Paul Vann to Baldwin, September 23, 1963, ibid., box 18, folder 940.

8. Ibid.

9. Baldwin to Sulzberger and others, April 13, 1964, E. Clifton Daniel papers, *NYT* Archives, Baldwin file, 1 and 3.

10. Ibid., 3

11. Baldwin to Oakes, memorandum, April 17, 1964, Baldwin papers, Yale, series 1, box 11, folder 573.

12. Baldwin, a speech, April 30, 1964, Baldwin papers, ibid., box 25, folder 10.

13. Ibid.

14. Baldwin, "United States Global Strategy," June 11, 1964, an address given at the sixteenth global strategy discussions at the U.S. Naval War College, Newport, R.I., Baldwin papers, Yale, series 2, box 25, p. 10.

15. Ibid., 11.

16. Baldwin to Oakes, December 11, 1964, Baldwin papers, Yale, series 1, box 11, folder 10. One of the editorials that bothered Baldwin was entitled "Morality Is Realism," *NYT*, December 12, 1964, 30.

17. James Reston, "Washington: The Agonies of Vietnam," February 21, 1965, *NYT*, IV, 8.

18. George Donelson Moss, *Vietnam: An American Ordeal*, 3rd edition (Upper Saddle River, NJ: Prentice Hall, 1998), 181. The president's words were attributed to Jack Valenti, an aide.

19. Ibid., 180–82. He had promised that he sought no wider war during the 1964 presidential campaign against Barry Goldwater.

20. Ibid., 182.

21. Hanson W. Baldwin, "We Must Choose—(1) Bug Out (2) Negotiate (3) Fight," February 21, 1965, *NYT Magazine*, 9.

22. Ibid.

23. Ibid., note 9.

24. Ibid.

25. Ibid.

26. Ibid., 32.

27. Ibid.

28. Ibid., 63.

29. Ibid.

30. Ibid.

31. Ibid.

32. Frankel, *The Times of My Life and My Life With the Times*, 263 and 265.

33. Beschloss, ed., *Reaching for Glory*, 194. In a telephone conversation with Robert McNamara on February 26, 1965, the president said, "I don't think anything is going to be as bad as losing and I don't see any way of winning."

34. "The Debate on Vietnam," editorial, February 21, 1965, *NYT*, E8. See also *Time*, July 23, 1965, 60.

35. "Alarming Distortion," letter to the editor, March 14, 1965, *NYT*, VI, 16.

36. Ron Smith to Edward Mossien, March 2, 1965, Baldwin papers, Yale, series 1, box 22, folder 1040. Mr. Mossien was Baldwin's office manager and assistant since 1943. General Greene to Arthur Ochs Sulzberger, February 25, 1965, Catledge papers, Mitchell Memorial Library, Mississippi State University, Baldwin file, series IIC. A total of 144 letters were received; 88 percent were opposed to Baldwin, while only 12 percent were in favor. The highest-ranking officer who praised Baldwin's expert "acute appraisal of the situation" was General Wallace M. Greene Jr., the commandant of the U.S. Marine Corps (1964–68).

37. Hilsman to the *Times* editors, February 25, 1965, Baldwin papers, Yale, series 1, box 10, folder 140.

38. "Vietnam: Looking Back," editorial, March 30, 1973, *Wall Street Journal*, 8.

39. *NYT*, June 14, 1965, 8.

40. Baldwin to Oakes, memorandum, June 22, 1965, John B. Oakes private file on Hanson Baldwin. See also Baldwin papers, Yale, series 1, box 11, folder 573.

41. Ibid.

42. Frankel to Catledge, memorandum, August 9, 1965, Catledge papers, Mississippi State University, ibid., series 11, C/D Vietnam, 1962–68.

43. Baldwin, "Vietnam: New Policy in the Making," August, 12, 1965, *The Reporter*, 16.

44. Ibid., 19.

45. Ibid.

46. Ibid., 20

47. Arthur Ochs Sulzberger to Catledge, memorandum, February 9, 1965, Catledge papers, Mississippi State University, Baldwin file, series 11C. The publisher had urged him for months to make the trip, but the continuing illness of his younger daughter, Elizabeth, had delayed his departure.

48. *NYT*, December 26, 1965, 1.

49. *NYT*, December 27, 1965, 10.

50. For Baldwin's detailed comments on the editing of his pieces, see Baldwin papers, Yale, series 2, box 27, folders 30–32.

51. "Silencing the Guns," editorial, *NYT*, December 23, 1965, 26.

52. Baldwin to E. C. Daniel, memorandum, January 7, 1966, E. Clifton Daniel papers, *NYT* Archives, Vietnam file, 1965–70.

53. Baldwin to E. C. Daniel, memorandum, February 3, 1966, ibid.

54. Baldwin to Sulzberger and John Oakes, memorandum, January 10, 1966, Oakes private file on Baldwin.

55. Ibid.

56. "The Vietnam Commitment," editorial, February 20, 1966, *NYT*, 6, 12E.

57. Baldwin, "The Information War in Saigon," February 24, 1966, *The Reporter*, 31.

58. Baldwin, "The Case for Escalation," February 27, 1966, *NYT Magazine*, 79.

59. Ibid., 81.

60. Baldwin to Edward Fitch Hall, July 11, 1967, Baldwin papers, Yale, series 1, box 3, folder 37.

61. Ibid.

62. Baldwin to Daniel, memorandum, December 27, 1966, E. Clifton Daniel papers, *NYT* Archives, Baldwin file.

63. Ibid.

64. *NYT*, December 27, 1966, 23.

65. "The Truce Ends," editorial, *NYT*, December 27, 1966, 34.

66. Baldwin to Daniel, memorandum, December 27, 1966, Daniel papers, *NYT* Archives.

67. Moss, *Vietnam: An American Ordeal*, 242.

68. George C. Herring, *America's Longest War: The United States and Vietnam, 1950–1975*, 3rd edition (New York: McGraw-Hill, 1996), 198.

69. Baldwin to Abe Raskin, memorandum, August 10, 1967, Baldwin papers, Yale, series 1, box 10, folder 155.

70. Ibid.

71. Ibid.

72. Ibid., 4.

73. Ibid.

74. Ibid.

75. Baldwin, "A Vietnam Balance Sheet," *The Reporter*, October 19, 1967, 18.

76. Herring, *America's Longest War*, 198–99.

77. Ibid. See also Moss, *Vietnam: An American Ordeal*, 246.

78. Bruce E. Jones to Baldwin, November 11, 1986, Baldwin papers, Yale, series 1, Box 10, folder 143.

79. *NYT*, December 26, 1967, 18.

80. Ibid., December 26, 1967, 16.

81. Ibid.

82. Ibid., December 27, 1967, 22.

83. Ibid., December 28, 1967, 16.

84. Worthington to Baldwin, December 28, 1967, Baldwin papers, Yale, series 1, box 32, folder 38.

85. Ibid., July 13, 1966 (or 1968), Baldwin papers, Yale, series 1, box 3, folder 43.

86. General William C. Westmoreland to Baldwin, January 17, 1968, Baldwin papers, ibid., folder 42.

87. Sidle to Baldwin, January 16, 1968, Lester Markel papers, The State Historical Society of Wisconsin, Madison, Wisconsin. When I used this collection in 1987, no box or folder number had been assigned. The call number for this collection is MCHC77–005.

88. Baldwin to Markel, January 19, 1968, Markel papers, ibid.

89. Peter Braestrup, *Big Story*, abridged edition (New Haven, CT: Yale University Press, 1978), 439.

90. Sulzberger to Baldwin, January 15, 1968, Baldwin papers, Yale, series 1, box 3, folder 43.

91. Baldwin to Arleigh Burke, November 11, 1968, ibid., box 4, folder 52.

92. Walter Cronkite, *A Reporter's Life* (New York: Alfred A. Knopf, 1966), 257–58.

93. *NYT,* February 3, 1968, 10.

94. Clark Clifford, *Counsel to the President: A Memoir* (New York: Random House, 1991), 517.

95. Baldwin to Sulzberger, September 15, 1967, Baldwin papers, Yale, series 1, box 10, folder 154.

96. Oakes to Baldwin, memorandum, October 4, 1967, A. H. Sulzberger papers, *NYT* Archives, Baldwin, file, 1933–67.

97. Baldwin to A. H. Sulzberger, September 19, 1967, A. H. Sulzberger papers, *NYT* Archives, Baldwin file, 1933–67.

98. Baldwin to Sulzberger, February 1, 1967, ibid.

99. Baldwin to E. C. Daniel, February 19, 1968, Baldwin papers, ibid.

100. Baldwin to Dabney, September 9, 1976, Baldwin papers, George C. Marshall Library, Lexington, Virginia, box 7, folder 20.

Chapter 18 ⌒ AN OLD-FASHIONED FELLOW, 1969-80s

1. Mark Skinner Watson, *The War Department: Chief of Staff: Prewar Plans and Preparations* (Washington, D.C.: Government Printing Office, 1950), 12.

2. Hanson W. Baldwin, *Strategy for Tomorrow* (New York: Harper and Row, 1970), 12.

3. Ibid., 17.

4. *Reminiscences*, 725 and 729.

5. Interview with Vincent Demma, June 1987. He was a staff member at the U.S. Army Center of Military History, who specialized in the U.S. Army in Vietnam. See also Lewis Sorley, *Honorable Warrior: General Harold K. Johnson and the Ethics of Command* (Lawrence: University Press of Kansas, 1998), 213. The story behind that decision occurred on July 28, 1965, at Camp David, where two influential U.S. senators, Richard Russell and John Stennis, convinced the president not to call up the Reserves. A call-up would lead to a congressional debate on our policy in Vietnam. They argued also that the Reserves had a limited military value in war, and that they could only be mobilized for one year of active military duty. Their most telling argument was the precedent set in 1961 of the hostile public reaction of Reservists and their families, who wrote to members of Congress when called to active duty by President Kennedy during the Berlin Wall crisis.

6. Sorley, *Honorable Warrior*, 213.

7. Baldwin, written testimony, November 20, 1969, Baldwin papers, Yale, series 1, box 6, folder 67, 1 and 4. In July 1969 Melvin Laird, secretary of defense, appointed the Blue Ribbon Defense Panel to assess the Pentagon's procurement practices and to recommend reforms. Baldwin was asked to submit written testimony to the panel.

8. Ibid., 4A.

9. *Reminiscences*, 704.

10. Ibid.

11. Ibid., 705, and Baldwin, *Strategy*, 41.

12. Baldwin, *Strategy*, 30.

13. Ibid., 31–32.

14. Ibid., 32.

15. Baldwin to Rosenthal, April 27, 1970, Baldwin papers, series 1, box 8, folder 70. See also Rosenthal to Baldwin, April 22, 1970, ibid.

16. His previous ties to the magazine were largely through his friendship with Hobart Lewis, its senior editor. Though he submitted a number of articles to the magazine, not many were published. In truth, he was never comfortable with the punchy writing style of that magazine, which limited his ability to elaborate.

17. Baldwin to Markel, May 24, 1977, Baldwin papers, Yale, series 1, box 10, folder 148.

18. Baldwin, "Where Have the Flowers Gone?" *Shipmate*, September–October 1970, 7.

19. Ibid., 8.

20. Baldwin to General Wallace M. Greene Jr., USMC (Ret.), *Reminiscences*, appendix. He was the commandant of the U.S. Marine Corps, 1964–68.

21. Baldwin, *Shipmate*, 9–10.

22. Ibid., 13.

23. Baldwin to Burke, August 28, 1969, Baldwin papers, Yale, series 1, box 8, folder 93.

24. Baldwin to Mr. Dempsey, March 19, 1968, ibid., box 3, folder 42.

25. Baldwin, "The Best and Brightest?" *Intercollegiate Review*, Winter 1973–74, 44.

26. Ibid., 46.

27. Ibid., 47.

28. Ibid., 48.

29. Ibid., 49.

30. Ibid., 50.

31. Ibid.

32. William L. Kostar to Baldwin, June 9, 1974, Yale, series 1, box 10, folder 143. See Baldwin to Rosenthal, April 27, 1970, ibid.

33. Baldwin to "Ted," September 29, 1970, ibid., box 6, folder 73. See also Baldwin to Rosenthal, April 27, 1970, ibid.

34. Baldwin to David B. Benham, April 2, 1977, Baldwin papers, George C. Marshall Library, Lexington, Virginia, box 7, folder 16.

35. Baldwin, "Troubled Waters in the Navy," *Saturday Evening Post*, May 1974, 52–57 passim.

36. Baldwin to David B. Benham, April 12, 1977, Baldwin papers, George C. Marshall Library, Lexington, Virginia, box 7, folder 16. He was the president of the U.S. Naval Academy Alumni Association.

37. Baldwin, "On US Intelligence," *NYT*, May 5, 1975, op-ed page.

38. Ibid.

39. Lester Markel to Baldwin, May 21, 1975, Baldwin papers, Yale, series 1, box 8, folder 99.

40. David Rockefeller to Baldwin, May 12, 1975, ibid. He was the chairman and chief executive officer of the Chase Manhattan Bank.

41. *Reminiscences*, 770–71. See also Baldwin to Lester Markel, May 24, 1975, Baldwin papers, Yale, series 1, box 8, folder 99.

42. Baldwin to Joseph Worthington, June 7, 1977, Worthington family papers. See also Baldwin to Worthington, February 4, 1978, and September 14, 1977.

43. Ibid., September 14, 1977.

44. Baldwin to Captain Paul B. Ryan, USN (Ret.), October 13, 1975, Baldwin papers, Yale, series 1, box 8, folder 100.

45. Baldwin, "The Panama Canal: Sovereignty and Security," *AEI Defense Review*, October 1977, 33–34.

46. *Time*, August 23, 1977, 11.

47. Jeff Potter to Barbara Potter, n.d. This recollection is from the Baldwin/ Potter family papers. I am thankful to Mrs. Potter for this and other family records.

48. Ibid.

49. Ibid.

50. Baldwin to Joe Worthington, July 7, 1986, Worthington family papers.

51. Ibid., September 10, 1984.

52. Ibid., July 23–25, 1975, Worthington family papers.

53. Ibid., April 29, 1986.

54. Baldwin to Kathy Worthington, November 4, 1986, Worthington family papers. The verse is by Algernon Charles Swinburne (1837–1909) from his "The Garden of Proserpine," (1865), Louis Untermeyer, ed., *Modern British Poetry: A Critical Anthology*, 3rd ed., rev. (New York: Harcourt Brace and Company, 1930), 100.

55. His wife, Helen, died on June 1, 1994, at the age of eighty-seven.

56. Taped interview with Hanson Baldwin, July 10, 1986, in author's possession.

Selected Bibliography

MANUSCRIPT SOURCES

Enoch Pratt Free Library, Special Collections, Baltimore, Maryland
H.L Mencken papers
Oliver Perry Baldwin papers

Houghton Library, Harvard University
Oswald Garrison Villard papers
John Mason Brown papers

John Fitzgerald Kennedy Library, Columbia Point, Massachusetts
Robert F. Kennedy oral history

Library of Congress, Manuscript Division, Washington, D.C.
Bernard L. Austin papers
Hanson W. Baldwin papers
Alan G. Kirk papers
William D. Leahy papers
Elwood R. Quesada papers
Nathan F. Twining papers
Thomas D. White papers

**Mitchell Memorial Library, Mississippi State University,
Starkville, Mississippi**
Turner Catledge papers
Turner Catledge oral history

New York Times Archives, New York, New York
Edwin Leland James papers
Arthur Hays Sulzberger papers
E. Clifton Daniel papers
John Bertram Oakes papers

**Princeton University, Seeley G. Mudd Manuscript Library,
Princeton, New Jersey**
Hamilton Fish Armstrong papers
Bernard Baruch papers

Allen W. Dulles papers
John Foster Dulles papers
Ferdinand Eberstadt papers
James V. Forrestal papers
Arthur Krock papers

Syracuse University Library, Department of Special Collections, Syracuse, New York
Robert Lee Sherrod papers
Thomas D. White papers
John S. Wood papers

United States Naval Academy, Nimitz Library, Special Collections Department
Hanson W. Baldwin papers

United States Naval Institute, Oral History Program, Annapolis, Maryland
Bernard L. Austin
Hanson W. Baldwin
Arleigh A. Burke
Charles D. Griffin
Fitzhugh Lee
Charles J. Moore
William J. Sebald
Joseph M. Worthington

University of Illinois at Urbana—Champagne, Illinois
James B. Reston papers

Virginia Historical Society, Richmond, Virginia
Oliver Perry Baldwin papers

Yale University, Sterling Memorial Library, Manuscripts and Archives Division, New Haven, Connecticut
All *New York Times* and *Baltimore Sun* articles not found elsewhere
    were accessed here.
Hanson W. Baldwin papers
Hugh Byas papers
Walter Lippmann papers

BOOKS, ARTICLES, AND DISSERTATIONS

Alden, John D. *Flush Decks and Four Pipes.* Annapolis: U.S. Naval Institute Press, 1965.

Baer, George W. *One Hundred Years of Sea Power: The U.S. Navy, 1890–1990.* Stanford: Stanford University Press, 1994.

Baldwin, Hanson W. *Sea Fights and Shipwrecks: True Tales of the Seven Seas.* Garden City, NY: Hanover House, 1938.

———. *The Caissons Roll: A Military Survey of Europe.* New York: Alfred A. Knopf, 1938.

———. *Great Mistakes of the War.* New York: Harper and Brothers, 1950.

———. *Battles Lost and Won: Great Campaigns of World War II.* New York: Konecky and Konecky, 1966.

———. *Strategy for Tomorrow.* New York: Harper and Row, 1970.

———. "America Rearms," *Foreign Affairs* (April 1938).

———. "Our New Long Shadow," *Foreign Affairs* (April 1939).

———. "The New American Army," *Foreign Affairs* (October 1940).

———. "U.S. Air Power," *Fortune* (March 1941).

———. "Blueprint for Victory," *Life* (August 4, 1941).

———. "Impregnable America," *The American Mercury* (July 1939).

———. "Too Much Wistful Thinking About China," *Reader's Digest* (August 1943).

———. "Our Army in Western Europe," *Life* (December 4, 1944).

———. "Conscription for Peacetime?" *Harper's* (March 1945).

———. "The Military Move In," *Harper's* (December 1947).

———. "Our Worst Blunders of the War," *Atlantic Monthly* (January and February 1950).

———. "Strategy for Two Atomic Worlds," *Foreign Affairs* (April 1950).

———. "We're Not the Best in the World," *Saturday Evening Post* (July 15, 1950).

———. "Let's Quit Talking Nonsense About the Cold War," *Saturday Evening Post* (September 11, 1954).

———. "Limited War," *Atlantic Monthly* (May 1959).

———. "Our Fighting Men Have Gone Soft," *Saturday Evening Post* (August 8, 1959).

———. "The Proper Use of Power to Preserve Peace," *Reader's Digest* (September 1962).

———. "Critical Tomorrows," U.S. Naval Institute *Proceedings* (December 1962).

———. "Speaking Out—The McNamara Monarchy," *Saturday Evening Post* (March 9, 1963).

———. "Managed News," *Atlantic Monthly* (March 1963).

———."Vietnam: New Policy in the Making," *The Reporter* (August 12, 1965).

———."The Information War in Vietnam," *The Reporter* (February 24, 1966).

———."A Vietnam Balance Sheet," *The Reporter* (October 19, 1967).

———."The Best and Brightest?" *Intercollegiate Review* (Winter 1973–74).

———."Troubled Waters in the Navy," *Saturday Evening Post* (May 1974).

———."The Panama Canal: Sovereignty and Security," *AEI Defense Review* (October 1977).

———."D-Day Remembered: The Greatest Martial Drama in History," *Army* (June 1980).

Benning, Kendall. *Annapolis Today.* New York: Funk and Wagnalls Company, 1938.

Berger, Meyer. *The Story of the New York Times, 1851–1951.* New York: Simon and Schuster, 1951.

Beschloss, Michael R. *May Day: Eisenhower, Khruschev and the U-2 Affair.* New York: Harper and Row, 1986.

———.*Reaching for Glory: Lyndon Johnson's Secret White House Tapes, 1964–1965.* New York: Simon and Schuster, 2001.

Boettcher, Thomas D. *First Call: The Making of the Modern U.S. Military, 1945–1953.* Boston: Little, Brown and Company, 1992.

Boyer, Paul. *By the Bomb's Early Light: American Thought and Culture at the Dawn of the Atomic Age.* New York: Pantheon Books, 1985.

Braestrup, Peter. *Big Story.* (Abridged edition.) New Haven: Yale University Press, 1978.

Braley, Russ. *Bad News: The Foreign Policy of the New York Times.* Chicago: Regnery Gateway, 1984.

Buck, Tom. *Jack Williams and Boys' Latin School, 1926–1978.* Baltimore: Gateway Press, Inc. 1983.

Burlingame, Roger. *Don't Let Them Scare You: The Life and Times of Elmer Davis.* Philadelphia: J. B. Lippincott Company, 1961.

Buzzanco, Robert. *Masters of War: Military Dissent and Politics in the Vietnam Era.* Cambridge: Cambridge University Press, 1996.

Carruth, Gorton, ed. *The Encyclopedia of American Facts and Dates.* 6th ed. New York: Crowell, 1972.

Catledge, Turner. *My Life and the Times.* New York: Harper & Row, 1971.

Clifford, Clark. *Counsel to the President: A Memoir.* New York: Random House, 1991.

Cohen, Bernard C. *The Press and Foreign Policy.* Princeton: Princeton University Press, 1963.

Coletta, Paolo E. *The American Naval Heritage in Brief.* Washington: University Press of America, 1978.

Collier, Richard. *Fighting Words: The War Correspondents of World War Two*. New York: St. Martin's Press, 1989.

Cronkite, Walter. *A Reporter's Life*. New York: Alfred A. Knopf, 1996.

The Cruise of the Class of 1924. Annapolis: U.S. Naval Academy, 1974.

Current Biography. New York: H. W. Wilson Company.

Dawson, Joseph G., ed.. *Commanders in Chief: Presidential Leadership in Modern Wars*. Lawrence: University Press of Kansas, 1993.

Dizer, John T., Jr. *Tom Swift and Company: Boys Books by Stratemeyer and Others*. Jefferson, NC: McFarland and Company, 1982.

Emery, Michael C., and Edwin Emery. *The Press in America*, 6th edition. New York: Prentice Hall, 1988.

Ferrell, Robert H. *The Diary of James C. Hagerty: Eisenhower in Mid-Course 1954–1955*. Bloomington: Indiana University Press, 1983.

Frank, Richard B. *Guadalcanal*. New York: Random House, 1990.

Frankel, Max. *The Times of My Life: and My Life with the Times*. New York: Random House, 1999.

Freeman, Douglas Southall. *Robert E. Lee: A Biography*. New York: Scribner's, 1934.

Freeman, Robert Selph. *The Story of the Confederacy*. New York: Grosset and Dunlop, 1936.

Gabriel, Richard A., and Paul L. Savage. *Crisis in Command: Mismanagement in the Army*. New York: Hill and Wang, 1978.

Gelb, Arthur. *City Room*. New York: G. P. Putnam's Sons, 2003.

Gingrich, Arnold. *Nothing But People: The Early Days at Esquire: A Personal History, 1928–1958*. New York: Crown Publishers, Inc., 1971.

Goulden, Joseph C. *Fit to Print: A. M. Rosenthal and His Times*. Secaucus, NJ: Lyle Stuart, Inc., 1988.

GrayBar, Lloyd. "Admiral King's Toughest Battle," *Naval War College Review* (February 1979).

Guthman, Edwin O., and Jeffrey Schulman. *Robert Kennedy in His Own Words*. New York: Bantam Books, 1988.

Hallin, Daniel C. *The "Uncensored War": The Media and Vietnam*. Berkeley: University of California Press, 1989.

Hammer, Ellen J. *The Struggle for Indochina*. Stanford: Stanford University Press, 1954.

Hammond, William M. *Reporting Vietnam: Media and Military at War*. Lawrence: University Press of Kansas, 1998.

Hancock, Harrie Irving. *Dave Darin Fourth Year at Annapolis*. Akron: Saalfield Publishing Company, 1911.

———.*Dave Darin on Asiatic Station*. Philadelphia: Henry Attemus Company, 1919.

Herring, George C. *America's Longest War: The United States and Vietnam, 1950–1975*, 3rd edition. New York: McGraw-Hill, Inc., 1996.

Herspring, Dale R. *The Pentagon and the Presidency: Civil Military Relations from FDR to George W. Bush*. Lawrence: University Press of Kansas, 2005.

Hessen, Robert, ed. *Berlin Alert: The Memoirs and Reports of Truman Smith*. Stanford: Hoover Institution Press, 1984.

Johnson, Gerald W., Frank R. Kent, Hamilton Owens, and H. L. Mencken. *The Sunpapers of Baltimore, 1837–1937*. New York: Alfred A. Knopf, 1937.

Kaufman, Burton I. *The Korean War: Challenges in Crisis, Credibility, and Command*. New York: Alfred A. Knopf, 1986.

Keegan, John. *The Second World War*. New York: Penguin Books, 1989.

Kennedy, William V. *The Military and the Media: Why the Press Cannot Be Trusted to Cover a War*. Westport, CT: Praeger, 1993.

Kinnard, Douglas. *The War Managers: American Generals Reflect on Vietnam*. Hanover, NH: University Press of New England, 1977.

Kluger, Richard. *The Paper: The Life and Death of the New York Herald Tribune*. New York: Alfred A. Knopf, 1986.

Knebel, Fletcher. "Kennedy vs. The Press," *Look* (August 28, 1962).

Krock, Arthur. *Memoirs: Sixty Years on the Firing Line*. New York: Funk and Wagnalls, 1968.

Larrabee, Eric. *Commander in Chief: Franklin Delano Roosevelt, His Lieutenants, and Their War*. New York: Harper and Row, 1987.

Liebling, A. J. *The Press*. New York: Pantheon Books, 1964.

———. "The Oracles of Mars," *The New Yorker* (October 28, 1950).

Linn, Brian McAllister. *Guardians of Empire: The U.S. Army and the Pacific, 1902–1940*. Chapel Hill: University of North Carolina Press, 1997.

Luckett, Margie H. *Maryland Women*, II. Baltimore, 1937.

Lydgate, William A. "Funeral March," *New Republic* (March 30, 1938).

Lyons, Michael J. *World War II: A Short History*, 2nd ed. Englewood Cliffs, NJ: Prentice Hall, 1994.

Markel, Lester. *Public Opinion and Foreign Policy*. New York: Harper, 1949.

Marolda, Edward J., ed. *FDR and the U.S. Navy*. New York: St. Martin's Press, 1998.

Matloff, Maurice. *American Military History*. Washington, D.C.: The Office of the Chief of Military History, 1969.

McMaster, H. R. *Dereliction of Duty: Lyndon Johnson, Robert McNamara, the Joint Chiefs of Staff, and the Lies That Led to Vietnam*. New York: Harper Collins, 1997.

McNamara, Robert S. *In Retrospect: The Tragedy and Lessons of Vietnam*. New York: Random House, 1995.

Millett, Allan R., and Peter Maslowski. *For the Common Defense: A Military History of the United States of America*. New York: The Free Press, 1984.

Mohr, Charles. "Once Again—Did the Press Lose Vietnam?" *Columbia Journalism Review* (November–December 1983).

Mollenhoff, Clark R. *The Pentagon: Politics, Profits and Plunder*. New York: G. P. Putnams's Sons, 1967.

Morison, Samuel Eliot. *The Struggle for Guadalcanal August 1942–February 1943*. Boston: Little, Brown and Company, 1949.

Morris, James M. *America's Armed Forces: A History*. Englewood Cliffs, NJ: Prentice Hall, 1991.

Moss, George Donelson. *Vietnam: An American Ordeal*, 3rd ed. Englewood Cliffs, NJ: Prentice Hall, 1998.

Nafalti, Timothy, ed. *John F. Kennedy's the Great Crises I*. New York: Norton and Company, 2001.

The National Cyclopedia of American Biography. vol. 22. New York: James T. White Company, 1932.

Olson, James S., and Randy Roberts. *Where the Domino Fell: America and Vietnam, 1945–1990*. New York: St. Martin's Press, 1991.

Padover, Saul K. "The Generals Take Over," *PM* (December 22, 1947).

Perry, Mark. *Four Stars*. Boston: Houghton Mifflin Company, 1989.

Peterson, Theodore. *Magazines in the Twentieth Century*. Urbana: University of Illinois Press, 1964.

Pollard, James E. "The Kennedy Administration and the Press," *Journalism Quarterly* (Winter 1964).

Pope, Dudley. *Graf Spee: The Life and Death of a Raider*. New York: J. B. Lippincott Company, 1957.

Potter, E. B. *Sea Power: A Naval History*. Annapolis: U.S. Naval Institute Press, 1981.

Report of the Secretary of the Navy. Washington, D.C.: U.S. Government Printing Office, 1928.

Reston, James. *Deadline: A Memoir*. New York: Random House, 1991.

Roeder, George H., Jr. *The Censored War: American Visual Experience During World War Two*. New Haven: Yale University Press, 1993.

Roosevelt, Franklin D. *The Complete Presidential Press Conferences of Franklin D. Roosevelt*, II. New York: DaCapo press, 1972.

Salinger, Pierre. *With Kennedy*. Garden City, NY: Doubleday and Company, 1966.

Salisbury, Harrison E. *Without Fear or Favor: The New York Times and Its Times*. New York: Ballantine Books, 1980.

———. *A Time of Change: A Reporter's Tale of Our Time*. New York: Harper and Row, 1988.

Schlesinger, Arthur M., Jr. *Robert Kennedy and His Times*, I. Boston: Houghton Mifflin Company, 1978.

Schulzinger, Robert D. *A Time for War: The United States and Vietnam, 1941–1975*. New York: Oxford University Press, 1997.

———."Whatever Happened to the Council on Foreign Relations?" *Diplomatic History* (Fall 1981).

Sheehan, Neil. *A Bright Shining Lie: John Paul Vann and America in Vietnam*. New York: Random House, 1988.

Shepard, Richard F. *The Paper's Paper: A Reporter's Journey Through the Archives of the New York Times*. New York: Times Books, 1996.

Sheridan, Philip H. *Personal Memoirs*. New York: C. L. Webster, 1888.

Sorley, Lewis. *Honorable Warrior: General Harold K. Johnson and the Ethics of Command*. Lawrence: University Press of Kansas, 1998.

Sweeney, Michael S. *Secrets of Victory: The Office of Censorship and the American Press and Radio in World War II*. Chapel Hill: University of North Carolina Press, 2001.

———. *The Military and the Press: An Uneasy Truce*. Evanston, IL: Northwestern University Press, 2006.

Sweetman, Jack. *The U.S. Naval Academy: An Illustrated History*. Annapolis: U.S. Naval Institute Press, 1955.

Talese, Gay. *The Kingdom and the Power*. New York: The World Publishing Company, 1969.

Tifft, Susan E., and Alex S. Jones. *The Trust: The Private and Powerful Family Behind the New York Times*. Boston: Little, Brown and Company, 1999.

U.S. Senate, Foreign Relations Committee, Executive Sessions, 86th Congress, 2nd Session vol. 12, 1960.

Villard, Oswald G. "Wanted: A Sane Defense Policy," *Harper's*, April 1939.

———."The Press and the War News," *Christian Century*, March 1, 1944.

Watson, Mark Skinner. *The War Department: Chief of Staff: Prewar Plans and Preparations*. Washington, D.C.: U.S. Government Printing Office, 1950.

Whelan, Richard. *Drawing the Line: The Korean War, 1950–1953*. Boston: Little, Brown and Company, 1990.

Who Was Who in America, 1. Chicago: A.M. Marquis Company.

Wyatt, Clarence R. *Paper Soldiers: The American Press and the Vietnam War*. New York: W.W. Norton and Company, 1993.

———."At the Cannon's Mouth," *Journalism History* (1986).

Young, Peter. *The World Almanac Book of World War II*. New York: Almanac Publications, 1981.

Index

About the Author

ROBERT B. DAVIES is a professor emeritus, Minnesota State University Moorhead, where he taught many courses in U.S. history for thirty-two years. His interest in military journalism developed from his popular college courses in World War II and American journalism history. An NEH summer seminar in 1983 gave Davies the opportunity to meet Hanson Baldwin at his home. Other interviews with him followed during that decade.

Davies is the author of *Peacefully Working to Conquer the World: Singer Sewing Machines in Foreign Markets, 1854–1920*. He now lives with his wife, Mary, in New Hampshire.